ACTOR'S ENCYCLOPEDIA OF DIALECTS

DONALD H. MOLIN

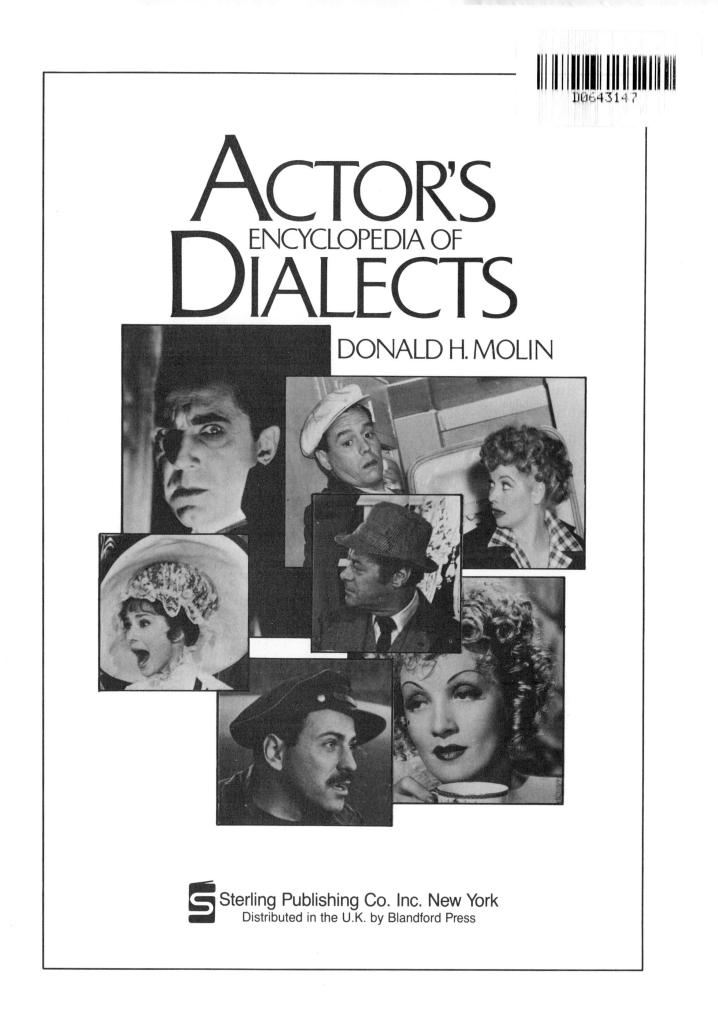

Sterling Publishing Co. Inc. New York
Distributed in the U.K. by Blandford Press

Dedication

To the memory of Jack Wormser; to the many others who have given their support, advice and encouragement; to my brother, Armin; my friends, Tony, John, Roger and Adèle; but most of all, to Sheila Anne Barry who made it work, and Signhild who made it worthwhile.

Library of Congress Cataloging in Publication Data

Molin, Donald H.
Actor's encyclopedia of dialects.

Includes index.
1. Acting. 2. English language—Dialects.
3. Dialectology. I. Title.
PN2071.F6M57 1984 417′.2 84-92
ISBN 0-8069-7044-8
ISBN 0-8069-7628-4 (pbk.)

Two Park Avenue, New York, N.Y. 10016
Distributed in Australia by Oak Tree Press Co., Ltd.
P.O. Box K514 Haymarket, Sydney 2000, N.S.W.
Distributed in the United Kingdom by Blandford Press
Link House, West Street, Poole, Dorset BH15 1LL, England
Distributed in Canada by Oak Tree Press Ltd.
% Canadian Manda Group, P.O. Box 920, Station U
Toronto, Ontario, Canada M8Z 5P9
Manufactured in the United States of America

TABLE OF CONTENTS

NOTES TO THE READER

The sound symbols used in the *GUIDE PAGES* and the *PRACTICE WORD LIST* (see pages 248–253) represent Standard American English pronunciation as found in any American dictionary and used by most American network radio and television announcers.

If you speak a regional variety of American English (or a non-American variety of English), you must first understand Standard American English in order to comprehend the sounds represented in the text and in the *GUIDE PAGES*. To aid this understanding, readers from the U.K., Canada, Australia, and New Zealand will find a further explanation of sound representations on the next page.

I have intentionally omitted all American regional varieties from this book. The influence of television, radio, and films, the mobility of Americans within the borders of the U.S. and the rise (and fall) of fads in pronunciation (such as the current "country-western" fad) all combine to make these varieties change rapidly. With minor exceptions, this means that current transcriptions of any American regional variety soon will be obsolete and/or inaccurate. Exploring the varieties and their changes would be a book in itself.

Also omitted are several other varieties and dialects which do not have a marked effect on the dialect scene in America today, including Welsh, Danish, and Dutch. I have excluded the oriental dialects, those of Africa, the Middle East, and Southeast Asia. They too would be a volume in themselves.

When I refer to an "educated" dialect in the text or in the *GUIDE PAGES*, I don't mean that the person holds a Ph.D., but merely that his or her education in English is more extensive than most.

The cassette that has been prepared to accompany this book may be purchased by writing to:

Donald H. Molin
℅ Sterling Publishing Co., Inc.
Two Park Avenue
New York, New York 10016

VOWEL SYMBOL GUIDE

<table>
<tr><th rowspan="2">Symbol</th><th colspan="3">How to Pronounce the Symbol if You Are from</th></tr>
<tr><th>the U.S.</th><th>the U.K. Canada</th><th>Australia N.Z.</th></tr>
<tr><td rowspan="2">A</td><td rowspan="2">as in "day" or "baby"</td><td colspan="2">e+E; both the "eh" (e) and "ee" (E) elements receive *equal* stress and value.*</td></tr>
<tr><td></td><td>(like the a in "comrade" as pronounced in Brisbane or in N.Z.)</td></tr>
<tr><td>*A*</td><td>as in "father" or "garden"</td><td colspan="2">Similar to the a in "are" or "swan" but shorter, like the a in "was"</td></tr>
<tr><td>a</td><td>as in "happy" or "had"</td><td>As pronounced at Oxford in the words "act," "happy" and "had"</td><td>As in "after" or "ask"</td></tr>
<tr><td>*a*</td><td>as in "after," "ask," "plant" or "France"</td><td>Doubled (or longer) Oxford "a" (see above); like the a in "after" or "can't" in the Norfolk dialect.</td><td>Similar to the "a" of "ask" or "after," but doubled or longer.</td></tr>
<tr><td>E</td><td colspan="3">as in "free," "please," "eat" or "steam"</td></tr>
<tr><td>*E*</td><td>as in "learn" or "herb"</td><td colspan="2">Like the e in "her" and the "o" in "word"</td></tr>
<tr><td>e</td><td colspan="2">as in "bed" and "next"</td><td>Similar to the e in "end" or "well" but longer.</td></tr>
<tr><td>*e*</td><td colspan="3">as in "level" or "gorgeous"</td></tr>
<tr><td>I</td><td>as in "island" or "light"</td><td colspan="2">A+E; the second element is the long sound "ee" (E); both the "ah" (A) and "ee" (E) elements receive equal stress and value.*</td></tr>
<tr><td>*I*</td><td colspan="3">like the e in "predict" and the o in "propose"</td></tr>
<tr><td>i</td><td colspan="2">as in "lift"</td><td>As in "in," "with," or the second syllable of "insist."</td></tr>
<tr><td>*i*</td><td colspan="3">as in "ago"</td></tr>
</table>

*The elements of an American diphthong are so closely tied that the two parts always blend into a single sound.

VOWEL SYMBOL GUIDE

<table>
<tr><th rowspan="2">Symbol</th><th colspan="3">How to Pronounce the Symbol if You Are from</th></tr>
<tr><th>the U.S.</th><th>the U.K. Canada</th><th>Australia N.Z.</th></tr>
<tr><td>O</td><td>as in “old,” “only” and “show”</td><td colspan="2">o + U; both the “aw” (o) and “oo” (u) elements receive equal stress and value.*</td></tr>
<tr><td>O</td><td>as in “out” and “clown”</td><td colspan="2">A + U; both the “ah” (A) and the “oo” (U) elements receive equal stress and value.*</td></tr>
<tr><td>o</td><td>as in “stop” and “trot”</td><td colspan="2">Similar to the “a” in “father” but only half as long.</td></tr>
<tr><td></td><td></td><td></td><td>the o of “off”</td></tr>
<tr><td>o</td><td>as in “horse” or “warm”</td><td>Similar to the “aw” sound of “off” or “loss” only longer.</td><td>Shorter version of the “aw” sound in “order” or “for.”</td></tr>
<tr><td>oE</td><td>as in “boy” or “oil”</td><td colspan="2">Both elements receive equal stress and value; the second element is a full “ee” (E) sound.*</td></tr>
<tr><td>U</td><td>as in “you” or “music”</td><td colspan="2">Y + U; the “y” as in “yet” is short and, together with the “oo” (U) element, is formed entirely in the front of the mouth.*</td></tr>
<tr><td>U</td><td>as in “fool” and “brew”</td><td>This is a pure “oo” sound as in “fool” with no other vowel elements involved. The vowel is not sounded until the lips have been rounded. Having only one part, no part of it originates in the back of the mouth cavity.</td><td>Longer version of the “oo” in “fool” produced entirely in the front of the mouth.</td></tr>
<tr><td>u</td><td>as in “up” and “color”</td><td>As a London executive pronounces the u of “up” and “cut”; as one from Suffolk pronounces the u of “pull.”</td><td>As in “up” or “cut”</td></tr>
<tr><td>u</td><td>as in “cook” and “could”</td><td colspan="2">Similar to the u in “full” and “push,” but farther back in the mouth.</td></tr>
</table>

*The elements of an American diphthong are so closely tied that the two parts always blend into a single sound.

KEY TO SYMBOLS

&	as indicated previously
$	when spelled
4	for the sound; in place of
"	when
#	open sound; mouth open
`;	pronounced forward in the mouth
%	liquid sound
!	excepting; except
-	initially; at the beginning of a word
--	at the beginning of a sentence
/	medially; in the middle of a word
.	finally; at the end of a word
..	at the end of a phrase
@	glottal stop; air stopped in the throat
(	preceding
{	in a prefix
Ɪ	before or after
)	following
}	in a suffix
+	add to
,	nasalized
:	stronger; more drawn out
½	weakened; shortened
¼	dropped; omit the sound
?	when used in a monosyllable
?:	in polysyllable
¢	consonant(s)
¢:	voiced "
¢½	unvoiced "
₵	between "
*	vowel(s)
✱	between "
C	as in church
n	as in bank, ink
S	as in shop, sure
s	as in outset, sits
t	as in think, bath
T	as in this, that
z	as in measure
=	interdentalized; pronounced with the tongue between the teeth
±	upperdentalized; pronounced with the tongue touching and behind the upper teeth
∓	lowerdentalized pronounced with the tongue touching and behind the lower teeth
h	as in the Scottish loch, or the German ich; the position of G or K with air hissing through a narrow opening
R	trilled "r"; tongue rapidly tapping the upper palate behind the teeth, as when imitating a steam drill's sound
r	uvular "r"; as when one makes a gargling sound

DIRECTIONS FOR USING THIS BOOK

Why bother learning dialects?

The most important reason is employment. The minute you master a new dialect or variety, you broaden your employment possibilities in television, film, and stage. An American actor who learns a "Latino" dialect is automatically *two* actors. And for every dialect that actor acquires, the demand for that person's talent increases while the competition decreases. Why? Because for every one of you who becomes proficient in a new dialect, there are a hundred competitors who won't bother.

Then there is the area of dubbing: an entire subcategory of acting where competition is minimal, employment easier to come by, and residuals more frequent (see the closing chapter: "Now That You're a Dialectician . . .").

Who should learn dialects?

Every thespian—professional or amateur—*but especially women*. Current statistics show only one-fifth as many women skilled in dialects as men. Therefore, the actress who excels in dialects gains even more respect from the entertainment industry for her professionalism than her male counterpart.

Now that you know the *"Why?"* and *"Who?"* let's get down to the *"What?"*

The pages that follow these directions have a specific pattern. Each chapter starts with an overview of the "Master Category" and then goes into two or more *GUIDE PAGES*.

The *GUIDE PAGES* serve four purposes: (1) they nail down the specifics of a given dialect; (2) they provide practice in all the sound changes you meet in that dialect (especially when you use them in conjunction with the *PRACTICE WORD LIST*); (3) they give the actor who is studying a master dialect (General German, General Italian, for example) an overview of other, associated dialects (thus the chance to pick up a couple of bonus dialects); and (4) they supply the actor with a ready "dialect shorthand" so that all the notes on any dialect can usually be jotted onto one 3″ × 5″ card, a handy study guide for odd moments while you're "waiting" (and aren't there a lot of them!) and an even more useful refresher guide for assisting you before you attempt a dialect role.

At this point, it is important to understand that a dialect (or a variety) is only a tool for use in creating a character; it is not the "key" to the role. Only deep research into what motivates and what frustrates a character can give an actor that.

As an alumnus of Actors Studio, I'm well acquainted with "the Method" of constructing a role internally. At the same time I have an equal knowledge of—and an equal respect for—the use of "external creation": that is, developing the outward expression of a character and allowing these manifestations to influence the internal understanding of a character. As a matter of fact, the latter is precisely the method Stanislavski describes as being his approach to creating a character fifty-seven years older than himself.

To use a dialect as a tool, first you need to master the outward manifestations of the dialect; then you need to internalize it. Whether your character speaks in a variety of English or in a foreign dialect, it is because your character *thinks* in that variety or dialect. In other words, that speech is organic to the role—as integral a part of the character as his or her complexion, height, age, or sex.

In everyday life, a dialect is often an

obstacle to our understanding. We find ourselves asking people with accents to repeat what they said. We unconsciously acknowledge the poor quality of the communication by raising our voices and speaking slowly (as if the individuals also *heard* with an accent!).

As actors, however, we can't allow our communication to break down or the dialect to "take over" a role. Several years ago I was among a group of "voice actors" asked to dub in Chinese voices for the pilot of a proposed TV series. When the dubbing directors said they wanted *real, authentic* dialects, three of us looked at each other in modified horror. We ventured a few hesitant protests, but soon we gave in and recorded what they *said* they wanted—authentic as a day in Peking.

When we left Warner Bros. that evening, one of the other pros said, "Well, see you back here in a couple of weeks!"

"Yup," I replied, "same place—different dialect."

Two weeks later, when we answered the call-back to redub *Kung Fu*, we were told that the network had rejected the pilot as being "unintelligible." Naturally. Now, finally, we three "troublemakers" were allowed to finish the objections we raised at the first session. They gave me the floor.

"It's not *authentic* Chinese dialect you want," I explained. "In the first place, Buddhist monks don't wander around China speaking to each other in English with a Chinese dialect." I heard David Carradine sigh in relief. "Of course, pure American would also sound strange coming out of those Oriental mouths on the screen. . . ."

"Then what *do* we want?" asked one director peevishly.

"What you want is the Oriental *intonation* and the very precise way in which the educated Chinese speaks English. In other words, what you want is the Chinese *flavor*." I had been demonstrating as I explained. The directors smiled; they knew their pilot was saved.

The basic rule, then, in employing and internalizing *any* dialect or variety is: *Your character must be understood. You* are the line of communication between author and audience. If you lack clarity, if the audience has a hard time understanding you—if, in essence, you fail to communicate—then the production fails.

By using "Oriental intonation" rather than totally authentic Chinese dialects, Kung Fu*—and its star David Carradine (shown here)—was able to reach and influence millions of TV viewers. Its action content opened the door to the import of dozens of Hong Kong-made martial arts films, while its philosophical content influenced Carradine so much that he dropped out of the glamor routine of Hollywood, opting for a life closer to nature and governed by his understanding of Oriental mysticism.*

Variety or Dialect?

Of the 136 so-called "dialects" you will find in this book, twenty-nine are actually "varieties." A London shopkeeper, a Dublin truck driver, a Glasgow tour guide, a Liverpool dockworker, and a Jamaican customs official all speaks different *varieties* of English. None speaks with a dialect; what comes out of their mouths is the English they grew up with, the accepted speech of their society and their peers. For them it is absolutely correct English.

On the other hand, people from Mexico City, Berlin, Rome, Stockholm, Warsaw, or Moscow are obviously not speaking their native tongue when they speak English. Their differences from Standard American speech are unintentional and so make up what can truly be called a "dialect." Ninety-day visitors to the U.S. from any of these cities will most probably return home speaking American English much better than when they left, since their aim will be to come as close as they can to the English they heard spoken in the States.

In contrast, someone from London, Dublin, or Melbourne will return from America with their version of English unaltered. After all, they wouldn't want their family and friends remarking that they'd picked up an "American accent."

The intention, therefore, of most people with a true dialect is to speak American English well. Their dialect will not necessarily be consistent, since any time they try to remember the American pronunciation, they will come as close to it as they can at that moment.

Alternatively, varieties are consistent: their users are speaking English well as far as they are concerned, and have no reason to change their speech—not unless they intend to emigrate, that is. Even then, most Britons of the middle and upper classes will retain the speech with which they arrived, encouraged as they are by the majority of Americans—who find such English "distinguished," "beautiful," and a mark of status.

Producing New Sounds

Before learning the techniques and "the rules," you had better learn how to remember them. And the best way to remember something is to *use* it:

1. For each sound change you learn in a specific dialect (or variety), string two or more words together which incorporate that change. For instance, saying "saw law" for "so low" would illustrate the Spanish substitution of the "aw" sound for the "oh" sound. If you can, come up with a phrase, preferably one that is common (or, better yet, characteristic).

2. For any entire dialect (or variety), compose a key phrase or sentence containing the most important (to you) sound changes and incorporating the characteristic music, rhythm, and pace.

Now you're ready for some of the rules.

We create the sounds of speech by impelling air from the lungs through the vocal cords. The shaping of those sounds is accomplished by combining positions of the throat, palate, tongue, lips, and teeth. If this sounds involved, it's because *it is*. Speaking is one of the most complicated sets of physical maneuvers possible—much more difficult to learn than driving a car or flying a plane—but you have learned it, and that means that you can master dialects as well, and with a lot less trouble.

Take new consonant combinations—BV, FW, or TS, to mention a few. These appear the hardest to learn, but are actually the easiest. Let's try TS as a sample.

In the chapters where you encounter this combination, you're given the examples "outset" and "its." It has probably occurred to you by now that you've been using this combination every day of your life. Pronounce the examples a couple of times and notice what your tongue and lips are doing. Now eliminate whatever comes before the sound ("ou" from "outset"). Next, eliminate whatever follows the sound ("et" from "outset"). Now you have the sound isolated and have added one more consonant to your range.

What about vowels? The problem usually arises when you find a vowel sound you know in a place you're not used to seeing it. Let's take the vowel sound in "good" when it's replacing the vowel in the word "too."

First turn to the *PRACTICE WORD LIST* on page 248. Find the appropriate examples of the vowel in "good"—*u*—and pronounce them aloud: "book"—"bush"—"foot," and so forth.

Second, repeat these examples, dropping the parts which follow the vowel: the "k" in "book," the "sh" in "bush," the "t" in "foot."

Third, take your example word, "too," change to the new vowel sound, and add a consonant at the end (the most common final consonant you can find among the Practice Words)—"k," for example. So "too" becomes "too-k."

Finally, pronounce the example word while dropping the added, final consonant.

Now let's tackle changes in everyday consonant sounds like L, G, D, or T. Since the tongue is the instrument that shapes most of the sounds we make (combined with the gums, teeth, or palate), let's observe it in action. Pronounce "lie," "guy," "die," and "tie," paying careful attention to where your tongue is. Did you notice that the tip of your tongue was in the same place for both "die" and "tie" (touching your gums just behind your upper teeth)? English is one of the few languages that produces the D and T sounds this way. Many more languages form these sounds with the tip of the tongue against the upper teeth themselves, making a "thicker" sound. In the text, I call this "upperdental." Other languages make even thicker sounds by placing the tip of the tongue *between* the teeth. I call this approach "interdental."

Practice all four of these variations (upperdental D and T and interdental D and T). You now have learned four new sounds, one or more of which you will use in the overwhelming majority of dialects you acquire.

Now let's take an *old* sound: the rapid vibrating of the tip of the tongue against the upper gum ridge that we made as children when imitating car and motorcycle motors, pneumatic drills, or machine guns. Remember it? Make like a car again. Feel where the vibrating sound is coming from. This is how much of the world makes its R sounds. (Even British English uses a "single tap" variety of this R between vowels, as in "very" or "story.")

Amazing how quickly you're learning new sounds, isn't it? Well, not really. You are equipped with the same basic sound-making and sound-shaping instruments as the rest of the human race, and any sound the foreign-born can make in their version of English, you can make. All it takes is practice and a knowledge of how and where the sound is made.

Take the CH in the Scottish "loch" and the German "ich." The first time they came across it, some of my students swore they'd never be able to master it. Others tried the advice they had heard somewhere of "clearing the throat like you're going to spit." Then I had them pronounce "good" and "could," noticing where the back of the tongue was. You try it. See? The tongue closes off the back of the mouth—for the G in "good" with some voice added (a "voiced consonant"), and for the C in "could", with just a small explosion of air (an "unvoiced consonant"). And that's the exact position for producing the elusive "ich" sound, except that instead of closing off the back space entirely, you leave a small opening and let the air hiss through (as the air hisses through the space between tongue and teeth for a SH).

I've just referred to "voiced" and "unvoiced" consonants. Since this distinction affects many foreign dialects, you'd better know which is which. The *unvoiced* consonants (those made with a small explosion of air) are CH, F, K (or hard C), P, S, SH, T, and TH as in "think."

Every *unvoiced* consonant has a voiced counterpart, made in the same position of the tongue and teeth, but with the voice as an aid rather than an explosion of air. These *voiced* counterparts are J, V, G, B, Z, and S as in "measure," D, and TH as in "that."

In several languages there are very few pure consonants. Their speakers will start voicing a "b" sound, but end by exploding it

	Trilled R		loch ich	Interdental	Upperdental	Open						Uvular R	sits outset	Nasalized			Liquid	Voiced Consonants	Unvoiced Consonants	Glottal Stop	Lowerdental
SYMBOL	*R*	BV	*h*	=	±	#	BP	DT	VF	GK	ZS	*r*	*s*	,	FW	VW	%	¢:	¢½	@	≠
BRITISH	X																				
Spanish	x	x	x	x	x	x															
GERMAN	X		X	X	X	X	X	X	X	X	X	X	X								
Italian	x				x		x		x	x					x						
POLISH	X												X		X	X					
Yiddish	x		x							x		x	x			x					
RUSSIAN	X		X	X			X			X	X					X	X	X	X		
Lithuanian	x			x			x	x		x	x					x	x	x	x		
IRISH	X			X													X				
Swedish	x			x	x							x									
SCOTTISH	X																			X	
French	x			x			x		x	x		x		x					x		x
COCKNEY	X																			X	
Anzac	x																				
CZECH	X			X												X		X	X		X
Jugoslav	x		x	x			x	x	x	x	x					x		x	x		
HUNGARIAN	X															X					
Finnish	x						x		x		x		x			x					
GREEK	X	X	X	X									X								
India	x						x									x					
WEST INDIES	X															X					
Portuguese	x	x	x		x									x					x	x	

This chart indicates the consonant changes which are encountered in the major categories.

into a "p." Similarly, they will start voicing a "d" and slip into the explosion of a "t." For such speakers, the English word "bad" comes out "BPaDT." Other voiced/unvoiced combinations are VF, GK, and ZS. The rule for these combinations is usually to "buzz" (or voice) the sound first and then "explode" it. When this doesn't apply, I've indicated so in the text and *GUIDE PAGES* by spelling the combination differently (ZS and DT in German, for example).

The VW combination is found in several dialects, including all the Slavic ones. For this, first repeat "vet" several times. Notice how your upper teeth form the V sound by touching your lower lip. Now repeat "wet" a few times. See how the W is made by pursing your lips? In the VW combination, purse your lips as for a W, while your upper teeth *almost* make full contact with your lower lip—almost, but not quite. Now voice the whole thing using the V part of this combination (if you didn't voice it, you'd be making the FW combination).

A number of new sounds (such as the FW) are listed in the *KEY TO SYMBOLS* (on page 8). These include "liquid L," "open F," "uvular R," and the "glottal stop," but as these appear in only a few of the dialects and varieties in this book, they are explained only in the chapters in which you meet them.

There is more to studying dialects than merely altering the sounds of vowels and consonants: You need to have an ear for the *music* and *rhythm* that the speaker carries over from the native language. But don't worry, you don't need perfect pitch: If you can sing "Happy Birthday" (even off-key), you can grasp what is needed.

Music, Rhythm, and Pace

If you have an accompanying cassette at hand, this is the time to use it. If not, please have patience with an explanation of something that should be heard rather than read.

Every language has its own characteristic music; thus all dialects (and many varieties) have *their* own music. If the "native" music is differentiated sharply enough from Standard American (Italian, Yiddish, Swedish, Russian, Hungarian, for instance), then even second-generation Americans may carry this music over into English.

Though American English is generally thought of (especially by the foreign groups mentioned above) as being a monotone (single note) language, we can find examples of music in it. "He didn't leave," with a falling inflection (lowered note) at the end, is obviously a statement, while "He *didn't leave*?!" expresses both surprise and a question by stressing (lengthening the tone of) the last two words and ending on a rising inflection (higher note).

Often the entire language (and therefore the dialect) is spoken at a different pitch from American English, which is basically a baritone language. Italian, Yiddish, and Irish are tenor, while Russian is a bass-baritone dialect compared to American speech.

Generally, American English has a tendency to stick to a small range of notes. British English offers a far wider range. Listen to Rex Harrison in *My Fair Lady* as he delivers the lines: "Look at her, a victim of the gutters, condemned by every syllable she utters. . . ." The Italian dialect tends to climb the scale as it approaches the most important part of a phrase, and then go back down the scale to the end of the phrase. Swedish (and even more often, Norwegian) may go up and down the scale several times in one phrase, giving it that so-called singsong quality. "Please tell me how to get to the railroad station," as an example, is made up of twelve syllables that could be played on a piano, thus:

F, *E*, D, rest, F, F, *E*, F, F, *E*, D, *E*, D

with the italicized notes held longer than the others.

This holding of a tone is one form of stress in all dialects and varieties; loudness is another. Together, they define the *rhythm* of a dialect. German has a tendency to stress many more words than English does, and so the dialect has a slower, more ponderous rhythm. Spanish stresses the last vowel before a consonant, and therefore has a more regular, identifiable rhythm. Of course, Iberian (European) Spanish and American Spanish are widely separated by the speeds with which they are spoken, and this differentiation we'll call "pace."

European Spanish is staccato and spoken rapidly; American Spanish is spoken in a more leisurely style. The dialects of Spain evoke a picture of a flamenco dancer's heels rapping out a staccato accompaniment to the guitar; those of Mexico and most of Latin America call up the image of a small, laden burro, slowly clip-clopping along a dusty road.

As with the pace of Spanish, the pace with which your character speaks English can point not only to the native tongue, but even identify speakers of the same language who came from different countries or regions. Someone from Lisbon is going to have a much brisker pace than someone from Rio de Janeiro, for example, despite the fact that they both speak Portuguese. And though their speech is similar in many ways, the people of New Zealand tend to speak more rapidly than their often "drawling" Australian neighbors.

A heavy, stolid pace is characteristic of Polish dialects, whereas the Irish varieties flow more rapidly over the tongue, like a stream dancing over pebbles. Change that stream into the slow and stately Volga, and you have a picture to evoke the Russian dialects.

Another example of a star choosing "communication" over "authenticity." Had Audrey Hepburn's Cockney variety been true to the background and status of the role of Eliza Doolittle in the 1964 film, My Fair Lady *(CBS/Warner), very few American filmgoers would have been able to understand half of what she said. Still, her speech was much closer to "Cockney Worker" than that of Wendy Hiller, who portrayed the original film Eliza in* Pygmalion.

In some cases, pace seems determined by climate. The farther south you go in the U.S., the more slowly the natives speak. Conversely, the farther north you travel in Sweden, the more the native speech slows down.

Cultural influences may also have an impact on a speaker's pace, music, and even rhythm. So when cultural, geographic, or climatic factors affect the way a dialect (or subdialect) is spoken, they will be pointed out.

Observation and Notes

A natural question by now (if not when you first picked up this book) must be: *"Can I really learn a dialect from a book?"* And the answer is: *"Not from a book alone." Active* observation (as with all acting) is necessary for perfecting a dialect.

I stress "active," because note-taking is essential both for impressing things on our memories, and later for refreshing those memories. This is one of the uses to which you can put your "dialect shorthand" once you've learned it from the *KEY TO SYMBOLS* and the *PRACTICE WORD LIST*. Use that shorthand as much as possible, because it will make it easier for you to mentally "hear" the changes that you need to make.

Access to a cassette recorder (an inexpensive one will do very well) can be of great help in observing dialects. First, it will enable you to observe *your own* use of a dialect. Second, you can use it to record "samples" of authentic dialects.

These samples are available all around you, believe it or not. Often someone's parent, grandparent, or old friend speaks with the dialect you want to collect. Just get your "samples" to talk about the subject that interests them the most (usually themselves), and you can collect samplings that are both extensive and increasingly (as the interviews continue) unselfconscious.

This unselfconsciousness is not that common in another source of samples—TV news and interview shows. I have acting colleagues who seldom watch either type of show without a cassette recorder at their elbows—but they realize that almost anyone appearing before those cameras is likely to have a certain amount of self-consciousness.

This caution does not apply to a third source: TV drama and comedy, including *The Late Show*. Consulting my *TV Guide*, I find that in a typical week I can hear (and tape) twenty-seven different examples of dialects and varieties including Oxford-Graduate-British, Russian, Turkish, Mexican, African, Portuguese, German, London-Shopkeeper-British, Filipino, Israeli, South-American Spanish, Yiddish, Japanese, West Indian, Italian, Cuban, Australia/New Zealand, French, Pakistani, Danish, Chinese, Irish, Austrian, Asian Indian, and European-Spanish. This is in addition to the varieties of Western, Southern, New York, and Down-East American English I can hear and record.

A couple of things to watch out for: first, forget any film that has been dubbed into English. Second, be very careful that what you're taping is as close to the "authentic" dialect as possible. Smaller character roles are more apt to deliver the right dialect. Watch out for big stars speaking foreign dialects, be they British or American; in most cases, what they're speaking is not what you're looking for. Obvious exceptions are Peter Ustinov, Alan Arkin, and Laurence Olivier. In most cases, the late Peter Sellers also delivered reasonably authentic dialects, but not in the *Pink Panther* films.

In all instances, remember: Your dialect "model" should not become the model for the *role* you are creating, but only a pattern for the linguistic makeup you are going to apply.

The final source of samples and examples is the cassette that was made to go with this book.

Using the Cassette

The cassette necessarily follows this book quite closely, but is much more extensive.

Oral examples of every dialect change in the book are given by experts. In addition, there are passages of dialogue for each Master Category, so that you will have samples of music, rhythm, and pace. When there are (as in Spanish) wide differences between some of the dialects within the Master Category, more than one sample passage is recorded.

It is, of course, a great advantage to have such an extensive "library of dialects" available whenever you want to listen; it is also a great temptation. "*Why put in all this time studying the book? How much easier just to listen to the cassette and imitate what I hear.*" But you're setting yourself up for problems that way. First of all, you will be *imitating* rather than *acquiring* a dialect. Second, unless you follow the steps outlined in these Directions and each chapter, once you have mastered three dialects, you run the risk of getting additional dialects mixed up with each other. Last, unless you really *master* them, dialects have an annoying habit of slipping out the back door of memory when you're not looking.

Sure, it's more work to do it "the right way"—but it will leave you with solid tools for your acting, skills that you can never lose. From time to time you may have to "hone your tools"—review the material you have learned—but each review will leave your tools—and you—that much sharper.

Now, pick the dialect or variety you want to start with and let's get to work!

Surrounded by impossibly zany characters and goings-on, the authenticity of Alan Arkin's portrayal made much of the madness in The Russians Are Coming, the Russians Are Coming *(MGM/United Artists, 1966) believable and therefore successful. Arkin's carefully crafted and integrated Russian dialect reflects the thoroughness which has made him one of the top dialecticians of American entertainment.*

Again, comedy made believable by use of an authentic dialect. Peter Sellers's title role in Dr. Strangelove *(Columbia, 1963) called for an outrageous madness which could never have worked in the hands of a less capable actor and dialectician. Though the actions of his character often crossed the line into implausibility, his German dialect never did.*

MASTER CATEGORY 1

BRITISH ENGLISH

A certain status is attached to some British varieties, and not only in the United States. Canada and Australia both number native-born citizens whose British English sets them apart from their fellows. In the majority of cases, these are people who have been educated in England, and whose speech is a prime example of the consistency which any variety demands.

For example, I have a Canadian-born-and-bred friend who studied, worked, and wrote in England. Every time I hear the (even to my ear) pleasingly clipped phrases flow from him, I can't help but compare his English with that attempted by Marlon Brando as Mr. Christian in *Mutiny on the Bounty*. This role was well below his usual standard—and why? Because of his unsuccessful imitation of Oxford-graduate-British. My friend John, on the other hand, became English in everything but citizenship. He thinks British, acts British, and therefore speaks British. In other words, while Brando *learned* the changes that make up British English, John *internalized* them. And this is exactly what you must do—but you don't have to move to England to do it.

In Mutiny on the Bounty *(MGM/United Artists, 1962), Marlon Brando's British variety suffered by comparison with Trevor Howard's. Howard's British English was native and integral to his speech, but while Brando's "Mr. Christian" was thoroughly internalized, his adopted variety was not, resulting in one of his less successful film portrayals.*

General British and all the subcategories you'll see in the following four *GUIDE PAGES* are varieties, remember. As such they require much more consistency than dialects. Whichever type of British English your character speaks, it must be because he or she *thinks* those particular sounds.

The British varieties were not always so different from what was being spoken in America—after all, the English language was brought to these shores by colonists from the British Isles. Not all of them were English, true; there were the Welsh, the Irish, and the Scots. In addition, a sizable number of those from England did not speak "the King's English," but rather the variety associated with their shire (Kent, Wessex, Yorkshire, and so forth) or their particular section of London (see Cockney varieties). Then, of course, there were the influences of other colonists whose native language wasn't English: the Dutch, the French, the Germans, and others.

Actually, the surprising thing is that it wasn't American English that moved away from the mother tongue as much as it was the language spoken in Britain that changed. All languages continuously go through fads, generally established by the social leaders of the times. But in Britain, many of these fads were incorporated into daily speech. Thus the influences of Oxford, Cambridge, and the Royal Court itself carried British English a long way away from the language of the time of Queen Elizabeth the First.

When scholars reconstructed the sound of Shakespeare's words as spoken by the players in the Bard's own time, the results proved closer to American English than to anything spoken in England today. If you have any doubts on this point, listen to some of the excellent recordings made of Shakespeare's plays in Elizabethan English. You'll have quite a surprise.

The first thing you'll probably note is that the Elizabethan vowel sounds are much closer to American English than they are to British. It is in this vowel production (and the handling of R) that the basis of British English lies.

First of all, the British vowels are produced much farther forward in the mouth than the American. To see what is meant by "forward," pronounce "pole," "pull," and "pool," observing where the vowel sounds originate. Now repeat the series a couple of times. You see how the sounds progress from the back of the mouth to the forward part? Now that you've identified the position of the "shift," you are much better equipped to give your dialogue a decidedly British flavor.

As for the individual vowel changes, we'll take up ten of them here; the rest will be found in the GUIDE PAGES that follow. Throughout this book, we will use the sound symbols illustrated in the PRACTICE WORD LIST (pages 248–253). You'll know when these sound symbols are being used rather than normal spelling because they will be set off in parentheses. The word "love," for example, might appear as (LuV).

Vowel Changes

We'll start with diphthongs. All the word "diphthong" means is two sounds combined. An example is the first letter of the alphabet, (A)—as in "aid came late." The two sounds that are combined to produce (A) are the (e) in "bet" and the (E) in "beat." In British English, the *first* element is stressed. This changes the sentence to:

(e:ED Ke:EM Le:ET).

The only exception to this in General British English is when the (A) sound at the end of a word is weak. Then it changes into (i) as in "bit." Thus "yesterday was Saturday" becomes:

(YeST*E*¼Di W*A*Z SaT*E*¼Di).

Both these changes tend to give the British sounds a "clipped" quality.

An even better example of this is the diphthong (I), which is made up of (*A*) as in "far" and (E) as in "fear." In British English this (*A*E) sound is shortened into (*A*i). Thus, "I like twilight time" becomes:

(*A*i L*A*iK TW*A*il*A*iT T*A*iM).

Compare the American and the British sounds, repeating them one after the other. You'll find that the British sound *is* farther forward in the mouth.

A third example is the diphthong (O) as in "boat." It is made up of the elements (*o*) as in "bought" and (*U*) as in "boot." In this case, the *first* element is brought forward, changing it to the (e) in "bet." Thus, what was (*oU*) becomes (e*U*), changing "he owns an old boat" into:

He (e*U*NZ eN e*U*LD Be*U*T).

Next is the diphthong (*O*) as in "found" and "ground." This is a combination of the (*A*) in "wand" and "swan" with the (*U*) in "swoon." Here, the British drop the second element entirely while lengthening the first one into (*A*:). A "crowd outbound" from "town" becomes:

A (KR*A*:D *A*:TB*A*:ND) from (T*A*:N).

In a final example of diphthong change, neither element is altered or dropped. This is the sound (U) as in "use," composed of the (Y) in "yes" and the (*U*) in "do." Both elements are retained, and a *third* sound is placed between them: the (i) in "hip." As with all diphthongs, the sounds are not kept separate, but are glided into a continuous whole. This makes the producer's comment that he could "use" a "few cute tunes" into:

He could (Yi*U*Z) a (FYi*U* KYi*U*T TYi*U*NZ).

A word of caution here: listen very carefully to the new sound you're making; be very *sure* you are not changing it into (iYi*U*). It's an easy error to make, but it changes the variety from General British English into Cockney (see Master Category 14).

Other characteristic vowel changes have nothing to do with diphthongs. For example, one of them alters the sound in the observation "odd" the "clock was not on top" by bringing the (o) sound forward into an (*o*½) sound. To do this, take the (*o*) of "bought" and make the sound only half as long—(*o* ½). The above observation then becomes:

(*o*½D) the (KL*o*½K W*A*Z N*o*½T *o*½N T*o*½P).

A second change is so striking that even nonactors use it when imitating (or mocking) the British; this is what happens to the (*a*) of "laugh." In British English it is often broadened into the (*A*) of "far" and then made longer—(*A*:). This occurs only when the (*a*) is found before F, FF, FT, NCE, NCH, SK, SP, or TH (*t*). Thus, the tree-climber's complaint that he "can't grasp" the "last branch" becomes:

He (K*A*:NT GR*A*:SP) the (L*A*:ST BR*A*:NCH).

Unfortunately, this is one of those rules that you simply have to memorize. Take all the words in the *PRACTICE WORD LIST* under (*a*) and repeat them with the British pronunciation. Keep doing so until the British pronunciation begins to sound more natural to you than the American one. Now you are well on your way to "organic memorization" (what happens when "rote" learning becomes internalized).

Other vowel changes are minor, or apply only to some of the British varieties, so the last one we'll consider actually has to do with a consonant change: the vanishing (R).

The sound is (*E*), as with the young lady who "heard her first German word." The rules applying to (R) require that we drop (¼) all the (R)s in that phrase. When we do so, we see that this changes the vowel sound itself, bringing it forward in the mouth. Thus, in British English, she:

(H*E*¼D H*E*¼ F*E*¼ST G*E*¼M*i*N W*E*¼D).

Consonant Changes

This is not the only place where the (R) disappears in British speech. Whenever the (R) follows a vowel and precedes a consonant, we drop (¼) it. Thus, the bandleader who explains that the "march's first part" is "short," in British English says:

(M*A*:¼*C*Z F*E*¼ST P*A*:¼T) is (*S*o½¼T).

What's more, unless the following word starts with a vowel, all final (R)s are dropped, so that the fireman who spotted a "fire near" the "far door," in British English saw:

(F*A*i¼NE¼) the (F*A*:¼ D*o*½¼).

In between two vowel sounds, however, the (R) changes radically. Some people hear the new sound as being a (D), and imitate British speech by saying "veddy" for "very." It's an easy trap to fall into, since the new sound is a short trill (*R*½), produced just behind the place where an American makes a (D). The trilled (*R*), you'll remember, is one in which the tongue vibrates (or flaps) rapidly against the gums behind the upper front teeth. In this case, the tongue taps only once. Thus the Briton speaks *not* of a "veddy roodal stoddy"—a very rural story—but of:

a (Ve*R*½i R*U**R*½eL ST*o*½*R*½i).

This new sound may be a little hard to master at first, but it's worth the trouble. *All* British varieties use it, and to employ an American (R) in its place would remove the British character of a word, no matter what other changes were made.

The three remaining consonant changes we will look at here all concern consonants in positions preceding "u." Americans have a tendency toward a lazy tongue, which may result in speaking of "moving pickcherz," "the gradjooating class" and "Kleenex tishooz." The British follow the spelling more carefully.

Thus the "ch" (*C*) sound of a "lecture" with "pictures," in British reverts to:

a (LeKTYi*U*¼) with (PiKTYi*U*¼Z).

Likewise, the (J) sound of each "individual, gradual procedure" becomes:

each (iNDiViDYi*U*L, GReDYi*U*L PR*I*SEDYi*U*¼).

And, finally, a Briton observing that the June *Playboy* "issue was sensual" would say:

the (iSSYi*U* W*A*Z SeNSYi*U*L)

rather than the "ishoo wuz senshool."

Music, Rhythm, and Pace

The music of British English differs from the American in two major aspects. First, the average Briton speaks two tones higher than his American counterpart. This not to say that the Briton is basically a tenor, but rather that the chronic tone of British speakers (the tone from which they start out) is higher.

Second, there is a greater range in British English. While they may start higher than Americans, they also have the ability to slide into lower notes quite easily. I have cited an example of this in the "Directions" (page 14).

As for rhythm, British English is generally "clipped." Whereas Americans "glide" one word into another, Britons tend to complete each word distinctly. Though "Did you hear what he said?" in America is liable to come out: "D'ja hear whadee said?," in London every consonant will be crisp and clear.

Not that Britons always handle their vowels so carefully—far from it. While Americans retain all four syllables when pronouncing "dictionary" and "secretary," the British drop the vowel of the third syllables, rendering them "diction'ry" and "secret'ry." This "single-syllable stress" applies to all polysyllables, so that the British come up with pronunciations such as "sep'rate," "priv'lege," "int'rupt," "pr'post'rous," and "vig'lance."

Because the average pace of British speech is much more rapid, the dialogue in British films is sometimes hard for Americans to understand. Since, as actors, *we* don't wish to present our audiences with this problem, it's best to speed up the British dialogue only to the point where it's still easily understood. As there is much "drawl" in American speech, you can accomplish this and still give your lines the British "pace."

Observation and Notes

Observing the British varieties in action is fairly easy. You probably hear them every day of your life, if you're in a metropolitan center. Merely turn on your television set and listen to the language of the films made in Britain (especially those with no Americans in them). Listen, too, to the programs from the BBC or other British television producers.

You will even hear some of the "subvarieties" of British English, if you pay close enough attention. As to which subvariety, that depends on where the drama takes place. If it is rural and a countrified character is being played by Trevor Howard or Peter Cushing, they're apt to play it in their native "Kent" or "Surrey" variety. On the other hand, if the character is being played by John Mills, the variety is more likely to be *Norfolk-Suffolk*.

Except for rural or Cockney varieties, however, most of the English you hear in British films exemplifies the best of General British English—so don't forget your notebook or your recorder.

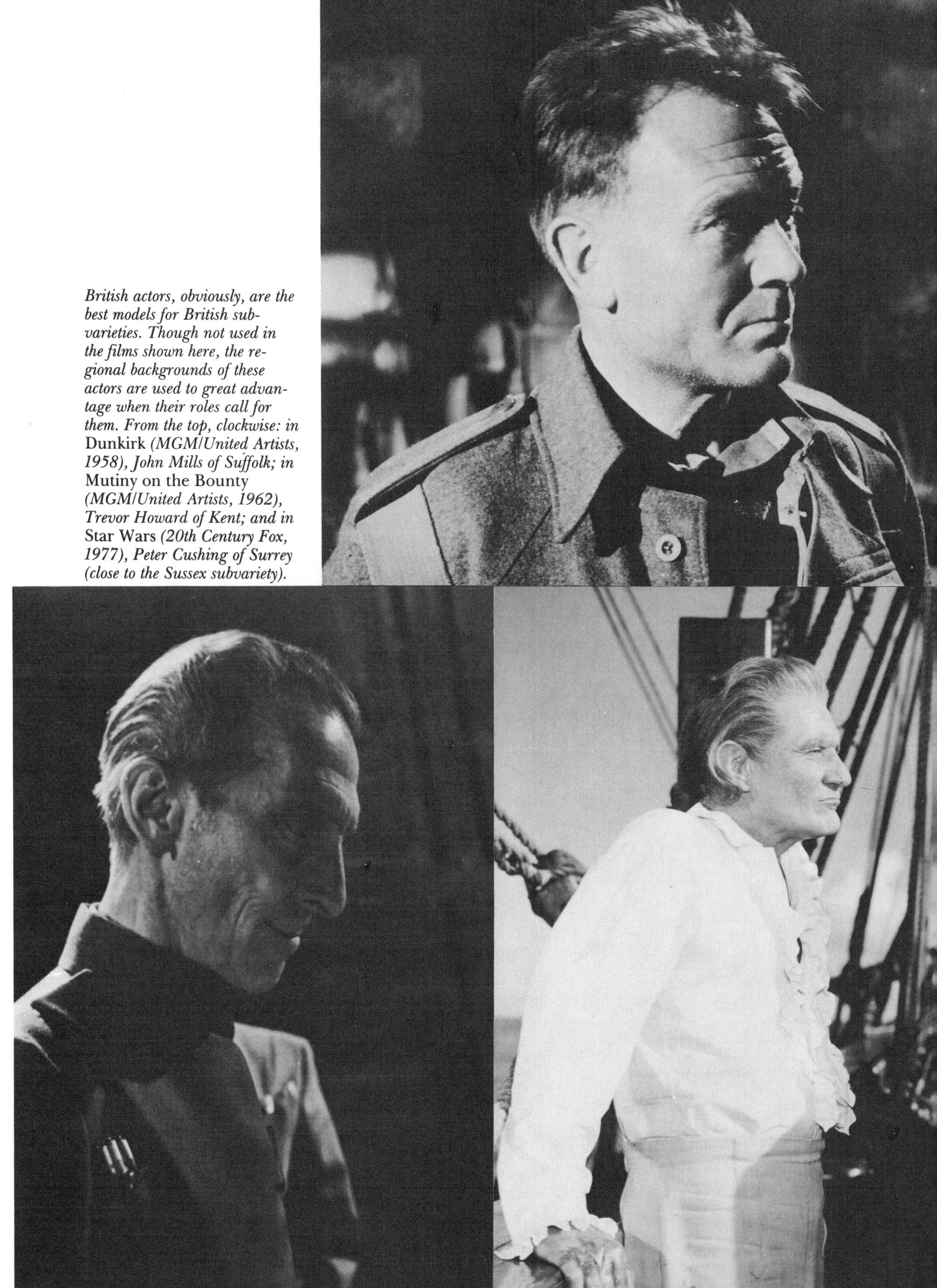

British actors, obviously, are the best models for British subvarieties. Though not used in the films shown here, the regional backgrounds of these actors are used to great advantage when their roles call for them. From the top, clockwise: in Dunkirk *(MGM/United Artists, 1958), John Mills of Suffolk; in* Mutiny on the Bounty *(MGM/United Artists, 1962), Trevor Howard of Kent; and in* Star Wars *(20th Century Fox, 1977), Peter Cushing of Surrey (close to the Sussex subvariety).*

GENERAL BRITISH ENGLISH - OXFORD GRADUATE - LONDON EXECUTIVE

GUIDE PAGES	SOUND	General British Engl.	Oxford Graduate	London Executive
STRESS first element: (aid) e:ED (late) Le:ET	A	e:E	&	&
CHANGE when weak at the end of a word: (yesterday) YeSTE¼Di, (Saturday) SaTE¼Di	A	.i"½	&	&
No change when spelled ea except before R: (eat) ET, (steam) STEM, (east) EST	E	E$ea !(r	&	&
CHANGE at the beginning of a word before a consonant: (erase) iR½AS, (emit) iMiT	E	-i(¢	&	&
CHANGE when in prefix: (prefix) PRiFiX, (believe) BiLEV, (degree) DiGRE	E	i{	&	&
CHANGE when spelled "y" at the end of a word (secretary) SeKR¼TRi, (library) LIBReR½i	E	.i$y	&	&
WEAKEN second element: (ice) AiS, (like) LAik, (try) TRAi, (mind) MAiND, (I) Ai	I	Ai	&	&
Change in all positions: (own) eUN, (boat) BeUT, (no) NeU, (whole) HeUL, (old) eULD	O	eU	&	&
Interpolate i sound in all positions: (use) yiUZ, (cute) KyiUT, (few) FyiU, (you) yiU	U	YiU	&	&

Change in all positions: (act) eKT, (happy) HePi, (angry) eNGRi, (as) eZ, (had) HeD	a	e		&
OR no change: aKT, HaPi, aNGRi, aZ	a		a	
WEAKER in prefixes: (endure) e½NDyiUR, (enact) e½NeKT, (endanger)e½NDe:ENJE	e	e½{	&	&
CHANGE in "again" *i*GAN, "against" *i*GANST	e	A	&	&
No change: (in) iN, (lift) LiFT, (sympathy) SiMPeti, (women) WiMeN, (busy) BiZi	i	i	&	&
Change in all positions: (odd) o½D, (clock) KLo½K, (not) No½T, (on) o½n, (top) To½P	o	o½	&	&
DROP when weak: (combine) K¼MBAin, (concoct) K¼NKo½KT, (compact) K¼MPaKT	o	¼"½	&	&
Change in all positions: (up) AP, (cut) KAT, (was) WAZ, (ugly) AGLi, (blood) BLAD	u	A	&	
OR no change: uP, KuT, WuZ, uGLi, BLuD	u			u

Longer sound: (are) A:¼, (palm) PA:LM (swan) SWA:N, (watch) WA:C, (spa) SPA:	A	A:	&	&
Retain vowel while dropping R: (her) HE¼, (earn) E¼N, (word) WE¼D, (first) FE¼ST	E	E¼	&	&
No change: (predict) PRIDiKT	I	I	&	&
Change in all positions: (out) A:T, (town) TA:N, (now) NA:, (how) HA:, (loud) LA:D	O	A:	&	
OR change to: eUT, TeUN, NeU, HeU, LeUD	O			eU
Interpolate short i sound: (fool) Fi½UL, (boot) Bi½UT, (do) Di½U, (rule) Ri½UL	U	i½U	&	&
OR interpolate Yi when spelled u, ue, eu or ew and NOT after J, R, W or C: (glue) GLyiU (flew) FLyiU, (clue) KLyiU, (knew) NyiU	U	YiU$u ue,eu ew!)J	&	&

Key:

& as shown	- initially	(preceding	" when	R trilled R
$ spelled	. finally	{ in prefix	: longer	¼ drop
			½ weakened	¢ consonant

GENERAL BRITISH ENGLISH, OXFORD GRADUATE AND LONDON EXECUTIVE

GUIDE PAGES		All 3
CHANGE before F, FF, FT, NCE, NCH, NT, SK, SP, SS, ST or TH: (laugh) LA:F, (after) A:FTE, (dance) DA:NS, (branch) BRA:NC, (can't) KA:NT, (ask) A:SK, (grasp) GRA:SP, (brass) BRA:S, (last) LA:ST, (bath) BA:*t*	*a*	A:(Fnce FFftNT NCH SK SPssST
AND medially before ND in polysyllable: (handshaking) HA:NDSe:EKiNG, (handwriting) HA:NDRAiTiNG, (sandpiper) SA:NDPAiPE, (bandleader) BA:NDLEDE	*a*	/A:(ND ?:
No change: (gorgeous) Go¼JeS, (level) LeVeL	*e*	*e*
DROP between consonants when weak: (family) FeM¼Li, (system) SiST¼M, (company) KuMP¼Ni	*i*	¼₵½
OTHERWISE, no change: (ago) *i*GO, (idea) IDE*i*	*i*	*i*
Shorter sound: (off) *o*½F, (all) *o*½L, (loss) L*o*½S, (war) W*o*½¼, (door) D*o*½¼, (ought) *o*½T, (board) B*o*½¼D	*o*	*o*½
FORWARD placement: (full) F*u*;L (push) P*u*;S (good) G*u*;D	*u*	*u*;

Shorten E sound: (oil) *o*iL, (boy) B*o*i, (point) P*o*iNT	*o*E	*o*i

No change	B	B
Retain T when spelled T before "*u*" (picture) PiKTYE, (lecture) LeKTYE; otherwise no change (change) CeENJ	C C	TY$tu C
Drop finally between consonants (mind reader) MIN¼REDE	D	.¼₵
Change to V medially when spelled PH (nephew) NeVyi*U*	F	/V$ph
No change: (go) GO, (grain) GRe:EN, (get) GeT	G	G
No change	H	H
Retain D when spelled D before "u" (gradual) GReDYi*U*L, (individual) iNDiViDYi*U*L, (residual) RiZiDYi*U*L	J	DYi$du
No change: (kill) KiL, (ache) e:EK, (cane) Ke:EN	K	K
No change	L	L
No change	M	M
No change	N	N
No change: (uncle) u*n*K*i*L, (drink) DRi*n*K, (ink) i*n*K	*n*	*n*
No change	P	P
No change	Q	Q
A light tap between vowels: (very) Ve*R*½i (story) ST*oR*½i	R	*R*½⁑
DROP after vowel before consonant: (park) PA¼K	R	¼)*(¢
DROP finally except before a vowel (are not) A:¼-N*o*½T	R	.¼!(*
No change: (say) Se:E, (civil) SiViL, (face) Fe:ES	S	S
When medial CI, SU or SSU, change: (sensual) SeNSYi*U*L, (official) *i*FiSYeL, (tissue) TiSYi*U*, (issue) iSYi*U*	*S*	/SY$ci su ssu
No change: (outside) *O*s*A*:D (waits) We:E*s* (sits) Si*s*	*s*	*s*
No change	T	T
No change: (thief) *t*EF, (mouth) M*O**t*, (lethal) LE*t**i*L	*t*	*t*
No change: (they) *T*e:E (sooth) SU*T*, (other) u*T*E	*T*	*T*
No change	VW	V W
No change	XZ	X Z
Change before U: (azure) eZYi*U*¼, (pleasure) PLeZYi*U*¼, (measure) MeZYi*U*¼, (treasure) TReZYi*U*¼	z	ZYi(u

Key: ?: polysyllable

! except	/ medially	) after	¢ consonant	* vowels
$ spelled	. finally	½ weaken	₵ between "	⁑ between "
; forward	(before	¼ drop	: longer	*R* trilled R

LONDON SHOPKEEPER - SUSSEX-KENT - NORFOLK-SUFFOLK

GUIDE PAGES		LON-DON SHOPK	SUSSEX -KENT	NOR-FOLK SUFFK
STRESS first element (aid) e:ED (late) le:ET	A	e:E	&	&
CHANGE when weak at the end of a word (yesterday) YeSTƐ¼Di, (Saturday) SeTƐ¼Di	A	.i"½	&	&
OR change before L and consonant (tailgate) TƐLGe:ET (sailboat) SƐLBOT (mailman) MƐLMeN	A	Ɛ(L¢		
No change when spelled ea (except before R): (eat) ET, (steam) STEM, (east) EST	E	E	&	&
CHANGE at the beginning of a word before a consonant: (erase) iR½e:ES, (emit) iMiT	E	-i(¢	&	&
CHANGE if in a prefix: (believe) BiLEV, (prefix) PRiFiX, (degree) DiGRE	E	i{	&	&
CHANGE when spelled "y" at the end of a word: (secretary) SeKR¼TRi, (library) LAiBReR½i	E	.i$y	&	&
OR change before R and consonant: (earlobe) Ɛ¼LOB, (fearsome) FƐ¼SuM, (merely) MƐ¼li			Ɛ(R¢	
WEAKEN second element: (ice) Ais, (like) LAiK, (try) TRAi, (mind) MAiND, (I) Ai	I	Ai		&
OR change all AS, LAK, TRA, MAND,	I		A	
OR change before ND (mind) MuEND (kind) KuEND	I			uE(ND
Change in all positions: (own) eUN, (boat) BeUT, (no) NeU, (hole) HeUL, (old) eULD	O	eU		&
OR change: uUN, BuUT, NuU, HuUL, uULD			uU	
Interpolate i sound in all positions: (use) yiUZ, (cute) KyiUT, (few) FyiU, (you) yiU	U	yiU	&	&
CHANGE in all positions: (act) eKT, (happy) HePi, (angry) eNGRi, (as) eZ, (had) HeD	a	e	&	&
WEAKER in prefixes: (endure) e½NDyiU¼, (enact) e½NeKT, (endanger) e½NDe:ENJƐ¼	e	e½{	&	&
CHANGE in "again" iGAN, "against" iGANST	e	A$ai	&	&
No change: (in) iN, (sympathy) SiMPeti	i	i	&	&
Change in all positions: (odd) o½D, (clock) KLo½K, (not) No½T, (on) o½N, (top) To½P	o	o½	&	&
DROP when weak: (combine) K¼MBAiN, (concoct) K¼NKo½KT, (compact) K¼MPeKT	o	¼ ½	&	&
Change in all positions: (up) AP, (cut) KAT, (was) WAZ, (ugly) AGLi, (blood) BLAD	u	A	&	&
Longer sound: (are) A:¼, (palm) PA:LM (swan) SWA:N, (watch) WA:C, (spa) SPA:	A	A:	&	&
Retain vowel while dropping R: (her) HƐ¼, (earn) Ɛ¼N, (word) WƐ¼D, (first) FƐ¼ST	Ɛ	Ɛ¼	&	&
No change: (predict) PRIDiKT	I	I	&	&
Change in all positions: (out) A:T, (town) TA:N, (now) NA:, (how) HA:, (loud) LA:D	O	A:	&	&!
OR except before ND (round) RuUND (sound) SuUND	O			uU(ND
Interpolate short i sound: (fool) fi½UL, (boot) Bi½UT, (do) Di½U, (rule) Ri½UL	U	i½U	&	&
OR change before R: (poor) Po:¼ (tour) To:¼	U		o:(r	
OR change before L: (fool) FuL, (tool) TuL				u(L

Key:

& as shown	- initial	(preceding	" when	R trilled R
$ spelled	. final	{ in prefix	: longer	¼ dropped
			½ weaken	¢ consonant

LONDON SHOPKEEPER - SUSSEX-KENT - NORFOLK-SUFFOLK - *GUIDE PAGES*

		SHOPK	SUSSEX	NORFK
CHANGE before F, FF, FT, NCE, NCH, NT, SK, SP, SS, ST or TH (laugh) LA:F (after) A:FTE (dance) DA:NS (branch) BRA:NC (can't) KA:NT (ask) A:SK	a	A:(nce FffNT etc.	&	
AND medially before ND in polysyllable: (handwriting) HA:NDRAiTiNG	a	/A: (ND?:	&	
OR no change: LaF, aFTE, DaNS, BRaNC, KaNT	a			a
No change: (level) LeVeL, (gorgeous) Go¼JeS	e	e	&	&
DROP between consonants when weak: (family) FeM¼Li, (system) SiST¼M, (company) KuMP¼Ni	i	¼₵½	&	&
Shorter sound: (off) o½F, (all) o½L, (loss) Lo½S, (war) Wo½¼, (ought) o½T, (door) Do½¼	o	o½	&	&
FORWARD placement: (full) Fu;L, (good) Gu;D	u	u;		
OR change before R: (insurance) iNSo:R½iNS	u		o:(r	
OR change before L: FuL, (wool) WuL	u			u(L
No change	B	B	&	&
Retain T sound when spelled "tu" (picture) PiKTYE, (lecture) LeKTYE	C	TY$tu	&	&
OTHERWISE, no change: (change) Ce:ENJ	C	C	&	&
DROP finally between consonants: (mind reader) MAiN¼REDE, (send for) SeN½Fo½¼	D	.¼₵	&	&
OR change to J finally before Y: (did you) DiDJyiU, (wild youth) WAiLJUt	D	.J(Y		
CHANGE to V medially when spelled PH (nephew) NeVyiU, (zephyr) ZeVE, (symphony) SiMV¼Ni	F	/V$ph	&	&
No change: (go) GeU, (get) GeT, (grain) GRe:EN	G	G	&	&
No change	H	H	&	&
Retain D sound when spelled "du" (gradual) GReDYiUL (individual) iNDiViDYiUL	J	DYi $du		
No change (cut) KAT, (kill) KiL, (ache) e:EK	K	K	&	&
When weak, drop after vowel & before consonant: (field) FE¼D, (told) TeU¼D, (calm) KA:M	L		¼"½)*(¢	
No change	MNnPQ	M	N n P	Q
A light tap between vowels: (very) VeR½i	R	R½✱	&	&
DROP after vowel before consonant: (park) PA¼K	R	¼)*(¢	&	&
DROP finally except before vowel: (are not) A:¼No½T	R	.¼!(*	&	&
No change: (say) Se:E (civil) SiViL (face) Fe:ES	S	S	&	&
CHANGE medial CI,SU,SSU: (sensual) SeNSYiUL, (official) FiSYeL, (tissue) TiSYiU	S	/SY$ci su ssu	&	&
No change: (outside) A:sAid, (waits) We:Es	s	s	&	&
No change	T	T	&	&
No change: (thief) tEF, (mouth) MA:t	t	t	&	&
No change: (they) Te:E (sooth) SUT (other) uTE	T	T	&	&
OR except "the" which becomes "Du"	T		"Du"	
OR except "the" which becomes "T" before a consonant: (the bit) T-BiT (the meat) T-MET	T			T(¢
AND T¼ before a vowel (the ice) T¼-Ais	T			T¼(*
CHANGE to WV initially and medially: (living) LiWViNG, (vest) WVeST, (visit) WViZiT	V		-/WV	
STRONG HW when spelled WH: (when) H:WeN (why) H:WAi, (where) H:We:E¼, (what) H:WAT	W			H:W $WH
No change	XZ	X		Z
CHANGE before U: (measure) MeZYi ¼	z	ZYi(u	&	&

Key:

		& as shown	(preceding	¢ consonants
" when	- initial	$ spelled	) following	₵ between "
¼ drop	/ medial	; forward	* vowels	R trilled R
: longer	. finally	½ weakened	✱ between "	?: polysyllable

AMERICAN SPANISH

The number of "Latino" roles written for U.S. TV and films seems to be increasing geometrically each year. This reflects the steadily rising immigration from Spanish-speaking America, the higher natural growth in the Latino community, and the growing power and voice of that community. Then, too, countries such as Colombia, El Salvador, Cuba, Puerto Rico, Nicaragua, and Chile dominate newspaper and TV headlines—giving rise to even more Spanish-American roles and stories.

Naturally, many of these roles go to Latin Americans—but it seldom happens that all these parts are cast on a Latino-only basis. Indeed, when those of Latin heritage like Martin Sheen (né Ramón Estevez) and Raquel Welch (née Raquel Tejada) reach the top of their profession, we don't often see them playing Spanish-American roles.

I myself have tutored actors of Italian and of French heritage in American Spanish, simply because it made it possible for them to get movie parts otherwise beyond their reach. And, since extending your reach as an actor is what this book is all about, American Spanish dialects should be among the first in your list of priorities.

The fact that American Spanish is a dialect rather than a variety, means that the demand for consistency is not as great. As long as the "sound" is there, an occasional lapse into pure American speech can be written off as your character's having remembered the American sound better at that particular time. Don't take this as an encouragement to be lazy; to learn *any* dialect or variety, you really have to apply yourself. Once you master it, however, you can concentrate more on sustaining your character than on maintaining your dialect.

You may have been surprised to see that there are two chapters on Spanish dialects: one on American Spanish and one on European Spanish. This is because the differences in these two branches of Spanish are as great as the differences between American varieties and British ones.

Indeed, the split between the American and European branches of Spanish bears a strong resemblance to what happened to English. In both instances the "colonial" language preserved more of the original tongue than the European version. In both cases the nobility and the court led the "mother country" into wider and wider departures from the original tongue. Finally, the European versions of both Spanish and English are spoken more rapidly and crisply than the American types.

As you study and compare, the differences will become more and more apparent. The greatest number of them, you'll find, will emerge as you study the vowels.

Vowel Changes

Part of the Latin-American modification of vowel sounds has nothing to do with any inability to produce American vowels; it is strictly psychological. For several years I was acquainted with a Colombian girl. She was highly intelligent, had studied at one of the most distinguished universities in the U.S., graduated from an American college, worked at the UN in New York and was married to an American. Despite all this, she still talked of "the bold man" when she meant "the bald man," and of "sawing a dress" when she meant "sewing a dress."

This was probably a type of "compensation": subconsciously aware she had replaced one sound with another, she reversed the procedure to compensate when the other sound came up.

The reversal resulted in the (O) sound of "so" and the (*o*) sound of "saw" being substituted for each other. In other words, "so," "coal," and "low" become "saw," "call," and "law"—and vice versa. Taking the substitutions one at a time, this means that a Latino observing that one can't play "polo solo" would say:

one can't play (PoL±*o* SoL±*o*).

On the other hand, a Spanish-American commentator who "foresaw" a "long war" would say he:

(FO*R*½S:O) a (L±ON¼ *i*WO*R*:).

Except for those most highly educated in American English, Spanish speakers also reverse the (A) of "late" and the (e) of "let." This turns "main," "raid," and "wail" into "men," "red," and "well"—and vice versa. Taking these changes singly, a boy born into a wealthy Latin American family might have "eight namesakes," but his father would say he had:

(eT NeM*i*S:eKS).

Contrariwise, the caution to "expect them" would turn out:

(A:K*i*SPA:K¼ D±A:M).

You might have noted in the last example that the (e) doesn't merely turn into an (A), but into a *long* (A:). This is because the Spanish American lengthens certain sounds. First of all there's the (E) sound in "heat," which is lengthened into (E:). As a result, all the diphthongs (double sounds)—of which (E) is a part—are likewise lengthened. (A), a diphthong made up of (e) and (E), becomes (eE:) or (A:). (I), which could be written (*A*E), becomes (*A*E:). Finally, the diphthong (*o*E) stretches into (*o*E:).

You'll find another instance of this lengthening effect in the (*u*) of "full" and "pull." This becomes the "oo" (*U*) of "fool" and "pool." Thus, a gardener doing replanting might want to know where he "should put" the "good bush," but if he were Latino he would ask:

where he (*SU*D± P*U*T) the (G*U*D± B*US*).

This lengthening influence also affects the (i) of "it," "is," "fill," and "lick," turning them into "eat," "ease," "feel," and "leak." Actually, the sound is longer (:) than the American (E). An impression that "is still distinct" becomes one which:

(E:S: *i*STE:L± DE:STE:NKT).

There's a good reason for this lengthening: in Spanish the letter "i" is pronounced "ee," so that "Si, si" comes out "See, see."

The Spanish sound also dominates when a Latino reads the letter "a." In Spanish, this is the (*A*) of "father." Consequently, despite the fact that there are three different "a" sounds in American speech, the Latin American changes the "a"s of "as," "fast," and "balance" *all* into (*A*). Thus (aZ) becomes (*A*S:), (F*a*ST) becomes (F*A*ST), and (BaL*i*NS) becomes (B*A*L±*A*NS).

This "native language" change also effects the (o) of "odd." Since in Spanish the "o" is pronounced "aw," the words "odd," "cot," and "pod" come out "awed," "caught," and "pawed." In this way, someone who's "got topnotch stock," in American Spanish has:

(G*o*T T*o*PN*o*C *i*ST*o*K).

Because there may be many different spellings for a single sound in American English, sometimes a vowel-sound change affecting one spelling spreads to others in the same sound group. For instance, the (u) of "love" and "does" is changed again to the Spanish "aw" (*o*) sound of "o" and comes out (L±*o*BV) and (D±*o*S:). But this change *also* affects *other* spellings of (u), so that "but," "dug," and "lung" become "bought," "dog," and "long." So, an electrician asking "what was unplugged?" if he were Latino would ask:

(*i*W*o*T *i*W*o*S: *o*NPL±*o*G'D±?).

Consonant Changes

The native Spanish pronunciation is so strong in its effect that the American sound (*E*) as in "urge" has four different pronunciations in American Spanish. Just how this sound is translated depends on its spelling. If spelled "e" as in a "perverse merger," it becomes the (e) of "end" and forms a

(Pe*R*½BVe*R*½S Me*R*½Ce*R*:).

If it is spelled "i" as in what got the "girl's skirt dirty," it becomes (E:) to get:

the (GE:*R*½L±S: *i*SKE:*R*½¼ D±E:*R*½TE:).

Spelled "o," naturally the pronunciation becomes (*o*), so that the fellow who doesn't know a "worse word" than "work," in American Spanish doesn't know a

(*i*W*o**R*½S *i*W*o**R*½D±) than (*i*W*o**R*½K).

Finally, when spelled "u," the sound becomes the (*u*) of "pull"; so while you might find that the "burn hurt," the Latino would find that

the (B*uR*½N *huR*½T).

In all the phonetic spellings of the "r" above, you must have noticed that the symbol (*R*) was substituted. This is because the Latin Americans trill their (*R*)s. To review the "trill": you make it by placing your tongue against the gum ridge behind your upper front teeth, and then voicing the sound so that the tongue flaps (or taps, or vibrates) like the sound a child makes when imitating a pneumatic drill. In most positions, this (*R*) is pronounced long and strong (:), so that the editor who found "very real stories rare," if Spanish-speaking found:

(BVe*R*:E: *R*:E:L± *i*STO*R*:E:S: *R*½e*R*:).

In that last phrase, notice that one of the (*R*)s—the first one in "rare"—is *not* a long (:) trill, but rather a short (½) one. This *light tap* of the (*R*½) occurs whenever you find an (*R*) before or after a consonant. The reason will become clear to you if you try trilling the (*R*) strongly (:) in that position. You see? It's very difficult—if not nearly impossible. So, if after a rain we might want to go to a "drier part" of the "park," in American Spanish we'd seek:

a (D±*R*½AE:*R*½ PA*R*½T) of the (PA*R*½K).

Some students object that the last (*R*) in "drier" didn't come *before or after* a consonant any more than the first (*R*) in "rare." But they're wrong in both cases. With "rare," the (*R*) followed the "s" of "stories"; with "drier" it preceded the "p" of "part." True, those were separate words, but Latin Americans have the same tendency as their northern neighbors: they run their words together. This is why some of the rules in the following *GUIDE PAGES* apply only to final consonants in relation to the words which follow them. As these are minor changes, we won't concern ourselves with them here.

Instead, we'll move on to a few more "carry-overs" from the original Spanish. In that language, it is impossible to start a word with an "s" followed by another consonant. All such "s"s are preceded by a vowel: *espina* is Spanish for "spine," *escuela* for "school," *esquirol* for "squirrel," and *estampa* for "stamp." Therefore, whenever the "s" at the beginning of a word is followed (or even preceded by) a consonant, we insert the (*i*) sound of "ago" in front of it. That means if we observed that "students" in "school stopped speaking," in American Spanish, the

(*i*ST*U*D±A:NTS) in (*i*SK*U*L± *i*ST*o*P'T *i*SPE:KE:N¼).

This small vowel sound, (*i*), also comes before any word starting with "w." The Spanish language has no letter "w," but it has a similar sound: the "ooW" found in *huevo* (egg), pronounced "ooWave-aw." Even here a preceding vowel is needed—a "help" sound in order to make the "w." If we wanted to ask someone "why" he "was weak-willed," in American Spanish we must ask:

(*i*WAE:) he (*i*WAS: *i*WE:K *i*WE:L±D±).

This same "help" sound is inserted into (Q) or "kw." Since "qu" in Spanish is pronounced (K), our way of pronouncing the letter is quite strange to the Spanish speaker. Where we might talk of a "frequent question," in American Spanish we'd mention:

a (F*R*½E:K*i*WANT K*i*WA:SCAN).

The Spanish language also has a different way of pronouncing "j"; it becomes (*h*), a sound nowhere near the American (J). However, there is a sound in Spanish that originates in the same position as (J): the (*C*) in "church." This is the "unvoiced" version of the "voiced" (J). So, where we might hope that the "judge enjoyed logic," if we were Latino we'd hope that:

the (*CoC* A:N*Co*E:D± L±*oC*E:K).

Another letter that doesn't employ American pronunciation in Spanish is "h." In fact, it doesn't have any pronunciation at all; it's silent. Still, Latin Americans try to approximate our (H) by using (*h*), thus cutting off the (H)'s flow of air by arching the back of the tongue. You'll remember that (*h*) is pronounced at the same place as (G) and (K); except , instead of cutting the air off entirely, the back of the tongue narrows the opening and thus imparts a hissing sound to this unvoiced letter. So, where an American might speak of "his unhappy household," in American Spanish it would be:

(*h*E:S: *o*N*hA*PE: *hO*S:*ho*L±D±).

The letter "z" is also handled differently in Spanish—and differently in Madrid—than in the New World. Latin Americans pronounce it "s," so that "zip" and "zeal" sound more like "sip" and "seal." Actually, the (S) in this case is decidedly longer (:). An American might be put off by "his lazy gaze," but a Latino would be irked by

(*h*E:S: L±eS:E: GeS:).

Other Spanish letters, though similar to their American counterparts, sound different because the tongue is in another position. The letter "d," for example, is not produced as we produce it—with the tongue touching the upper gum ridge behind the front teeth—but with the tongue touching the upper teeth (±) themselves. This imparts a slightly "thicker" sound, which goes a long way toward giving the dialect an authentic flavor. We can practice by remembering exam day in school, and how we "did dread that day"—or, in American Spanish, how we:

(D±E:D± D±*R*½A:D± D±*A*¼ D±e).

You may have noticed in that last sentence that the (*T*) of "that" was also turned into an "upperdentalized D" (D±). This is the closest the Spanish American can come to that English sound. So if he or she wants a belt made out of "that other leather," they will ask for one made of:

(D±*A*T *o*D±*eR*½ L±A:D±*eR*:).

From the treatment of "l" in "leather" (above), you can see that this letter also gets an "upperdental" (±) handling. This is not surprising in view of the fact that—as with the "d" and the "r"—the English language forms the "l" in unique ways. I write "ways" because there is more than one "l" in English; just pronounce "love" and "bulb" and watch what your tongue does. In the first instance, the tip of the tongue touches the upper gum ridge; in the second, the middle of the tongue touches it. For the Spanish (L), all we do is move the tongue forward until it touches the front upper teeth (±) themselves. Thus, the boss who requires a "list of skillful help," in American Spanish needs:

a (L±E:S:T *o*BV SKE:L±F*U*L± *h*A:L±P).

Did you notice how the (V) sound in "of" changed just then? This is because the mouth position of the Latino is different for (V) than ours is. Instead of forming (V) with the front upper teeth touching the lower lip, it is made by *almost* bringing the lips together as for a (B), and then, with the lips taut but still slightly apart, voicing the sound as one would with a (V). The resulting letter we describe as (BV). And the churchgoer who "gave" a "private vow," if Latino:

(GeBV) a (P*R*½AE:BV*e*T BV*O*).

The letter "b," in the *middle* of a word, is formed the same way (unless it follows "m" or "n" as in "number"). Thus, a young woman who is trying to "obtain" a "husband," if Spanish-speaking, will be trying:

to (*o*BVTeN) a (*ho*S:BV*A*ND ±).

You might object that Latinos couldn't distinguish between the two letters if they *were* both produced that way. Well, the fact is *they can't.* During the year I spent in South America, every time I sent a telegram in which those letters were used, the question always came back as to whether I meant "BVeh" as in *burro,* or "BVeh" as in *vaca* (cow).

Music, Rhythm, and Pace

In general, the music of American Spanish is marked by two distinctions: a placement *one tone higher* than American speech, and a falling inflection (lowered tone) at the end of a phrase. An exception to the "falling inflection" rule is found among Mexicans. They tend to end a phrase on a *double note,* going up, then down. Often this takes place in the middle of a syllable, if that final syllable ends in a consonant. (You'll see why in the next paragraph). This tendency is most pronounced among speakers from Baja California (Tijuana) and Sonora (Nogales).

The Spanish language is marked by a very definite rhythm that is carried over into American Spanish dialects. This is because the stress in a word is *always* placed on *the last vowel to come before a consonant.* Thus "*base*ball" becomes "base*ball*" and "*foot*ball," "foot*ball*"—but "*hock*ey" remains "*hock*ey" because the last vowel to come before a consonant in that case is in the first syllable.

Despite the fact that they were married in real life, Desi Arnaz and Lucille Ball (shown here in MGM's 1954 The Long, Long Trailer*) had a hard time convincing network executives that Arnaz, with his heavy Cuban-Caribbean dialect, would be accepted by television viewers as Lucy's husband. So the two of them toured the U.S., performing before live audiences, and then produced a pilot with $5,000 of their own money. The result—*I Love Lucy*—became one of the most successful shows in television history.*

Katy Jurado's immense talent brought her international recognition in High Noon, *her American film debut. In every role since then (such as in Paramount's 1961* One-Eyed Jacks, *shown here), her native Mexican dialect added to her portrayal, because she never allowed it to interfere with what she was communicating with her character's lines.*

Study this rhythm carefully; mark off some well-known poems or speeches, and recite them aloud with the Spanish emphasis. You might start with: "Four score and se*ven* years *a*go, our fa*thers* came to this conti*nent* to esta*blish* a new na*tion*, con*ceived* in li*ber*ty and dedica*ted* to the proposi*tion* that all men are crea*ted* e*qual*."

While you are doing these rhythm exercises, you can also practice your American Spanish pace: an easier, slower, flowing pace that reflects the more reasonable tempo of life in Latin America.

Observation and Notes

The observation and study of American Spanish dialects depends partly on your geographic location. In California and the Southwest, the opportunities to hear and record Mexican dialects are there for the taking. The same applies to Cuban and Colombian dialects in the urban centers of Florida. Besides Mexican and Cuban, New Yorkers and Chicagoans have the chance to study the Puerto Rican dialect (nearly the same as Cuban).

If you lack these nearby concentrations of Latinos—or want to supplement the observations you *can* make—there is always TV. *I Love Lucy* will probably be in rerun forever, and the dialect of Desi Arnaz is a prime example of Cuban (Santiago more than Havana). For the Argentinian, there are the many films of Fernando Lamas; for Mexican, those of Katy Jurado and Ricardo Montalban, who can also be seen on every rerun of *Fantasy Island*.

In the *GUIDE PAGES* that follow for the section on Mexican dialects, *Distrito Federal* represents those Spanish Americans most educated in American English.

GENERAL AMERICAN SPANISH - BOGOTÁ COLOMBIAN - CARIBBEAN: PUERTO RICAN and CUBAN - BUENOS AIRES-MONTEVIDEO

GUIDE PAGES	SOUND	General American Spanish	Bogotá Colombian	Caribbean: Puerto Rican & Cuban	Buenos Aires Montevideo
Change in all positions: (air) eR:, (able) eBVuL±, (pain) PeN, (they) D±e	A	e	&	&	&
Longer sound: (eat) E:T, (teach) TE:C, (me) ME: (emit) E:ME:T (steel) iSTE:L±	E	E:	&	&	&
Stress second element: (I'm) AE:M, (side) SAE:D±, (try) TR½AE:	I	AE:	&	&	&
Change in all positions: (old) oL±D±, (bone) BoN, (no) No, (only) oNL±E:	O	o	&	&	&
No change: (you) U, (mule) MUL±	U	U	&	&	&
OR change initially: zU, (unit) zUNE:T (useless) zUS:L±eS, (youth) zUS	U				-zU
Change in all positions (as) AS: (bad) BAD± (at) AT (magic) MACE:K (act) AKT	a	A	&	&	&
Change in all positions: (end) A:ND±, (leg) L±A:G, (every) A:BVeR:E:	e	A:		&	&
OR change: aND=, L±aG, aBVeR:E:	e		a		
Change in all positions: (it) E:T, (women) iWE:MAN, (busy) BE:S:E:	i	E:	&	&	&
Change in all positions: (odd) oD±, (clock) KL±oK, (not) NoT, (on) oN	o	o	&	&	&
Change in all positions: (love) L±oBV, (up) oP, (does) D±oS:, (was) iWoS:	u	o	&	&	&
No change: (are) AR:, (calm) KALM	A	A	&	&	&
When spelled "er": (earn) eR½N (heard) heR½D± (were) iWeR: (butter) BoTeR:	E	e$er	&	&	&
When spelled "ir" (stir) iSTE:R: (first) FE:R½ST (dirty) D±E:R½TE: (girl) GE:R½L	E	E:$ir		&	&
OR: iSTo½R: Fo½R½ST D=o½R½TE: Go½R½L±			o½$ir		
When spelled "or" (work) iWoR½K (world) iWoR½L±D±, (comfort) KoMFoR½T	E	o$or		&	&
OR: iWo½R½K, iWo½R½L±D=, KoMFo½R½T	E		o½$or		
When spelled "ur": (current) KuR:iNT, (burn) BuR½N, (return) R:E:TuR½N	E	u$ur	&	&	&
No change: (predict) PR½ID±E:KT	I	I	&	&	&
No change: (out) OT, (down) D±ON	O	O	&	&	&
No change: (do) D±U, (soon) SUN	U	U	&	&	&
Change in all positions:(after) AFTeR: (and) AND± (fast) FAS:T (half) hAL±F	a	A	&	&	&
When spelled "le" after a consonant: (simple) SE:MPuL± (title) TAE:TuL±	e	uL± $le)¢	&	&	&
Change in all positions: (balance) BALANS:, (ago) AGo (system) SE:S:TAM	i	A	&	&	&

Key: - initially; C church; R trilled R; & as shown;) following; ½ weakened; $ spelled; : longer; ¢ consonant

GENERAL AMERICAN SPANISH - BOGOTÁ COLOMBIAN - CARIBBEAN: PUERTO RICAN and CUBAN - BUENOS AIRES- MONTEVIDEO

GUIDE PAGES

	SOUND	General American Spanish	Bogotá Colombian	Caribbean: Puerto Rican & Cuban	Buenos Aires Montevideo
Change in all positions: (off) OF, (all) OL±, (cause) KOS:, (long) L±ON¼	*o*	O	&	&	&
Change in all positions (could) K*U*D±, (push) P*U*S, (foot) F*U*T, (put) P*U*T	*u*	*U*	&	&	&
Lengthen: (joy) C*o*E:, (oil) *o*E:L±	*o*E	*o*E:	&	&	&
Change medially: (husband) *ho*S:BVAND± (habit)*h*ABVE:T, (absent) ABVS:A:NT	B	/BV	&	&	&
BUT no change after M or N (rainbow) *R*:eNB*o*, (number) N*o*MBe*R*:	B	B)MN	&	&	&
OR drop finally before consonant (club room) KL±*oR*:*U*M (scrub lady) SK*R*½*o*L±eD±E	B			.¼(¢	
No change: (change) CeNC, (much) M*o*C	C	C	&	&	&
Against upper teeth: (day) D±e, (body) B*o*D±E:, (need) NE:D±, (did) D±E:D±	D	D±		&	&
OR between teeth: D=e, B*o*D=E:, D=E:D=	D		D=		
AND drop finally before T: (bad time) BA¼TAE:M, (good taste) G*U*¼TeS:T	D	.¼(T	&		&
OR drop finally before or after consonant: (cold) K*o*L±¼ (bad back) BA¼BVAK	D			.¼Ɪ¢	
No change	F	F	&	&	&
Drop finally following "N": (sing) SE:N¼ (going) G*o*E:N¼ (along) AL±ON¼	G	.¼)N	&	&	&
OR becomes *h* before I or E, (get) *h*A:T (give) *h*E:BV, (general) *h*A:Ne*R*:AL±	G			*h*(IE	
OR drop finally before consonant: (big boy) BE:¼BV*o*E:,(dig for) D±E:¼FO*R*:	G			.¼(¢	
Change in all positions: (he) *h*E: (anyhow) A:NE:*h*O, (have) *h*ABV	H	*h*		&	&
OR change: *h*½E:, A:NE:*h*½O, *h*½ABV			*h*½		
Change in all positions: (judge) *CoC* (enjoy) A:NC*o*E:, (logic) L*o*CE:K	J	C	&	&	
OR change: *zoz*, A:Nz*o*E:, L*o*zE:K					z
No change: (keep) KE:P, (ache) eK	K	K	&	&	&
Against upper teeth: (lead) L±E:D±, (ill) E:L± (blue) BL±*U* (call) KOL±	L	L±	&	&	&
Change when spelled "LLI": (million) ME:Y*o*N, (brilliant) B*R*½E:YANT	L	Y$ lli	&	&	
OR change: ME:z*o*N, B*R*½E:zANT					z$lli
Drop finally before consonant: (arm band) A*R*½¼BVAN¼ (seem to) SE:¼T*U*	M			.¼(¢	
Drop finally before consonant: (sun sign) S*o*¼S:AE:N, (pen pal) PA¼PAL±	N			.¼(¢	
No change: (bank) BA*n*, (think) TE:*n*	*n*	*n*	&	&	&
No change	P	P	&	&	&

Key:

				R trilled R
& as shown	z measure	(preceding	: longer	¢ consonant
h loch, ich	/ medially	Ɪ before/after	½ weakened	= interdental
$ spelled	° finally	) following	¼ dropped	± upper "

GENERAL AMERICAN SPANISH - BOGOTÁ COLOMBIAN - CARIBBEAN: PUERTO RICAN and CUBAN - BUENOS AIRES-MONTEVIDEO

GUIDE PAGES

	SOUND	General American Spanish	Bogotá Colombian	Caribbean: Puerto Rican & Cuban	Buenos Aires Montevideo
Change initially: (quake) K*i*WeK, (question) K*i*WA:S:C*o*N (quit) K*i*WE:T	Q	-K*i*W	&	&	&
Strong Trill: (read) R:E:D±, (very) BVA:R:E:, (for) FOR:, (rich) R:E:C	R	R:	&	&	
OR trill RE:D±, BVA:RE: FOR, RE:C	R				R
BUT a light tap before or after a consonant: (dry) D±R½AE:, (part) PAR½T	R	R½ʃ¢	&	&	&
ADD "*i*" sound initially before or after consonant: (sleep) *i*SL±E:P (what say) *i*WAT*i*Se, (smile) *i*SMAE:L±	S	-*i*Sʃ¢	&	&	&
Longer medially: (insect) E:NS:A:KT, (basin) BeS:E:N, (decide) D±E:S:AE:D±	S	/S:	&	&	&
OR change medially AND finally before B, D, G, L, M, N, R or V: (disband) D±E:z½BVAND± (dismiss) D±E:z½ME:S	S				/.z½(B,D,G L etc
No change: (ship) SE:P, (sure) S*U*R:	*S*	*S*	&		&
OR change: CE:P, C*U*R:, (dish) D±E:C	*S*			C	
No change: (outset) *O*sA:T (waits) *i*Wes	s	s	&	&	&
Drop finally before "D": (get done) GA:¼D±*o*N, (sat down) SA¼D±*O*N	T	.¼(D	&	&	&
OR drop finally after consonant (fact) FAK¼ (salt) SOL±¼ (rest) R:A:S¼	T			.¼)¢	
Change in all positions: (thing) TE:N, (bath) BAT, (healthy) *h*A:L±TE:	*t*	T	&	&	
OR change: SE:N, BAS, *h*A:LSE:	*t*				S
Change in all positions: (mother) M*o*D±eR: (that) D±AT (smooth) *i*SM*U*D±	*T*	D±	&	&	
OR change: M*o*ZeR:, ZAT, *i*SM*U*Z	*T*				Z
Change in all positions: (vote) BV*o*T (never) NA:BVeR: (of) OBV (give) GE:BV	V	BV	&	&	&
ADD "*i*" sound: (week) *i*WE:K, (subway) S*o*BV*i*We, (will) *i*WE:L±, (why) *i*WAE:	W	*i*W	&	&	&
"GS" for "GZ" sound (see exceptions below) (example) A:GSAMP*u*L± (executive) A:GSA:KUTE:BV (exist) A:GSE:S:T	X	GS 4 gz!	&	&	&
AND "S" finally before consonant: (tax man) TASMAN, (six times) SE:STAE:MS:	X	.S(¢	&	&	&
ALSO "S" in "exact" and "examine": A:SAKT, A:SAMAN	X	S in exact	&	&	&
Change in all positions: (zone) S:*o*N, (busy) BE:S:E: (use) US: (his) *h*E:S:	Z	S:	&	&	&
OR change finally before B, D, G, L, M, N, R or V: (his bed) *h*E:zBVA:D±, (wise man) *i*WAE:zMAN (size nine) SAE:zNAE:N	Z				z.(B D,G,L M etc

Key:

		± upperdental		C church
h loch, ich	- initially	(preceding	: stronger	¢ consonant
z measure	/ medially	ʃ before/after	½ weakened	R trilled R
4 for	. finally	) following	¼ drop	& as shown

GENERAL MEXICAN - MEXICO CITY - NOGALES-SONORA-BAJA - DISTRITO FEDERAL (EDUCATED)

GUIDE PAGES	SOUND	General Mexican	Mexico City Less Educated	Nogales Sonora-Baja	Distrito Federal Educ.
Change in all positions: (air) eR:, (able) eBVuL±, (pain) PeN, (they) D±e	A	e	§	§	
OR shorten: A½R:, A½BVuL, PA½N, D±TA½	A				A½
Longer sound: (eat) E:T, (teach) TE:C, (me) ME: (emit) E:ME:T (steel) iSTE:L±	E	E:	§	§	§
Stress second element: (I'm) AE:M, (side) SAE:D±, (try) TR½AE:	I	AE:	§	§	§
Change in all positions: (old) oL±¼ (bone) BoN, (no) No, (only) oML±E:	O	o	§	§	
OR no change: OL±D±, BON, ONL±E:	O				O
No change: (you) U, (mule) MUL±	U	U	§	§	§
Change in all positions (as) AS: (bad) BAD± (at) AT (magic) MAhE:K (act) AK¼	a	A	§		§
OR no change: aS:,BaD±,aT,MaCE:K,aK¼				a	
Change in all positions: (end) A:N¼, (leg) L±A:G, (every) A:BVeR:E:	e	A:	§	§	§
Change in all positions: (it) E:T, (women) iWE:MAN, (busy) BE:S:E:	i	E:	§	§	§
Change in all positions: (odd) OD±, (clock) KL±OK, (not) NOT, (on) ON	o	O	§		
OR change: oD±, KL±oK, NoT, oN	o			o	o
Change in all positions: (love) L±oBV (up) oP, (does) D±oS:, (was) iWoS:	u	o		§	§
OR change: L±ABV, AP, D±AS:, iWAS:	u		A		
No change: (are) AR:, (calm) KAL±M	A	A	§		§
OR change: aR:, KaL±M, (watch) iWaC	A			a	
When spelled "er": (earn) eR½N (heard) heR½, (were) iWeR:, (butter) BoTeR:	E	e$er	§	§	§
When spelled "ir" (stir) iSTE:R: (first) FE:R½S¼ (dirty) D±E:R½TE: (girl) GE:R½L±	E	E:$ir	§	§	
OR: iSTo½R:, Fo½R½ST, D±o½R½TE:, Go½R½L±	E				o½$ir
When spelled "or" (work) iWoR½K (world) iWoR½L±¼, (comfort) KoNFoR:¼	E	o$or	§	§	
OR: iWo½R½K, iWo½R½L±D±, KoMFo½R½T	E				o½$or
When spelled "ur": (current) KuR:iN¼, (burn) BuR½N, (return) R:E:TuR½N	E	u$ur	§	§	§
No change: (predict) PR½ID±E:K¼	I	I	§	§	§
No change: (out) OT, (down) D±ON	O	O	§	§	§
No change: (do) D±U, (soon) SUN	U	U	§	§	§
Change in all positions (after) aFTeR: (and) aN¼ (fast) FaS:¼, (half) ¼aL±F	a	a	§		
OR change: AFTeR:, AND, FAS:¼, ¼AL±F	a			A	A

Key: C church R trilled R
§ as shown $ spelled h loch, ich : stronger ½ weakened ¼ dropped

GENERAL MEXICAN - MEXICO CITY - NOGALES-SONORA-BAJA - DISTRITO FEDERAL (EDUCATED)

GUIDE PAGES	SOUND	General Mexican	Mexico City Less Educated	Nogales Sonora-Baja	Distrito Federal Educ.
When spelled "le" after a consonant: (simple) SE:MP*u*L±, (title) TAE:T*u*L±	*e*	*u*L± $1e)¢	&	&	&
Change in all positions: (system) SE:S:TAM (ago) AG*o* (balance) BALANS:	*i*	A	&	&	&
When spelled "a, au" or "aw": (cause) KOS:, (awful) OF*u*L±, (all) OL±	*o*	O$a au,aw	&	&	&
NO change spelled "o, oa, oo" or "ou": (off) *o*F, (door) D±*o*R:, (court) K*o*R:¼	*o*	*o*$oa o etc	&	&	&
Change in all positions: (could) K*U*D±, (push) P*U*S, (foot) F*U*T, (put) P*U*T	*u*	*U*	&	&	&
Lengthen: (boy) B*o*E:, (oil) *o*E:L±	*o*E	*o*E:	&	&	&
Change medially: (husband) *ho*S:BVAN¼, (habit) *h*ABVE:T, (absent) ABVS:A:N¼	B	/BV	&	&	&
BUT no change after M or N: (rainbow) *R*:eMB*o*, (number) N*o*MBe*R*:	B	B)MN	&	&	&
No change: (change) *C*eN*C*, (much) M*oC*	*C*	*C*	&	&	&
Against upper teeth: (day) D±e, (body) BOD±E:, (need) NE:D±, (did) D±E:D±	D	D±	&	&	&
AND drop finally before T: (bad time) BA¼TAE:M, (good taste) G*U*¼TeS:T	D	.¼(T	&	&	&
AND drop finally after a consonant: (cold) K*o*L±¼ (and) aN¼(word) *i*W*o*R:¼	D	.¼)¢	&		
No change	F	F	&	&	&
DROP finally following "N": (sing) SE:N¼ (going) G*o*E:N¼ (along) AL±*o*N¼	G	.¼)N	&	&	
CHANGE to *h* before I or E: (get) *h*A:T (give) *h*E:BV, (general) *h*A:N*e*R:AL±	G	*h*(i,e	&		
DROP initially: (he) ¼E:, (have) ¼aBV	H	-¼	&		
Change in all other positions (anyhow) A:NE:*h*O, (behind) BE:*h*AE:N¼	H	*h*	&	&	
OR change: A:NE:*h*½O BE:*h*½AE:ND±	H				*h*½
Change in all positions: (edge) A:*C* (enjoy) A:M*C*oE:, (logic)L±OCE:K, (judge) *C*o*C*, (giant) *C*AE:AN¼	J	*C*	&	&	
OR change: A½*C*½, A:N*C*½*o*E:, L±*o*C½E:K	J				*C*½
No change: (keep) KE:P, (ache) eK	K	K	&	&	&
Against upper teeth: (lead) L±E:D± (ill) E:L± (blue) BL±*U* (call) KOL±	L	L±	&	&	&
Change when spelled "LLI" (million) ME:Y*o*N, (brilliant) BR½E:YANT	L	Y$ 11i	&	&	&

Key:

& as shown	- initially	: stronger	¢ consonant
$ spelled	/ medially	½ weakened	± upperdental
(before	. finally	¼ dropped	*h* loch, ich
) after			*R* trilled R

GENERAL MEXICAN - MEXICO CITY - NOGALES SONORA-BAJA - DISTRITO FEDERAL (EDUCATED)

GUIDE PAGES	SOUND	General Mexican	Mexico City Less Educated	Nogales Sonora-Baja	Distrito Federal Educ.
Change finally before consonant: (arm band) AR½NBVaN¼ (seem to) SE:NTU	M	.N(¢	&		
Change medially before consonant (onto) OMTU (until) oMTE:L± (inmate) E:MMeT	N	/M(¢	&		
No change: (bank) BA*n*, (think) TE:*n*	*n*	*n*	&	&	&
No change	P	P	&	&	&
Change initially: (quake) K*i*WeK, (question) K*i*WA:S:CoN (quit) K*i*WE:T	Q	-K*i*W	&	&	&
Strong trill: (read) *R*:E:D±, (very) BVA:*R*:E:, (for) Fo*R*:, (rich) *R*:E:C	R	*R*:	&	&	&
BUT a light tap before or after a consonant: (dry) D±*R*½AE:, (park) PA*R*½K	R	*R*½I¢	&	&	&
ADD "*i*" sound initially before or after consonant: (sleep) *i*SL±E:P (what say) *i*WAT*i*Se, (smile) *i*SMAE:L±	S	I¢	&	&	&
Longer medially: (insect) E:NS:A:K¼, (basin) BeS:E:N (decide) D±E:S:AE:D±	S	/S:	&	&	&
CHANGE (shut) CoT (cash) KaC (sure) CUR:	S	C	&		
OR no change: SoT, KAS, SUR:	S			S	S
No change: (outset) O*s*A:T (waits) *i*We*s*	*s*	*s*	&	&	&
DROP finally before "D": (get done) *h*A:¼D±oN, (sat down) SA¼D±ON	T	.¼(D	&	&	&
AND drop finally after consonant (fact) FAK¼ (salt) SOL±¼ (rest) *R*:A:S¼	T	.¼)¢	&	&	
Change in all positions: (thing) TE:N, (bath) BAT, (healthy) *h*A:L±TE:	*t*	T	&	&	
OR change: T*t*E:NG, BAT*t*, *h*½A:LT*t*E:	*t*				T*t*
Change in all positions: (mother) MoD±e*R*:, (that) D±AT, (smooth) *i*SMUD±	T	D±		&	
OR change: MATe*R*:, TAT, *i*SMUT	T		T		
OR change: MoD±Te*R*:, D±TAT, *i*SMUD±T	T				D±T
Change in all positions: (vote) BVoT (never) NA:BVe*R*: (of) OBV (give) *h*E:BV	V	BV	&	&	&
ADD "*i*" sound: (week) *i*WE:K, (subway) SoBV*i*We, (will) *i*WE:L±, (why) *i*WAE:	W	*i*W	&	&	&
"GS" for "GZ" sound (see exceptions below) (example) A:GSAMPuL, (executive) A:GSA:KUTE:BV, (exist) A:GSE:S:¼	X	GS 4 gz!	&	&	&
AND "S" finally before consonant (tax man) TASMAN, (six times) SE:STAE:MS:	X	.S(¢	&	&	&
ALSO in "A:SAK¼" and "A:SAMAN"	X	exact	&	&	&
Change in all positions: (zone) S:oN, (busy) BE:S:E: (use) US: (his) *h*E:S:	Z	S:	&	&	&

Key:

				C church
& as shown	- initial	(preceding	: stronger	¢ consonant
h loch, ich	/ medially	I before/after	½ weakened	± upperdental
4 for	. finally	) following	¼ dropped	*R* trilled R

Ricardo Montalban and Herve Villechaize, stars of TV's Fantasy Island. *Montalban's highly educated Mexican dialect is so refined that it can almost serve as a "cosmopolitan Latin-American" model, and it has a clarity that contrasts sharply with Herve Villechaize's native Parisian French dialect.*

MASTER CATEGORY 3

IBERIAN (EUROPEAN) SPANISH

The annual number of immigrants from Spain to the U.S. has always been far below the number from Germany, Italy, or Poland. Why then should Iberian (European) Spanish occupy such an important place in our studies and in this book?

Prospective roles is one reason. Due to the poverty that Spain suffered under the decades-long dictatorship of Francisco Franco, tens of thousands of Spanish youths left their country to seek their livelihoods in lands that enjoyed higher standards of living. Then too, the depressed wages and the consequent cheapness of Spanish labor and services turned several parts of Spain into tourist havens for the rest of the Western world.

Both situations contributed to the creation of a large group of people who speak English with a European Spanish accent, and many acting roles that require—or allow—Iberian Spanish dialects to be used.

In addition, historical plays and films that take place between the late fifteenth and early nineteenth centuries very often have Iberian Spanish characters, since Spain was a leading world power during this period.

There are a great number of similarities between European Spanish and American Spanish, so, of course, if you have absorbed the Latin-American dialect, mastering the Iberian one will be much easier than learning a brand new dialect.

Naturally, there are differences between American Spanish and Iberian Spanish as well as similarities. When I first moved to Spain, I expected my ear to be well attuned to both Spanish and to the English spoken by Spaniards. After all, I had lived in Central and South America for over a year, and it was the same language, wasn't it? I was in for a big surprise. Neither the rhythm, pace, nor sound were similar.

Vowel Sounds

Where Latin Americans produce longer vowel sounds than those in English, and originate them from farther forward in the mouth, the Spaniard speaking English has the opposite tendencies. Thus the European Spanish will take the sound of "e" as in "bed," "leg," "men," and "pet" and move it back in the mouth until it becomes the "a" of "bad," "lag," "man," and "pat." This means that if one would "expect" a "wet smell" after a rain, a Spaniard would:

(aKS:PaKT=) a (*i*WaT= *i*SMaL±).

Likewise, the European Spanish will move the "oo" of "fool" back until it becomes the "u" of "full." The Spanish rendition of "mood" thus rhymes with the American "good," and that of "boot" with the American "put." So, a student from Spain complaining of "a poor schoolroom," would speak of:

a (P*uR*½ *i*SK*u*L± *R*½*u*M).

You will find it harder to make this substitution for words that *end* in the "oo" (*U*) sound, since there are no words in English that end in (*u*). However, by using the following method (also described on page 12), even this obstacle can be overcome.

Say that you have the words "too," "who," "shoe," and "knew" in your dialogue. Simply add the letter that will make the changed sound into a familiar word. In this case, the letter "k" changes the above words into "took," "hook," "shook," and "nook." Now pronounce the new words aloud until you get the feel and placement of the vowel sound. Then merely drop the final "k" to get your completed vowel substitution.

The diphthong (two sounds combined) "yoo" (U) as in "use" undergoes a similar change. Thus the high school coed who wants to invite a "few cute youths" to her party, if Spanish, will invite:

a (FY*u* KY*u*T= Y*ut*:S)

to the gathering.

Placing the sounds farther back in the mouth shortens many vowels—as you can hear in the words "poor" and "few," mentioned earlier. This effect goes so far with certain diphthongs that it strips them of their second sounds entirely.

Take the "ay" (A) of "late," main," and "raid." This sound is made up of "eh" (e) as in "bed" followed by "ee" (E) as in "bead." The Iberian completely drops the second sound, so that the above examples become "let," "men," and "red." In other words, if "they vacated" the "place" because of floods, to the Spaniard:

(*T*:e BVeKeT=*e*D=) the (PL±eS).

Another example is the "oh" (O) of "own"—made up of "aw" (*o*) and "oo" (*U*). This is the vowel in "so," "coal," and "low." The European Spanish omit the second sound, making these words into "saw," "call," and "law." Thus, if your character wants to "grow potatoes," if Spanish, he or she will:

(G*R*½*o* P*o*T=eT=*o*S:).

You can see from this change that the Spanish often pronounce vowels as they would in their native tongue. When they do, they are in complete agreement with their Latin-American cousins. Consequently, if you have already mastered the section on American Spanish, you can treat the remaining information on vowels as a review and refresher.

The Spanish pronunciation of the letter "o" being "aw" (*o*), the sound of "odd" and "cot" changes to "awed" and "caught." This means that if the game the children were playing was "not hopscotch," for the Spanish, it was:

(N*o*T= *ho*PSK*oC*).

Again, since the Spanish pronunciation of the letter "u" is "oo," the sound of "full" and "pull" becomes that of "fool" and "pool." When your character thinks something "would look pitiful," if from Spain you would say it:

(*i*W*U*D= L±*U*K PE:T=*e*F*U*L±).

Did you notice how the "*I*" *sound* in "pitiful" changes? This is because the Spaniard reads the letter "i" as a long "ee" sound, pronouncing "it," "is," "fill," and "lick" as though they were "eat," "ease," "feel," and "leak." So, if you think someone is being a "bit inquisitive," If Spanish, you would say that they were being a:

(BE:T= E:NK*i*WE:S:E:T=E:BV).

Note that the "i" is changed not merely into "ee" (E), but into something longer: "eee" (E:). This extension applies not only to the sound in "eat" (E:T=) and "east" (E:ST=), but to *both* diphthongs of which "ee" (E) is a part. This means that the (I) of "pipe" becomes the (*A*E:) of (P*A*E:P) and the (*o*E) of "boy" becomes the (*o*E:) of (B*o*E:).

Since the Spanish pronounce any letter "a" as "ah," three different American sounds change. The "a"s of "bad," "fast," and "ago" all become "ah"s: (B*A*D=), (F*A*S:T=) and (*A*G*o*).

Finally, though "earn," "girl," "work," and "blur" all share the same vowel sound—(*E*)—in American English, in the Spanish dialect they receive four different vowels because of their spellings. Thus, if the latest reports you "heard were better," the ones the Spaniard:

(*he**R*½D= *i*We*R*½ BaT=e*R*:).

And when the recipe tells you to "stir first," someone from Spain would read it as:

(*i*ST=E:*R*½ FE:*R*½S:T=).

A travel agent offering a "world" of "comfort," if Spanish would be offering a:

(*i*W*oR*½L±D=) of (K*o*MF*oR*½T=).

And someone undergoing a "burning urge," as a Spaniard would suffer a:

(B*uR*½NE:NG½ *uR*½*z*).

Consonant Changes

In the above examples, you may have noted that the Spanish "r" is trilled (*R*) lightly (*R*½) before or after another consonant. This trill is made by placing the tip of the tongue against the gum ridge behind the upper front teeth, and then voicing the sound. If you are doing this right, the tongue will vibrate, or "tap." If it is a strong trill (*R*:)—as with a Spanish "r" in *any* position *except* before or after another consonant—the sound will be much like the one we made as children when imitating a pneumatic drill, a motorcycle, or a machine gun.

So, the selective short-story fan who only "reads very rare stories," if Spanish, only:

(*R*:E:D=S: BVa*R*:E: *R*:e*R*:
*i*ST=o*R*:E:S:).

When the book fell in the pool, we might find selecting a "dry part hard," while a Spaniard would say:

(D=*R*½AE: PA*R*½T= *hAR*½D=).

Certain American consonant sounds are totally missing from Spanish. This includes "h," "j," "q," "w," and any initial "s" when followed by a consonant. In this latter case, since it is not possible to start a word in Spanish with an "s" and then a consonant, the Spaniards insert the "i" from "family" (*i*) before all such initial "s"s. If this news makes you "slowly stop smiling," in Spanish dialect it would make you:

(*i*SL±oL±E: *i*ST=oP
*i*SM*A*E:L±E:NG½).

This same help sound (*i*) is used by Spaniards when they try to pronounce the American "w." So, if you are still trying to find out "what will work," with an Iberian role, you will seek:

(*i*WoT= *i*WE:L± *i*Wo*R*½K).

The American initial and medial "qu"s are actually pronounced "kw" by us. Since there is that "w" in there, the (*i*) sound is again inserted. In other words, if the students were all "equally quiet," the Spanish would find them all:

(E:K*i*W*A*L±E: K*i*W*A*E:aT=).

We also mentioned "h" as being missing from the Spaniard's repertoire. The closest sound the Spanish can manage is (*h*), restricting the "h"s flow of air by arching the back of the tongue. This sound is produced in the same place as our (G) or (K). In the case of (*h*) however, the air is not cut off entirely. Instead, a narrow opening is left by the arched tongue, producing a friction as the air hisses through. To speak of the lucky amateur gardener "who has his" own "hothouse" in Spanish dialect, we would say:

(*hu hA*S: *h*E:S:) own (*ho*T=*hAU*S).

While the Spanish alphabet does contain the letter "h," it is silent. The Spanish letter "j," on the other hand, *is* spoken aloud—however as (*h*); nowhere near the American "j." Distinct from the Latin Americans, the European Spanish substitute the (*z*) sound of "measure." So an officer complaining of serving under a "strange major general," if from Spain would complain of a:

(*i*ST=*R*½eN*z* Me*zoR*½ *z*ANe*R*:*a*L±).

Except in Andalusia, the Iberian pronunciation of the letter "z" is "th" as in "bath." Since seeing a "theebra at the thoo" strays far from the American sound, the Spanish substitute a strong "s" (S:) for our "z." This means that "zeal" and "zip" end up sounding much more like "seal" and "sip." And a visitor who wants to see the "zoo's laziest zebra," if from Spain would watch the:

(S:*u*S: L±eS:E:aS:T= S:E:BV*R*½*A*).

As with the Latin American, the Iberian does not place the tip of the tongue in the same position as Americans do for the letters "d," "l," and "t." For the "d," as an example, the tongue is even farther forward than in Latin American. Instead of forming this letter by touching the gum ridge behind the upper teeth, the tip of the tongue goes *between* (=) the teeth. Thus, a premed student who "needs good credits" to go on to medical school, being from Spain finds he:

(NE:D=S: G*U*D= K*R*½aD=E:T=S).

Quite possibly you noticed that the "t" in "credits" above also received an interdental (=) treatment; that is to say, it is pro-

Fernando Rey's portrayal in The French Connection *(20th Century Fox, 1971) gave contemporary American movie-goers their first taste of the Iberian Spanish dialect. Suppressed here (because of role requirements), Rey's dialect was allowed more latitude in his starring role in* Monsignor. *It will be interesting to see if movie-makers will ever cast him as a Spaniard, rather than a French Corsican or Italian.*

nounced with the tongue *between* (=) the teeth. Since the Iberian Spanish handle all "t"s this way, a hostess serving a "taste treat" for "dessert," if in Spain would offer a:

(T=eS:T= T=*R*½E:T=) for
(D=E:S:e*R*½T=).

As with American Spanish, Iberian Spanish forms the "l" with the tip of the tongue touching the upper teeth (±). Experiment with this for a while: You will hear a *thicker* sound than the American "l." This means that when we speak of movie audiences who "like blue-collar films," in Spanish dialect we would speak of those who:

(L±*AE*:K BL±*u* *Ko*L±*AR*½
FE:L±MS:).

When you review this material in the *GUIDE PAGES* that follow, you will come across a number of additional changes in pronunciation. However, these are all either minor, conditional, or restricted to the Filipino dialects. So the last major change we will examine here has to do with the Spanish rendition of the American "b" and "v" sounds. For the "v" as in "view," the Spaniard uses a mouth position halfway between "b" and "v." This is to say, the Spanish *almost* bring their tensed lips together as for a "b," but then, with the lips still taut but slightly apart, they voice the letter as one does with a "v." So if the quiet man had "never voiced" a "view," the Spaniard would describe him as having:

(NaBVe*R*½ BV*o*E:S:T=) a (BVY*u*).

This same treatment is given the letter "b" in the middle of a word. The only exception is when the "b" follows an "m" or an "n"—as in "number" and "rainbow." Thus the woman who complains that her "husband's absence" is a "habit," if Spanish would say that her:

(*ho*S:BV*A*ND=S: *A*BVS:aNS) is a (*h*ABVE:T=).

Music, Rhythm, and Pace

As with American Spanish, Iberian Spanish has a music marked both by placement (one tone higher than American speech) and a falling inflection (lowered tone) at the end of a phrase or sentence. Also, the rhythm of speech is borrowed from the mother tongue. The stress in a word is *always placed on the last vowel to come before a consonant*. A fuller explanation and description of this, plus a practice paragraph, can be found in the preceding chapter (pages 32–33).

In contrast to American Spanish, the Iberian Spanish dialect has a decidedly staccato feel to its rhythm. What's more, it is spoken at a much brisker pace than either American Spanish or American English. Naturally, this pace is carried over into English when spoken by Spaniards. If you have the accompanying cassettes, this would be a good time to play the examples of rhythm and pace—for both American Spanish and Iberian Spanish. The contrast might surprise you.

Observation and Notes

Observation is a little more difficult with the Iberian dialects than with the Latin-American ones. Not that there aren't plenty of films made in Spain, but nearly all of them that come to our television and theater screens have been dubbed into English by other actors. Nor are there any top stars—aside from Fernando Rey—who come from Spain, but instead many feature players whose faces are much more familiar than their names.

For this reason, the cassettes devote a proportionately longer section to Spain and her many dialects. Here, too, you will find the dialects of the Philippines, a Spanish possession for hundreds of years. These dialects are also included in the following GUIDE PAGES.

Since television will not serve its usual role as home tutor when it comes to Iberian dialects, you'll need to attune your ear to what you hear from the cassettes and/or what you hear in person. This means checking your local Spanish-speaking community and the Spanish-language teachers of your local colleges. It can be time consuming to track down dialect models, but like everything in acting that gives you a true sense of security and authenticity, it will be well worth it.

Note: The *Madrid* dialect in the GUIDE PAGES represents those Spaniards most educated in American English.

GENERAL IBERIAN SPANISH - SEVILLE, ANDALUSIAN - TOLEDO, LESS EDUCATED - MADRID, EDUCATED

GUIDE PAGES

		General Iber.	Seville Anda.	Toledo Less Educ.	Madrid Educated
Change in all positions: (pain) PeN, (air) e*R*:, (they) *T*:e, (able) eBV*u*L±	A	e	&	&	
OR shorten: PA½N, A½*R*:, *T*:A½, A½BV*u*L±	A				A½
					All 4
LONGER: (eat) E:T=, (teach) T=E:*C*, (emit) E:ME:T=	E				E:
STRESS 2nd element: (I'm) AE:M, (side) SAE:D=, (by) BAE:	I				AE:
CHANGE: (old) *o*L±D=, (bone) B*o*N, (no) N*o*, (only) *o*NL±E:	O				*o*
CHANGE: (you) Y*u*, (mule) MY*u*L±, (new) NY*u*, (use) Y*u*S:	U				Y*u*
CHANGE: (as) *A*S:, (bad) B*A*D=, (at) *A*T=, (magic) M*A*zE:K	a				*A*
CHANGE: (end) aND=, (leg) L±aG, (every) aBVe*R*:E:	e				a
CHANGE: (it) E:T=, (women) *i*WE:MAN, (busy) BE:S:E:	i				E:
CHANGE: (odd) *o*D=, (clock) KL±*o*K, (not) N*o*T=, (on) *o*N	o				*o*
Change in all positions: (was) *i*W*o*S:, (love) L±*o*BV, (up) *o*P, (does) D=*o*S:	u	*o*	&		&
OR change: *i*WAS:, L±ABV, AP, D=AS:	u			A	
No change: (are) AR:, (calm) KAL±M	A	A	&	&	&
When spelled ER: (earn) e*R*½N, (heard) *h*e*R*½D= (were) *i*We*R*: (butter) B*o*T=e*R*:	*E*	e$er	&	&	&
When spelled IR: (dirty) D=E:*R*½T=E:, (stir) *i*ST=E:*R*:, (first) FE:*R*½ST=	*E*	E:$ir	&	&	
OR: D=*iR*½T=E:, *i*ST=*iR*:, F*iR*½ST=	*E*				*i*$ir
When spelled OR: (comfort) K*o*MF*oR*½T=, (work) *i*W*oR*½K, (world) *i*W*oR*½L±D=	*E*	*o*$or	&	&	
OR: K*o*MF*iR*½T=, *i*W*iR*½K, *i*W*iR*½L±D=	*E*				*i*$or
When spelled UR: (current) K*uR*:*i*NT=, (burn) B*uR*½N, (return) R:E:T=*uR*½N	*E*	*u*$ur	&	&	&
					All 4
No change: (predict) P*R*½*I*D=E:KT=	*I*				*I*
Separate sounds: (out) *AU*T=, (down) D=*AU*N, (now) N*AU*	*O*				*AU*
CHANGE: (do) D=*u*, (soon) S*u*N, (rule) *R*:*u*L±, (soup) S*u*P	*U*				*u*
CHANGE: (after) *A*FT=e*R*:, (and) *A*ND=, (fast) F*A*S:T=	*a*				*A*
When spelled LE after consonant: (simple) SE:MP*u*L±	*e*				*u*$1e)¢
CHANGE: (system) SE:S:T=*A*M, (ago) *A*G*o* (balance) BAL±*A*NS:	*i*				*A*
When spelled A,AU,AW: (cause) K*o*S:, (awful) *o*F*u*L±	*o*				o$a au
OTHERWISE no change: (off) *o*F, (court) K*oR*½T=, (or) *oR*:	*o*				*o*$o
CHANGE: (could) K*U*D=, (push) P*U*S, (foot) F*U*T= (put) P*U*T=	*u*				*U*
LENGTHEN: (boy) B*o*E:, (oil) *o*E:L±, (join) z*o*E:N	*o*E				*o*E:
CHANGE medially: (husband) *h*oS:BVAND=, (habit) *h*ABVE:T=	B				/BV!
EXCEPT after M or N: (number) N*o*MBe*R*:, (rainbow) *R*:eNB*o*	B				B)mn
No change: (change) *C*eNz, (much) M*oC*, (which) *i*WE:*C*	C				*C*
INTERDENTAL: (day) D=e, (need) NE:D=, (did) D=E:D=	D				D=
AND drop finally before T: (bad time) BA¼T=AE:M	D				.¼(t
OR drop finally after a consonant: (cold) K*o*L±¼ (and) AN½ (word) *i*W*oR*:¼	D			.¼)¢	
No change	F	F	&	&	&
WEAKEN in ING suffix: (going) G*o*E:NG½ (coming) K*o*ME:NG½ (morning) M*oR*½NE:NG½	G	G½ ing)	&	&	&
OR change before I or E: (get) *h*aT=, (give) *h*E:BV, (general) *h*a*N*e*R*:AL±	G			*h*(i,e	

Key:

		¼ dropped		
z measure	*h* loch,ich	(preceding	: stronger	= interdental
& as shown	/ medially	) following	½ weakened	± upper "
$ spelled	. finally	) in suffix	¢ consonant	*R* trilled R

GENERAL IBERIAN SPANISH - SEVILLE - TOLEDO - MADRID - *GUIDE PAGES*

		Genl.	Sevil.	Toledo	Madrid
Change in all positions: (anyhow) aNE:*hAU*, (have) *h*ABV, (he) *h*E:	H	*h*	&	&	
OR change: aNE:*h*½*AU*, *h*½ABV, *h*½E:	H				*h*½
OR drop initially: ¼ABV, ¼E:	H			- ¼	
Change in all positions: (edge) az, (enjoy) aNz*o*E:, (logic) L±*o*zE:K	J	z	&	&	
OR change: az½, aNz½*o*E:, L±*o*z½E:K	J				z½
No change: (keep) KE:P, (ache) eK	K	K	&	&	&
Against upper teeth: (lead) L±E:D=, (ill) E:L± (blue) BL±*u* (call) KOL±	L	L±	&	&	&
Change finally before consonant (arm band) *AR*½NBVAN¼, (seem to) SE:NT=*u*	M			.N(¢	
Change medially before consonant : (into) E:MT=*u*, (until) AMT=E:L±	N			/M(¢	
No change: (bank) BA*n*, (think) *t*:E:*n*	*n*	*n*	&	&	&
No change	P	P	&	&	&
CHANGE initially: (quake) K*i*WeK (question) K*i*WaS:*C*AN (quit) K*i*WE:T=	Q	-K*i*W	&	&	&
Strong trill: (read) *R*:E:D=, (very) BVa*R*:E:, (for) F*oR*:, (rich) *R*:E:*C*	R	*R*:	&	&	&
BUT a light tap before or after a consonant: (dry) D=*R*½AE:, (part) PA*R*½T=	R	*R*½][¢	&	&	&
ADD "*i*" sound initially before or after consonant (sleep) *i*SL±E:P (what say) *i*WAT=*i*Se (smile) *i*SMAE:L±	S	*i*S][¢	&	&	&
Longer medially: (insect) E:NS:aKT=, (basin) BeS:E:N (decide) D=E:S:AE:D=	S	/S:	&	&	&
CHANGE: (shut) *C*oT=, (sure) *C*u*R*:	S			*C*	
No change (outset) *AUs*aT= (waits) *i*We*s*	*s*	*s*	&	&	&
Between teeth: (take) T=eK, (into) E:NT=*u*, (sit) SE:T=, (ten) T=aN	T	T=		&	&
OR no change: TeK, E:NT*u*, SE:T, TaN	T		T		
AND drop finally before "D": (get done) Ga¼D=*o*N, (sat down) SA¼D=*AU*N	T	.¼(d	&	&	&
OR drop finally after consonant (fact) FAK¼ (salt) SOL±¼ (rest) *R*:aS¼	T			.¼)¢	

		All 4
STRONGER (thing) *t*:E:NG (bath) BA*t*: (healthy) *h*aL±*t*:E:	*t*	*t*:
STRONGER (mother) M*oT*:e*R*: (that) *T*:AT= (smooth) *i*SM*uT*:	*T*	*T*:
CHANGE all: (vote) BV*o*T=, (never) NaBVe*R*:, (of) ABV	V	BV
ADD "*i*" sound (week) *i*WE:K (subway) S*o*BV*i*We (will) *i*WE:L±	W	*i*W
"GS" for "GZ" sound (exceptions noted below) (executive) aGSaKY*u*T=E:BV, (example) aGSAMP*u*L± (exist) aGSE:S:T=	X	GS 4gz
AND S finally before consonant (tax man) T=ASMAN	X	∘S(¢
ALSO in (exact) aSAKT=, (examine) aSAMAN	X	exact

		Genl.	Sevil.	Toledo	Madrid
Change in all positions: (zone) S:*o*N (busy) BE:S:E: (use) Y*u*S: (his) *h*E:S:	Z	S:	&	&	&

Key:

h loch, ich	- initial	(preceding	: stronger	¢ consonant
z measure	/ medially	][before/after	½ weakened	= interdental
& as shown	∘ finally	) following	*C* church	± upper "
4 for		¼ dropped		*R* trilled R

GUIDE PAGES	SOUND	Manila Filipino	Bataan (Less Educated)	La Coruña Galicia
Change in all positions: (able) eBVuL±, (say) Se, (pain) PeN, (late) L±eT=	A	e	&	&
Change in all positions (eat) E:T= (steel) iST=E:L± (be)BVE: (each) E:C (seed) SE:D=	E	E:	&	&
Change in all positions: (I) AE:, (mind) MAE:N¼, (try) T=R½AE:, (right) R:AE:T=	I	AE:	&	&
Change in all positions: (own) oN, (gold) GoL±¼, (know) No, (boat) BVoT=	O	o	&	&
Change in all positions: (value) BVoL±U, (use) US:, (cute) KUT=, (pure) PU:R:	U	U	&	
OR change: BAL±Yu, YuSS, KYuT:, PYuR	U			Yu
Change in all positions (at) oT= (had) hoD= (happy) hoPE:, (as) oS:, (angry) oNGR½E:	a	o	&	
OR change: AT:, hAD=, hAPE:, AS , ANGR½E:	a			A
Change in all positions: (end) AN¼, (leg) L±AG, (dead) D=AD=, (sense) SANS	e	A	&	
OR change: aN¼, L±aG, D=aD=, SaNSS	e			a
Change in all positions: (it) E:T=, (in) E:N, (women) iWE:MAN, (busy) BVE:S:E:	i	E:	&	&
Change in all positions: (on) oN, (odd) oD= (drop) D=R½oP, (knot) NoT=, (lock) L±oK	o	o	&	&
Change in all positions: (up) oP, (cut) KoT=, (us) oS, (love) L±oBV, (touch) T=oC	u	o	&	&
LENGTHEN in all positions: (are) A:R:, (heart) hA:R½T=, (watch) iWA:C, (car) KA:R:	A	A:	&	
When spelled "er": (her) heR:, (were) iWeR:	E	e$er	&	&
When spelled "ir" (dirt) D=ER½T= (girl) GER½L±	E	E$ir	&	&
When spelled "or" (work) iWoR½K (word) iWoR:¼	E	o$or	&	&
When spelled "ur" (turn) T=uR½N (burn) BVuR½N	E	u$ur	&	&
No change: PR½ID-E:KT=, (produce) PR½ID=uS	I	I	&	&
Change in all positions: (count) KAuNT=, (out) AuT=, (town) T=AuN, (now) NAu	O	Au	&	
OR change: KAUNT:, AUT:, T±AUN, NAU				AU
Change in all positions: (room) R:uM, (soup) SuP, (move) MuBV, (true) T=R½u	U	u	&	&
Change in all positions (and) oN¼ (ask)oS:K (dance) D=oNS (last) L±oS:T= (can't) KoNT=	a	o	&	
OR change: AN¼, ASK, D=ANSS, L±AST:, KANT:				A
When spelled "le": (trouble) T=R½oBVuL±, (simple) SE:MPuL±, (title) T=AE:T=uL±	e	uL± $le	&	&
Change in all positions: (opinion) APE:NYAN, (ago) AGo, (system) SE:S:T=AM	i	A	&	&

Key:

h loch,ich	$ spelled	: stronger	= interdental	C itch,chew
& as shown	¼ dropped	½ weakened	± upper "	S show,sure
				R trilled R

MANILA FILIPINO - BATAAN (LESS EDUCATED) - LA CORUÑA, GALICIAN

GUIDE PAGES	SOUND	Manila Filipino	Bataan (Less Educated)	La Coruña Galicia
When spelled "a,au,aw": (all) OL±, (cause) KOS: (law) L±O (war) iWOR: (walk) iWOL±K	o	O$a au,aw	&	
OR change: oL±, KoS, L±o, iWoR:, iWoL±K				o$a
Change in all positions (could) KUD= (good) GUD=, (pull) PUL±, (look) L±UK, (put) PUT=	u	U	&	&
Change in all positions: (oil) oiL± (boy BVoi, (join) zoiN, (loyal) L±oieL±	oE	oi	&	
OR change: oE:L±, BVoE:, zoE:N, L±oE:eL±	oE			oE:
Change in all positions: (by) BVAE:, (but) BVoT= (submit) SoBVME:T= (maybe) MeBVE:	B	BV	&	&
OR except before M or N: SoBME:T:	B			B(MN
No change: (much) MoC, (change) CeNz	C	C	&	&
Change in all positions: (day) D=e, (body) BVoD=E:, (need) NE:D=, (did) D=E:D=	D	D=	&	&
AND drop finally before "T": (bad time) BA¼T=AE:M, (good taste) GU¼T=eS:T=	D	.¼(d	&	&
AND drop finally after consonant (hard) hA:R:¼ (cold) KoL±¼ (bird) BVE:R:¼ (lord) L±oR:¼	D	.¼)¢	&	&
OR except after R: hAR½D=, BE:R½D=, L±oR½D=	D			.D=)R
TEETH DO NOT touch lower lip: (fear) F#E:R: (off) oF#, (left) L±AF#T= (from) F#R½oM	F	F#		
OR change: P½E:R:, oP½, L±AP½T=, P½R½oM	F		P½	
Or no change: FE:R, oF, L±aFT:, FR½oM	F			F
Soften in "ing" suffix: (going) GoE:NG½ (coming) KoME:NG½, (singing) SE:NGE:NG½	G	G½ ing)	&	&
Change in all positions: (he) hE:, (how) hAu (behind) BVE:hAE:N¼ (ahead) AhAD=	H	h	&	&
Change in all positions (judge) zoz (edge) Az, (logic) L±ozE:K, (enjoy) ANzoi	J	z	&	&
No change: (keep) KE:P, (ache) eK	K	K	&	&
Against upper teeth (low) L±o (tell) T=AL± (lead) L±E:D= (clean) KL±E:N (halt) hOL±T=	L	L±	&	&
No change	MNnP	M	N n	P
Change initially: (quick) KiWE:K, (quite) KiWAE:T= (quart) KiWOR½T= (quit) KiWE:T=	Q	-KiW	&	&
STRONG trill: (read) R:E:D=, (are) A:R:, (wrong) R:oNG, (tomorrow) T=UMoR:o	R	R:	&	
BUT light tap before or after consonant: (try) T=R½AE: (park) PA:R½K (art) A:R½T=	R	R½][¢	&	&
OR trill: AR, PARK, ART±, (for) FoR	R			R
BUT strong trill initially and between vowels: R:E:D= (very) BaR:E: (rich) R:E:C	R			-R: R:ƒ
ALSO when spelled RR or following L,N or S: t±UMoR:O (alright) oL±R:AE:T± (inroad) E:NR:oD=	R			R:$rr (1Ns

Key:

h loch,ich	# open	(preceding	: stronger	¢ consonant
z measure	- initial	][before/after	½ weakened	= interdental
& as shown	. finally	) following	¼ dropped	± upper "
$ spelled		ƒ betwn vowels	) suffix	R trilled R

MANILA FILIPINO - BATAAN (LESS EDUCATED) - LA CORUÑA GALICIAN

GUIDE PAGES		Manila	Bataan	Galician
Add "ɩ" sound initially before or after consonant: (sleep) ɩSL±E:P, (speak) ɩSPE:K	S	-ɩS)(¢	ξ	
Longer medially: (decide) D=E:S:AE:D= (ask) oS:K (instead) E:NS:T=AD= (basis) BVeS:E:S	S	/S:	ξ	
OR no change initially or after a consonant: SL±E:P, (say) Se, (inside) E:NSAE:D=	S			-S S)¢
OR no change after a prefix or when spelled SS: D=E:SAE:D=, (class) KL±AS	S			S){ S$ss
OR change finally before K,F,P,S,T or at end of phrase: (ice caps.) AE:SSKAPSS		S		..SS
OR change between vowels: (basin) beZE:N, (leases) L±E:ZaS, (pricing) PRAE:ZE:NG½	S			Z#
OR change medially and finally before B,D,G, L,M,N,R or V: (useless.) Yuz½L±aSS, (dismiss) D=E:z½ME:S, (baseball) BVez½BVoL±	S			z½/. (bDlG mNrV
Change in all positions: (sure) SuR:, (special) ɩSPASeL±, (wish) ɩWE:S, (rush) R:oS	S	S	ξ	
OR no change: SuR, ɩSPaSeL±, ɩWE:S, RoS	S			S
No change: (outset) AusAT=, (waits) ɩWes	s	s	ξ	ξ
Between teeth: (take) T=eK, (into) E:NT=u (sit) SE:T=, (ten) T=AN, (test) T=AST=	T	T=	ξ	
AND drop finally before "D": (get done) GA¼D=oN, (sat down) So¼D=AuN	T	.¼(d	ξ	
AND add "ɩ" sound between TT: (better) BVATɩTeR:, (little) L±E:TɩTuL±	T	TɩT $tt	ξ	
OR against upper teeth: T±eK, E:NT±u, T±aN	T			T±
OR stronger finally: SE:T:, TaST:, GaT:, SAT:	T			.T:
Change in all positions: (thing) SE:NG (bath) BVAS, (healthy) ħaL±SE:	ŧ			S
OR no change: ŧE:NG, BVoŧ, ħAL±ŧE:	ŧ	ŧ	ξ	
Change in all positions: (that) T±oT=, (mother) MoT±eR:, (smooth) ɩSMuT±	T	T±	ξ	
OR change: ZAT:, MoZeR, ɩSMuZ	T			Z
Change in all positions (vote) BVoT= (never) NABVeR:, (of) oBV, (private) PR½AE:BVeT=	V	BV	ξ	
OR change: BoT:, NaBeR, oB, PR:AE:BeT:	V			B
ADD "ɩ" sound: (week) ɩWE:K, (subway) SoBVɩWe, (will) ɩWE:L±, (walk) ɩWOL±K	W	ɩW	ξ	ξ
GS for GZ sound (exceptions below): (executive) AGSAKUT=E:BV (example) AGSoMPuL±	X	GS 4 gz	ξ	ξ
AND "S" finally before a consonant: (tax man) T=oSMoN, (six times) SE:S:T=AE:MS:	X	.S(¢	ξ	ξ
ALSO (exact) ASoKT= (examine) ASoMAN	X	exact	ξ	ξ
Change in all positions: (busy) BVE:S:E:, (zone) S:oN, (use.) US:, (his.) ħE:S:	Z	S:	ξ	
OR finally before F,K,P,S or T or end of phrase: (was put) ɩWoSPUT, YuS, ħE:S	Z			..S .S(fK
OR change finally before B,D,G,L,M,N,R or V: (size nine) SAE:zNAE:N (his leg) ħE:zLaG	Z			.z(bD gLmNr

Key:

ħ loch, ich	4 for	(preceding	: stronger	.. end of senten
z measure	- initial	{ in prefix	½ weakened	# between vowels
ξ as shown	/ medial	) following	¼ dropped	= interdental
$ spelled	. final	R trilled R	¢ consonant	± upper "

MASTER CATEGORY 4

GERMAN & AUSTRIAN

In the 1950s London Films had a young Hungarian actress under contract. Naturally her boss, Sir Alexander Korda, made sure she was studying English with the best tutors money could buy. Yet there was a limitation placed upon what the tutors were allowed to teach that young actress: "Don't let her lose her accent entirely!" Seems contradictory, doesn't it? But in motion picture terms it made a great deal of sense. Here was a "talent" that London Films was investing in *as a foreign actress*. As long as she retained any sort of dialect (*Continental* preferred) she was a natural "loan out" to any of the American film companies that were trying to free their frozen assets in Europe by making motion pictures there. It was no coincidence that this actress's first big starring part in the West was in an American picture made in Italy. A dialect is not always a disadvantage.

It certainly was no disadvantage to my grandfather. His Berliner-German accent sounds in my memory's ear even today. Grandfather had been on the general staff of the Prussian Army, was very proud of his German heritage, and lived in a part of Pennsylvania where Germans made up the largest foreign minority. My mother's father was a brilliant man, with a sharp ear and a deep enjoyment of music. Undoubtedly he could have learned to speak perfect American English any time he wanted to. Indeed, when one of his visiting grandchildren stepped out of line, his reprimands were generally in flawless English, so that we wouldn't be able to pretend that we didn't understand him. But the sound of his own accent in his ears was undoubtedly comfortable for him, and his dialect was most probably retained as a very real part of his German heritage.

So it is with many people who speak with an accent; when they think through a sound, and when they *want* to communicate in clear American English, they can. But when the pressures abate, they go right back to their dialect.

My grandfather's influence on my life was minor, since he lived in Pennsylvania and my closest family lived in Chicago. Consequently, Grandfather's German accent was only one of many I heard in my formative years. Chicago has thousands of German-born people. My friends' parents often spoke with such dialects; one fellow's father even made his living operating a typical German *Biergarten* in our neighborhood. This, then, was my first introduction to the fact that my grandfather's Berlin dialect was not typical of all Germans.

My second submergence in German dialects came when I was barely seventeen, in Germany itself where I served just following World War II. At various times I was stationed in the north, the south, and even in central Germany. Since my initial assignment was in the Counter Intelligence Corps, I quickly reached the point where I could identify where a German had been born and raised by the way he or she spoke either German or English. The only ones who slipped by me were those who grew up speaking correct or "High" German. As this is the accepted tongue all over Germany, it naturally forms the basis for our study of General German Dialect.

On the whole, the German dialect is one of the easiest for the American ear to comprehend. This is because its speakers (and especially those who converse in "High" German) are used to pronouncing their consonants distinctly and their vowels clearly.

Vowel Changes

The handling of vowel sounds especially characterizes the German accent. Nearly eighty percent of German-dialect vowel sounds are the same or longer than the American ones; of those, three-quarters are longer.

Since lengthening a vowel consists merely in holding the sound longer than normal, we don't need to go into examples in this section; simply listing the longer vowel sounds should be sufficient.

First of all, the "ee" (E) of "he" and "she" is lengthened (:) into "eee" (E:). This also applies to the diphthongs (double sounds) that are made with (E). Thus, the "ay" (A) of "cake" becomes "ayee" (A:), and the "oy" (*o*E) of "boy" becomes "oyee" (*o*E:). The "ahee" (I) of "bite" and "sight" is stretched even longer, into "ahhh-eee" (*A*:E:).

You can deduce from that final "double stretching" that the "ah" element is also longer. This applies as well when "ah" (*A*) is by itself, as in "watch." That sound is lengthened into "ahh" (*A*:). This also happens to "ah" (*A*) when it's a part of other diphthongs. Thus "ow" (*O*), which is made up of "ah" (*A*) and "oo" (*U*), is stretched into "ahh-ooo" (*O*:).

Since you saw the "oo" (*U*) element lengthened into "ooo" (*U*:) above, it's a safe bet that this happens as well when the sound is found by itself, as in "too" (which becomes "too-oo"). We make two more diphthongs with "oo" (*U*); one is "yoo" (U) as in "use." Again, the sound is drawn out, making it into "yoo-oo" (U:). The other diphthong is made up of "aw" (*o*) and "oo" (*U*), and we combine these two elements to arrive at *our* sound "oh" (O), as in "boat." The German dialect, however, lengthens both of the component sounds until the diphthong becomes "aww-ooo" (O:).

The first sound in that diphthong, "aw" (*o*), is also stretched when found by itself *and when spelled with the letter "o."* Thus the "aw" (*o*) sound of "long" and "for" becomes "aww" (*o*:).

Another single sound that the Germans draw out is the short "oo" (*u*) of "book." Thus, if the director wants more extras in the hall because it "should look full," in German dialect it would be because it:

(*SU*:D:T L± *U*:G:K V:F*U*:L±).

Back in the American Spanish dialect we first encountered the phenomenon we called *reversal*: where the speaker exchanges two different vowel sounds for each other. In the German dialect, this applies to the "aw" (*o*) sound of "caught" and the short "ah" (o) sound of "cot." The first change takes place only when the "aw" (*o*) is spelled "a" as in "war," "au" as in "caught," or "aw" as in "law." This means that if the officer was a poor strategist who never "foresaw all losses," then in German dialect he never:

(V:F*o*:*r*So: o:L± L±*o*:ZS:*e*S::).

Notice that the "aw" (*o*) sounds in "fore-" and "losses" do not change, but merely lengthen (*o*:). This is because, in both instances, the "aw" (*o*) is spelled with an "o."

The reverse of the "aw" (*o*) becoming short "ah" (o), would be for that "ah" (o) of "not" and "clod" to come out sounding like the "aw" (*o*) of "naught" and "clawed"—and this is exactly what happens. So that if someone who touched an exposed wire "got" a "solid shock," in German dialect we'd say they:

(G:K*o*DT) a (ZS:*o*L±iD:T S*o*G:K).

There are four major vowel changes that reflect neither a "reversal" nor the lengthening tendency. The first is the "a" of "pack," "shall," "sat," and "tan." The German-speaking move this vowel forward in the mouth to become the "e" of "peck," "shell," "set," and "ten." So a comedy team who were known for their "madcap act," in German dialect would be famous for their:

(MeD:TG:KeB:P eG:KDT).

The next major vowel change is in the "uh" (u) sound of "cut," "bus," "done," and "fun." The Germans change this to the "aw" (*o*) sound of "caught," "boss," "dawn," and "fawn." Actually, as with the "aw" (*o*) sound itself, this changed vowel is drawn out into "awww" (*o*:). This means that if a carpenter

Lilli Palmer and Laurence Olivier in a scene from The Boys from Brazil *(20th Century Fox, 1978). Two authentic Austrian-German dialects: Palmer's was her heritage, but Lord Olivier's was learned and internalized—to the extent of having a slight trace of Germanic Yiddish. Though rather few, his dialect roles have always reflected the same kind of exactitude and self-discipline that brought him the Academy Award.*

thought his apprentice "was" a "young numbskull," if German he would tell his friends that the youth:

(V:Fo:S::) a (Yo:NG:K No:MSG:Ko:L±).

The third major vowel change affects the "aa" (*a*) of "hand" and "hatch" so that it rhymes with the "ah" (*A*) of "wand" and "watch." In other words, if a young man explains that he "can't dance fast," in German dialect he is complaining that he:

(G:KA:NDT D:TA:NS V:FA:SDT).

The last vowel sound we will examine here (though you'll find more in the *GUIDE PAGES*) is the (*E*) sound of "merger." Oddly enough, though the Germans have a sound in their own language that's similar—ö—they change the American sound into the "eh" (e) of "bell." Thus, if your daughter's "first words were 'burn' and 'earn,'" the German-speaking would say her:

(V:Fer:SDT V:Fer:D:TS:: V:Fer: 'B:Per:N') and ('er:N').

Consonant Changes

You may have noted that the last-mentioned vowel sound occurs only in conjunction with the letter "r"—but, as you saw from the above, the Germans make their "r"s entirely differently than we do. To be specific, the German "r" is heavily uvular (*r*:)—meaning that we employ the uvula to make this sound. The uvula is the small fleshy projection hanging down from the middle of the soft palate above the back of the tongue. For our purposes, it is more important for you to *feel* where it is than to see it. If you simply make a gargling sound, you will feel the back of your tongue vibrating against (or very near to) the uvula. If you arch the very back of your tongue into the position you use to clear your throat to spit, you will find the air hissing between the back of your tongue and your uvula. This is where the German "r" is formed and, since it is a voiced sound, the vibration of tongue and uvula produce a sound very similar to that of gargling, although softer. If you're not sure whether you're making the right sound, just check to see if the back of your tongue is vibrating against the soft palate above it. If it is, then you've got your uvular "r" (*r*:). Thus, if the zoo keeper can tell that the lions need feeding when he "hears their regular roars," when the zoo's in Germany, he:

(HE:*r*:S:: D:TA:*r*: *r*:eG:KU:L±e*r*: *r*:*o*:*r*:S::).

Another carry-over from the German language is the double sound of many of the consonants. Though "b," "d," and "g" are all single, voiced consonants, in German dialect (as in German), they are all double consonants; i.e., combined with their unvoiced counterparts "p," "t," and "k." This is to say that the first consonantal sound is the voiced one, immediately followed by the small explosion of air that makes up the unvoiced part. Since, in these combinations, the voiced part receives the emphasis, this means that both the letter "b" and the letter "p" are pronounced "bb-p" (B:P), "d" is pronounced "dd-t" (D:T), and both "g" and "k" are pronounced "gg-k" (G:K).

For the letter "t," although the voiced and unvoiced positions are combined, they receive *equal* emphasis, resulting in a "d-t" (DT) sound. The letter "f" also receives this voiced/unvoiced handling, resulting in a substituted sound of "vv-f" (V:F) with the emphasis on the voiced "v" (V) portion.

The letter "v" itself has a sound closer to "f" in German. Therefore the double-consonant sound that is substituted for the American "v" has the emphasis on the *unvoiced* part, thus: "v-ff" (VF:). So, the lady executive whose decisions "never involve love," if German would say that they:

(NeVF:e*r*: iNVF:*o*L±VF: L±*o*:VF:).

The German letter "w" is pronounced similarly to our own letter "v," so that "whim" and "wine" come out closer to "vim" and "vine." Since, however, this is also a double consonant sound, the result is actually "vv-f" (V:F), with the voiced "v" (V) being dominant. Thus, if someone wants to know "why we will" be "away," if German they would want to know:

(V:F*A*:E: V:FE: V:FiL±) be (*i*:V:F*A*:).

Since our double-consonant sound "q" is actually pronounced "kw," the changes that affect each sound separately combine, making our "q" into "gg-k-vv-f" (G:KV:F). This means that a runner who was "quite quick" would be referred to by German-speaking people as being:

(G:KV:F*A*:E:DT G:KV:FiG:K).

At the beginning of a word, or when found between two vowels, the letter "s" also gets the double-consonant treatment. However, in this case, the unvoiced element is the strongest, making the sound "z-ss" (ZS:). In other words, if we observe that the child "decided" to "say something sassy," the German dialect would have it that he:

(D:TE:ZS:*A*E:D:T*e*D:T) to (ZS:A: ZS:*o*:MDT:iNG:K ZS:eZS:E:).

Another native carry-over from German is the pronunciation of the English letter or sound "z." At the beginning of a word, the Germans pronounce this "ts" (*s*) as in "outset." Thus an astronaut in a weightless en-

Though Marlene Dietrich (seen here in Destry Rides Again, *Universal, 1939) has been a model for "pure" German dialect during her 40-year film career in America, her speech still bears the traces of her Berlin upbringing whenever her roles call for her to become excited.*

vironment might be able to "zip" and "zoom" around the "zero zone," but if German could:

(*s*iB:P) and (*sU*:M) around the (*s*E:*r*:O: *s*O:N).

At the end of a word, however, the "z" sound becomes "sss" (S::).

Like the Spanish dialects in earlier chapters, the German dialect "upperdentalizes" (±) its "l"s; it pronounces them with the tip of the tongue touching the upper front teeth. This means that a cynic's definition of effective propaganda being "well-told lies," in Germany would come out being:

(V:FeL± DTO:L±D:T L±*A*:E:S::).

In the last two consonant changes we'll discuss here, the German changes voiced sounds into unvoiced ones. In the first one, instead of holding back the breath for the voiced sound of "j" (J) as in "jump" and "gin," the Germans let the air explode into the unvoiced "ch" (*C*) of "chump" and "chin." This means that thrill seekers who "enjoy major dangers," if German-speaking would:

(eN*C*o*E*: MA:*Cer*: D:TA:N*Cer*:S::).

The second conversion from voiced to unvoiced consonant concerns the "zh" (*z*) sound in "azure" and "treasure." This becomes the "sh" (*S*) sound of "sure." So, while an eager young optometrist might have his own "version" of "vision measurement," in Germany he would have his:

(VF:*er*:*Si*:N) of (VF:i*Si*N Me*SU*:*r*:MeNDT).

Two more examples of the Austrian-German dialect: on the left, Maximilian Schell (in Julia, *20th Century Fox, 1977); on the right, Oskar Werner (in Universal's 1966* Fahrenheit 451*). While Werner's dialect always retains the soft, flowing feeling of his native tongue (enhancing his image as a romantic figure), Schell's can become as hard and brittle as a Berlin subdialect, when the role requires it.*

Music, Rhythm, and Pace

The German music has two characteristics that distinguish it from American English. First, it is pitched one tone lower. Second, there is very little lilt in the German dialect. Indeed, in the north of Germany the language is spoken almost in a monotone—and so are the dialects originating there.

Those of you who have studied German know that all nouns are capitalized in that language. More important for actors is the fact that much of German itself is spoken "in capitals." In other words, we encounter heavier stress in German dialects, and emphasis that is much more spread out among different words. There is no rule governing this; it is the actor's choice. However, it's a good idea to go over a German dialect speech, looking for every word your character could logically emphasize, and then, to some degree, stress each one. Remember though, a dialect never should be spoken at the expense of meaning or characterization; let that idea guide your choices.

German dialect is decidedly slower-paced than American English. This slowness is not due to slow mental processes or to the careful deliberation of deep minds. It is entirely the result of the large number of words that are stressed, combined with the German emphasis on clarity in speech. It may, at times, be heavy on the ear, but it doesn't reflect dullness.

Observation and Notes

Along with local patriotism, the local dialects have been kept alive. For example, though most Berliners know the universally accepted High German, most cling to the Berliner dialect, especially in their daily lives. You can find this dialect in some of the roles played by Fritz Feld, Hardy Kruger, and Marlene Dietrich. On the other hand, the Austrian dialect is often evident in characters played by Paul Henreid, Lilli Palmer, Maria and Maximilian Schell, Romy Schneider, and Oskar Werner. In many instances, you may observe the Bavarian (or Munich) dialect in the work of Curt Jurgens, while both Ursula Andress and Marthe Keller sometimes fall into their native Swiss cadences. All the actors named above most often speak with what we call the General German dialect.

Naturally, it's best to use a German- or Austrian-born actor as your dialect model,

Above: Curt Jurgens in The Enemy Below *(20th Century Fox, 1957). Though he played many romantic roles in German films, in the U.S. he played mostly military ones. Below: Two prime examples of the Swiss-German subdialect—close to the Bavarian, but softer: Ursula Andress (left) in United Artists' 1962* Dr. No. *(Right) The dynamic Marthe Keller in* Fedora *(United Artists, 1978).*

though such actors as Laurence Olivier (in *The Marathon Man*), Rod Steiger (in *The Girl and the General*), and Marlon Brando (*The Young Lions*) have managed starring roles while maintaining creditable German dialects. Many American actors and actresses, however, tend toward caricature when they affect a German accent. This is particularly true of TV sit-com characters, with the exception of Werner Klemperer's POW Camp Commandant in *Hogan's Heroes*.

Note: In the *GUIDE PAGES* that follow, the dialect that represents the speech of a German well-educated in American English is that of *Berlin, Educated*.

Lasting a respectable six years (and still in syndication 18 years after its debut), Hogan's Heroes *introduced the TV public to the comedic and dialect talents of Werner Klemperer (shown here with Bob Crane). Klemperer's Col. Klink contrasted sharply with John Banner's Sgt. Schultz. Banner's dialect was generally broad and rather burlesqued, while Klemperer's dialect was consistently authentic—due, perhaps, to his studying the speech of his father, Otto Klemperer, the conductor.*

GENERAL GERMAN - HAMBURG, NORTH SEA - BERLIN (EDUCATED)

GUIDE PAGES		All 3
LONGER SOUND: (aim) A:M, (maybe) MA:B:PE:, (day) D:TA:	A	A:
LONGER SOUND: (east) E:SDT, (seem) ZS:E:M, (we) V:FE:	E	E:
LONGER SOUND: (I) A:E:, (right)ʀ:A:E:DT, (by) B:PA:E:	I	A:E:
LONGER SOUND: (only) O:NL±E:, (road)ʀ:O:D:T, (so) ZS:O:	O	O:
LONGER SOUND: (you) U:, (tune) D:TU:N, (new) NU:	U	U:

		Genl.	Hmbg.	Berlin
Change in all positions: (bad) B:PeD:T, (at) eDT, (man) MeN, (am) eM, (map) MeB:P	a	e	&	
OR change: Be½D:T, e½T, Me½N, e½M, Me½P:	a			e½
No change: (end) eND:T, (let) L±eDT	e	e	&	&
No change: (it) iDT, (ring) iNG:K	i	i	&	&
Change in all positions: (on) oN, (shop) SoB:P, (not) NoDT, (clock) G:KL±oG:K	o	o	&	&
Change in all positions: (up) o:B:P, (cut) G:Ko:DT, (love) L±o:VF:, (does) D:To:S::	u	o:	&	
OR change: oP:, K:oT, L±oV:F, D:ToS	u			o
LONGER SOUND: (far) V:FA:ʀ:(calm) G:KA:L±M (art) A:ʀ:DT(mark) MA:ʀ:G:K(watch) V:FA:C	A	A:		&
OR change: F#aʀ:,G:KaL±M,aʀ:DT, Maʀ:G:K,V½aC	A		a	
Change in all positions: (her) Heʀ: (were) V:Feʀ: (turn) D:Teʀ:N (first) V:Feʀ:SD:T	E	e	&	
OR no change: HEʀ:,V½Eʀ:,TEʀ:N VF:Eʀ:ST	E			E

		All 3
No change: (pretend)B:Pʀ:IDTeND:T (propose)B:Pʀ:IB:PO:S::	I	I
LONGER SOUND: (out) O:DT, (down) D:TO:N, (now) NO:	O	O:
LONGER SOUND: (room)ʀ:U:M, (true) DTʀ:U: (soon) ZS:U:N	U	U:

		Genl.	Hmbg.	Berlin
Change in all positions: (laugh) L±A:V:F, (and) A:ND:T, (last) L±A:SDT, (ask) A:SG:K	a	A:		&
OR change: L±aF#, aND:T, L±aSDT, aSG:K	a		a	
No change: (level) L±eVF:eL± (added) eD:TeD:T	e	e	&	&
LONGER SOUND: (family)V:FeMi:L±E:, (system) ZS:iSDTi:M (ago) i:G:KO: (idea) A:E:D:TE:i:	i	i:	&	
OR no change: VF:e½MiL±E:, ZS:iSTiM, iG:KO:	i			i
Change when spelled "a,au,aw": (all) o:L±, (cause) G:Ko:S:: (law) L±o: (war) V:Fo:ʀ:	o	o:$a, au,aw	&	
OR longer: o:L±, K:o:S, L±o:, V½o:ʀ:	o			o:
AND LONGER otherwise:(off) o:V:F, (broad) B:Pʀ:o:D:T (door) D:To:ʀ:(court) G:Ko:ʀ:DT	o	o:$oa oOOou	&	&
Change in all positions: (look) L±U:G:K, (could) G:KU:D:T, (full) V:FU:L±	u	U:	&	
OR longer: L±u:G:K, K:u:D:T, VF:u:L±				u:
LONGER SOUND: (oil) oE:L±, (boy) B:PoE:, (point) B:PoE:NDT, (soil) ZS:oE:L±	oE	oE:	&	&

Change in all positions: (by) B:PA:E: (rub) ʀ:o:B:P (maybe) MA:B:PE:, (but) B:Po:DT	B	B:P	&	
OR no change: BA:E:,ʀ:oB, MA:BE:, BoT	B			B
Change in all positions: (cheap) SE:P:, (future) F#U:Seʀ: (speech) ZS:P:E:S	C		S	
OR no change: CE:B:P, V:FU:Ceʀ: ZS:B:PE:C	C	C		C
Change in all positions: (did) D:TiD:T, (body) B:PoD:TE:, (food) V:FU:D:T	D	D:T	&	&

Key:

& as shown	: longer	± upperdental	S sure
$ spelled	½ weaker	ʀ uvular R	# open

GENERAL GERMAN - HAMBURG, NORTH SEA - BERLIN (EDUCATED)

GUIDE PAGES		Genl.	Hmbg.	Berlin
Change in all positions: (fine) V:FA:E:N, (lcft) L±cV:FDT (rough) *r*:*o*:V:F (off) *o*:V:F	F	V:F		
OR mouth open: F#A:E:N, L±eF#DT, *r*:*o*:F#, *o*:F#	F		F#	
OR change: VF:A:E:N, L±eVF:T, *r*:*o*VF:, *o*:VF:	F			VF:

		All 3
CHANGE: (go) G:KO:, (big) B:PiG:K, (again) *i*:G:KeN	G	G:K
No change	H	H
CHANGE: (judge) *C**o*:*C*, (edge) e*C*, (enjoy) eN*C**o*E:	J	*C*

		Genl.	Hmbg.	Berlin
Change in all positions: (keep) G:KE:B:P, (make) MA:G:K, (come) G:K*o*:M, (neck) NeG:K	K	G:K	&	
OR stronger: K:E:P:, MA:K:, K:*o*M, NeK:	K			K:
Against upper teeth: (low) L±O:, (told) DTO:L±D:T, (well) V:FeL±, (lead) L±E:D:T	L	L±	&	&
No change	M	M	&	&
No change	N	N	&	&
Change in all positions: (cup) G:K*o*:B:P, (open) O:B:P*e*N, (poor) B:P*U*:*r*:, (pin) B:PiN	P	B:P		
OR stronger: G:K*o*:P:, O:P:*e*N, P:*U*:*r*:, P:iN	P		P:	P:
Change in all positions: (quit) G:KV:FiDT, (equal) E:G:KV:F*e*L±, (quick) G:KV:FiG:K	Q	G:K V:F		
OR change: KViDT, E:KV*e*L±, KViG:K	Q		KV	
OR change: K:V½iT, E:K:V½*e*L±, K:V½iK:				K:V½

		All 3
Heavy uvular: (read) *r*:E:D:T: (very) VF:e*r*:E: (or) *o*:*r*:	R	*r*:
Change initially: (say) ZS:A: (sleep) ZS:L±E:B:P (see) ZS:E:	S	-ZS:
AND between vowels: (decide) D:TE:ZS:A:E:D:T	S	ZS:ǂ
BUT no change otherwise, medially or finally	S	∘/S

		Genl.	Hmbg.	Berlin
No change: (show) *S*O:, (sure) *SU*:*r*:	*S*	*S*	&	&
Change in all positions: (take) DTA:G:K, (into) iNDT*U*:, (sit) ZS:iDT, (rest) *r*:eSDT	T	DT	&	
OR no change: TA:K:, iNT*U*:, ZS:iT, *r*:eST	T			T
Change in all positions: (thin) DT:iN, (death) D:TeDT:, (bath) B:PA:DT:	*t*	DT:	&	&
Change in all positions: (they) D:TA:, (mother) M*o*:D:T*er*: (smooth) ZS:M*U*:D:T	*T*	D:T	&	&
Change in all positions: (five) V:FA:E:VF: (view) VF:U:, (over) O:VF:*er*: (of) *o*:VF:	V	VF:	&	
OR change: VF:A:E:V:F, V:FU:, O:V:F*er*:, *o*V:F	V			V:F
Change in all positions: (will) V:FiL±, (away) *i*:V:FA:, (why) V:FA:E:, (we) V:FE:	W	V:F		
OR change: V½iL±, *i*:V½A:, V½A:E:, V½E:	W		V½	V½

		All 3
"KS" for "GZ" sound: (exact) eKSeG:KDT (exude) eKS*U*:D:T	X	KS4gz
"GZ" for "KS" sound: (next) NeGZDT (fix) V:FiGZ	X	GZ4ks

		Genl.	Hmbg.	Berlin
Change initially: (zero) *s*E:*r*:O:, (zone) *s*O:N, (zoom) *sU*:M, (zip) *s*iB:P	Z	-*s*	&	&
AND change medially and finally: (busy) B:PiS::E:, (his) HiS::, (use) U:S::	Z	/∘S::	&	
OR change: BiSE:, HiS, U:S	Z			/∘S
Change in all positions: (pleasure) B:PL±e*SU*:*r*: (vision) VF:i*S*eN	z	*S*	&	&

Key:

& as shown	- initial	*C* church	ǂ between vowels
4 for	/ medial	*s* outset	± upperdental
# open	∘ finally	: stronger	*r* uvular R
		½ weakened	

SAARBRÜCKEN, WESTERN GERMAN - KIEL, BALTIC - COLOGNE, RHINELAND

GUIDE PAGES

		Saar.	Kiel	Cologn
LONGER SOUND: (aim) A:M, (maybe) MA:B:PE:, (day) D:TA: (air) A:*r* (table) D:TA:B:PeL±	A	A:	&	&
LONGER SOUND: (eat) E:DT, (we) V:FE:, (me) ME:, (east) E:SDT, (seem) ZS:E:M	E	E:	&	&
MUCH LONGER: (I) A:E:, (mind) MA:E:ND:T (by) B:PA:E:, (ice) A:E:S, (right) *r*A:E:DT	I	A:E:	&	
OR longer: AE:, MAE:ND:T, B:PAE:, R:AE:DT	I			AE:
LONGER SOUND: (only) O:NL±E:, (road) *r*O:D:T (so) ZS:O: (old) O:L±D:T (smoke) ZS:MO:G:K	O	O:	&	&
LONGER SOUND: (you) U:, (cute) G:KU:DT, (tune) DTU:N (new) NU: (use) U:S::	U	U:	&	&
Change in all positions: (bad) B:PeD:T, (am) eM, (map) MeB:P, (fact) VF:eG:KDT	a	e		
OR change: B:PAD:T, AM, MAB:P, V:FAG:KDT	a		A	A
AND change before F,N,S,T: (at) ADT, (man) MAN, (afghan) AV:FG:KAN, (angry) ANG:K*r*E:	a	A(F, N,S,T	&	&
Change in all positions: (end) aND:T, (men) MaN, (bell) B:PaL±, (leg) L±aG:K	e			a
OR no change: eND:T, MeN, B:PeL±, L±eG:K	e	e	&	
Change in all positions: (it) EDT, (ring) R:ENG:K, (milk) MEL±G:K, (if) EV:F (in) EN	i			E
OR no change: iDT, *r*iNG:K, MiL±G:K, iV:F, iN	i	i	&	
Change in all positions: (on) oN, (shop) SoB:P, (not) NoDT, (clock) G:KL±oG:K	o	o	&	
OR change: AN, SAB:P, NADT, G:KL±AG:K	o			A

		All 3
CHANGE: (up) o:B:P, (cut) G:Ko:DT, (love) L±o:VF:	u	o:
LONGER SOUND: (far) V:FA:*r* (watch) V:FA:C (calm) G:KA:L±M	A	A:
CHANGE: (her) He*r*, (turn) DTe*r*N, (first) V:Fe*r*SDT	E	e
No change: (pretend) B:P*r*IDTeND:T (propose) B:P*r*IB:PO:S::	I	I
LONGER SOUND: (out) O:DT, (down) D:TO:N, (now) NO:	O	O:
LONGER SOUND: (room) *r*U:M, (true) DT*r*U:, (soon) ZS:U:N	U	U:
CHANGE: (laugh) L±A:V:F, (and) A:ND:T, (last) L±A:SDT	a	A:
No change: (level) L±eVF:eL±, (added) eD:TeD:T	e	e
LONGER SOUND: (family) V:FeMi:L±E:, (system) ZS:iSDTi:M	i	i:
When spelled "a,au,aw": (all) o:L±, (cause) G:Ko:S::	o	o:$a
OTHERWISE LONGER: (off) o:V:F, (court) G:Ko:*r*DT	o	o:$o

		Saar.	Kiel	Cologn
Change in all positions: (look) L±U:G:K, (could) G:KU:D:T, (full) V:FU:L±	u	U:	&	
OR longer: L±u:G:K, G:Ku:D:T, V:Fu:L±	u			u:
LONGER SOUND: (oil) oE:L±, (boy) B:PoE: (point) B:PoE:NDT, (soil) ZS:oE:L±	oE	oE:	&	&

		Saar.	Kiel	Cologn
Change in all positions: (by) B:PA:E:, (rub) *r*o:B:P, (maybe) MA:B:PE:, (but) B:Po:DT	B	B:P		&
OR no change: BA:E:, *r*o:B, MA:BE:, Bo:DT	B		B	
Change in all positions: (cheap) SE:B:P, (future) V:FU:SeR:, (speech) ZS:B:PE:S	C			S
OR no change: CE:B:P, V:FU:Ce*r*, ZS:B:PE:C	C	C	&	
Change in all positions: (did) D:TiD:T, (body) B:PoD:TE:, (food) V:FU:D:T	D	D:T		&
OR no change: DiD, BoDE:, V:FU:D	D		D	

Key:

& as shown	S sure, show	: longer	R trilled R
$ spelled	(preceding	± upperdental	*r* uvular R

SAARBRÜCKEN, WESTERN GERMAN - KIEL, BALTIC - COLOGNE, RHINELAND

GUIDE PAGES		Saar.	Kiel	Cologn
Change in all positions: (fine) V:FA:E:N, (left) L±eV:FDT, (rough) *ro*:V:F (off) *o*:V:F	F	V:F	&	&
Change in all positions: (go) G:KO:, (big) B:PiG:K, (again) *i*:G:KeN, (get) G:KeDT OR no change: GO:, BiG, *i*:GeN, GeDT	G G	G:K	 G	&
No change	H	H	&	&
Change in all positions: (judge) *Co*:*C*, (edge) e*C*, (enjoy) eN*Co*E:, (page) B:PA:*C* OR change: *zo*:z, az, aN*zo*E:, B:PA:z	J	*C*	&	 z
Change in all positions: (keep) G:KE:B:P, (make) MA:G:K, (come) G:K*o*M, (neck) NeG:K OR no change: KE:B:P, MA:K, K*o*:M, NeK	K K	G:K	 K	&
				All 3
Against upper teeth: (lead) L±E:D:T, (told) DTO:L±D:T	L			L±
No change	M			M
No change	N			N
CHANGE: (cup) G:K*o*:B:P, (open) O:B:P*e*N, (poor) B:P*U*:*r*	P			B:P
CHANGE: (quit) G:KV:FiDT, (equal) E:G:KV:F*e*L±	Q			G:KV:F
Uvular, light gargle: (read) *r*E:D:T, (or) *o*:*r*, (right) *r*A:E:DT, (very) VF:e*r*E: OR strong trill: *R*:E:D:T, *o*:*R*:, *R*:AE:DT	R R	*r*	&	 *R*:
				All 3
Change initially: (say) ZS:A:, (sleep) ZS:L±E:B:P	S			-ZS:
AND between vowels: (decide) D:TE:ZS:A:E:D:T	S			ZS:≠
BUT no change otherwise, medially or finally	S			/.S
No change: (show) *S*O:, (sure) *SU*:*r*	*S*			*S*
CHANGE: (take) DTA:G:K, (into) iNDT*U*:, (sit) ZS:iDT	T			DT
Change in all positions: (thin) TiN, (path) B:PA:T, (death) D:TeT, (mouth) M*O*:T OR change: DT:iN, BA:DT:, DeDT:, M*O*:DT: OR change: SEN, B:PAS, D:TaS, M*O*:S	*t* *t* *t*	T	 DT:	 S
Change in all positions: (they) D:TA:, (mother) M*o*:D:T*er*, (smooth) ZS:M*U*:D:T OR change: DA:, M*o*:D*er*, ZS:M*U*:D OR change: ZA:, M*o*:Z*eR*:, ZS:M*U*:Z	*T* *T* *T*	D:T	 D	 Z
Change in all positions: (five) V:FA:E:VF:, (view) VF:U:, (over) O:VF:*er*, (of) *o*:VF:	V	VF:	&	&
Change in all positions: (will) V:FiL±, (away) *i*:V:FA:, (why) V:FA:E:, (we) V:FE:	W	V:F	&	&
"KS" for "GZ" sound: (exact) eKSaG:KDT, (examine) eKSeM*i*:N, (exude) eKS*U*:D:T	X	KS4gz	&	&
"GZ" for "KS" sound: (expert) eGZB:Pe*r*DT, (next) NeGZDT, (fix) V:FiGZ, (sex) ZS:eGZ	X	GZ4ks	&	&
Change initially: (zero) *s*E:*r*O:, (zone) *s*O:N, (zoom) *sU*:M, (zip) *s*iB:P	Z	-*s*	&	&
AND change medially and finally: (busy) B:PiS::E:, (his) HiS::, (use) U:S::	Z	/.S::	&	&
Change in all positions: (pleasure) B:PL±e*SU*:*r*, (vision) VF:i*S*e*N* OR no change: B:PL±az*u*:*R*:, VF:Ez*e*N	z z	*S*	&	 z

Key:

z measure	- initially	*s* outset, sits	*C* church
& as shown	/ medially	: stronger	± upperdental
	∘ finally	≠ between vowels	*R* trilled R
			r uvular R

NAUEN, RURAL GERMAN - MUNICH, BAVARIAN - VIENNA, AUSTRIAN

GUIDE PAGES

	SOUND	Nauen Rural German	Munich Bavarian	Vienna Austrian	All 3
LONGER SOUND: (aim) A:M, (maybe) MA:B:PE:, (day) D:TA:	A				A:
LONGER SOUND: (east) E:SDT, (seem) ZS:E:M, (we) V:FE:	E				E:
LONGER SOUND: (I) A:E:, (right)*r*:A:E:DT, (by) B:PA:E:	I				A:E:
LONGER SOUND: (only) O:NL±E:, (road)*r*:O:D:T, (so) ZS:O:	O				O:
LONGER SOUND: (you) U:, (tune) DTU:N, (new) NU:	U				U:
Change in all positions: (bad) B:PeD:T, (am) eM, (map) MeB:P, (fact) V:FeG:KDT	a	e			
OR change: B:PAD:T, AM, MAB:P, V:FA*h*DT	a		A	A	
AND change before F,N,S,T: (at) ADT, (man) MAN, (afghan) AV:FG:KAN, (angry) ANG:K*r*:E:	a	A(F, N,S,T	&	&	
No change: (end) eND:T, (leg) L±eG:K	e	e	&	&	
Change in all positions: (it) EDT, (ring) *r*:ENG:K, (milk) MEL±K, (if) EV:F, (in) EN	i		E	E	
OR no change: iDT,*r*:iNG:K, MiL±G:K, iV:F, iN	i	i			
Change in all positions: (on) *o*N, (shop) z*o*B:P, (not) N*o*DT, (clock) G:KL±*o*G:K	o	*o*			
OR change: AN, zAB:P, NADT, *h*L±A*h*	o		A	A	
Change in all positions: (up) *o*:B:P, (cut) G:K*o*:DT, (love) L±*o*:VF:, (does) D:T*o*:S::	u	*o*:			
OR change: A½B:P, *h*A½DT, L±A½VF:, D:TA½S::	u		A½		
OR change: *o*BP:, GK:*o*T, L±*o*VF:, DT*o*S::	u			*o*	
LONGER SOUND: (far) V:FA:*r*: (watch) V:FA:C (calm) G:KA:L±M	A				A:
CHANGE all: (her) He*r*: (turn) DTe*r*:N (first) V:Fe*r*:SDT	E				e
No change: (pretend)B:P*r*:IDTeND:T (propose)B:P*r*:IB:PO:S::	I				I
MUCH LONGER SOUND: (out) O::DT (down) D:TO::N (now) NO::	O				O::
LONGER SOUND: (room)*r*:U:M, (true) DT*r*:U: (soon) ZS:U:N	U				U:
CHANGE: (laugh) L±A:V:F, (and) A:ND:T, (last) L±A:SDT	a				A:
No change: (level) L±eVF:eL±, (added) eD:TeD:T	e				e
LONGER SOUND: (family) V:FeM*i*:L±E:, (system) ZS:iSDT*i*:M (mama) MA:M*i*: (idea) A:E:D:TE:*i*:	*i*	*i*:	&	&	
OR change initially: (ago) aG:KO:, (above) aB:P*o*:VF:, (afraid) aV:F*r*:A:D:T	*i*	-a			
OR change initially: AG:KO:, AB:P*o*VF:	*i*			A	
When spelled "a,au,aw": (all) o:L±, (cause) G:Ko:S::	*o*				o:$a
OTHERWISE LONGER: (off) *o*:V:F, (court) G:K*o*:*r*:DT	*o*				*o*:$o
CHANGE: (look) L±U:G:K, (good) G:KU:D:T, (put) B:PU:DT	*u*				U:
MUCH LONGER SOUND: (oil) *o*E::L± (boy) B:P*o*E:: (joy) C*o*E::	*o*E				*o*E::
CHANGE: (by) B:PA:E:, (rob)*r*:*o*:B:P, (maybe) MA:B:PE:	B				B:P
No change: (cheap) CE:B:P, (speech) SB:PE:C, (each) E:C	C				C
Change in all positions: (did) D:TiD:T (body) B:P*o*D:TE: (food) V:FU:D:T (day) D:TA:	D	D:T	&		
OR change: DTEDT, B:PADTE:, VF:U:DT, DTA:	D			DT	
Change in all positions: (fine) V:FA:E:N, (left) L±eV:FDT (rough)*r*:*o*:V:F (off) *o*:V:F	F	V:F	&		
OR change: VF:A:E:N, L±eVF:T,*r*:*o*VF:, *o*:VF:	F			VF:	

Key:
& as shown — S show,sure — - initially
$ spelled — *h* loch,ich — : longer — ± upperdental
(preceding — ½ shorter — *r* uvular R

GUIDE PAGES	SOUND	Nauen Rural German	Munich Bavarian	Vienna Austrian
Change in all positions: (go) G:KO:, (big) B:PiG:K, (again) *i*:G:KeN, (get) G:KeDT	G	G:K	&	&
No change	H	H	&	&
Change in all positions: (enjoy) eN*Co*E::, (edge) e*C*, (judge) *Co*:*C*, (page) B:PA:*C*	J	*C*	&	&
Change in all positions: (keep) G:KE:B:P (make) MA:G:K, (come) G:K*o*:M, (neck) NeG:K	K	G:K		
OR change: *h*E:B:P, MA:*h*, *h*A½M, Ne*h*	K		*h*	
OR change: GK:E:BP:, MA:GK:, GK:*o*M, NeGK:	K			GK:
Against upper teeth: (low) L±O:, (told) DTO:L±D:T, (well) V:FeL±, (lead) L±E:D:T	L	L±	&	&
No change	M	M	&	&
No change	N	N	&	&
Change in all positions: (cup) G:K*o*:B:P (open) O:B:P*e*N, (poor) B:P*U*:*r*: (pin) B:PiN	P	B:P	&	
OR change: GK:*o*BP:, O:BP:*e*N, BP:*U*:¼, BP:EN	P			BP:
Change in all positions: (quit) G:KV:FiDT, (equal) E:G:KV:F*e*L±, (quick) G:KV:FiG:K	Q	G:K V:F	&	&
Heavy uvular: (read) *r*:E:D:T, (road) *r*:O:D:T (right) *r*:A:E:DT, (very) VF:e*r*:E:	R	*r*:	&	&
OR drop finally: (car) G:KA:¼ (or) *o*:¼	R		¼.	¼.
Change initially: (say) ZS:A:, (see) ZS:E:, (civil) ZS:iVF:*e*L±, (sale) ZS:A:L±	S	-ZS:	&	
AND between vowels: (decide) D:TE:ZS:*A*:E:D:T	S	ZS:≠	&	
BUT no change otherwise, medially or finally	S	/.S	&	&
OR change initially before L,M,N,P,T,W: (swim) *S*V:FiM, (sleep) *S*L±E:B:P, (stop) *S*DTAB:P	S	-*S*(L, MNPTW		
OR no change: SA:, SE:, SVF:EM, SL±E:BP:	S			S
Change in all positions: (show) zO:, (sure) z*U*:*r*, (tissue) DTizU:, (wish) V:Fiz	*S*	z	&	
OR no change: *S*O:, *SU*:¼, TESU:, V:FE*S*	*S*			*S*
Change in all positions: (take) DTA:G:K, (into) iNDT*U*:, (sit) ZS:iDT, (rest) *r*:eSDT	T	DT	&	
OR no change: TA:GK:, ENT*U*:, SET, *r*:eST				T

		All 3
CHANGE: (thin) DT:iN, (death) D:TeDT:, (bath) B:PA:DT:	*t*	DT:
CHANGE: (they) D:TA:, (this) D:TiS, (smooth) *S*M*U*:D:T	*T*	D:T
CHANGE: (view) VF:U:, (over) O:VF:*er*: (of) *o*:VF:	V	VF:
CHANGE: (will) V:FiL±, (away) *i*:V:FA:, (why) V:FA:E:	W	V:F
"KS" for "GZ" sound: (exact) eKSeG:KDT, (exude) eKS*U*:D:T	X	KS4gz
"GZ" for "KS" sound: (next) NeGZDT, (expert) eGZB:Pe*r*:DT	X	GZ4ks

Change initially: (zero) *s*E:*r*:O:, (zone) *s*O:N, (zoom) *sU*:M, (zip) *s*iB:P	Z	-*s*	&	&
AND change medially and finally: (busy) B:PiS::E:, (his) HiS::, (use) U:S::	Z	/.S::	&	&
Change in all positions: (pleasure) B:PL±e*SU*:*r*: (vision) VF:i*Se*N	z	*S*	&	&

Key:	*C* church		(preceding
h loch,ich	- initial	*s* outset	≠ between vowels
& as shown	/ medial	: stronger	± upper dental
4 for	. finally	¼ dropped	*r* uvular R

ITALIAN

Some thirty years ago I lived for a while in the Greenwich Village section of New York. At the time, "the Village" had its itinerant minority and its resident majority. The former were artists, actors, dancers, and musicians from all over America; the latter were overwhelmingly Italians, both first-generation and immigrants.

My closest friend was an ex-Army buddy who lived uptown with his parents. Enrico was Italian-born, but from age ten on had grown up in the United States.

The superintendent of my building was an old Italian woman, long-faced and withdrawn. Withdrawn, that is, until Enrico visited me; then, from his very first words to her in Italian, she brightened as though someone had turned on a switch inside her. I couldn't understand it: wasn't she living in an all-Italian neighborhood? Why did she seem so isolated and lonely until Enrico showed up?

He explained: the Village *was* made up of Italians, true; but they were Sicilians and Calabrese (from the southern "boot" of Italy). The caretaker was an uneducated widow from a small town outside Milan—in northern Italy. Not only were her customs and manners different from those of her neighbors, but the very language she spoke was not quite the same. Enrico, a "cosmopolitan" Roman (well, at least his parents were), actually could handle the Milanese dialect as easily as he could the Roman or Sicilian. So he spoke Milanese to her—and he was a touch of home.

You will find this fragmentation well represented in the *GUIDE PAGES* that follow. Not only are eight distinct "subdialects" represented, but you will see that the differences among them are sometimes quite extreme. For example, there are three totally diverse regional pronunciations for the letter "a" in "all," and three very distinct ways in which different regions pronounce the "d" in "credit."

This divergence is easier to understand when you look at the history of what is now Italy after the fall of the Roman Empire. The entire peninsula broke up into a number of small, independent states, some so small, in fact, that they consisted solely of one city and its environs. Yet each state, no matter how small, had its own government, its own army, and sometimes even its own navy.

Add to this the fact that various parts of Italy came under outside influences, which sometimes amounted to outright colonization. There were the incursions of the Germanic tribes from the north, as well as the resurgence of the old (some pre-Roman) Greek colonies in the south. At various times, Arabs occupied Sicily and parts of Calabria. They were replaced by armies led by Norman adventurers, who also occupied central Italy. In their turn, the Spanish took over central Italy and parts of northern Italy.

Not until 1861, under Victor Emmanuel II, was Italy once again independent and "unified." But, by then the regional influences were so strong and so diversified that my Milanese caretaker could (and did) feel like a foreigner among fellow Italians who were from Sicily and Calabria.

Vowel Changes

How then can we speak of a General Italian Dialect? The answer lies in the Italian language itself, in its "Italianate" sound and its Italian music. Glancing through an English-Italian dictionary, one is struck by the preponderance of words ending in vowel sounds—over ninety percent of the Italian lexicon, as a matter of fact. Naturally enough, almost all native Italian speakers carry over this tendency into English in the form of an interpolated (*e*½). This is a short version of the "e" in "often" and "dozen"; it is *not* the "ah" of the burlesque Italian: "Wot-sah dah mattah wid-ah all-ah you-ah?" The real sound is much closer to a voiced breath—an echoing reminder of the missing vowel ending. Also, the interpolation or addition of this (*e*½) follows very definite rules.

Rule #1: When one word of a phrase ends in a consonant, and the next one begins in a consonant, the aspirate (*e*½) is inserted in between. So "seem to," "sun sign," and "stoplight," when found in the middle of a phrase become:

(SE:M*e*½ T± *U*:), (So:N± *e*½ *SA*:EN±) and (ST±*o*:BP:*e*½ L±*A*:ET±).

Rule #2: When a phrase or sentence ends in a consonant, this same aspirate (*e*½) is added (+); thus "love," changes to (L±o:V*e*½).

In the above examples, you probably noticed the lengthening (:) of most of the vowels: (E:), (*U*:), (o:), (*A*:E), and (*o*:). This is because the Italian language generally has longer vowel sounds than those found in American English. The (E) of "tea," the (I) of "tie," (U) of "tune," (*A*) of "tar," (*U*) of "too," and (*o*E) of "toy" are all drawn out until they become (T±E:), (T±*A*:E), (T±U:N±), (T±*A*:*R*), (T±*U*:), and (T±*o*E:).

In one case, the vowel is extended doubly until it actually becomes a new sound. This is the (*u*) of "full" and "pull," which is turned into the (*U*:) of "foo-ool" and "poo-ool." If the Italian-born wants his house re-painted because it "would look good," he would say he wants it because it:

(*e*½W*U*:T±*e*½ L±*U*:GK:*e*½ G*U*:D±*e*½).

Likewise, the (i) of "sin" is stretched to the point where it too becomes a new sound. The kindergarten teacher might "insist" her children "sit still," but if she's Italian she'll:

(E:N±SE:Z¼) they (SE:D±*e*½ ST±E:L±*e*½).

This particular conversion is an "Italianizing"—giving the Italian pronunciation to the letter the speaker sees. The same process goes on when Italians look at the letter "a." To their eye, this letter always represents the (*A*:) or (*A*) sound. Thus, despite the fact that the American pronounces the "a"s of "had," "aunt," and "ago" in three distinctly different ways, the Italian-speaking person makes them all into (*A*:) or (*A*). (HaD) becomes (H:*A*:D±), (*a*NT) becomes (*A*:N±¼), and (*i*GO) becomes (*A*G*o*:).

A word of caution: don't jump to conclusions! Not all vowels in the Italian dialect are longer; there are three different diphthongs (double vowels) that are shorter.

The (A) of "bait" is made up of the (e) of "bet" and the (E) of "beat." The Italian cuts this down to (e:)—so that if you want the movers to "take" the "table away," in the Italian dialect you'd tell them to:

(T±e:GK:*e*½) the (T±e:B*e*L± *A*We:).

The second of these diphthongs is the (*O*) of "wowed," which combines the (*A*) of "wad" with the (*U*) of "wooed." This becomes shortened to (*A*:), so that the playground director who "allows loud sounds" if Italian-speaking will:

(*A*L±*A*: L±*A*:D±*e*½ S*A*:N±D±Z).

The last of this trio is the (O) of "boat," made up of the (*o*) of "bought" and the (*U*) of "boot." The Italian chops this down to (*o*:), so that if Grandpa "dozes over" his "cocoa," if we're from Italy we remark that he:

(D±*o*:Z*e*Z *o*:V*eR*) his (GK:*o*:GK:*o*:).

The "reversal" effect we saw at work in the Spanish and German dialects also takes place in the Italian. As you saw above, the (O) of "boat" becomes the (*o*:) of "bought." The reverse is also true, so that the "long, broad door" is described by an Italian as:

a (L±O:N±G*e*½ B*R*O:T±*e*½ D±O:*R*).

There are four remaining major vowel changes that reflect neither lengthening, shortening, nor reversal. In the first of these, the Italian takes the (e) sound of "bet" and moves it back in the mouth to become the (a) sound of "bat." Of course, the Italian-born have the tendency to draw this out into (a:), so that if the professors of the university at Florence tend to be "well read men," *they* would speak of themselves as:

(*e*½Wa:L ± *e*½ *R*a:T ± *e*½ Ma:N ±).

The second change is from the (o) of "cot" to the (*o*) of "caught." Again, the new sound is stretched into (*o*:), so that if a night watchman notices that someone's "shop's not locked," if he's from Italy, he would tell them their:

(*So*:BP:S*e*½ N ± *o*:D ± *e*½ L ± *o*:GK:T ± *e*½).

Change number three makes the (u) of "shut" into the (o) of "shot." Once more, the lengthening effect takes over and this becomes (o:), so that the Italian-speaking would talk of a tyrant who "governed unjustly" as one who:

(Go:V*iRe*½N ± ¼ o:N ± Jo:ST ± L ± E:).

The final vowel conversion we'll consider here turns the (*E*) of "urge" into the (*i*) of "ago." Thus the Italian mother who's worried that her boy will "learn dirty words" from his friends would say she feared he would:

(L ± *iRe*½N ± *e*½ D ± *iRe*½T ± E: *e*½W*iRe*½D ± Z*e*½).

Consonant Changes

In these phonetic spellings, you've no doubt noticed that the symbol (*R*) is used for all the Italian pronunciations of the letter "r." As the Spanish-speaking do, Italians trill their (*R*)s, but rather than send you back to former chapters, we'll review how to accomplish that (*R*) right here.

Place your tongue against the gum ridge behind your upper front teeth. Then voice the sound so that your tongue vibrates, making a sound like the imitation of a pneumatic drill, a motorcycle or a machine gun.

In the vowel examples, you saw this trill followed by the soft aspirate (*e*½). This takes place whenever an "r" in the middle of a word is followed by a consonant—as in "poorly" (BP:*U*:*Re*½L ± E:) and "organ" (O:*Re*½G*e*N ±). When the "r" is used to begin a word, the aspirate *precedes* it (*e*½*R*). So an Italian father who notes his son "rarely writes regularly" would complain that the boy:

(*e*½*Re*:*Re*½L ± E: *e*½*RA*:ET ± S *e*½*R*a:GU:L ± *eRe*½L ± E:).

This is only one of several carry-overs from Italian consonant pronunciation. Another is the pronunciation of "k" (or "hard c"). For an American, this is a simple expulsion of air; for the Italian, the air is *stopped* first, and then expelled, resulting in a (GK:) sound. Thus the old slang term "to kick the bucket," when voiced by the Italian-speaking would be to:

(GK:E:GK:*e*½) the (BoGK:*e*T ± *e*½).

The explosive "p" goes through the same process to become (BP:). The decorator who wants to brighten a child's room and "put up pretty paper," in Italian dialect would wish to:

(BP:*U*:D ± o:BP:*e*½ BP:*R*E:T ± E: BP:e:BP:*eRe*½).

Another typically Italian habit is to change the letter "s" to a (Z) when it occurs between vowels in the middle of a word. Therefore, one who enjoys "spicy sauces," if from Italy, would like:

(SBP:*A*:EZE: SO:Z*e*Z).

In many of the examples given so far, you have seen the symbol (±) used to indicate the "upperdentalization" of consonants. In their native language, the Italians pronounce these sounds with the tip of the tongue against the upper teeth. This gives the consonant a "thicker" sound, and naturally the Italians carry this over when they speak American English.

As an example, there are two tongue positions possible in English for the letter "l": 1) the tip of the tongue against the upper gum ridge for (L) in "love," and 2) the middle of the tongue against the same spot for (L) in "bulb." For the Italians there is only one position: (L ±), with the tip of the tongue against the upper teeth. So a bird that has a "low, lilting call" would be described by the Italian-born as having a:

(L±*o*: L±E:L±*e*½T±E:N±¼ GK:O:L±).

As you saw in this last example, the tongue is also moved from the upper gum ridge to the upper teeth for the Italian (N±). Thus a doctor might observe that his patient's alcoholism is a "known condition," but as an Italian would refer to her state as: a (N±*o*:N±*e*½ GK:*A*N±D±E:*SA*N±).

That last phrase also provides a sample of the Italian handling of the "d"; again, the tongue migrates from the upper gum ridge to the upper teeth (D±). So if running short of money makes one face the end of the month with "added dread," the Italian dialect would turn that into:

(*A*:D±*e*T±*e*½ D±*R*a:D±*e*½).

(To learn why the final "d" in "added" became a (T±), see the *GUIDE PAGES*.)

Finally, the letter "t" undergoes this same "upperdentalization" (T±), so that a soldier who has been "battle tested," if in the Italian army, would have been:

(B*A*:T±*e*L±*e*½ T±a:ST±*e*D±*e*½).

Other than the American "r," there are three consonant sounds in American English that don't exist in Italian at all, so that Italians speaking our tongue can only approximate them. The first is the (*T*) of "smooth." In Italian dialect this is made into an upperdentalized "d" (D±). Therefore, if we are told to choose "either this or that," an Italian would tell us to select:

(E:D±*eRe*½ D±E:S) or (D±*A*:D±*e*½.).

The next sound that is nonexistent in Italian is the (*t*) of "both." This is converted into an upperdentalized "t" (T±), so that if a decision is "worth thinking through," someone from Italy would consider it:

(*e*½W*iRe*½T±*e*½ T±E:N±GK:E:N±¼ T±*RU*:):

As you see, Italians are incapable of pronouncing a "w" without a "help" (*e*½) sound. Again, this is because the American consonant sound doesn't exist in their language. Thus, if in hiking to California "we walked west," the Italian-speaking would observe that:

(*e*½WE: *e*½WO:GK:T± *e*½Wa:Z¼).

Music, Rhythm, and Pace

Back on page 65, I referred to a definite Italian music. This music is so distinctive that, in my early days in Chicago, I had already noticed that some of my young peers from Chicago's West Side spoke differently than I did. Years later I realized that these were "first generation" Italians, speaking with an Italian accent, but *without any vowel or consonant changes*. In other words, the Italian music by itself provided the Italian flavor.

First, as may be expected from the profusion of great Italian tenors, the language is spoken at a center point of from one-and-a-half to two tones higher than American English; naturally, this applies to the dialect as well.

Next, the typical Italianized sentence will cover quite a range, for Italian is a truly musical language. The predominant pattern is to start at the center point, go up the scale until you reach the word or meaning you want to stress, and then glide down the scale toward the end of the phrase to a point below the middle tone.

This "musical stress" is important in keeping your dialogue from sounding monotonous, for Italian has a distinct and almost rigid rhythmic pattern. First, the penultimate syllable (the one next to the last) is always the one that receives the rhythmic stress. Second, there is only one emphasized syllable in any given word so that "dic-tion-a-ry" and "sec-re-ta-ry" come out in the Italian dialect as:

(D±E:GK:*SA*N±a:*R*E:) and (Sa:GK:*Re*T±a:*R*E:).

Third, the interpolated "uh" (*e*½) that we discussed on page 66 serves as a kind of unobtrusive, melodic "glue" that furthers the flow of the music.

Overall, holding sway over both rhythm and pitch, stress and flow, is a verve that is typical not only of the language but of the tenor of Italian life itself.

Observation and Notes

For models of Italian dialect (when not dubbed by others), there are Marcello Mastroianni, Claudia Cardinale, Rossano Brazzi, and Gina Lollobrigida. For models of subdialects (when they are playing "local" parts), there is Vittorio Gassman for Genoa, Raf Vallone for Turin, and Sophia Loren for Naples.

And finally, for those who may still entertain some notion that there is "really only one Italian dialect" (probably the caricatured one you heard as a child), I refer you to the film *The Godfather*. Not only was Francis Ford Coppola a stickler for having every possible Italian role played by an Italian but he gathered Italians (and actors of Italian descent) from all over America. The result (except for the native American actors like Brando) is a beautiful mélange of different Italian dialects, and a vivid demonstration that when the peoples of "the many Italys" immigrated to America, they each brought their own Italy with them.

Note: Of the subdialects in the *GUIDE PAGES*, the one that comes closest to American English, the "lightest," so to speak, is *Florentine, Educated*.

With actors of all types of Italian backgrounds, the cast of The Godfather *(Paramount, 1971) often sounded like a meeting of the Italian National Assembly. However, with his acquaintance with the Sicilian community of New York and his total dedication to internalizing the accent as well as the role, Marlon Brando (seen here with other members of the cast) gave us a title role that was consistently and authentically Sicilian.*

After over 50 films, Sophia Loren (shown here in The Millionairess, *20th Century Fox, 1960) established herself as the top comedic actress of her time. Under the right director, her dramatic abilities, too, became noticeable, but the more intense the role, the more her true Neopolitan subdialect showed through. This was especially so (and especially appropriate) when she played her own mother in the TV mini-series* Sophia.

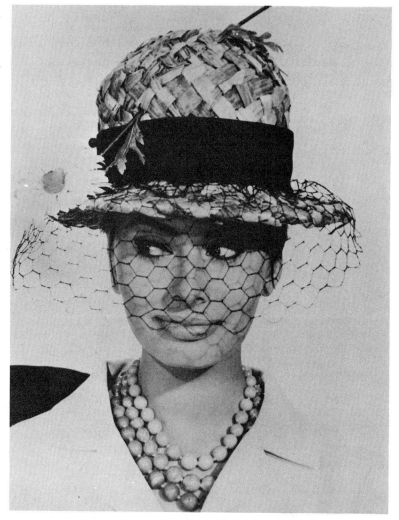

Because the "spoken music" is not nearly so heavy in Northern Italy, we do not always identify the speakers of the Northern Italian subdialects as Italians, and they are often given non-Italian roles in American films. Two examples: (left) In a scene from Universal's The Nude Bomb, *Vittorio Gassman of Genoa (similar to the Milano subdialect); (right) In a scene from* The Other Side of Midnight *(20th Century Fox, 1977) Raf Vallone of Turin. Vallone was often chosen to play Spaniards, Russians or Greeks, while Gassman portrayed Mexicans, Russians and Frenchmen.*

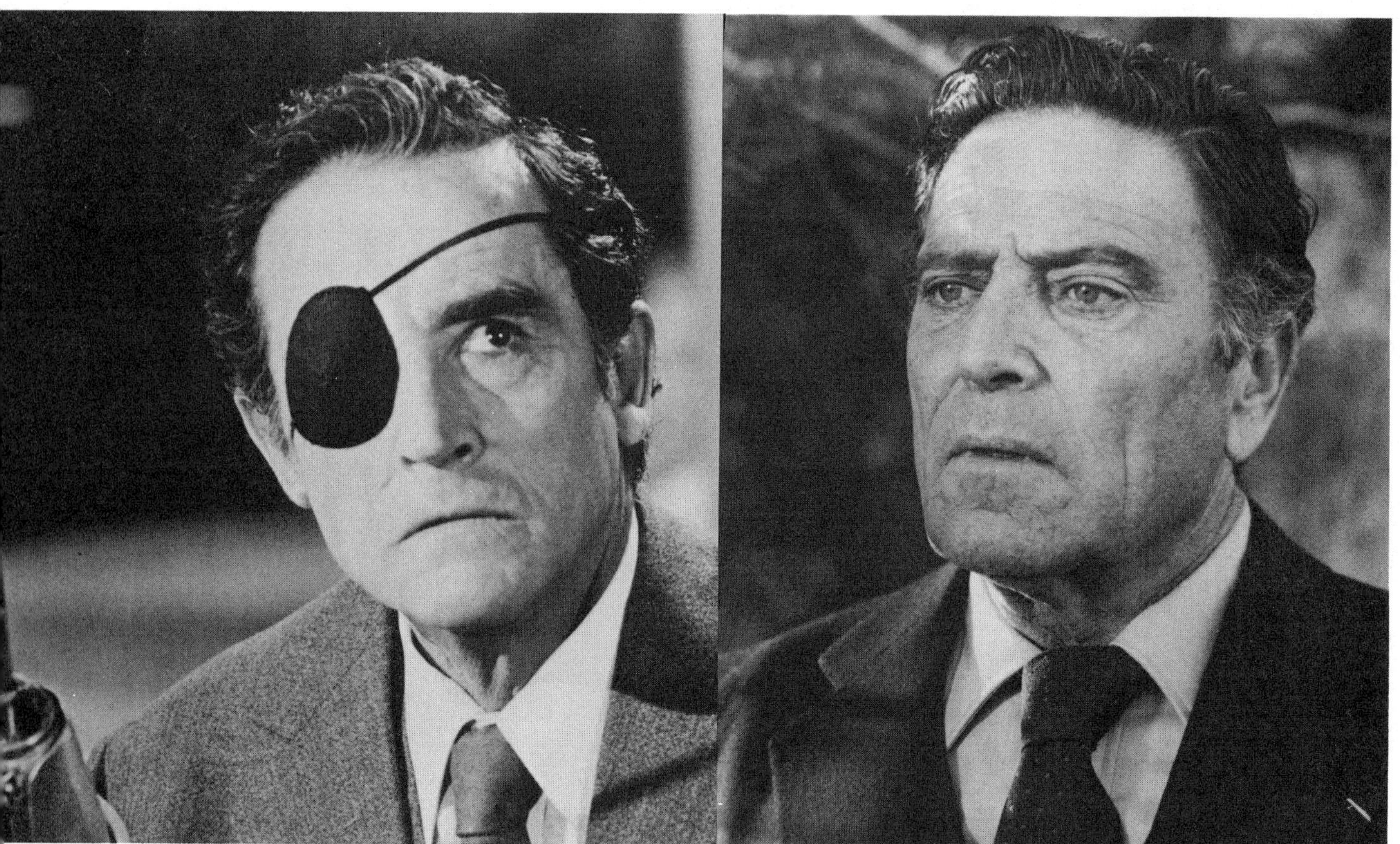

GENERAL ITALIAN - ROMAN ITALIAN - FLORENTINE (EDUCATED)

GUIDE PAGES	SOUND	General Italian	Roman Italian	Florentine Educated
				All 3
CHANGE: (age) e:J, (shame) *S*e:M, (say) *S*e:, (ate) e:D±*e*½	A			e:
LONGER SOUND: (eat) E:D±*e*½, (leave) L±E:V, (see) SE:	E			E:
CHANGE: (I'm) *A*:EM, (like) L±*A*:EGK:, (ice) *A*:ES	I			*A*:E
Change in all positions: (own) *o*:N±, (whole) H:*o*:L±, (old) *o*:L±¼, (note) N±*o*:D±*e*½	O	*o*:	&	
OR shorter sound: O½N±, H:O½L±, N±O½D±*e*½	O			O½
				All 3
LONGER SOUND: (use) U:Z, (tune) T±U:N±, (new) N±U:	U			U:
CHANGE: (had) H:*A*:D±, (act) *A*:GK:T±, (angry) *A*:N±G*R*E:	a			*A*:
CHANGE: (let) L±a:D±*e*½, (well) *e*½Wa:L±, (said) Sa:D±	e			a:
CHANGE: (in) E:N±, (women) ½WE:M*e*N±, (if) E:VF:	i			E:
Change in all positions: (on) *o*:N±, (solid) S*o*:L±E:D±, (got) G*o*:D±*e*½, (drop) D±*Ro*:BP:	o	*o*:	&	
OR no change: oN±, SoL±E:D±, GoD±*e*½, D±*R*oBP:	o			o
				All 3
CHANGE: (us) o:S, (cut) GK:o:D±*e*½, (love) L±o:V	u			o:
LONGER SOUND: (are) *A*:*R*, (watch) *e*½W*A*:C, (calm) GK:*A*:L±M	A			*A*:
CHANGE: (her) H:*i**R*, (first) F*i**R**e*½Z¼, (turn) T±*i**R**e*½N±	*E*			*i*
No change: (predict) BP:*RI*D±E:GK:T± (propose) BP:*RI*BP:*o*:Z	*I*			*I*
CHANGE: (out) *A*:D±*e*½, (down) D±*A*:N±, (count) GK:*A*:N±¼	*O*			*A*:
LONGER SOUND: (room) *RU*:M, (soon) S*U*:N±, (do) D±*U*:	*U*			*U*:
CHANGE: (and) *A*:N±¼, (can't) GK:*A*:N±¼, (last) L±*A*:Z¼	*a*			*A*:
No change: (simple) S:MBP:*e*L±, (person) BP:*i**R*S*e*N±	*e*			*e*
CHANGE: (ago) *A*G*o*:, (system) SE:ST±*A*M, (idea) *A*:ED±E:*A*	*i*			*A*
Change in all positions: (talk) T±O:GK:, (all) O:L±, (off) O:VF:, (door) D±O:*R*	*o*	O:	&	
OR longer sound: T±*o*:GK:, *o*:L±, *o*:VF:, D±*o*:*R*	*o*			*o*:
				All 3
CHANGE: (could) GK:*U*:D±, (put) BP:*U*:D±*e*½, (look) L±*U*:GK:	*u*			*U*:
LONGER SOUND: (oil) *o*E:L±, (boy) B*o*E:, (join) J*o*E:N±	*o*E			*o*E:
No change	B			B
No change: (cheap) CE:BP:, (which) *e*½WE:C	C			C
UPPERDENTAL: (day) D±e:, (did) D±E:D±, (dress) D±*R*a:S	D			D±
AND change finally before consonant: (bad for) BA:T±VF:O:*R*, (freed from) FRE:T±VF:*R*o:M	D	.T±(¢	&	&
AND drop finally after consonant: (bird) B*i**R*¼, (cold) GK:*o*:L±¼, (mind) MA:EN±¼	D	.¼)¢	&	&
OR change between vowels: (body) BoT±E:, (credit) GK:*R*a:T±E:D±*e*½, (added) A:T±*e*D±	D			T±♯
				All 3
Change medially & finally: (left) L±a:VF:T± (safe) Se:VF:	F			VF:
DROP from ING suffix: (living) L±E:VE:N±¼	G			¼ing)
VERY STRONG: (hair) H:e:*R*, (high) H:*A*:E, (house) H:*A*:S	H			H:
BUT drop at start of sentence: (He has) ¼E:H:*A*:Z	H			--¼

Key:

¼ drop	(preceding	: stronger	± upperdental	♯ between vowels
½ weak	) following	& as shown	-- initially in sentence	*S* show, sure
. final	) in suffix	*R* trilled R		¢ consonant(s)

GENERAL ITALIAN - ROMAN ITALIAN - FLORENTINE (EDUCATED)

GUIDE PAGES	SOUND	General Italian	Roman Italian	Florentine Educated
No change: (judge) Jo:J, (edge) a:J	J	J	&	&
Change in all positions: (keep) GK:E:BP:, (ache) e:GK:, (sky) SGK:*A*:E, (ask) *A*:SGK:	K	GK:		&
OR change: GE:BP:, e:G, SGA:E, *A*:SG	K		G	
Against upper teeth: (law) L±O: (blue) BL±*U*: (land) L±A:N±¼ (till) T±E:L± (well) *e*½Wa:L±	L	L±	&	&
BUT change medially before a consonant: (bulb) Bo:L±*e*½B, (silver) SE:L±*e*½Ve*R*	L	/L±*e*½ (¢	&	&
AND drop finally before R: (well read) *e*½Wa:¼*R*a:D±, (all wrong) O:¼*R*O:N±G	L	.¼)r	&	&
		All 3		
No change	M	M		
Against upper teeth: (not)N±*o*:T± (any) a:N±E: (run) *R*o:N±	N	N±		
CHANGE: (put) BP:*U*:T±, (open) *o*:BP:*e*N±, (step) ST±a:BP:	P	BP:		
No change	Q	Q		
TRILL: (gray) G*R*e:, (very) Va:*R*E:, (for) FO:*R*	R	*R*	&	&
BUT change initially: (read) *e*½*R*E:D± (write) *e*½*R*A:ED±*e*½ (rich) *e*½*R*E:C (ready) *e*½*R*a:D±E:	R	-*e*½*R*	&	&
AND medially before a consonant: (poorly) BP:*U*:*Re*½L±E:, (organ) O:*Re*½G*e*N±	R	/*Re*½ (¢	&	&
Change between vowels: (decide) D±E:ZA:ED±	S	Z‡		
AND before dropped T: (best) Ba:Z¼, (cost) GK:O:Z¼	S	Z(¼t		
BUT no change spelled SS: (classy) GK:L±A:SE:	S	S$ss		
No change: (show) *S*o:, (sure) *SU*:*R*	*S*	*S*		
Against upper teeth: (take) T±e:GK:, (tell) T±a:L±, (winter) *e*½WE:N±T±*eR*, (tie) T±A:E	T	T±	&	&
BUT drop finally following N or S: (test) T±a:Z¼, (can't) GK:*A*:N±¼, (don't) D±*o*:N±¼	T	.¼)NS	&	&
AND change finally after vowel: (sit) SE:D±*e*½ (but) Bo:D±*e*½ (late) L±e:D±*e*½ (meet) ME:D±*e*½	T	.D±*e*½)*	&	&
		All 3		
CHANGE: (thing) T±E:N±G, (bath) BA:T±, (three) T±*R*E:	*t*	T±		
CHANGE: (they) D±e:, (this) D±E:S, (smooth) SM*U*:D±	*T*	D±		
No change	V	V		
Change initially: (will) *e*½WE:L± (why) *e*½WA:E (was) *e*½Wo:Z	W	*e*½W		
Change KS sound: (next) N±a:K*e*½Z¼, (expert) a:K*e*½ZBP:*i*RT±, (fix) FE:K*e*½Z, (sex) Sa:K*e*½Z	X	K*e*½Z 4ks	&	&
Change GZ sound: (examine) a:G*e*½SA:MAN, (exist) a:G*e*½SE:Z¼, (exact) a:G*e*½SA:GK:T±	X	G*e*½S 4gz	&	&
Change KS sound: (luxury) L±o:K*e*½*Si*RE:, (complexion) GK:AMBP:L±a:K*e*½*S*AN±	X	K*e*½*S* 4k*S*	&	&
No change: (zero) ZE:*Ro*:, (his) H:E:Z	Z	Z	&	&
When spelled "sure": (pleasure) BP:L±a:*ze*, (measure) Ma:*ze*, (treasure) T±*R*a:*ze*	*z*	*ze*$ sure	&	&
INSERT ASPIRATE after final consonant when followed by consonant: (seem to) SE:M*e*½T±*U*: (sun sign) So:N±*e*½SA:E:N± (stop light) ST±*o*:BP:*e*½L±A:ED±*e*½		.)¢(¢ +*e*½	&	&
SAME at end of sentence: (love.) L±o:V*e*½.		..+*e*½	&	&

Key:

& as shown	*C* church	(preceding	: stronger	.. end of sentence
$ spelled	- initial	) following	½ weakened	* vowels
4 for	/ medial	¢ consonant	¼ dropped	‡ between "
+ add to	. finally	*R* trilled R		± upperdental

ITALIAN: MILANO, LOMBARDY - TORINO, NORTHWEST - RIETI, RURAL

GUIDE PAGES	SOUND	Milano Lombardy Ital.	Torino North West Ital.	Rieti Rural Italian
Change in all positions: (age) eJ, (shame) SeM, (say) Se, (eight) eD±e½, (nail) N±eL±	A	e	&	
OR change: e:J, Se:M, Se:, e:D±e½, Ne:L±	A			e:
LONGER SOUND: (eat) E:D±e½, (theory) T±E:iRE:, (believe) BE:L±E:V, (she) SE:, (each) E:C	E	E:	&	&
Change in all positions: (line) L±A:EN± (I'm) A:EM (like) L±A:EGK: (my) MA:E (ice) A:ES	I	A:E	&	
OR change: L±A:N±, A:M, L±A:GK:, MA:, A:S				A:
Change in all positions: (own) o:N±, (whole) H:o:L± (so) So: (old) o:L±¼ (note) N±o:D±e½	O	o:	&	&
LONGER SOUND: (value) VA:L±U:, (tune) T±U:N±, (use) U:Z, (cute) GK:U:D±e½, (new) N±U:	U	U:	&	&
Change in all positions: (had) H:A:D±, (act) A:GK:T±, (magic) MA:JE:GK:, (angry) A:ŊGRE:	a	A:		&
OR change: H:e:D±, e:GK:T±, Me:zE:GK:, e:ŊGRE:	a		e:	
Change in all positions: (end) a:N±¼, (let) L±a:D±e½, (well) e½Wa:L±, (said) Sa:D±-	e	a:	&	&
Change in all positions: (in) E:N±, (if) E:VF:, (still) ST±E:L±, (women) e½WE:MeN±	i	E:	&	&
Change in all positions: (on) o:N±, (solid) So:L±E:D±, (got) Go:D±e½, (drop) D±Ro:BP:	o	o:	&	&
Change in all positions: (us) o:S, (cut) GK:o:D±e½, (love) L±o:V, (touch) T±o:C	u	o:		
OR change: oS, GK:oD±e½, L±oV, T±oC	u		o	o
LONGER SOUND: (are) A:R (mark) MA:RGK: (calm) GK:A:L±M, (large) L±A:Re½J, (watch) e½WA:C	A	A:	&	&
Change in all positions: (her) H:iR, (learn) L±iRe½N±, (first) FiRe½Z¼, (turn) T±iRe½N±	E	i	&	
OR when spelled ER: H:eR, L±eRe½N±				e$er
When spelled IR: FE:Re½Z¼, (girl) GE:Re½L±				E:$ir
" " OR: (work) e½Wo:Re½GK:, (comfort) GK:o:MVF:o:Re½T±, (word) e½Wo:R¼				o:$or
When spelled UR: TU:Re½N±, (hurt) H:U:Re½T±				U:$ur
No change: (predict) BP:RID±E:GK:T±	I	I	&	&
Change in all positions: (down) D±A:N± (out) A:D±e½, (now) N±A:, (count) GK:A:N±¼	O	A:	&	&
LONGER SOUND: (room) RU:M, (soon) SU:N±, (do) D±U:, (group) GRU:BP:, (blue) BL±U:	U	U:	&	&
Change in all positions: (and) A:N±¼, (last) L±A:Z¼, (can't) GK:A:N±¼, (after) A:VF:T±eR	a	A:	&	&
No change: (simple) SE:MBP:eL±	e	e	&	&
Change in all positions: (ago) AGo:, (idea) A:ED±E:A, (system) SE:ST± M, (awake) WeGK:	i	A	&	&!
OR drop at start of phrase: ¼Go:, e½We:GK:				--¼

Key:

& as shown	C church	S show, sure
$ spelled	, nasalized	-- initially in sentence
¼ dropped	: longer	± upper dental
	½ weakened	R trilled R

ITALIAN: MILANO, LOMBARDY - TORINO, NORTHWEST - RIETI, RURAL

GUIDE PAGES	SOUND	Milano Lombardy Ital.	Torino North West Ital.	Rieti Rural Italian
When spelled "a,au,aw": (talk) T±O:GK:, (cause) GK:O:Z, (law) L±O:, (all) O:L±	*o*	O:$a, au,aw		
OR change: T±*o*:GK:, GK:*o*:Z, L±*o*:, *o*:L±	*o*		*o*:$a	
OR change: T±A:GK:. GK:A:S, L±A:, A:L±	*o*			A:$a
OTHERWISE: (off) O:VF:, (door) D±O:*R*	*o*	O:$o	&	&
Change in all positions: (could) GK:*U*:D± (look) L±*U*:GK: (wolf) *e*½W*U*:L±VF:	*u*	*U*:	&	&
OR when spelled U: (put) BP:E*U*T± (full) VF:E*U*L±	*u*	E*U*$u	E*U*$u	
LONGER SOUND: (oil) *o*E:L±, (boy) B*o*E:, (join) J*o*E:N±, (enjoy) a:ŊJ*o*E:, (spoil) SBP:*o*E:L±	*o*E	*o*E:	&	&
No change	B	B	&	&
No change: (cheap) CE:BP:, (which) *e*½WE:C	C	C	&	&
Against upper teeth: (day) D±e, (did) D±E:D±, (food) F*U*:D±, (dress) D±*R*a:S, (made) MeD±	D	D±	&	&
AND change finally before consonant: (bad for) BA:T±*e*½VF:O:*R*, (freed from) F*R*E:T±*e*½VF:*R*o:M	D	.T± (¢	&	&
AND drop finally after a consonant: (bird) B*i*R¼, (cold) GK:*o*:L±¼, (mind) MA:EN±¼	D	.¼) ¢	&	&
Change medially and finally: (safe) SeVF:, (left) L±a:VF:T±, (coffee) GK:O:VF:E:	F	/.VF:	&	&
DROP from "ing" suffix: (living) L±E:VE:N±¼, (meeting) ME:T±E:N±¼ (coming) GK:*o*:ME:N±¼	G	¼ing)	&	&
VERY STRONG: (hair) H:e*R*, (high) H:A:E, (house) H:A:S, (unhappy) o:N±H:A:BP:E:	H	H:	&	&
BUT drop at the start of a sentence: (He has) ¼E:H:A:Z, (How high) ¼A:H:A:E	H	--¼	&	&
OR drop initially after consonant (beach house) BE:C¼A:S, (long hair) L±O:ŊG¼e*R*	H			-¼) ¢
OR drop medially: *o*N±¼A:BP:E: (somehow) S*o*M¼A:	H			/¼
Change in all positions: (judge) z*o*z, (edge) a:z, (stage) ST±ez, (gradual) G*R*e:zU:*e*L±	J		z	
OR no change: Jo:J, a:J, ST±eJ, G*R*A:JU:*e*L±	J	J		&
Change in all positions: (keep) GK:E:BP:, (ache) eGK:, (sky) SGK:A:E, (make) MeGK:	K	GK:	&	&
OR drop from KS when spelled CC: (accent) A:¼Sa:N±¼, (accept) A:¼Sa:BP:T±	K			¼$cc
Against upper teeth: (law) L±O: (blue) BL±*U*: (land) L±A:N±¼ (till) T±E:L± (well)*e*½Wa:L±	L	L±	&	&
BUT drop finally before R: (well read) *e*½Wa:¼*R*a:D±, (all wrong) O:¼*R*O:N±G	L	.¼(r	&	&
AND change medially before a consonant: (bulb) Bo:L±*e*½B, (silver) SE:L±*e*½V*e*R	L	/L±*e*½ (¢	&	
OR drop medially ditto: B*o*¼B, SE:¼V*eR*	L			/¼(¢
Nasalize medially and finally after vowel and before consonant: (empty) a:M̦BP:T±E:	M	/.M̦)*(¢	&	
OTHERWISE no change	M	M	&	&

Key:

& as shown	- initially	z measure	, nasalize
$ spelled	-- " in sentn.	(preceding	¢ consonants
: stronger	/ medially	) following	* vowels
½ weakened	. finally ¼ dropped	) in suffix	*R* trilled R
			± upperdental

ITALIAN: MILANO, LOMBARDY - TORINO, NORTHWEST - RIETI, RURAL

GUIDE PAGES	SOUND	Milano Lombardy Ital.	Torino North West Ital.	Rieti Rural Italian
Against upper teeth: (none) N±o:N±, (name) N±eM (not) N±o:D±e½ (any) a:N±E: (run) Ro:N±	N	N±	&	&
Nasalize medially & finally after vowel & before consonant: (into) E:ŊT±U:, (until) o:ŊT±E:L±	N	/.Ŋ)*(¢	&	
Change in all positions: (page) BP:eJ, (put) BP:U:D±e½, (open) o:BP:eN±, (step) ST±a:BP:	P	BP:	&	&
Change in all positions: (quick) GK:e½WE:GK:, (equal) E:GK:e½WeL±, (quiet) GK:e½WA:EeD±e½	Q			GK: e½W
TRILL: (gray) GRe, (very) Va:RE:, (dry) D±RA:E	R	R	&	&
BUT change initially: (read) e½RE:D±, (write) e½RA:ED±e½, (rich) e½RE:C, (ready) e½Ra:D±E:	R	-e½R	&	&
AND medially before a consonant: (organ) O:Re½GeN±, (poorly) BP:U:Re½L±E:	R	/Re½ (¢	&	&
OR drop finally: (for) FO:¼ (are) A:¼ (or) O:¼				¼.

	SOUND	All 3
Change between vowels: (decide) D±E:ZA:E:D±	S	Z⁑
AND before dropped T: (best) Ba:Z¼, (cost) GK:O:Z¼	S	Z(¼T
BUT no change spelled SS: (classy) GK:L±A:SE:	S	S$ss
No change: (show) So:, (sure) SU:R	S	S

	SOUND	Milano Lombardy Ital.	Torino North West Ital.	Rieti Rural Italian
Against upper teeth: (take) T±eGK:, (tell) T±a:L±, (winter) ½WE:ŊT±eR, (tie) T±A:E	T	T±	&	&
BUT drop finally following N or S: (test) T±a:Z¼, (can't) GK:A:N±¼, (don't) D±o:N±¼	T	.¼)NS	&	&
AND change finally after vowel: (sit) SE:D±e½ (but) Bo:D±e½ (late) L±eD±e½ (meet) ME:D±e½	T	.D±e½)*	&	&
OR change between vowels: (better) Ba:D±eR	T		D±⁑	

	SOUND	All 3
CHANGE: (thing) T±E:ŊG, (bath) BA:T±, (three) T±RE:	t	T±
CHANGE: (they) D±e, (this) D±E:S, (smooth) SMU:D±	T	D±
No change:	V	V
Change initially: (will) e½WE:L± (why) e½WA:E (was) e½Wo:Z	W	e½W

	SOUND	Milano Lombardy Ital.	Torino North West Ital.	Rieti Rural Italian
Change KS sound: (next) N±a:Ke½Z¼, (expert) a:Ke½ZBP:iRT±, (fix) FE:Ke½Z, (sex) Sa:Ke½Z	X	Ke½Z 4ks	&	
OR change: N±a:Ge½Z, a:G ½ZBP:eRT±, FE:Ge½Z	X			Ge½Z4ks
Change GZ sound: (examine) a:Ge½SA:MAN±, (exist) a:Ge½SE:Z¼, (exact) a:Ge½SA:GK:T±	X	Ge½S 4gz	&	
OR change: a:Ke½SA:MAN, a:Ke½SE:Z¼	X			Ke½S4gz
Change KS sound: (luxury) L±o:Ke½SeRE:, (complexion) GK:AMBP:L±a:Ke½SAN±	X	Ke½S 4kS		
OR change Gz: (luxurious) LoKe½SU:RE:eS	X			Ke½S4Gz
Change in all positions: (zero) SE:Ro:, (his) H:E:S, (zone) So:N±, (use) U:S, (was) e½WoS	Z			S
When spelled "sure": (pleasure) BP:L±a:ze, (measure) Ma:ze, (treasure) T±Ra:ze	z			ze$ sure
INSERT ASPIRATE after final consonant when followed by consonant:				
(seem to) SE:Me½T±U: (sun sign) So:N±e½SA:EN± (stop light) ST±o:BP:e½L±A:ED±e½		.)¢(¢ +e½	&	&
SAME at end of sentence: (love.) L±o:Ve½.		..+e½	&	&

Key:

4 for	: stronger	- initial	¢ consonant	(preceding
¼ drop	& as shown	/ medial	* vowels	) following
C church	$ spelled	. finally	⁑ between "	R trilled R
½ weaken	+ add to	.. end of sentence	, nasalized	± upperdental

NAPLES ITALIAN - REGGIO, CALABRIAN ITALIAN - VENICE ITALIAN

GUIDE PAGES	SOUND	Naples Italian	Reggio Calabrian Ital.	Venice Italian
		All 3		
CHANGE: (age) e:J, (shame) Se:M, (say) Se:, (ate) e:T±	A			e:
LONGER SOUND: (eat) E:T±, (believe) BE:L±E:V, (each) E:C	E			E:
CHANGE: (I'm) A:EM, (like) L±A:EGK:, (ice) A:ES	I			A:E
Change in all positions: (own) *o*:N±, (whole) H:*o*:L±, (so) S*o*:, (old) *o*:L±D±, (note) N±*o*:T±	O	*o*:	&	
OR shorter sound: O½N±, H:O½L±, SO½, N±O½T±	O			O½
		All 3		
LONGER SOUND: (use) U:S, (tune) T±U:N±, (new) N±U:	U			U:
CHANGE: (had) H:A:D±, (act) A:GK:T±, (angry) A:N±GRE:	a			A:
Change in all positions: (end) a:N±D±, (let) L±a:T±, (well) *e*½Wa:L±, (said) Sa:D±	e	a:	&	
OR change: eiN±¼, L±eiT±, *e*½WeiL±, SeiD±	e			ei
		All 3		
CHANGE: (in) E:N± (women) *e*½WE:M*e*N± (if) E:VF: (it) E:T±	i			E:
CHANGE: (on) *o*:N±, (solid) S*o*:L±E:D±, (got) G*o*:T±	o			*o*:
CHANGE: (us) o:S, (cut) GK:o:T±, (love) L±o:V, (up) o:BP:	u			o:
LONGER SOUND: (are) A:*R*, (watch) *e*½WA:C, (calm) GK:A:L±M	A			A:
CHANGE: (her) H:*ɩR*, (first) F*ɩRe*½ST±, (turn) T±*ɩRe*½N±	*E*			*ɩ*
No change: (predict) BP:*RI*D±E:GK:T±, (propose) BP:*RI*BP:*o*:S	*I*			*I*
CHANGE: (out) A:T±, (down) D±A:N±, (count) GK:A:N±T±	*O*			A:
LONGER SOUND: (room) *RU*:M, (soon) S*U*:N±, (do) D±*U*:	*U*			*U*:
CHANGE: (and) A:N±D±, (can't) GK:A:N±T±, (last) L±A:ST±	*a*			A:
No change: (simple) SE:MBP:*e*L±, (person) BP:*ɩR*S*e*N±	*e*			*e*
CHANGE: (ago) AG*o*:, (system) SE:ST±AM, (idea) A:ED±E:A	*ɩ*			A
CHANGE: (talk) T±O:GK: (off) O:VF: (door) D±O:*R* (all) O:L±	*o*			O:
CHANGE: (could) GK:*U*:D±, (put) BP:*U*:T±, (look) L±*U*:GK:	*u*			*U*:
LONGER SOUND: (oil) *o*E:L±, (boy) B*o*E:, (join) J*o*E:N±	*o*E			*o*E:
No change	B			B
No change: (cheap) CE:BP:, (which) *e*½WE:C, (church) C*ɩR*C	C			C
Against upper teeth: (day) D±e:, (did) D±E:D±, (food) F*U*:D±, (dress) D±*R*a:S, (made) Me:D±	D	D±	&	&
OR change medially: (body) B*o*:*R*E:, (address) A:*R*a:S, (middle) ME: L± (credit) GK:*R*a:*Re*T±	D	/*R*		
OR change medially: B*o*:T±E:, A:T±*R*a:S, ME:T±*e*L	D		/t	
OR drop finally after consonant: (bird) B*ɩR*¼, (cold) GK:O½L±¼, (mind) MA:EN±¼	D			.¼)¢
		All 3		
Change medially & finally: (left) L±a:VF:T±, (safe) Se:VF:	F			VF:
DROP from "ing" suffix: (living) L±E:VE:N±¼	G			¼ing}
VERY STRONG: (hair) H:e:*R*, (high) H:A:E, (house) H:A:S	H			H:
BUT drop at start of sentence: (He has) ¼E:H:A:S	H			--¼
No change: (judge) Jo:J, (edge) a:J	J			J
Change in all positions: (keep) GK:E:BP:, (ache) e:GK:, (sky) SGK:A:E, (ask) A:SGK:	K	GK:	&	&
OR drop before T: (fact) FA:¼T± (sect) Sa:¼T±	K			/.¼(t

Key:

& as shown	(preceding	± upper dental	¼ dropped	/ medially
: stronger	) following	*R* trilled R	*S* show, sure	. finally
½ weakened	} in suffix	-- initially in sentence		¢ consonant

NAPLES ITALIAN - REGGIO, CALABRIAN ITALIAN - VENICE ITALIAN

GUIDE PAGES	SOUND	Naples Italian	Reggio Calabrian Ital.	Venice Italian
Against upper teeth: (law) L±O:, (blue) BL±U: (land) L±A:N±D± (till) T±E:L± (well) e½Wa:L±	L	L±	§	§
BUT change medially before a consonant: (bulb) Bo:L±e½B, (silver) SE:L±e½VeR	L	/L±e½ (¢	§	§
AND drop finally before "R": (well read) e½Wa:¼Ra:D±, (all wrong) O:¼RO:N±G	L	.¼(r	§	§
No change	M	M	§	§
Against upper teeth: (none) N±o:N±, (name) N±e:M (not) N±o:T± (any) a:N±E: (run) Ro:N±	N	N±	§	§
Change in all positions: (page) BP:e:J, (put) BP:U:T±, (open) o:BP:eN±, (step) ST±a:BP:	P	BP:	§	§
No change	Q	Q	§	§
TRILL: (gray) GRe:, (very) Va:RE:, (for) FO:R	R	R	§	§
BUT change initially: (read) e½RE:D±, (write) e½RA:ET±, (rich) e½RE:C, (ready) e½Ra:D±E:	R	-e½R	§	§
AND change medially before a consonant: (poorly) BP:U:Re½L±E:, (organ) O:Re½GeN±	R	/Re½ (¢	§	§

	SOUND	All 3
Change between vowels: (decide) D±E:ZA:ED±, (basis) Be:ZE:S	S	Z‡
AND before dropped T: (best) Ba:Z¼, (cost) GK:O:Z¼	S	Z(¼t
BUT no change spelled "SS": (classy) GK:L±A:SE:	S	S$ss
No change: (show) So:, (sure) SU:R	S	S

	SOUND	Naples Italian	Reggio Calabrian Ital.	Venice Italian
Against upper teeth: (take) T±e:GK:, (tell) T±a:L±, (ticket) T±E:GK:eT± , (tie) T±A:E	T	T±	§	§
OR change medial TT: (better) Ba:ReR, (battle) BA:ReL±, (little) L±E:ReL±	T	/R$tt		
OR change after N or R: (can't) GK:A:N±D±, (hurt) H:iRe½D±, (won't) e½Wo:N±D±	T		D±)nr	
OR change finally before vowel: (shut up) So:Ro:BP:, (get off) Ga:RO:VF:	T	.R(*		

	SOUND	All 3
CHANGE: (thing) T±E:N±G, (bath) BA:T±, (three) T±RE:	t	T±
CHANGE: (they) D±e¼, (smooth) SMU:D±, (this) D±E:S	T	D±
No change	V	V
Change initially: (will) e½WE:L± (why) e½WA:E (was) e½Wo:S	W	e½W

	SOUND	Naples Italian	Reggio Calabrian Ital.	Venice Italian
Change "KS" sound: (next) N±a:Ke½ZT±, (fix) FE:Ke½Z (expert) a:Ke½ZBP:iRT± (sex) Sa:Ke½Z	X	Ke½Z 4ks	§	§
CHANGE "GZ" sound: (examine) a:Ge½SA:MAN, (exist) a:Ge½SE:ST±, (exact) a:Ge½SA:GK:T±	X	Ge½S 4gz	§	§
Change "KS" sound: (luxury) L±o:Ke½SiRE:, (complexion) GK:AMBP:L±a:Ke½SAN±	X	Ke½S 4kS	§	§
Change in all positions: (zero) SE:Ro:, (his) H:E:S, (wise) e½WA:ES, (lazy) L±e:SE:	Z	S	S	
No change: (measure) Ma:zeR, (azure) A:zeR	z	z	§	§
INSERT ASPIRATE after final consonant when followed by consonant: (seem to) SE:Me½T±U: (sun sign) So:N±e½SA:EN± (stop light) ST±o:BP:e½L±A:ET±		.)¢(¢ +e½	§	§
SAME at end of sentence: (love.) L±o:Ve½.		..+e½	§	§

Key:

§ as shown	C church	◦. end of sent.	: stronger	* vowels
$ spelled	/ medially	(preceding	½ weakened	‡ between "
4 for	◦ finally	) following	½ dropped	± upperdental
	- initially	+ add to	¢ consonant	R trilled R

MASTER CATEGORY 6

POLISH

In the last chapter I referred to my Italian friends from Chicago's West Side. That section of the city, the stronghold of Chicago's Roman Catholics, also provided me with many first-generation Polish friends. Unlike my Italian buddies, they had no distinctive music that shaded their speech, and they were reluctant to invite me to their homes. I eventually found out why. First, their parents all spoke Polish at home and, as a result, their sparse English was heavily accented—a source of deep shame to my friends. Second, their parents often and openly discussed their feelings about Jews, and my buddies knew how their families would react to their children's Jewish friends. I wasn't concerned with all this family conflict; I was keeping my ears open for that distinctive Polish accent.

At first the dialect sounded like the speech of the parents of my best friend, Alex Boas. But Alex's folks were Russian, and surely that was an entirely different language. Gradually I became able to distinguish between the two dialects—to pick out the differences as well as the surface similarities that had made me confuse them.

Let's examine these factors—with the hope that you'll never fall into the trap of using a Russian dialect when a Polish one is called for (or vice versa)—a frequent acting "crime."

Similarities and Differences between Polish and Russian Dialects

The first element that both dialects have in common is a "Y-glide" that precedes "e" and "i" sounds. In Russian it also happens (often) after "d," "l," "t," soft "th" (*t*), hard "TH" (*T*), and "n." In Polish, the Y-glide only follows an "n."

Second, neither dialect distinguishes between "v" and "w." But where the Russian combines the two sounds into (V:W) with the emphasis on the "v," Polish gives equal value to both elements and comes out with a (VW).

Third, though both dialects trill their "r"s (*R*), the Russian does it much more strongly (*R*:).

Finally, two vowel sounds distinguish the Polish dialect from the Russian (and most other dialects). The first is the double sound, or diphthong (*u*i), which the Poles use to replace the (*o*E) of "boy." The second is the use of the (o) sound of "hot" to replace thirty percent of the remaining twenty vowel sounds of American English.

Vowel Changes

Besides standing for itself, as in (oN) and (SToP), the ubiquitous (o) takes the place of (a), (*a*), (*i*), and (*o*) when spelled "a" and (*A*).

The myth "that Thor had a magic hammer" for the Polish thus becomes:

(DoT) Thor (HoD) a (Mo*C*iK HoM*eR*).

Likewise, if my oldest "aunt can't dance fast," and I were from Poland, I'd say my old:

(oN¼ KoN¼ DoNS FoS¼).

If you wanted to tell your overnight guest that there was an "extra pair of pajamas atop the sofa," using Polish dialect you'd tell him there was:

(aXT*R*o Po*C*oMoS oToP) the (S*o*FWo).

If we saw that the TV commentators "talked of war all autumn" long, if Polish-speaking we might remark that they:

(ToK¼) of (VWo*R* oL oToM).

And finally, if our friends wanted to tell us about "watching the gala Mardi Gras march" in New Orleans, as Polish-born, they would describe:

(VWo*C*iN¼) the (GoLo Mo*R*Di G*R*o Mo*RC*).

This last substitution, that of (o) for (*A*), is significant of a whole category of changes, since that (o) of "fox" is more or less a shortened version of the (*A*) of "father." This vowel shortening affects, first of all, the (*U*) of "Luke" and "pool," turning them into the (*u*) of "look" and "pull." Thus if someone wanted to paint the "schoolroom blue," in the Polish dialect they would want to paint:

the (SK*u*¼*Ru*M BL*u*).

This shortening also affects the (U) sound, since this is a diphthong (double-vowel sound) made up of (Y) and (*U*). So an arranger who found only a "few music cues" in a screenplay, if Polish would find only a:

(FWY*u* MY*u*SiK KY*u*S).

Again, the "ee" (E) sound is shortened into (i), so that "peak" and "lead" rhyme with "pick" and "lid." Thus someone observing that a spotlight "released heat," as a Pole would say it:

(*R*iLiS¼ HiT).

This tendency covers a number of other diphthongs as well, shortening their second elements or cutting them off entirely. For example, the sounds that combine to make the (A) of "mate" are the (e) of "met" and the (E) of "meet." Poles shorten the second element to (i), making the diphthong (ei). Thus if a party to an accident might admit that "maybe they tailgated," if they were Polish, their confession would come out that:

(MeiBi Dei Tei¼GeiTeD).

The (I) sound of "wine" is also a diphthong, made up of the (*A*) of "wan" and the (E) of "wean." Again the second element is weakened into an (i), producing the sound (*A*i), so that a young woman bragging that her boyfriend had a "dynamite line," if Polish-speaking would say he had:

a (D*A*iNoM*A*iT L*A*iN).

As noted, some diphthongs lose their second elements entirely in the Polish dialect. For example, the (*O*) of "brow" is a combination of the (*A*) of "bra" and the (*U*) of "brew," but the Polish drop the (*U*) completely. Thus a poet may curse the "foul ounce of doubt" that robs him of his confidence, but as a Pole, he would rail against the:

(FW*A*:L *A*:NS) of (D*A*:T).

The (*U*) sound is also lost from the diphthong (O) as in "flow," which is made up of the (*o*) in "flaw" and the (*U*) of "flew." This change is quite organic since, in the Polish language, the letter "o" is pronounced "aw" (*o*). It converts "boat" and "pose" into something like "bought" and "pause." So if the guest star will be late arriving at the club, we might have to "postpone the show"—but in Polish dialect we'd have to:

(P*o*STP*o*N) the (*S*Y*o*).

This same "aw" (*o*) sound replaces the (u) of "gun" and "done," turning them into "gone" and "dawn." So if in taking over my son's lawn-mowing chores I look for "what was uncut," if I were Polish, I would keep an eye out for:

(VW*o*T VW*o*S *o*NK*o*T).

Just as this change moves the vowel sound farther back in the oral cavity, so does the change of the (e) move it back to become an (a), so that in Polish dialect, "head" and "bet" sound more like "had" and "bat." Thus if an army hospital decided to "sell their excess beds," as Poles their decision would be to:

(SaL) their (aXaS BaDS).

Now for the other characteristic Polish sound that I mentioned at the beginning of this chapter: the substitution for the (*o*E) of "boy." This case is the only instance I know of in which both elements of a diphthong change: the (*o*) of "fall" changes to the (*u*) of "full" and the (E) of "feel" to the (i) of "fill." The result? A brand new Polish diphthong: (*u*i). So if a Polish chef were to instruct his assistant to "avoid boiling oysters," he would tell him to:

(HoVW*u*iD B*u*iLiN¼ *u*iST*eR*S).

You'll find a few more specialized vowel changes in the *GUIDE PAGES*, but we'll only concern ourselves here with the last major change: the (*E*) sound. This is the sound of "bird" and "were," and the Polish dialect changes it into the (*o*) sound of "board" and "war." So if a four-year-old has reached the stage where she says no to every request, a Polish child psychologist observing "her turn perverse," would talk of seeing:

(H*oR* T*oR*N P*oR*VW*oR*S).

Consonant Changes

As you can see from that last line, when the Poles *do* pronounce their "r"s, they trill (*R*) them. A trilled "r" (*R*), as we have seen before, is one that is produced by a vibration (or flapping) of the tongue. It happens when the tongue is placed against the gum ridge behind the upper front teeth, and the sound is voiced, so that it resembles a pneumatic drill, a motorcycle, or a machine gun.

I emphasized "when the Poles *do* pronounce their 'r's" because they always drop (¼) them in the middle of a word when the "r" follows an (o) sound and precedes another consonant. Putting these two rules of the Polish "r" together, we find that a professor who admonished his students not to "disregard rural art," if he were Polish would ask them not to:

(DiS*R*iGo¼D *R*u*R*oL o¼T).

Just as the trilled "r" (*R*) is a carry-over from the native Polish language, so is the Y-glide that was mentioned at the beginning of this chapter. The Y-glide takes place when an (N) is followed by an "i" or an "e" sound and becomes an (NY). For example, if the man "needs a nip," the Polish-speaking will say he:

(NYiDS) a (NYiP)

And if on a nature walk we "named snakes," in the Polish dialect we:

(NYeiM¼D SNYeiKS).

A third carry-over is the distinctly Polish pronunciation of "f." In English, this sound is made with the upper teeth touching the lower lip while breath is expelled through the narrow opening. In Polish the teeth come nowhere near closing that gap, though the breath is still aspirated through slightly rounded lips. The result is an (FW) sound; thus a comedy routine that got "fifteen laughs" would be described by a Polish-born critic as having gotten:

(FWiFWTiN LoFWS).

Since "v" is actually a voiced version of "f," it is not surprising that it receives exactly the same treatment. In the case of "v," the consonant sound is made in the same mouth positions, but it is voiced rather than aspirated; the result is a (VW). Thus a romantic movement that brings about the "revival of love verses," in the Polish quarter will start up a:

(*R*iVW*A*iVW*e*L oVW LoVW VW*oR*S*e*S).

As the Polish language makes no distinction between "v" and "w" sounds, they are handled in precisely the same way. In other words, if I tried to explain "which way we went," in this dialect I'd be telling:

(VWi*C* VWei VWi VWaN¼).

Since the letter "j" stands for the (Y) sound in the Polish language, the closest the Pole can come to the American voiced "j" sound is "ch" (*C*), the unvoiced sound made in the same mouth position. This makes "jump" and "edge" sound more like "chump" and "etch." So a thrill-seeker who could "enjoy the jolt of danger," as a Pole would:

(HaN*C*ui) the (*C*oL¼) of (DeiN*C*e*R*).

In Polish, the letters "sz" stand for a sound something like the American "sh" (*S*). Actually, the Polish sound is closer to "shY" (*SY*), and this is what the Pole substitutes for our (*S*)—most of the time. So a review so terrible that it would "shut the show for sure," in this dialect would:

(*SY*oT) the (*SY*o) for (*SY*u*R*).

Notice that I said "most of the time"; the rule does not hold true when the "sh" sound is spelled "ch"—such as in the word "chef" (generally such words are of French origin). When the Poles see the "ch," it reminds them of the "cz" combination which in their language stands for the "ch" (*C*) sound. That is exactly what the Pole throws in (all the more ironic since the letter combination "ch" in French almost always indicates the "sh" (*S*) sound). So if someone complains that the "chauffeur drank the chef's champagne," if he were Polish his accusation would come out that the:

(*C*oFWo*R*) drank the (*C*aFWS *C*oMPein).

Another sound that *almost* exists in Polish is written in that language as "rz." The sound this stands for is like—but does not duplicate—the American (z) as in "azure." The Poles, however, substitute "sh" (*S*) for the American (z), so if a scholar speaks of the Koran's description of Paradise (mistakenly) as an "Asian vision of pleasure," in this dialect he would call it an:

(Hei*S*oN VWi*S*oN) of (PLa*S*e*R*).

Two more American consonant sounds do not exist at all in Polish: the soft "th" (*t*) and the hard "TH" (*T*). The Polish-speaking person converts the first "th" (*t*) into a (T), so that if the world faced "three breathless months" while the Polish Solidarity movement defied the Polish government, the Poles in America would refer to this period as:

(T*R*i B*R*aTLaS MoNTS).

The hard "TH" (*T*) becomes a (D) in the Polish dialect, so that while a sportsman looking for a carrier for his hunting knife might ask for "that leather sheath," if Polish-born he would ask for:

(DoT LaDe*R* *S*YiD).

In the GUIDE PAGES that follow, there are five subdialects to add to your repertoire: the Krakow dialect of southern Poland, the Lublin dialect of eastern Poland, the Poznan dialect of western Poland, the Zwolen dialect of rural central Poland, and the *Warsaw Educated* dialect. The last is the "lightest" one and comes closest to American English.

Music, Rhythm, and Pace

As for the music that guides all these sound changes, there are two outstanding characteristics. First, like most of the Slavic languages, Polish (and consequently its dialect) is spoken two to three tones lower than American English. Second, there is little natural variance in Polish except when the speaker becomes strongly emotional. When that happens, the music rises sharply on the verb or adjective expressing the character's emotion. For example, in "I just can't *stand* that man!", "stand" is a tone-and-a-half higher than the rest of the words. Likewise, in "I'm completely *crazy* about your kids!," "crazy" would be raised above the rest of the sentence. Remember, though you might not normally choose the emotion-word for emphasis, your Polish character will. In the normal sentence, there is a long rise to the focal point, followed by a gliding "fall," usually on a vowel sound.

The rhythm of the dialect is marked by a heavy stress on the next to the last syllable. Individual words that are stressed receive a much heavier handling than in American English. Finally, the pace of the Polish dialect is much slower than that of normal American speech. This slowness, combined with the heavy stress, lower tone, and lack of variance, makes for a fairly solemn, stolid music.

Observation and Notes

As actors we are fortunate in having many opportunities to observe Polish Americans, their customs and their attitudes, for almost every urban center in the country has a good representation of Poles and has its own Polish-American society, complete with folk festivals, dancing, and Polish music.

On the other hand, the opportunity to observe Polish-born actors on American TV and in American films is virtually nonexistent. A noted exception is Roman Polanski, who, though best known as a director, has taken parts (usually small character roles) in a few major films.

The Polish dialect Meryl Streep used in *Sophie's Choice* is also an excellent example, though not one-hundred percent authentic.

So for personal observation, look toward your own neighboring Polish-American community, and to the tapes that have been made in conjunction with this book.

One of the few American film stars ever to try a Polish dialect in a leading role, Meryl Streep (shown here in a scene from Sophie's Choice, *Universal, 1982), delivered such a riveting performance that her few lapses were hardly noticeable. Even these may have been by design, since—typical of the speech of an English-speaking Pole—they occurred only when she spoke slowly and calmly, never when her character was excited.*

GENERAL POLISH - KRAKOW SOUTHERN POLISH - WARSAW, EDUCATED POLISH

GUIDE PAGES	SOUND	General Polish	Krakow Southern Polish	Warsaw Educated Polish
Change in all positions: (able) eiB¼L, (pain) PeiN, (break) BReiK, (day) Dei	A	ei	&	&
Change in all positions: (eat) iT, (teach) TiC, (theory) TioRi, (we) VWi, (tree) TRi	E	i	&	&
Change in all positions: (I'm) AiM, (like) LAiK (right) RAiT (my) MAi (while) VWAiL	I	Ai	&	&
Change in all positions: (own) oN, (whole) HoL, (so) So, (road) RoD, (fellow) FWaLo	O	o	&	&
Change in all positions: (use) YuS, (tune) TYuN, (new) NYu, (value) VWoLYu, (you) Yu	U	Yu	&	&

Change in all positions: (had) HoD, (flat) FWLoT, (angry) oNGRi, (as) oS, (at) oT	a	o	&	&

		All 3
CHANGE: (men) Man, (let) LaT, (read) RaD, (bell) BaL	e	a
No change: (in) iN, (busy) BiSi, (women) VWiMoN	i	i
No change: (on) oN, (lock) LoK, (stop) SToP, (not) NoT	o	o
CHANGE: (us) oS, (love) LoVW, (does) DoS, (was) VWoS	u	o

CHANGE: (are) oR, (calm) Ko¼M, (watch) VWoC, (car) Ko¼	A	o
CHANGE: (her) HoR, (girl) GoRL, (word) VWoRD, (turn) ToRN	E	o
No change: (predict) PRIDiK¼, (propose) PRIPoS	I	I
CHANGE: (out) A:T, (loud) LA:D, (now) NA:, (how) HA:	O	A:
CHANGE: (room) RuM, (true) TRu, (drew) DRu, (do) Du	U	u

CHANGE: (and) oN¼, (last) LoS¼, (laugh) LoFW, (ask) oSK	a	o		
When spelled ON or EN: (reason) RiSoN, (frighten) FWRAiToN, (person) PoRSoN	e	oN$en or on	&	&
When spelled OR: (labor) LeiBoR, (major) MeiCoR, (glamor) GLoMoR, (tenor) TaNoR	e	oR$or	&	&
When spelled EL or LE: (level) LaVW¼L, (trouble) TRoB¼L, (simple) SiMP¼L	e	¼$el or le	&	&
Change in all positions: (family) FWoMoLi, (ago) oGo (system) SiSToM (extra) aKSTRo	i	o	&	&
When spelled A,AU,AW: (all) oL, (cause) KoS, (law) Lo, (war) VWoR, (tall) ToL	o	o$a au,aw	&	&
OTHERWISE: (off) oFW, (door) DoR, (board) BoRD, (court) KoRT, (dog) DoK, (loss) LoS	o	o$oOA oo,ou	&	&

		All 3
No change: (could) KuD, (pull) PuL, (book) BuK	u	u
CHANGE: (oil) uiL, (boy) Bui, (join) CuiN, (soil) SuiL	oE	ui

No change	B	B		
CHANGE: (cheap) CiP, (much) MoC, (future) FWYuCeR	C	C		
DROP finally after consonant (except R): (cold) KoL¼, (mind) MAiN¼, (field) FWiL¼	D	.¼)¢!r	&	&
Change in all positions: (after) oFWTeR, (laugh) LoFW, (fifteen) FWiFWTiN	F	FW	&	&

Key:

			. finally
& as shown	! excepting	: longer	¢ consonant
$ spelled	) following	¼ dropped	R trilled R

GENERAL POLISH - KRAKOW SOUTHERN POLISH - WARSAW, EDUCATED POLISH

GUIDE PAGES	SOUND	General Polish	Krakow Southern Polish	Warsaw Educated Polish
Change finally: (big) BiK, (leg) LaK, (fog) FWoK, (flag) FWLoK, (rug) RoK, (pig) PiK	G	°K	&	&
AND drop finally from ING or ONG (living) LiVWiN¼, (wrong) RoN¼, (along) oLoN¼	G	.¼ing .¼ong	&	
ADD before vowel at start of phrase: (all of) HoLoVW, (up at) HoPoT, (at all) HoToL	H	--+(*	&	&
Change in all positions: (judge) CoC (joy) Coi, (logic) LoCiK, (major) MeiCoR	J	C	&	&
No change: (make) MeiK, (keep) KiP	K	K	&	&
DROP medially before consonant: (silver) Si¼VWeR, (bulb) Bo¼B, (skillful) SKi¼FWuL	L	/¼(¢	&	
No change	M	M	&	&
"NY" before "i" or "e" sound: (need) NYiD, (name) NYeiM, (nip) NYiP, (nail) NYeiL	N	NY("i""e"	&	&
No change	P	P	&	&
Change in all positions: (quiet) KVWAieT (equal) iKVWoL, (square) SKVWeiR	Q	KVW	&	&
TRILL: (read) RiD (write) RAiT, (very) VWaRi, (disregard) DiSRiGo¼D, (for) FWoR	R	R	&	&
AND drop medially after "o" sound: (park) Po½K (heart) Ho¼T (army) o¼Mi (art) o¼T	R	/¼) "o"	&	
No change: (say) Sei, (face) FWeiS	S	S	&	&
OR change initally before consonant: (stop) SToP (sleep) SLiP (speak) SPiK (swim) SVWiM	S		-S(¢	
Change in all positions: (shut) SYoT (sure) SYuR, (motion) MoSYoN, (special) SPaSYeL	S	SY	&	
AND change when spelled CH: (champagne) CoMPeiN, (chef) CaFW, (charade) CoReiD	S	C$ch	&	
DROP finally after consonant (except R): (fact) FWoK¼, (left) LaFW¼, (rest) RaS¼	T	°¼)¢ !r	&	
OR change medially when spelled TT: (better) BaD R, (little) LiD¼L, (bottle) BoD¼L	T		/D$tt	
OR drop finally after vowel: (late show) Lei¼SYo (heat wave) Hi¼VWeiVW	T		.¼)*	
Change in all positions: (thing) TiN¼, (faithful) FWeiTFWoL, (bath) BoT	t	T	&	&
Change in all positions: (this) DiS (they) Dei, (either) iDeR, (smooth) SMuD	T	D	&	&
Change in all positions: (vote) VWoT (over) oVWoR (give) GiVW (voice) VWuiS (of) oVW	V	VW	&	&
Change in all positions: (was) VWoS (walk) VWoK (away) oVWei (swim) SVWiM (weak) VWiK	W	VW	&	&
No change	X	X	&	&
When spelled S: (wise) VWAiS, (his) HiS, (nose) NoS (music) MYuSiK (prison) PRiSoN	Z	S$s	&	&
Change in all positions: (treasure) TRaSoR, (vision) VWiSoN, (azure) oSoR	z	S	&	&

Key:

& as shown	- initially	C church ° finally	¢ consonant	R trilled R
$ spelled	--" in sentn.	(preceding	* vowels	+ add to
4 for	/ medially	) following	! excepting	¼ dropped

POLISH: LUBLIN, EASTERN - POZNAN, WESTERN - ZWOLEN, RURAL

GUIDE PAGES		Lublin East Poland	Poznan West Poland	Zwolen Rural Poland
				All 3
CHANGE: (able) eiB¼L, (pain) PeiN, (day) Dei, (ate) eiT	A			ei
CHANGE: (eat) iT, (teach) TiC, (degree) DiGRi, (we) VWi	E			i
CHANGE: (I'm) AiM, (like) LAiK, (right) RAiT, (my) MAi	I			Ai
CHANGE: (own) oN, (whole) HoL, (so) So, (fellow) FWaLo	O			o
CHANGE: (use) YuS, (tune) TYuN, (new) NYu, (you) Yu	U			Yu
CHANGE: (had) HoD, (angry) oNGRi, (flat) FWLoT, (as) oS	a			o
CHANGE: (men) MaN, (let) LaT, (read) RaD, (bell) BaL	e			a
No change: (it) iT, (busy) BiSi, (women) VWiMoN	i			i
No change: (on) oN, (lock) LoK, (stop) SToP, (not) NoT	o			o
CHANGE: (us) oS, (love) LoV:W, (does) DoS, (was) VWoS	u			o
CHANGE: (are) oR, (calm) Ko¼M, (watch) VWoC, (car) KoR	A			o
CHANGE: (her) HoR, (girl) GoRL, (word) VWoRD (turn) ToRN	E			o
No change: (predict) PRIDiK¼, (propose) PRIPoS	I			I
CHANGE: (out) A:T, (loud) LA:D, (now) NA:, (how) HA:	O			A:
CHANGE: (room) RuM, (true) TRu, (drew) DRu, (do) Du	U			u
CHANGE: (and) oN¼, (last) LoS¼, (laugh) LoFW, (ask) oSK	a			o
If spelled ON or EN: (reason) RiSoN, (frighten) FWRAiToN	e			oN$en
If " OR: (labor) LeiBoR, (major) MeiCoR , (tenor) TaNoR	e			oR$or
If " LE OR EL: (trouble) TRoB¼L, (level) LaV:W¼L	e			¼$le
Change in all positions: (family) FWoMoLi, (system) SiSToM, (natural) NoCoRoL	i	o	&	&
OR drop initially: (ago) ¼Go (above) ¼BoV:W	i			-¼
OR drop finally after vowel: (idea) AiDi¼	i			.¼)*
				All 3
If spelled A,AU,AW: (all) oL, (cause) KoS, (law) Lo	o			o$aAU
OTHERWISE: (off) oFW (door) DoR (board) BoRD (court) KoRT	o			o$oOA
No change: (could) KuD, (pull) PuL, (book) BuK	u			u
CHANGE: (oil) uiL, (boy) Bui, (join) CuiN, (soil) SuiL	oE			ui

Rule		Lublin East Poland	Poznan West Poland	Zwolen Rural Poland
No change	B			B
No change	C			C
DROP finally after consonant (except R): (cold) KoL¼, (mind) MAiN¼, (field) FWiL¼	D	.¼)¢ !r	&	&
OR change finally after vowel or R: (did) DiT, (bird) BoRT, (had) HoT, (card) KoRT	D			.T) * or r
Change in all positions: (laugh) LoFW, (fear) FWiR, (left) LaFW¼, (after) oFWTeR	F	FW	&	&
Change finally: (big) BiK, (leg) LaK, (fog) FWoK, (flag) FWLoK, (rug) RoK, (pig) PiK	G	.K	&	&
AND drop finally from ING or ONG: (living) LiV:WiN¼, (wrong) RoN¼, (along) oLoN¼	G	.¼ing .¼ong	&	&
ADD before vowel at start of phrase: (all of) HoLoV:W, (up at) HoPoT, (at all) HoToL	H	--+(*	&	&
Change in all positions: (major) MeiCoR, (judge) CoC, (joy) Cui, (logic) LoCiK	J	C	&	&
DROP finally after consonant (except R): (ask) oS¼, (think) TiN¼, (desk) DaS¼	K			.¼)¢!r

Key:

& as shown	- initially	(preceding	: stronger	¢ consonant
$ spelled	-- "in sentn.	) following	¼ dropped	* vowels
+ add to	. finally	! excepting		R trilled R

POLISH: LUBLIN, EASTERN - POZNAN, WESTERN - ZWOLEN, RURAL

GUIDE PAGES		Lublin	Poznan	Zwolen
DROP medially before consonant: (silver) Si¼V:WeR, (bulb) Bo¼B, (skillful) SKi¼FWoL	L	/¼(¢	&	&
No change	M	M	&	&
"NY" before "i" or "e" sound; (need) NYiD, (name) NYeiM, (nip) NYiP, (nail) NYeiL	N	NY("i"e"	&	&
No change	P	P	&	&
Change in all positions: (quiet) KV:WAiT (equal) iKV:WoL, (square) SKV:WeiR	Q	KV:W		
OR change: KVAiT, IKVoL, SKVeiR	Q		KV	
OR change, KVWAiT, iKVWoL, SKVWeiR	Q			KVW
TRILL: (read) RiD, (for) FWoR, (disregard) DiSReGo¼D, (write) RAiT, (very) V:WaRi	R	R	&	&
AND drop medially after "o" sound: (park) Po¼K, (heart) Ho¼T, (army) o¼Mi, (art) o¼T	R	/¼) "o"	&	&
No change: (say) Sei, (yes) YaS	S	S	&	&
OR change initially before consonant: (stop) SToP (sleep) SLiP (speak) SPiK (swim) SVWiM	S			-S(¢
OR change when spelled C: (civil) 𝓈iVW¼L, (decide) Di𝓈AiD, (face) FWei𝓈	S			𝓈$c
Change in all positions: (shut) SYoT (sure) SYuR, (motion) MoSYoN, (special) SPaSY¼L	S	SY	&	
BUT change when spelled CH: (champagne) CoMPeiN, (chef) CaFW, (charade) CoReiD	S	C$ch	&	
OR change: SYoT, SYuR, MoSYoN, SPaSY¼L				SY
DROP finally after consonant (except R): (fact) FWoK¼, (left) LaFW¼, (rest) RaS¼	T	.¼)¢ !r	&	&
OR change medially when spelled TT: (better) BaReR, (little) LiR¼L, (bottle) BoR¼L	T	/R$tt	&	&
OR change finally before vowel: (it is) iRiS, (at all) oRoL, (out of) A:RoVW	T			.R(*
Change in all positions: (thing) TiN¼, (faithful) FWeiTFWoL, (bath) BoT	*t*	T	&	&
Change in all positions: (this) Dis, (they) Dei, (either) iDeR, (smooth) SMuD	*T*	D	&	&
Change in all positions: (vote) V:WoT (over) oV:WoR (give) GiV:W (voice) V:WuiS (of) oV:W	V	V:W		
OR no change: VoT, oVoR, GiV, VuiS, oV	V		V	
OR change: VWot, oVWoR, GiVW, VWui𝓈, oVW	V			VW
Change in all positions: (was) VWoS (walk) VWoK (away) oVWei (swim) SVWiM (weak) VWiK	W	VW	&	&
No change:	X	X	&	
OR change in all positions: (next) NaKS¼, (exact) aKSoK¼, (luxury) LoKSuRi	X			KS
When spelled S: (his) HiS, (music) MYuSiK, (wise) V:WAiS, (nose) NoS, (prison) PRiSoN	Z	S$s	&	&
Change in all positions: (vision) V:WiSoN, (illusion) iLuSoN, (measure) MaSuR	z	S	&	&

Key:

& as shown	- initially	C church	: stronger	¢ consonant
$ spelled	/ medially	(preceding	𝓈 outset	* vowels
¼ dropped	. finally	) following		R trilled R
		! excepting		

MASTER CATEGORY 7

YIDDISH

Yiddish is not a dialect, it is a number of dialects. There are as many varieties of Yiddish as there are different countries in which the Jews of Central and Eastern Europe have lived. The word "Yiddish" itself points straight to the source of the language, for *Jüdisch* is the German word for Jewish. But why should Jews all over Europe speak different variations of Old High German? Certainly they didn't all come from Germany.

As a matter of historical fact, the majority of Eastern Jews had come from their own kingdom originally. No, not Judea—not from anywhere in the Middle East—nor from any Semitic land, but from the khanate of Khazaria. Sometime around the year 600 A.D., the great Khan of the Khazars married a Jewish woman and subsequently had all his people converted to that faith. At that time, the Khazars were still one of the most powerful of the Tatar tribes, ruling all of South Russia between the Volga and Dnieper, extending their power west to Krakow in Poland and south to include the Crimea.

A part of the "white Tatars," the Khazars were typically high cheek-boned, fair-skinned, and predominantly redheaded. Reference to the Khazar warriors who accompanied Attila the Hun referred to them as "the red beards." Racially, they had nothing at all in common with the Jews of the Middle East.

As their khanate fell apart from the pressure of other Tatar and Mongol nomads from the east, the Khazars drifted west. Some accompanied the Magyars to Hungary, others the Bulgars to the Balkans, still others—one of the largest groups—settled in Lithuania. And one last group straggled into Poland. There they met up with other Jewish people totally different from themselves. When the Inquisitions (yes, there were more than one) drove the Jews from Spain, Italy, and France, the King of Poland welcomed them with open (if calculating) arms. The Polish people were being drained steadily by foreign merchants. Poles themselves seemed to have no head for trade—and here were a people, the Jews, who came from the Western seats of learning and commerce.

So, there in Poland two peoples came together, neither of whom spoke much Polish—one spoke Tatar, a Turkic tongue, the other, a Latin one (even today called "Ladino").

Now, up to that time there was only one group of Jews in Europe who had lived a relatively unharassed existence, who had had their roots in their host nation long enough to assimilate its language (though with liberal sprinklings of Hebrew), and those were the Jews of Germany. Small in number, but enormously influential, especially in the intellectual community, the *Juden* of Germany provided the universal Jewish language that still survives today, both in its spoken and written forms.

This is not to say that all the Jews of Europe speak (or spoke) Yiddish. British Jews most often raised their children speaking the English of whichever British region and social strata they sprang from. The Sephardim (those from Spain and Portugal) kept Ladino alive as their Jewish language both in Italy and in the Turkish dominated lands of the Middle East. And assimilationist Jews in all parts of Europe raised their children speaking only the tongue of their native land.

Still, Yiddish is what we are concerned with here. The different forms represented in the eight subdialects you will find in the following *GUIDE PAGES* are each influenced by the "native tongues" of their speakers. Thus Berlin, Lübeck, and Vienna Yiddish all have traces of Germanic influences; the Yiddish of Bobrusk and Moscow of Slavic; the Yiddish of Warsaw, Polish; the Yiddish of Vilna, Lithuanian; and the Yiddish of New York, a melange of all of the above *plus* a slight overlay of Cockney and Dutch, both predominant in Old New York!

From my earliest days, I was exposed to most of these subdialects. Though my parents were American-born, *their* parents, uncles, aunts, and other relatives generally were not. This enormous double family (twenty-one uncles and aunts, plus their spouses) included emigrants from Lithuania, Germany, Poland, Russia, Austria, and Hungary (not counting a few French relatives, since they had to learn their Yiddish from the others).

If so many disparate elements have gone into Yiddish, what is the "phonetic glue" that binds them together—what makes the Yiddish dialect recognizable as such? If anything, it is the shortening of the vowel sounds.

Vowel Changes

Five of the six basic American diphthongs (double vowels) are shortened in the Yiddish dialect. The (A) of "mate" is made up of the (e) of "met" and the (E) of "meet." The second element is shortened to the (i) of "mitt," so if the landlady's afraid "maybe they'll vacate late," in Yiddish dialect she'd fear that:

(MeiBi DeiL VeiKeiT Leit).

The two sounds that combine to produce the (I) of "wine" are the (A) of "wan" and the (E) of "wean." Again the (E) becomes the briefer sound (i) of "win," so if "I'm likewise nice at night," if Yiddish, the boast would be:

(*A*iM L*A*iKV*A*iZ: N*A*iS:) at (N*A*iT).

Two of the diphthongs that have the (*U*) of "boot" as their second sound lose it entirely. So the (O) of "boat" is left with only its first element, the (*o*) of "bought," and if Gabriel "blows a golden note," in this dialect he: (BL*o*Z:) a (G*o*¼D*i*N N*o*T).

Since the (*O*) of "bout" has the (*A*) of "bark" as its first sound, that's what it's trimmed down to, and the famous enunciation exercise: "How now brown cow?" is converted to:

(H*A*: N*A*: B*r**A*:N K*A*:).

Finally, the second element of the (U) in "use" is shortened, making it into (Y*u*)—and if our friend daydreamed about "beautiful, lewd stewardesses," if Yiddish-speaking, he dreamed of:

(BY*u*DeFAL LY*u*T S:DY*u*V*i*¼T*e*S:¼Z:).

This same shortening takes place when the (*U*) is found by itself, changing "fool" and "suit" into "full" and "soot." Thus if Tevye of *Fiddler on the Roof* were to complain that his "boots were too loose" he would say his:

(B*u*TS:) were (T*u* L*u*S:).

The (*A*) of "father" is also abbreviated. Since Yiddish drops "r"s that come before consonants, this means that "sharp" becomes "shop" and "heart" becomes "hot." Thus if the hostess thinks it's time to "start the gala," in Yiddish she thinks they should:

(S:To:¼T) the (GoLo).

Finally, the (E) of "heal" and "green" is reduced to the (i) of "hill" and "grin." So if the mathematics professor tells us that Einstein took a long time to "reveal his theory," if the professor is Yiddish she'll talk of how long to:

(*r*iFiL) his (Ti*A**r*i).

Besides the characteristic vowel shortening, there are two cases of *reversals* in Yiddish. As we just saw, (i) is substituted for (E). The reverse is also true, so that "dip" and "fist" are made into "deep" and "feast"—and the warning that there's a "stiff critic" in the audience, in Yiddish dialect is converted into there's a:

(STEF K*r*EDEK) there.

The other reversal affects (e) and (a). In the first case, the (e) of "pen" and "met" turns into the (a) of "pan" and "mat." Thus if you wanted the "letter sent express," in this dialect you would have the:

(LaD*er* S:aN¼ *h*aXP*r*aS:).

Conversely, the (a) of "lad" and "bag" changes to the (e) of "led" and "beg"—and the hitchhiker who's carrying a "fat knapsack," in Yiddish dialect is described as carrying a:

(FeT NePS:eK).

Just as the short (a) is converted into (e), so is the longer (*a*) of "dance" and "laughed" made into the (e) of "dense" and "left"—and if the press conference isn't over until "after the last answer," to the Yiddish-speaking it's:

(*h*eFDe¼) the (LeS:T *h*eNS:e¼).

The next change turns the (u) of "crutch" and "one" into the (*A*) of "crotch" and "wan." So if flowers improve a hospital room by giving it a "sudden touch of color," in the Yiddish dialect they lend a:

(S:*A*T*i*N T*AC* *hA*F K*A*Le¼).

In the middle or at the end of a word, the (*i*) sound also changes to (*A*), so that if the grocer throws in an "extra banana," the Yiddish would call it an:

(*h*aXD*rA* B*A*NeN*A*).

In still another vowel shift, the (o) of "fond" and "rob" becomes the (u) of "fund" and "rub"—and if a rich suburb boasts some "topnotch shops," the Yiddish-speaking would turn this into some:

(TuPNu*C* *S*uPS:).

A similar alteration makes the (*o*) of "bought" and "dawn" into something like the (u) of "but" and "done." Actually, the substituted sound is a longer (u:), so that if you heard "all sorts of talk" at the party, in the dialect you would speak of hearing:

(*h*u:L S:u:¼TS:) of (Tu:K).

The last vowel change we'll consider concerns the (*E*) of "fur." In every Yiddish dialect—except one—this is made into the (*i*) of "ago." Thus if the job was the "girl's first work," in these dialects it was the:

(G*i*¼LZ: F*i*¼*S*:¼ V*i*¼K).

The one exception is New York Yiddish (soon acquired by any Jewish immigrant who settled there). In this case, the sound is converted into the (*o*E) of "boy," and the above phrase tells us that same job was the:

(G*o*E¼LZ: F*o*E¼S:¼ V*o*E¼K).

Consonant Changes

As you probably noticed, all the "r"s in the last phrase disappeared. This is true of an "r" in the middle of a word, before another consonant, and also at the end of a word. Otherwise, in General Yiddish, the "r" becomes the uvular (*r*) which we first encountered in German. To review this letter, if you make a sound as if you were gargling, you will feel the back of your tongue vibrating against the uvula—just as it does with the Yiddish uvular (*r*). Since this is a voiced sound, the vibration of the tongue and uvula brought together produce something like a soft light gargling. (For a more detailed description, see page 54.)

So you see there may be two (or even three) different "r"s in one sentence in Yiddish dialect. For example, if the "reporter wrote a story about a fire in the park," in dialect it would turn out that the:

(*r*iPu:¼Te¼ *r*oT) a (S:Tu:*r*i) about a (F*A*i*i*) in the (Po:¼K).

Yes, you *did* catch another variation: the "r" that follows an (*A*i) as in "fire" changes to (*i*). Admittedly, this is complex, and it takes study and practice to master the rules. Don't let it get you down. Remember, this is a *dialect* you're learning, and therefore it doesn't have to be completely consistent. When the Yiddish speaker remembers how to produce the American English sound, that's what he'll use.

Let's move on to something easier: the part-time reversal of (D) and (T). When (D) appears in the middle or at the end of a word, it becomes a (T)—so that a "dead body" becomes a:

(DaT BuTi).

The reverse is also true when a (T) is in the middle of a word, making an "empty bottle" into an:

(*h*aMPDi BuDeL).

As you may have noticed in the last examples (and many others before), we add a letter before an initial vowel. This sound, (*h*), is much the same as the one we encountered in Spanish. It is pronounced in the same place in the mouth as (G) and (K), except instead of cutting off the air entirely, the back of the tongue narrows the opening, creating a "hissing" unvoiced consonant. (For more about this, see page 31.) And remember: this (*h*) goes before all initial vowels—so that if we reach our goal by "aiming at it," in the Yiddish dialect, it is by:

(*h*eiMEN¼ *h*et *h*ET).

Another truly Yiddish characteristic is the strengthening and/or lengthening of some consonants. A (G) in the middle or at the end of a word, for example, and "peg leg" becomes:

(PaG: LaG:).

(S)s, as in "yes," are more strongly hissed: (YaS:); and (Z)s, as in "size," are more strongly buzzed: (S:*A*iZ:).

Since Yiddish originated as a form of German, it is hardly surprising that some consonants—like the (*r*)—receive Germanic handling. A (V) at the middle or at the end of a word converts into an (F)—so that if a piece of machinery has "over five valves," the Yiddish-speaking would say it had:

(*ho*Fe¼ F*A*iF Ve¼FS:).

Again, in the German manner, all (W)s turn into (V)s. If you wanted to know "toward which window" the chair should face, you'd inquire in the Yiddish dialect:

(T*A*Vu:¼T VE*C* VENT*o*).

As with many other dialects, there are certain American consonant sounds that are nonexistent in Yiddish. Since (W) is one, (Q), or (KW), is another. Predictably, the (Q)s are converted into (KV)s—and if two serenades have "equally quiet qualities," here we would say they had:

(*h*iKV*A*Li KV*A*i*A*T KVoL*A*TiZ:).

There being no (J) sound in Yiddish, this voiced consonant is exploded into "ch" (*C*), its unvoiced equivalent. If someone standing on a bridge had a "strange urge to jump," in this dialect we would say they had a:

(S:T*r*eiN*C* *hi*¼*C*) to (*C*AMP).

Likewise, the voiced (*z*) is turned into the unvoiced "sh" (*S*)—and an optometrist who "measures vision," may be said in dialect to:

(Ma*S*i¼ VE*S*AN).

Neither the soft (*t*) nor hard (*T*) "th" exists in Yiddish. So "three healthy athletes" may be spoken of as:

(T*r*i HaLTi *he*TLiTS:).

Likewise, when one's child beats up another's, a woman may seek for words "that soothe the other mother," but in the dialect, we would say she sought words:

(DeT S:*u*D Di *A*De¼ M*A*De¼).

All the above changes are true for "General Yiddish," but may vary for the different subdialects found in the following *GUIDE PAGES*. The "lightest" of these is *Warsaw, Educated*.

Music, Rhythm, and Pace

Another way of "lightening" a subdialect is by a less extreme use of the Yiddish music. This music is so distinctive that it can convey the feeling of a Yiddish dialect even when the speaker doesn't change a vowel or consonant sound. First, it's most often spoken two or three tones higher than American speech. Next, it has a decided singsong quality caused by radical climbs up and down the scale. Emphasis is achieved by raising the tone of words, rather than by stress. In the sentence, "I'm telling you, I just can't stand the man," the music rises sharply on "telling," then climbs down the scale, word by word, for nearly a full octave. In the question, "Do I look like a rich man?," it climbs upward nearly an octave, word by word. However, the last word, "man," drops a full tone in the middle. This is another characteristic of Yiddish music: the two-note close. The wide range of the music may be even more extreme than we have just seen. Under emotional pressure, it can go up even into the falsetto.

Since Yiddish emphasizes important words by raising or lowering tones, you don't need volume or pacing to serve that function. So, though the rhythm of the Yiddish dialect is rather close to that of American English, it is more regular, with fewer breaks and pauses. Finally, the pace of Yiddish is noticeably slower than that of English, creating a very definite Yiddish "drawl."

Observation and Notes

As for observation and study of the Yiddish dialects, this is almost as difficult a problem as with Polish. There are simply no film or TV stars anymore for whom Yiddish is a native tongue. True, in good productions of *Fiddler on the Roof*, Yiddish *intonation* can be heard and observed (indeed, Tehvye's lines lend themselves to no other type of speech-music). But that is one isolated example, and it is likely to remain so. While many of the characters in *The Godfather* spoke with Italian accents, and most of the black characters in *Roots* spoke black (either African or Southern) varieties, *not one* of the characters in *The Holocaust* had a Yiddish dialect.

So once more I must refer you to local sources: to Jewish community centers (especially on nights devoted to senior citizens) and to the homes for the Jewish aged. Aside from this, there are of course the accompanying tapes.

But a note of caution here: the Yiddish dialect (and any of its subdialects) is too subtle and too complex to allow you to achieve any level of proficiency without a good deal of observation. If you have a good ear, however, your observation and study will pay off handsomely.

Many forms of Yiddish dialect still exist in Israel today, giving the Israeli actor Topol a strong advantage in researching his lead role of Tevye in United Artists' 1971 Fiddler on the Roof *(this photo also shows actor-teacher Paul Mann, left). Of course, anyone reading the work from which* Fiddler *was drawn, "Tevye and His Daughters," knows that the lines are written in such a way as to draw forth a Yiddish inflection from anyone who has ever heard the Yiddish dialect spoken.*

GENERAL YIDDISH - NEW YORK YIDDISH - VILNA LITHUANIAN YIDDISH

GUIDE PAGES	SOUND	General Yiddish	New York Yiddish	Vilna Lithuanian Yid.
Change in all positions: (pain) PeiN, (cake) KeiK, (they) Dei, (ache) *h*eiK, (baby) BeiBi	A	ei	&	&
Change in all positions: (each) *h*iC, (degree) DiG:*r*i, (me) Mi, (we) Vi, (see) S:i, (be) Bi	E	i	&	&
Change in all positions: (I'll) *h*AiL, (like) LAiK, (die) DAi, (my) MAi, (ice) *h*AiS:	I	Ai	&	&
Change in all positions: (own) *h*oN, (whole) H*o*L, (slow) S:L*o*, (so) S:*o*, (coal) K*o*L	O	*o*	&	&
Change in all positions: (you'll) Y*u*L, (mule) MY*u*L, (use) Y*u*Z:, (tune) TY*u*N, (new) NY*u*	U	Y*u*	&	&
AND change medially before vowel: (dual) Du*e*L, (valuing) VeL*u*ENK, (fuel) Fu*e*L	U	/*u*(*	&	&
Change in all positions: (flag) FLeG: (angry) *h*eNG:*r*i, (magic) MeCEK, (as) *h*eZ, (map) MeP	a	e	&	&
Change in all positions: (smell) S:MaL, (men) MaN, (leg) LaG:, (every) *h*aF*ir*i, (let) LaD	e	a	&	&
Change in all positions: (if) *h*EF, (in) *h*EN, (women) VEM*i*N, (busy) BEZ:i, (bill) BEL	i	E	&	&
Change in all positions: (lock) LuK, (drop) D*r*uP, (not) NuD, (copy) KuPi, (on) *h*uN	o	u	&	&
Change in all positions: (gun) GAN, (love) LAF, (does) DAZ:, (what) VAD, (was) VAZ:	u	A	&	&
Change in all positions: (palm) Po¼M, (calm) Ko¼M, (watch) VoC, (swan) S:VoN, (spa) S:Po	A	o	&	&
AND change before dropped R: (mark) Mo:¼K, (card) Ko:¼T, (far) Fo:¼, (are) *h*o:¼	A	o:(¼r	&	&
Change in all positions: (earn) *hi*¼N, (her) H*i*¼, (girl) G*i*¼L, (work) V*i*¼K, (were) V*i*¼	*E*	*i*		&
OR change: *h*oE¼N, GoE¼L, VoE¼K	*E*		*o*E	
No change: (predict) P*r*ITEK¼	*I*	*I*	&	&
Change in all positions: (down) DA:N, (now) NA:, (loud) LA:T, (count) KA:N¼, (out) *h*A:D	*O*	A:	&	&
Change in all positions: (fool) F*u*L, (soon) S:*u*N, (group) G*r*uP, (lose) L*u*Z:, (do) D*u*	*U*	*u*	&	&
Change in all positions: (ask) *h*eS:K, (fast) FeS:T, (laugh) LeF, (can't) KeN¼	*a*	e	&	&
When spelled ED: (aided) *h*eiTiT (added) *h*eTiT	*e*	iT$ed	&	&
When " EN: (often) *h*u:FD*i*N (heighten) HAiD*i*N	*e*	*i*N$en	&	&
When " OR: (labor) LeiB*i*¼ (neighbor) NeiB*i*¼	*e*	*i*$or	&	&
When " ANCE: (fragrance) F*r*eiG:*R*iNGZ, (ambulance) eMBY*u*LiNGZ, (vigilance) VEG:ELiNGZ	*e*	iNGZ$ ance	&	&
When spelled ER: (paper) PeiPe¼ (caper) Keipe¼	*e*	e$er	&	
OR " " " : PeiP*i*¼, KeiP*i*¼	*e*			*i*$er

Key:
& as shown
¼ dropped
$ spelled
h loch, ich
/ medially
r uvular R
(preceding
* vowels
C church
: stronger

GUIDE PAGES	SOUND	General Yiddish	New York Yiddish	Vilna Lithuanian Yid.
Change medially and finally: (family) FeMALi, (system) S:ES:DAM, (idea) *h*AiTiA (sofa) S:*o*FA	*i*	/.A	&	&
BUT drop initially: (ago) ¼G:*o*, (afraid) ¼F*r*eiT, (above) ¼B*o*F, (attack) ¼DeK	*i*	-¼	&	&
Change in all positions: (off) *h*u:F, (tall) Tu:L, (cause) Ku:Z:, (door) Du:¼ (war) Vu:¼	*o*	u:	&	
OR no change: *ho*F, T*o*L, K*o*Z:, D*o*¼, V*o*¼	*o*			*o*
No change: (could) K*u*T, (put) P*u*D (foot) F*u*D	*u*	*u*	&	&
No change: (oil) *ho*EL (boy) B*o*E (join) C*o*EN	*o*E	*o*E	&	&

No change	B	B	&	&
Change in all positions: (cheap) *s*iP, (much) MA*s*, (church) *si*¼*s*, (which) VE*s*, (teach) Ti*s*	C			*s*
OR no change: CiP, MAC, C*i*¼C, VEC, TiC	C	C	C	
Change medially and finally: (did) DET (body) BuTi, (middle) MET*e*L, (had) HeT, (said) S:aT	D	/.T	&	&
BUT drop finally after a consonant: (and) *h*eN¼ (cold) K*o*L¼, (wild) VAiL¼, (mind) MAiN¼	D	.¼)¢	&	&
No change	F	F	&	&
STRONGER medially and finally: (big) BEG:, (forget) Fu:¼G:aT, (together) T*u*G:aDe¼	G	/.G:	&	&
BUT change in ING suffix: (living) LEFENK, (morning) Mu:¼NENK, (coming) KAMENK	G	King} !(*	&	&
EXCEPT dropped before vowel: (living at) LEFEN¼*h*eT, (coming up) KAMEN¼*h*AP	G	¼ing} (*	&	&
No change	H	H	&	&
ADD before initial vowel: (ache) *h*eiK, (as) *h*eZ:, (each) *h*iC, (I'll) *h*AiL, (own) *ho*N	*h*	+*h*(-*	&	&
Change in all positions: (judge) CAC, (jump) CAMP, (edge) aC, (page) PeiC, (logic) LuCEK	J	C	&	
OR change: *s*A*s*, *s*AMP, a*s*, Pei*s*, Lu*s*EK				*s*
No change: (keep) KiP, (ache) *h*eiK (come) KAM	K	K	&	&
DROP medially before consonant: (help) Ha¼P, (bulb) BA¼B, (silver) S:E¼Fe¼, (calm) Ko¼M	L	/¼(¢	&	&
No change	M	M	&	&
No change: (name) NeiM, (knife) NAiF	N	N	&	&
No change	P	P	&	&
Change in all positions: (square) S:KVei¼, (quit) KVET, (equal) iKV*e*L, (quite) KVAiT	Q	KV	&	&

Key:

& as shown
! excepting
- initially
/ medially
. finally

h loch, ich
(preceding
) following
} in suffix
+ add to
r uvular R

¢ consonant
s outset
: stronger
¼ dropped
* vowels

GUIDE PAGES	SOUND	General Yiddish	New York Yiddish	Vilna Lithuanian Yid.
UVULAR initially: (read) *r*iT, (write) *r*AiT, (ready) *r*aTi, (rich) *r*EC, (wrong) *r*u:NG:	R	-*r*	&	&
UVULAR medially except before consonant: (very) Va*r*i, (story) S:Tu:*r*i, (spring) S:P*r*ENG:	R	/*r* !(¢		&
OR drop medially: Va¼i, S:Tu:½i	R		/¼	
DROP medially before consonant: (park) Po:¼K (organ) *h*u:¼G:AN (poorly) P*u*¼Li (cork) Ku:¼K	R	/¼(¢	&	&
AND change medially after "Ai" sound: (fireproof) FAi*i*P*r*uF, (wireless) VAi*i*LaS:	R	/*i*) "Ai"		&
DROP finally except after "Ai" sound: (wore) Vu:¼, (near) Ni¼, (far) Fo:¼, (or) *h*u:¼	R	.¼!) "Ai"	&	&
AND change finally after "Ai" sound: (fire) FAi*i*, (wire) VAi*i*, (tire) TAi*i*, (hire) HAi*i*	R	.*i*) "Ai"	&	&
STRONGER in all positions: (say) S:ei, (yes) YaS:, (decide) DiS:AiT, (speak) S:PiK	S	S:	&	&
Change in all positions: (show) S:*o*, (sure) S:*u*¼, (tissue) TES:*u*, (action)	S			S:
OR no change: *So*, *Su*¼, TE*Su*,	*S*	*S*	*S*	
Change medially: (empty) *h*aMPDi, (into) *h*ENDu, (better) BaD*i*, (winter) VENDe¼ (little) LEDeL	T	/D	&	&
BUT drop medially between consonants except after S: (strictly) S:T*r*EK¼Li	T	/¼₵ !)s	&	
Change finally before vowel: (get up) GaDAP, (at all) *h*eDu:L, (sit on) S:EDuN	T	∘D(*	&	&
BUT drop finally after consonant (except S): (salt) S:u:L¼, (left) LaF¼, (fact) FeK¼	T	.¼)¢ !)s	&	&
AND drop finally before D or T except after S: (put down) Pu¼DA:N, (not done) Nu½DAN	T	∘¼(dt !)s	&	&
Change in all positions: (thing) TENG:, (healthy) HaLTi, (mouth) MA:T, (bath) BeT	*t*	T	&	&
Change in all positions: (they) Dei, (other) *h*AD*i*¼ (smooth) S:MuD, (this) DES: (that) DeT	*T*	D	&	&
Change medially and finally: (never) NaF*i*¼, (gave) GeiF, (private) P*r*AiF*i*T, (over) *ho*Fe¼	V	/.F	&	&
Change in all positions: (will) VEL, (when) VaN, (nowhere) N*o*Vei¼, (between) BiTViN	W	V	&	&
No change	X	X	&	&
STRONGER in all positions: (please) PLiZ:, (zero) Z:i*ro*, (use) YuZ:, (lazy) LeiZ:i	Z	Z:	&	&
Change in all positions: (vision) VE*S*AN, (measure) Ma*Si*¼, (perversion) P*i*¼F*i*¼*S*AN	z	*S*	&	&

Key:

& as shown
! excepting
\- initially
/ medially
. finally

(preceding
) following
¢ consonants
₵ between "
C church

* vowels
h loch,ich
r uvular R
: stronger
¼ dropped

YIDDISH: BOBRUSK, LESS EDUCATED RUSSIAN - MOSCOW, EDUCATED RUSSIAN WARSAW, POLISH

GUIDE PAGES

		All 3	Bobrusk	Moscow Educ.	Warsaw Polish
CHANGE: (pain) Pein, (baby) BeiBi, (main) Mein, (day) Dei	A	ei			
CHANGE: (me) Mi, (see) S:i, (beef) BiF, (leap) LiP	E	i			
CHANGE: (like) LAiK, (buy) BAi, (my) MAi, (pipe) PAiP	I	Ai			
CHANGE: (know) N*o*, (slow) S:L*o*, (sew) S:*o*, (own) *ho*N	O	*o*			
CHANGE initial & final: (you'll) Y*u*L (new) NY*u* (use) Y*u*S:	U	-.Yu			
AND change medial before vowel: (dual) D*ue*L, (fuel) F*ue*L	U	/*u*(*			
CHANGE: (map) MeP, (pan) PeN, (at) *h*eT, (as) *h*eS:	a	e			
CHANGE: (bell) BaL, (exam) *h*aXeM, (them) DaM, (men) MaN	e	a			
CHANGE: (busy) BES:i, (bill) BEL, (women) VWEM*i*N, (it) *h*ET	i	E			
CHANGE: (lock) LuK, (drop) DRuP, (not) NuT, (on) *h*uN	o	u			
Change in all positions: (gun) GAN, (love) LAVW (does) DAS:, (what) VWAT, (was) VWAS:	u		A	&	
OR change: G*o*N, L*o*F, D*o*Z:, V*o*T, V*o*Z:	u				*o*
		All 3			
CHANGE: (palm) Po¼M, (watch) VWoC, (swan) S:VWoN	A	o			
AND change before dropped R: (mark) Mo:¼K, (are) o:¼	A	o:(¼r			
CHANGE: (her) *hi*¼, (girl) G*i*¼L, (work) VW*i*¼K, (earn) *hi*¼N	*E*	*i*			
No change: (predict) PRITEK¼	*I*	*I*			
CHANGE: (down) DA:N, (out) *h*A:T, (now) NA:, (loud) LA:T	*O*	A:			
CHANGE: (soon) S:*u*N, (group) GR*u*P, (lose) L*u*S:, (do) D*u*	*U*	*u*			
CHANGE: (ask) *h*eS:K, (fast) FeS:¼, (laugh) LeF	*a*	e			
When spelled ED: (aided) *h*eiTiT (added) *h*eTiT	*e*		iT$ed	&	&
When " EN: (often) *h*u:FD*i*N, (dozen) DAS:*i*N	*e*		*i*N$eN	&	&
When " OR: (labor) LeiB*i*¼, (neighbor) NeiB*i*¼	*e*		*i*$or	$	$
When " ANCE: (fragrance) FReiKRiNGZ	*e*		iN$an	&	&
When " ER: (paper) PeiPe¼, (caper) GeiPe¼	*e*		e$er		&
OR " " ER: PeiP*i*¼, KeiP*i*½	*e*			*i*$er	
		All 3			
CHANGE medially & finally: (family) FeMALi, (sofa) S:*o*FA	*i*	/.A			
BUT drop initially: (ago) ¼G*o*, (above) ¼BAVW, (attack) ¼DeK	*i*	-¼			
Change in all positions: (cause) Gu:S:, (off) *h*u:F, (tall) Tu:L, (door) Du:¼	*o*		u:		&
OR no change: G*o*S:, *ho*F, T*o*L, D*o*¼	*o*			*o*	
No change: (could) KuT, (put) PuT	*u*		*u*	&	&
No change: (oil) *ho*EL (boy) B*o*E (join) C*o*EN	*o*E		*o*E	&	&
No change	B		B	&	&
No change: (cheap) CiP, (church) C*i*¼C	C		C	&	&
		All 3			
Change medial & final: (did) DET, (body) BuTi, (had) *h*eT	D	/.T			
BUT drop finally after consonant: (and) *h*eN¼, (cold) G*o*L¼	D	.¼)¢			
No change	F	F			
Change medial & final: (big) BEK, (forget) Fu:¼KaT, (together) TuKaDe¼, (leg) LaK	G		/.K	&	
OR stronger: BEG:, Fu:G:aT, TuG:aDe¼, LaG:	G				/.G:
BUT change in ING suffix: (coming) GAMENK, (morning) Mu:¼NENK, (living) LEVWENK	G		ing)K !(*	&	&
EXCEPT dropped before vowel: (living at) LEVWEN¼*h*eT, (coming up) GAMEN¼*h*AP	G		ing)¼ (*	&	&

Key:

$ spelled	*h* loch, ich	- initial	(preceding	! excepting
¼ dropped	& as shown	/ medial	) following	¢ consonant
* vowels	: stronger	. finally	) in suffix	*R* trilled R

YIDDISH: BOBRUSK RUSSIAN - MOSCOW, EDUCATED - WARSAW, POLISH

GUIDE PAGES		Bobrsk	Moscow	Warsaw
Change in all positions: (hate) *h*eiT, (his) *h*ES:, (overhear) oVWe¼*h*i¼, (how) HA:	H	*h*	&	
OR no change: HeiT, HEZ:, oFeHE¼, HA:	H			H
AND add before initial vowel: (own) *h*oN, (I'll) *h*AiL (as) *h*eS: (it) *h*ET (are) *h*o:¼	*h*	+*h*(-*	&	&
Change in all positions: (judge) CAC (jump) CAMP (edge) aC (page) PeiC (logic) LuCEK	J	C	&	&
Change initially: (keep) GiP, (kill) GEL	K	-G	&	
OR no change: KiP, KEL				K

		All 3
MEDIAL DROP before consonant: (silver) S:E¼VWe¼ (calm) Go¼M	L	/¼(¢
No change	M	M
No change: (name) NeiM, (knock) NuK, (knot) NuT	N	N
No change:	P	P
CHANGE: (quit) KVET, (equal) iKVeL, (square) S:KVei¼	Q	KV
TRILL initial & medial: (read) *R*iT (very) VWa*R*i (rich) *R*EC	R	-/*R*
DROP medial before consonant: (park) Po:¼K (organ) u:¼KAN	R	/¼(¢
DROP final except after Ai: (near) Ni¼ (far) Fo:¼ (or) u:¼	R	.¼!)Ai
CHANGE medial & final after Ai: (fireman) FAi*i*MeN, (wire) VWAi*i*, (choirboy) GVWAi*i*BoE, (tire) TAi*i*, (hire) *h*Ai*i*	R	/.*i*)Ai

		Bobrsk	Moscow	Warsaw
Change initial & medial: (say) *s*ei, (sit) *s*ET, (decide) Di*s*AiT, (civil) *s*EVWeL	S	/-*s*		
OR STRONGER: S:ei, S:ET, DiS:AiT, S:EVWeL	S		-/S:	&
AND stronger finally: (base) BeiS:	S	.S.	&	&
No change: (show) *So*, (sure) *Su*¼	*S*	*S*	&	&
Change initially before W: (twin) *s*VWEN, (twist) *s*VWES¼, (twice) *s*VWAiS:	T	-*s*(w	&	
OR no change: TVEN, TVES¼, TVAiS:	T			-T

		All 3
Change medially: (into) *h*ENDu (little) LEDeL (empty)*h*aMPDi	T	/D!₵
EXCEPT drop " between consonants: (strictly) S:TREK¼Li	T	/¼₵
Change finally before vowel: (get up) Ga*R*AP (sit on) S:E*R*uN	T	.*R*(*
AND drop " after consonant: (left) LaF¼, (fact) FeK¼	T	.¼)¢
AND drop " before D or T: (put down) Pu¼DA:N	T	.¼(dt
CHANGE: (thing) TENG, (bath) BeT, (healthy) *h*a¼Ti	*t*	T
CHANGE: (they) Dei, (other) *h*ADe¼, (smooth) S:MuD	*T*	D

		Bobrsk	Moscow	Warsaw
Change in all positions: (never) NaVWe¼, (vote) VWoT, (gave) GeiVW, (over) *h*oVWe¼	V	VW	&	
OR medial & final: NaFe¼, GeiF, *h*oFe¼	V			/.F
OR no change initially: VoT	V			-V
Change in all positions: (will) VWEL (when) VWaN (nowhere) NoVWei¼ (between) BiTVWiN	W	VW	&	
OR change: VEL, VaN, NoVer¼, BiTViN	W			V
No change	X	X	&	&
Change in all positions: (please) PLiS:, (zero) S:i*R*o, (lazy) LeiS:i, (use) YuS:	Z	S:	&	
OR stronger: PLiZ:, Z:i*R*o, LeiZ:i, Y Z:	Z			Z:
Change in all positions: (vision) VWE*S*AN (measure) Ma*Si*, (perversion) P*i*¼VW*i*¼*S*AN	z	*S*	&	&

Key:

		C church		
& as shown	- initial	(preceding	*s* outset, its	* vowels
+ add to	/ medial	) following	¢ consonants	*R* trilled R
¼ dropped	. finally	! excepting	₵ between "	: stronger

YIDDISH: BERLIN, EDUCATED GERMAN - LÜBECK, LESS EDUCATED GERMAN

VIENNA, AUSTRIAN

GUIDE PAGES

Rule	Sound	Berlin Educ. German	Lübeck Less Educ.	Vienna Austrian
		All 3		
CHANGE: (pain) PeiN, (baby) BeiBi, (main) MeiN, (day) Dei	A	ei		
CHANGE: (me) Mi, (see) S:i, (beef) BiF, (leap) LiP	E	i		
CHANGE: (like) LAiGK, (buy) BAi, (my) MAi, (pipe) PAiP	I	Ai		
CHANGE: (know) N*o*, (slow) S:L*o*, (own) *o*N, (pole) P*o*L	O	*o*		
CHANGE initial & final: (you'll) Y*u*L, (new) NY*u*, (use) Y*u*Z:	U	-.Y*u*		
AND change medially before vowel: (dual) D*ue*L, (fuel) F*ue*L	U	/*u*(*		
CHANGE: (map) MeP, (pan) PeN, (at) eT, (as) eZ:, (am) eM	a	e		
CHANGE: (bell) BaL, (exam) aXeM, (them) DaM, (men) MaN	e	a		
CHANGE: (busy) BEZ:i, (bill) BEL, (women) VEM*i*N, (it) ET	i	E		
CHANGE: (lock) LuGK, (drop) D*r*uP, (not) NuT, (on) uN	o	u		
CHANGE: (gun) GAN, (love) LAF, (does) DAZ:, (what) VAT	u	A		
CHANGE: (palm) Po¼M, (watch) VoC, (swan) S:Von, (spa) S:Po	A	o		
AND change before dropped R: (are) o:¼, (far) Fo:¼	A	o:		
CHANGE: (her) H*i*¼, (girl) G*ir*L, (work) V*ir*GK, (earn) *ir*N	*E*	*i*		
No change: (predict) P*rI*TEGK¼, (propose) P*rI*P*o*Z:	*I*	*I*		
CHANGE: (down) DA:N, (out) A:T, (now) NA:, (loud) LA:T	*O*	A:		
CHANGE: (soon) S:*u*N, (group) G*ru*P, (lose) L*u*Z:, (do) D*u*	*U*	*u*		
CHANGE: (ask) eS:GK, (fast) FeS:¼, (laugh) LeF, (and) eN¼	*a*	e		
When spelled ANCE: (fragrance) F*r*eiGK*r*iNGZ	*e*	iN$anc	&	&
OR " " ED: (aided) *h*eiTiT, (added) *h*eTiT	*e*			iT$ed
" " " EN: (often) *ho*FD*i*N, (dozen) DAZ:*i*N	*e*			*i*N$en
" " " OR: (labor) LeiB*i*¼, (neighbor) NeiB*i*¼	*e*			*i*$or
" " " ER: (paper) PeiP*i*¼, (greater) G*r*eiT*i*¼	*e*			*i*$er
		All 3		
CHANGE medially & finally: (family) FeMALi, (sofa) S:*o*FA	*i*	/.A		
BUT drop initially: (ago) ¼GK*o*, (above) ¼BAF, (attack) ¼DeGK	*i*	-¼		
When spelled A,AU,AW: (tall) Tu:L, (cause) GKu:Z:, (law) Lu:, (saw) S:u:, (war) Vu:¼	*o*	u:$au a or aw	&	&
OR otherwise no change: (off) *h*oF, (door) D*o*R	*o*			*o*$o oo
No change: (could) GK*u*T (put) P*u*T (foot) F*u*T	*u*	*u*	&	&
No change: (oil) *o*EL, (boy) B*o*E, (join) C*o*EN	*o*E	*o*E	&	&
Change in all positions: (bite) PAiT, (maybe) MeiPi, (grab) G*r*eP, (but) PAT	B		P	
OR no change: BAiT, MeiBi, G*r*eB, BAT	B	B		&
		All 3		
No change: (cheap) CiP, (church) C*ir*C, (future) FY*u*C*e*¼	C	C		
Change medial & final: (did) DET, (body) BuTi, (had) HeT	D	/.T		
BUT drop finally after consonant: (and) eN¼, (cold) GK*o*L¼	D	.¼)¢		
No change	F	F		
Change medial & final: (big) BEGK, (forget) Fu:*r*GKaT, (together) T*u*GKaD*e*¼, (leg) LaGK	G	/.GK	&	
OR stronger: BEG:, F*o*¼G:aT, T*u*G:aD*i*¼, LaG:	G			/.G:
DROP from ING suffix before vowel: (living at) LEFEN¼eT, (coming up) GKAMEN¼AP	G	ing}¼ (*	&	&
OR otherwise change: (living) LEFENK, (morning) M*o*¼NENK, (coming) KAMENK				ing}K! (*

Key:

& as shown	- initially	(preceding	: stronger	*h* loch,ich
$ spelled	/ medially	) following	¢ consonant	* vowel(s)
¼ dropped	. finally	} in suffix	! excepting	*r* uvular R

YIDDISH: BERLIN, EDUCATED GERMAN - LÜBECK, LESS EDUCATED GERMAN
VIENNA, AUSTRIAN

GUIDE PAGES

		Berlin Educ. German	Lübeck Less Educ.	Vienna Austrian
No change	H	H	&	&
ADD before initial vowel: (own) *h*oN, (as) *h*eZ:, (I'll) *h*AiL, (it) *h*ET, (are) *h*o:¼	*h*		-*h*(-*	&
Change in all positions: (judge) *C*A*C* (jump) *C*AMP (edge) a*C* (page) Pei*C* (logic) Lu*C*EGK	J	*C*	&	&
Change in all positions: (keep) GKiP (sky) SGKAi (ache) eiGK (come) GKAM (ink) ENGK	K	GK	&	
OR no change: KiP, S:KAi, eiK, KAM, ENK				K

		All 3
DROP medial before consonant: (silver) SE:¼Fe¼ (calm) GKo¼M	L	¼/(¢
No change	M	M
No change: (name) NeiM, (knock) NuGK, (knot) NuT	N	N
No change	P	P
CHANGE all: (quit) KFET, (equal) iKFeL, (square) S:KFei¼	Q	KF

		Berlin Educ. German	Lübeck Less Educ.	Vienna Austrian
Uvular initially and medially: (read) *r*iT (very) Va*r*i (rich) *r*EC (spring) S:P*r*ENGK	R	-/*r*	&	
OR no change anywhere: RiT, VaRi (car) KoR				-/.R
OR drop medially before consonant: (park) Po:¼GK, (organ) u:¼GKAN, (large) Lo:¼C	R		/¼(¢	
OR change medially after Ai: (fireman) FAi*i*MeN, (choirboy) GKAi*i*PoE	R		/*i*)Ai	
DROP finally except after Ai: (near) Ni¼, (far) Fo:¼, (or) u:¼, (care) GKei¼	R	.¼!)Ai	&	
AND change finally after Ai: (fire) FAi*i*, (hire) HAi*i*, (wire) VAi*i*, (buyer) BAi*i*	R	.*i*)Ai	&	
STRONGER in all positions: (civil) S:EFeL, (say) S:ei, (sit) S:ET, (decide) DiS:AiT	S	S:		S:
OR change: ZEFeL, Zei, ZET, DiZAiT	S		Z	
No change: (show) *S*o, (sure) *S*u¼	*S*	*S*	&	&
Change medially: (into) ENDu, (little) LEDeL, (empty) aMPDi, (bottle) BuDeL	T	/D		/D
OR change medial TT: LE*r*eL, Bu*r*eL	T		*r*$tt	
AND drop medially between consonants except after initial S: (strictly) S:T*r*EGK¼Li	T	/¼₵ !)-S		/¼₵ !)-S
AND change finally before vowel: (get up) Ga*r*AP, (sit on) S:E*r*uN, (at all) e*r*u:L	T	.*r*(*	&	
OR change: GaRAP, S:ERuN, *h*eRu:L	T			.R(*

		All 3
AND drop finally after consonant: (left) LaF¼ (fact) FeGK¼	T	.¼)¢
AND drop " before D or T: (put down) Pu¼DA:N	T	.¼(dt
CHANGE: (thing) TENGK, (bath) BeT, (healthy) Ha¼Ti	*t*	T
CHANGE: (they) Dei, (other) ADe¼, (smooth) S:MuD	*T*	D
CHANGE medial & final: (never) NaFe¼, of) AF, (over) *o*Fe¼	V	/.F
CHANGE: (will) VEL, (when) VaN, (between) BiTViN	W	V
No change	X	X

		Berlin Educ. German	Lübeck Less Educ.	Vienna Austrian
STRONGER in all positions: (please) PLiZ: (zero) Z:i*r*o, (lazy) LeiZ:i, (use) YuZ:	Z	Z:	&	
OR change: PLiS:, S:iRo, LeiS:i, YuS:	Z			S:
Change in all positions: (vision) VE*S*AN (measure) Ma*S*e¼, (perversion) P*i*¼F*i*¼*S*AN	z	*S*	&	&

Key:

C church	- initial	(preceding	: stronger	*h* loch, ich
& as shown	/ medial	) following	¢ consonants	* vowel(s)
¼ dropped	. final	! excepting	₵ between "	*r* uvular R

MASTER CATEGORY 8

RUSSIAN

In the chapter on Polish, I mentioned my boyhood friend, Alex Boas. He, his sister, and his parents had all been born in Leningrad and so, naturally, when I thought of a Russian dialect, I thought of the way they spoke—especially the parents. A couple of years later, I dated a girl in high school whose father and mother were both born and raised in Odessa, and I had to revise my ideas about the Russian dialect. Within two more years, I found myself writing for the Armed Forces Radio Service in Bremen, where my buddies and I made friends with several officers of the Russian Reparations Commission. The few Red Army officers who spoke some English (we conversed mainly in German) did so with a variety of Russian dialects—and so all my previous conceptions were shattered.

Although the Soviet Union boasts of many "native" languages, the official language is Russian, and it is spoken by close to three hundred million people. Yet this language has little in common with Western European tongues, being neither Latinate nor Germanic. Moreover, it is written in an alphabet quite different from that used in Western Europe (or even in Poland, Czechoslovakia, Hungary, or Rumania).

In this Cyrillic alphabet, four of the vowel symbols look like ours: Y, A, O, and E. The first of these is pronounced "oo"; the last "yeh," which we will discuss later when we get into the consonantal Y-glide. The pronunciation of the A and the O at least bears *some* resemblance to *some* of the American pronunciations of these letters, so we'll start our examination of Russian vowel sounds with them.

Vowel Changes

The Russians pronounce the first, A, like the (*A*) in "father." It should come as no surprise, then, that when a Russian encounters an "a" in English, he is likely to come out with an "ah" regardless of the American pronunciation. Thus the American sounds (a), (*a*), and (*i*) all turn into "ah" (*A*); a "glad man" becomes a:

(GL%*A*D= M*A*N),

the proverbial "last laugh" (L*a*ST L*a*F) becomes the:

(L%*A*ST= L%*A*F),

and to "avoid attack" (*i*V*o*ED *i*TaK) becomes to:

(*A*V:WoiD= *A*T=*A*K).

As for the O, Russians most often articulate it as the (*o*) in "for." It doesn't matter if it's the "oh" (O) of "note" and "coat" or the (o) of "not" and "cot"; the Russians see and hear only the "aw" (*o*) of "naught" and "caught." So if a farmer decides to "only grow oats," in Russian dialect he decides to:

(*o*NL%Yi G*R*:*o* *o*T=S).

And if the "shop's not locked," for the Russian, the:

(*So*PS N*o*T= L%*o*KT=).

Since a great number of words (done, among, blood, color, does, front, govern, onion, touch, and love, among others are spelled with an "o" in English but pronounced with a (u), the Russian also changes this (u) sound to an "aw" (*o*), so that "lunch" and "hunt" sound like "launch" and "haunt." Thus if a lover worries "what love was undone" by his angry words, in this dialect he worries about:

(V:W*o*T= L%*o*V:W V:W*o*S: *o*ND=*o*N).

Another instance of an American sound receiving a totally different handling is the (e). This is converted to (a), making "then" and "hem" rhyme with "than" and "ham." So if she "said 'I read them well'," if from Russia, she:

(SaD=) I (*R*:aD= D=aM V:WaL%).

However, because of the "consonantal Y-glide" that we'll look at later, when the (e) sound follows an "l" or an "n," it changes to (ia), turning "leg" into (L%iaG) and "neck" into (NiaK).

There are only two cases in which Russian makes an American vowel sound longer: (I) stretches into "ah-eee" (*A*E:) and "aw" (*o*) is drawn out into "aww" (*o*:). There are, however, several places where it *shortens* the American sound, as in the case of the "ah" (*A*) of "father," which is converted into the (o) of "fodder." Thus, to "calmly watch the march," for the Russian-speaking would be to:

(KoL%ML%YI V:Wo*C*) the (Mo*R*:*C*).

The effect is even more evident with diphthongs (double vowels). For example "ow" (*O*), which is made up of "ah" (*A*) and "oo" (*U*), drops the "oo" (*U*) entirely so that "brow" and "how" come out closer to "bra" and "hah!" So if the Russian tourist "found out about how" Americans live, she would say she:

(F*A*N¼ *A*T= AB*A*T= H*A*) they live.

Another chopped-off diphthong is "ay" (A), a combination of "eh" (e) and "ee" (E). Again, the second sound is omitted, so that "age" and "sail" resemble "edge" and "sell." Thus, if the "waiter maintains eight tables," the Russian-born would say the:

(V:WeTe*R*: MeNT=eNS: eT= T=eBeL%S:).

When (A) comes after an "l" or "n," the Y-glide changes it to (ie), making "late" into (L%ieT=) and "name" into (NieM).

In two cases, the second element of the diphthong is retained, but it is weakened. The "aw-ee" (*o*E) of "joy" is changed into "aw-i" (*o*i); and if a courtier "enjoys the royal voice," a Russian would say he:

(aN*C*oiZ) the (*R*:oieL% V:WoiS).

Likewise, the "oo" (*U*) of "y-oo" (U) is abbreviated, making the sound into (Y*u*). Thus a "purely useless feud" in the Russian dialect would be a:

(PY*uR*:L%Yi Y*u*SL%iaS: FY*u*T=).

That same effect applies to "oo" (*U*) when it appears without the "Y," making "pool" and "cooed" sound more like "pull" and "could." Thus a rural mother who had a problem because she only "knew of two poor schools" for her children, in this dialect only:

(N*u*) of (T=*u* P*uR*: S:K*u*L%s:).

However, the Russian realizes that something is amiss in this abridgment—after all, Russian *does* have an "oo" sound—so, in compensation, he *reverses* this effect: "soot" and "wood" thereby rhyme with "suit" and "wooed," and if a hasty berry-picker "overlooked a full bush," the Russian would observe that she:

(*o*V:We*R*:L%*U*KT=) a (F*U*L% B*U*S).

This same "reversal compensation" works on "ee" (E) and (i). Thus "scheme" and "ease" come to sound like "skim" and "is"—and the observation "she's easy to cheat" is made into:

(SiS: iS:i) to (*C*iT=).

Conversely, "fit" and "itch" resemble "feet" and "each"—and if a socialite "is busy visiting other women," then in the Russian dialect, she:

(EZ BES:i V:WES:ET=YEN¼) other (V:WEMAN).

However, the consonantal Y-glide affects both of these reversals, not only after "l" and "n" but also following "d," "t," and both "th"s (*t*) and (*T*). After any of these letters, (i) changes to (YE)—so that if we speak of "this English mystic," in the Russian dialect we'd talk of:

(D=YES: ENGL%YE*S* MEST=YEK).

Following the "reversal effect," (E) is turned into (Yi) after those consonants—so if an anti-Darwinist points out that it's dangerous to "teach these theories," being from Russia, he would cite the peril if one were to:

(T=YiC D=YiS: T=YiAR:iS:).

Consonant Changes

The consonantal Y-glide is one of the characteristic carry-overs from the Russian language that separates Russian dialect from most others. It's called the Y-glide because the speaker uses the "Y" position of the mouth to glide from the consonant into the vowel that follows. It cannot be emphasized too strongly that, when you apply the Y-glide, the Y is never a separate sound. It is (NiaK) not (N-i-aK), (L%ieT=) not (L%-i-eT=), (D=YES:) not (D=-Y-ES:) and (T=YiC) not (T=-Y-iC). This Y-glide is so integral a part of the Russian language that three different Y-vowels have their own characters in the Russian alphabet: E (Ye), Я (YA) and I-O (YU).

The letter (N) obviously lends itself easily to this Y-glide, since we have words like "onion" and "canyon" in English. But the letters (L), (D), and (T) would require some fancy linguistic gymnastics to produce a Y-glide if they were formed in the American way. Happily, they are not.

First, the (L) is "liquid" (%) rather than hard. It is *not* formed with the tip of the tongue against the upper gum ridge as in "let live," but with the middle of the tongue arched against the hard palate. Paying special attention to where your tongue is for the letter (L), pronounce the following words aloud: "self," "milk," "bulk," "valve," and "false." Pronounced in the normal American way, the tip of the tongue comes nowhere near the upper gum ridge; rather, the (L) is formed by arching the tongue. Now, arch the tongue even more, until the middle of it firmly presses the upper palate and repeat the same words. Do you hear how the (L) sound fills the mouth, rather than disappearing? Can you sense the "softness," the "liquidity" of it? This is the "liquid L" (L%). Thus a Russian describing Sweden as a "calm, clean land," would call that country a:

(KoL%M KL%YiN L%AN¼).

Likewise, both (D) and (T) have to be modified from the American position if the tongue is going to move easily into a "Y." Instead of the tip of the tongue touching the upper gum ridge to form (D), the forward part of the tongue rests against *both* the upper gum ridge and the back of the upper teeth. Since the tip of the tongue is *between* the teeth in this position, we call this an "interdental D" (D=)—so if your accountant allows you to "deduct bad debts" from your gross income, as a Russian, he will let you:

(D=YiD=oKD= BAD= D=iaT=S).

The (T) too becomes "interdentalized" (T=). Thus if someone gets impatient listening to your story and wants you "to tell the important part," then in Russian dialect they want you:

(T=u T=aL%) the (EMPo:R:T=ANT= PoR:T=).

In the (D) example in the word "deduct"—you may have noticed that the (T) became a Russian (D=). This is because of another characteristic Russian modification: the rule of consonant agreement. To understand how this rule works, you need to look at the letters as "pairs": each position has a voiced (or sounded) consonant and an unvoiced (or exploded) consonant. Just pronounce "bat" and "pat"; notice how they are formed in the same place, with the (B) voiced (:) and the (P) unvoiced (½). The same voiced/unvoiced pairing applies to (V) and (F); (G) and (K); (Z) and (S), and (D) and (T). This "voiced versus unvoiced" is what we mean when we speak of *conflicts* between consonant sounds. And the rule of consonant agreement is simply that when a word ends in a consonant, that consonant must not conflict with the consonant that starts the next word in the phrase. (Naturally, if the next word starts with a vowel, the rule doesn't apply.) Since the final consonant of a word seldom receives the same value (or stress) as the beginning consonant, it is the final consonant that has to change to agree with the one that follows: a final (V) before an unvoiced consonant is converted into (F), and a final (F) before a voiced consonant is made into a (V), and so forth for each one of the "pairs" listed. Too many examples would need to be given in order to explore all the possibilities! Look at the *GUIDE PAGES* and pay close attention to the final consonants that conflict with the following consonant in the same phrase.

Another distinctly Russian consonant is the "R"; this is strongly trilled (*R*:) in *all* cases, not just in some. This trill, you'll remember, is made by placing the tongue against the upper gum ridge and then voicing the sound until the tongue vibrates (or flaps)—in this case, strongly. The sound is much like an imitation of a pneumatic drill, a motorcycle, or a machine gun. So if the child loved to "hear stories read" aloud, the Russian would say she loved to:

(*hiR*: ST=*o*:*R*:iS: *R*:aD=) aloud.

You may have noticed just now that the "h" of "here" was turned into a (*h*). This symbol stands for the fricative sound we have already encountered in Spanish and Yiddish. To recapitulate: find the place in your mouth where you pronounce (G) and (K). Now, instead of letting the back of your tongue cut the air off entirely (as in those two letters), let it merely narrow the opening, allowing the air to hiss through to produce this unvoiced consonant. (For more on this, see page 31.) So if we describe a beginning medical student and "his high hopes," as Russians, we would tell of:

(*h*ES: *hA*E: *ho*PS).

Why do the Russian-speaking make this change? Simply because the American (H) sound does not exist in Russian. Likewise, there is no (J) sound in that language; trying to produce it, the closest they can come is J's unvoiced equivalent: "ch" (*C*), articulated in the same mouth and tongue position but with an explosion of air rather than being voiced. Thus if our debating opponent seems to "enjoy strange logic," someone from Russia would say she seemed to:

(aN*C*oi ST=*R*:eN*C* L%*o*CEK).

The frontal position (tip of the tongue against the upper gum ridge) of the American (N) is another sound that gives the Russian trouble. He compensates by using this position in a place where it is *never* used in American English: before a (K), thereby making the American (*n*) sound into two separate sounds (N K). So if he's describing someone he doesn't like as a "shrunken monkey's uncle," the Russian would call him a:

(*SR*:oN K*e*N MoN KiS: *o*N K*e*L%).

Neither the soft "th" (*t*) nor the hard one (*T*) exists in Russian. The soft "th" (*t*) is replaced by the interdentalized "t" (T=), so that if we use "both mouth and throat" to make speech sounds, in the dialect we would use:

(B*o*T= M*A*T=) and (T=*R*:*o*T=).

The hard "th" (*T*) receives the interdentalized "d" (D=) treatment—so that if one chooses her upholstery material from "that smooth leather," if she is Russian, she chooses if from:

(D=*A*T= SM*u*D= L%iaD=*eR*:).

Another sound the Russians don't have is (Q); instead they substitute (KVW). To make this sound, purse your lips as you would for (Q). Now exaggerate that pursing while pushing your lower lip upward until it touches your upper teeth. This is the mouth position for (KVW)—and please note, this is pronounced as one letter, not three. So if at the end of his address, the speaker only has time to "request a quick question," if Russian-born he would:

(*R*:iKVWaST=) a (KVWEK KVWaSC*A*N).

A similar adjustment is made by the Russian when pronouncing either the American (V) or the American (W). Neither exists by itself in Russian; in their alphabet the letter "B" stands for a (V:W) combination. This sound is produced from the same lip and teeth position as the above (KVW), but it is more voiced, giving it a stronger "v" value. This new sound stands in, as indicated, for either (V) or (W)—so, if the Russian is talking about "verse" and "vest" *or* "worse" and "west," they will both come out:

(V:W*oR*:S) and (V:WaST=).

There are a number of variations on all of the vowel and consonant changes depending on which subdialect you're looking at. You'll find them in the *GUIDE PAGES*. The "lightest" of the Russian subdialects is designated as *Leningrad, Educated.*

Music, Rhythm, and Pace

The music of Russian is slow, steady and stately. It evokes a picture of the majestic Volga, flowing under dark and brooding skies. The flowing feeling comes partly from the "Y-glide," partly from the rolling "r"s, and partly from the broad "aw"s and "ah"s. For example, "Let's hope their next rerun of *Love Boat* is only as bad as their last," flows forth as:

(L%ieT=S *ho*B D=e*R*: NiaXT= *R*:i*R*:*o*N *o*V:W L%*o*V:W B*o*T= ES: *o*NL%Yi AS: BAD= AS: D=e*R*: L%AST=).

Those frequently used "dark" vowels also add to the dark quality of the music—as does the placement: generally three tones below that of American English.

There is not much movement up and down the scale in the Russian dialect, and then not more than a couple of tones altogether. Raising a word even one tone indicates special emphasis.

The rhythm is heavy, ponderous and slightly monotonous, since the Russian achieves emphasis not by stress but by tone. The only stress used in the Russian dialect has nothing to do with the importance of a word but only with affixes. Generally only prefixes and suffixes receive more emphasis than they would get in American English.

Russia includes three Slavic peoples who, although ultimately absorbed by Greater Russia, kept much of their own customs and some of their own language. That is why you will find three additional subdialects in the *GUIDE PAGES*: *Minsk, White Russian*; *Kiev, Ukrainian*; and *Odessa, South Ukrainian.*

Observation and Notes

Besides the Russian diplomats on television news shows, an occasional Russian sports figure, and the ubiquitous Russian ballet dancer, we have little opportunity to observe the Russian dialect in action. The generation of Russian actors and actresses

Among the many Russian actors who figured strongly in the American films of the 30's and 40's, Maria Ouspenskaya (shown here in Universal's 1940 The Wolf Man*) gave performances which reflected her training under Stanislavski and also gave audiences the taste of a truly authentic Russian dialect.*

Although primarily known for his dancing, Mikhail Baryshnikov (shown here with Leslie Browne in a scene from The Turning Point, *20th Century Fox, 1977) brought considerable acting talent to his role. This was the first American film in a generation to treat audiences to the sound of a native Russian dialect in a leading role.*

that so heavily populated the early American cinema has passed on, and there has been no new influx of Russian talent to replace it—an obvious loss to American films. Just how great a loss will be apparent to anyone who sees some of those Russian "greats"—from tragedians to comedians—in the old movies that sometimes turn up on the *The Late Show*. Akim Tamiroff, Maria Ouspenskaya, Mischa Auer, Vladimir Sokoloff—these are some of the names to look for.

Recently a new group of Russians have been coming to our shores: Russian Jews who have been allowed to emigrate; and their dialects are decidedly Russian, not Yiddish. If you live in an urban environment, you may find such an enclave; there may even be a Russian community center in your city, and probably a Russian Orthodox church as well. Any of these can offer you the opportunity for firsthand dialect observation and study.

Lastly, of course, there are the tapes designed to accompany this book. Because of the lack of accessibility of other sources, this section of the tapes is more thorough and comprehensive than most other sections.

GENERAL RUSSIAN - MOSCOW - KOLOMNA, RURAL - LENINGRAD, EDUCATED

GUIDE PAGES	SOUND	General Russian	Moscow Russian	Kolomna Rural	Leningrad Educated
CHANGE: (air) e*R*:, (pain) PeN, (baby)	A	e	&	&	
BeBi, (say) Se, (aim) eM, (cake) KeK					
OR change: ei*R*:, PeiN, BeiBi, Sei, eM	A				ei
BUT after L or N: (late) L%ieT=, (nail)	A	ie)ln	&	&	
NieL%, (blade) BL%ieD=, (snake) SNieK					
OR change: L%ieiT=, NieiL%, BL%ieiD=	A				iei)ln
CHANGE: (ear) i*R*:, (be) Bi, (see) Si,	E	i	&	&	&
(eat) iT=, (free) F*R*:i, (me) Mi					
BUT after D,L,N,T,*t*,*T*: (teach) T=YiC,	E	Yi)dl	&	&	&
(indeed) END=YiT=, (theory) T=Yie*R*:i		nt*tT*			
Change in all positions: (I'm) AE:M,	I	AE:	&	&	&
(side) SAE:T= (like) L%AE:K (my) MAE:					
Change in all positions: (only) *o*NL%Yi,	O	*o*	&	&	
(road) *R*:*o*T=, (know) N*o*, (boat) B*o*T=					
OR change: *ou*NL%Yi, *R*:*ou*T=, N*ou*, B*ou*T=					*ou*
Change in all positions: (cute) KY*u*T=	U	Y*u*	&	&	&
(use) Y*u*S: (few) FY*u* (value) V:WAL%Y*u*					
Change in all positions: (flat) FL%AT=,	a	A	&	&	&
(bad) BAT=, (as) AS:, (angry) ANGR:i					
CHANGE: (end) aN¼ (bed) BaT= (men) MaN	e	a	&	&	
(wet) V:WaT=, (bell) BaL%, (said) SaT=					
OR no change: eN¼, BeT=, MeN, VWeT=	e				e
BUT after L or N: (let) L%iaT=, (next)	e	a)ln	&	&	
NiaXT=, (fled) FL%iaT=, (neck) NiaK					
OR change: L%ieT=, NieXT=, FL%ieT=	e				ie)ln
CHANGE: (in) EN, (busy) BES:i, (bill)	i	E	&	&	&
BEL%, (if) EF, (bit) BET=, (kick) KEK					
BUT after D,L,N,T,*t*,*T*: (stick) ST=YEK,	i	YE)dl	&	&	&
(dig) D=YEG (lid) L%YET= (till) T=YEL%		nt*tT*			
Change in all positions: (not) N*o*T=,	o	*o*	&	&	&
(on) *o*N, (lock) L%*o*K, (copy) K*o*Pi					
Change in all positions: (love) L%*o*V:W,	u	*o*	&	&	&
(up) *o*P, (touch) T=*o*C, (but) B*o*T=					
Change in all positions: (calm) KoL%M,	*A*	o	&	&	&
(watch) V:WoC, (are) o*R*:, (swan) SV:WoN					
Change in all positions: (were) V:W*oR*:	*E*	*o*	&	&	
(girl) G*oR*:L%, (work) V:W*oR*:K					
OR change: VWe*R*:, Ge*R*:L%, VWe*R*:K	*E*				e
No change: (predict) P*R*:*I*D=EKT=	*I*	*I*	&	&	&
Change in all positions: (count) KANT=	*O*	A	&	&	
(now) NA, (doubt) D=AT=, (found) FAN¼					
OR change: KA:NT=, NA:, D=A:T=, FA:N¼					A:
Change in all positions: (group) GR:*u*P,	*U*	*u*	&	&	&
(soon) S*u*N, (rule) *R*:*u*L%, (drew) D=*R*:*u*					
Change in all positions: (dance) D=ANS,	*a*	A	&	&	&
(laugh) L%AF (and) ANT= (last) L%AST=					

Key:

& as shown　) following　*C* church　% liquid sound

R trilled R　: stronger　= interdental

GENERAL RUSSIAN - MOSCOW - KOLOMNA, RURAL - LENINGRAD, EDUCATED

GUIDE PAGES	SOUND	General Russian	Moscow Russian	Kolomna Rural	Leningrad Educated
No change: (apple) APeL% (onion) oNYeN	e	e	&	&	&
Change in all positions: (above) ABoV:W (family) FAMAL%i, (system) SEST=AM	i	A	&	&	&
LONGER sound: (off) o:F, (false) Fo:L%S (law) L%o:, (door) D=o:R:, (all) o:L%	o	o:	&	&	&
Change in all positions: (could) KUT=, (put) PUT= (book) BUK (woman) V:WUMAN	u	U	&	&	&
Change in all positions: (noise) NoiS:, (boy) Boi, (spoil) SPoiL%, (coin) KoiN	oE	oi	&	&	&

Change finally before unvoiced consonant: (grab for) G:RAPFo:R:, (fib to) FEPT=u	B	.P(¢½	&	&	&
Change at end of phrase: (rub.) R:oP., (grab.) GR:AP., (club.) KL%oP.	B	..P	&	&	
OR change: R:oBP., GR:ABP., KL%oBP.	B				..BP
No change: (church) CoR:C, (each) iC	C	C	&	&	&
Interdentalize: (day) D=e (body) BoD=Yi (dress) D=R:aS, (deduct) D=YiD=oKT=	D	D=	&	&	&
AND drop finally after consonant except R: (cold) KoL%¼, (mind) MAE:N¼	D	.¼)¢ !r	&	&	&
AND change at end of phrase: (broad.) BR:o:T=. (mad.) MAT=., (said.) SaT=	D	..T=	&	&	&
& change finally before unvoiced consonant (had for) hAT=Fo:R: (bad cut) BAT=KoT=	D	.T= (¢½	&	&	
OR change: H:AD=T=Fo:R:, BAD=T=KoT=	D				.D=T=(¢½
Change finally before voiced consonant: (if they) EVD=e, (off by) o:VBAE:	F	.V(¢:	&	&	
OR change: EFVD=ei, o:FVBAE:	F				.FV(¢:
DROP from ING suffix: (morning) Mo:R:NYEN¼, (living) L%EV:WEN¼	G	ing}¼	&	&	&
& change finally before unvoiced consonan (big for) BEKFo:R:, (hug to) hoKT=u	G	.K(¢½	&	&	
OR change: BEGKFo:R:, H:oGKT=u	G				.GK(¢½
AND change at end of phrase: (strong.) ST=R:o:NK., (leg.) L%iaK., (bag.) BAK.	G	..K	&	&	
OR change: ST=R:o:NGK., L%iaGK., BAGK.	G				..GK
Change in all positions: (house) hAS, (somehow) SoMhA, (he) hi, (have) hAV:W	H	h	&	&	
OR change: H:A:S, SoMH:A:, H:i, H:AV	H				H:
Change in all positions: (judge) CoC, (joy) Coi (page) PeC (giant) CAE:eNT=	J	C	&	&	
OR change: zoz, zoi, Peiz, zAE:eNT=	J				z
Change finally before voiced consonant: (ink blot) ENGBL%oT= (ask them) ASGD=iaM	K	.G(¢:	&	&	
OR change: ENGK:BL%OT=, ASGK:D=iaM	K				.GK:(¢:

Key:

& as shown	% liquid sound	(preceding	¢ consonant
C church	. finally	) following	¢: voiced "
z measure	.. end of sent.	} in suffix	¢½ un- " "
¼ dropped	= interdental	: stronger	R trilled R

GENERAL RUSSIAN - MOSCOW - KOLOMNA, RURAL - LENINGRAD, EDUCATED

GUIDE PAGES	SOUND	General Russian	Moscow Russian	Kolomna Rural	Leningrad Educated
LIQUID sound: (laugh) L%AF (blue) BL%u (told) T=oL%¼ (well) V:WaL% (call) Ko:L%	L	L%	&	&	&
No change	M	M	&	&	&
No change	N	N	&	&	&
SEPARATE SOUNDS: (uncle) oN KeL (drink) D=R:EN K (thank) T=AN K (anchor) AN Ko:R:	n	N K	&	&	&
Change finally before voiced consonant: (stop gap) ST=oBGAP, (up the) oBD=e	P	.B(¢:	&	&	
OR change: ST=oBP:GAP, oBP:D=Ye	P				.BP:(¢:
Change in all positions: (equal) iKVWeL% (square) SKVWe:R, (quite) KVWAE:T=	Q	KVW	&	&	&
STRONG TRILL: (right) R:AE:T= (ready) R:aD=i, (very) V:WaR:i, (are) oR:	R	R:	&	&	&
Change finally before voiced consonant: (face down) FeZD=AN (nice boy) NAE:ZBoi	S	.Z(¢:	&	&	&
OR change: FeiS:ZD=A:N, NAE:S:ZBoi	S				.S:Z(¢:
No change: (show) *So*, (sure) *SuR:*	*S*	*S*	&	&	&
Interdentalize: (tea) T=Yi, (tell) T=aL% (trade) T=R:eT=, (title) T=AE:T=eL%	T	T=	&	&	&
OR drop medially before or after a consonant, except R or initial S: (into) EN¼u, (winter) V:WEN¼eR:, (partly) PoR:¼L%i	T			/¼Ĭ¢ !r -s	
& change finally before voiced consonant: (sit by) SED=BAE:, (get back) GaD=BAK	T	.D= (¢:	&	&	
OR change: SED=T=:BAE:, GeD=T=:BAK					.D=T=:(¢:
Change in all positions: (bath) BAT=, (nothing) NoT=YENG, (through) T=R:u	*t*	T=	&	&	&
Change in all positions: (other) oD=eR: (they) D=e (smooth) SMuD= (this) D=YES	*T*	D=	&	&	&
Change initial & medial: (voice) V:WoiS (over) oV:WeR: (view) V:WYu (vow) V:WA	V	V:W	&		
OR change: VWoiS, oVWeR:, VWYu, VWA	V			VW	
OR no change: VoiS, ouVeR:, VYu, VA:	V				V
& change finally before unvoiced consonant (of some) oFSoM, (give to) GEFT=u	V	.F(¢½	&	&	&
Change in all positions: (when) V:WaN, (away) AV:We, (will) V:WEL%, (we) V:Wi	W	V:W	&	&	
OR change: VWaN, AVWei, VWEL%, VWi	W				VW
No change	X	X	&	&	&
When spelled S: (busy) BES:i, (music) MYuS:EK, (please) PL%YiS:, (does) D=oS:	Z	S:$s	&	&	&
& change before unvoiced consonant finally (gaze to) GeS:T=u, (size ten) SAE:S:T=aN	Z	.S: (¢½	&	&	
OR change: GeiSZ:T=u, SAE:SZ:T=aN					.SZ:(¢½
No change: (measure) MazeR:	z	z	&	&	&

Key:

& as shown	! excepting	% liquid sound	¢ consonants
$ spelled	- initially	(preceding	¢: voiced "
: stronger	/ medially	Ĭ before/after	¢½ un- " "
¼ dropped	. finally	= interdental	R trilled R

KIEV, UKRAINIAN - ODESSA, SOUTH UKRAINIAN - MINSK, WHITE RUSSIAN

GUIDE PAGES	SOUND	Kiev, Ukrainian Russian	Odessa South Ukrainian Russian	Minsk White Russian
CHANGE: (air) e*R*:, (pain) PeN, (baby) BeBi, (say) S:e, (ache) eK, (break) B*R*:eK	A	e	&	&
BUT after L or N: (late) L%ieT=, (name) NieM, (blade) BL%ieD=, (snake) S:NieK	A	ie)1N	&	&
CHANGE: (ear) i*R*:, (be) Bi, (see) S:i, (eat) iT=, (free) F*R*:i, (me) Mi, (either) iD=*e**R*:	E	i	&	&
BUT after D,L,N,T,*t*,*T*: (teach) T=YiC, (need) NYiD=, (theory) T=Yi*e**R*:i, (believe) BiL%YiV:W	E	Yi)dL nT*tT*	&	&
Change in all positions: (I'm) AE:M, (side) S:AE:T=, (like) L%AE:K, (night) NAE:T=	I	AE:	&	&
Change in all positions: (only) *o*NL%Yi, (so) S:*o*, (road) *R*:*o*T=, (know) N*o*, (oak) *o*K	O	*o*	&	
OR change: oNL%Yi, S:o, *R*:oDZ, No, oK	O			o
Change in all positions: (cute) KY*u*T=, (few) FY*u*, (use) Y*u*S:, (music) MY*u*S:iK	U	Y*u*	&	&
CHANGE: (bad) BeT=, (as) eS:, (had) H:eT=, (map) MeP, (at) eT=, (angry) eNG*R*:i	a	e	&	&
BUT after L or N: (flat) FL%ieT=, (nap) NieP, (lad) L%ieT=, (snack) S:NieK, (glad) GL%ieT=	a	ie)1N	&	&
CHANGE: (end) aN¼, (bed) BaT=, (men) MaN, (wet) VaT=, (bell) BaL%, (said) S:aT=	e	a	&	&
BUT after L or N: (let) L%iaT=, (neck) NiaK, (leg) LiaK, (next) NiaXT=, (fled) FL%iaT=	e	ia)1N	&	&
CHANGE: (in) EN, (busy) BES:i, (bill) BEL%, (if) EF, (bit) BET=, (kick) KEK, (is) ES:	i			E
OR no change: iN, BiS:i, BiL%, iF, BiT=, KiK	i	i	&	
BUT after D,L,N,T,*t*,*T*: (stick) S:TYiK, (dig) D=YiK, (lid) L%YiT=, (this) D=YiS:	i	Yi)dL nT*tT*	&	
OR change: S:T=EK, DZEK, L%YET=, DZYES:	i			YE)dLn
Change in all positions: (not) NAT=, (on) AN, (lock) L%AK, (copy) KAPi, (pocket) PAK*e*T=	o			A
OR no change: NoT=, L%oK, KoPi, PoK*e*T=	o	o	&	
Change in all positions; (love) L%*o*V:W, (up) *o*P, (touch) T=*o*C, (but) B*o*T=, (was) V*o*S:	u	*o*		
OR change: L%*u*V:W, *u*P, T=*u*C, B*u*T=, V*u*S:	u		*u*	
OR change: L%oV:W, oP, T=oC, BoT=, VoS:	u			o
Change in all positions: (calm) KoL%M, (are) o*R*:, (watch) VoC, (quantity) KVWoNT=YiT=Yi	*A*	o	&	&
Change in all positions: (were) V*o**R*:, (girl) G*o**R*:L%, (work) V*o**R*:K, (learn) L%*o**R*:N	*E*	*o*	&	
OR change: Vo*R*:, Go*R*:L%, Vo*R*:K, L%o*R*:N	*E*			o
No change: (predict) P*R*:*I*D=iKT=	*I*	*I*	&	&
Change in all positions: (count) KANT=, (now) NA, (doubt) D=AT=, (sound) S:AN¼	*O*	A	&	&
Change in all positions: (soon) S:*u*N, (rule) *R*:*u*L%, (group) G*R*:*u*P, (truth) T=*R*:*u*T=	*U*	*u*	&	&

Key:

& as shown	% liquid sound	*C* church	*R* trilled R
¼ dropped	= interdental	) following	: stronger

KIEV, UKRAINIAN - ODESSA, SOUTH UKRAINIAN - MINSK, WHITE RUSSIAN

GUIDE PAGES	SOUND	Kiev, Ukrainian Russian	Odessa South Ukrainian Russian	Minsk White Russian
Change in all positions: (laugh) L%AF, (ask) AS:K, (dance) D=ANS:, (rather) R:AD=eR:	a	A	&	&
No change: (apple) ePeL%, (paper) PePeR:	e	e	&	&
Change in all positions: (sofa) S:oFA, (ago) AGo, (family) FeMAL%Yi, (above) ABoV:W	i	A	&	&
LONGER in all positions: (door) D=o:R:, (or) o:R:, (false) Fo:L%S:, (off) o:F, (all) o:L%	o	o:	&	
OR change: DZoR:, oR:, FoL%S:, oF, oL%	o			o
Change in all positions: (look) L%UK, (put) PUT=, (could) KUT=, (foot) FUT=	u	U	&	
OR change: L%oK, PoT=, KoDZ, FoT=	u			o
Change in all positions: (noise) NoiS:, (boy) Boi, (spoil) S:PoiL%, (enjoy) aNCoi	oE	oi	&	
OR change: NoiS:, Boi, S:PoiL%, aNCoi	oE			oi
Change finally before unvoiced consonant: (grab for) GR:ePFo:R:, (boob tube) BuPT=YuB	B	.P(¢½	&	&
AND change at end of a phrase: (robe.) R:oP., (crab.) KR:eP., (rib.) R:EP., (sob.) S:oP.	B	..P	&	&
No change: (church) CoR:C, (each) iC	C	C	&	&
Interdentalize: (day) D=e, (body) BoD=Yi, (dress) D=R:aS:, (deduct) D=YiD=oKT=	D	D=	&	
OR change: DZe, BADZYi, DZR:aS:, DZYiDZoKT=	D			DZ
AND drop finally after any consonant except R: (cold) KoL%¼, (mind) MAE:N¼, (held) H:aL%¼	D	.¼)¢ !r	&	&
AND change at end of a phrase: (mad.) MeT=., (road.) R:oT=., (said.) S:aT=., (odd.) oT=.	D	..T=	&	
OR change: Mes., R:os., S:as., As.	D			..s
AND change finally before unvoiced consonant: (had for) H:eT=Fo:R:, (said so) S:aT=S:o	D	.T= (¢½	&	
OR change: H:esFoR:, S:asS:o	D			.s(¢½
OR change finally: (raid) R:eT=, (bed) BaT=, (lid) L%YiT=, (glad) GL%ieT=, (did) D=YiT=	D	.T=	&	
OR change: R:eDZ, BaDZ, L%YEDZ, GL%ieDZ	D			.DZ
Change finally before a voiced consonant: (off base) o:VBeS:, (if this) iVD=YiS:	F	.V(¢:	&	&
Change finally before an unvoiced consonant: (big for) BiKFo:R:, (dog trot) D=o:KT=R:oT=	G	.K(¢½	&	&
AND change at the end of a phrase: (flag.) FL%ieK., (hug.) H:oK., (leg.), L%iaK.	G	..K	&	&
AND drop from ING suffix: (giving) GiV:WiN¼, (loving) L%oV:WiN¼, (smiling) S:MAE:L%YiN¼	G	ing)¼	&	&
STRONGER in all positions: (house) H:AS:, (somehow) S:oMH:A, (he) H:i, (ahead) AH:aT=	H	H:	&	&

Key:

& as shown	% liquid sound	! excepting	R trilled R
s gets, its	. finally	(preceding	¢ consonant
: stronger	.. end of phrase	) following	¢: voiced "
¼ dropped	= interdental	) in suffix	¢½ un- " "

KIEV, UKRAINIAN - ODESSA, SOUTH UKRAINIAN - MINSK, WHITE RUSSIAN

GUIDE PAGES	SOUND	Kiev, Ukrainian Russian	Odessa South Ukrainian Russian	Minsk White Russian
Change in all positions: (judge) *CoC*, (joy) *Co*i, (page) PeC, (gradual) GR:eC*ue*L%	J	*C*	&	&
Change finally before a voiced consonant: (make do) MeGD=*u*, (back door) BeGD=*o*:*R*:	K	.G(¢:	&	&
LIQUID SOUND: (laugh) L%AF, (older) *o*L%D=*eR*: (blue) BL%*u*, (well) VaL%, (leave) L%YiV:W	L	L%	&	&
No change	M	M	&	&
No change	N	N	&	&
SEPARATE SOUNDS: (uncle) *o*N K*e*L%, (thinking) T=YiN KiN¼, (bank) BeN K, (anchor) eN K*o*:*R*:	*n*	N K	&	&
Change finally before a voiced consonant: (up the) *o*BD=Yi, (step down) S:T=iaBD=AN	P	.B(¢:	&	&
Change in all positions: (square) S:KVWe*R*:, (equal) iKVW*e*L%, (quit) KVWiT=	Q	KVW	&	&
STRONG TRILL: (right) *R*:AE:T=, (are) o*R*:, (very) V:Wa*R*: i, (regular) *R*:aGY*u*L%*eR*:	R	*R*:	&	&
STRONGER SOUND: (seem) S:iM, (base) BeS:, (ask) AS:K, (stop) S:T=oP, (class) KL%ieS:	S	S:	&	&
BUT change finally before a voiced consonant: (iceberg) AE:ZB*o*R:G, (baseball) BeZB*o*:L%	S	.Z(¢:	&	&
No change: (show) *So*, (motion) M*oS*AN	*S*	*S*	&	&
Interdentalize: (title) T=AE:T=*e*L%, (taught) T=*o*:T=, (tea) T=Yi, (straight) S:T=*R*:eT=	T	T=	&	&
BUT change finally before a voiced consonant: (hot bath) H:oD=BAT=, (let go) L%iaD=G*o*	T	.D= (¢:	&	&
Interdentalized "t": (both) B*o*T=, (nothing) N*o*T=YiNG, (thank) T=ieN K, (mouth) MAT=	*t*	T=	&	&
Interdentalized "d": (this) D=YiS:, (other) *o*D=*eR*:, (smooth) S:M*u*D=, (father) FoD=*eR*:	*T*	D=	&	
OR change: DZYES:, oDZ*eR*:, S:M*u*DZ, FADZ*eR*:	*T*			DZ
CHANGE: (view) V:W*u*, (over) *o*V:W*eR*:, (love) L%*o*V:W, (involve) iNV:WoL%V:W, (of) *o*V:W	V	V:W	&	&
BUT change finally before unvoiced consonant: (give to) GiFT=*u*, (have some) H:eFS:*o*M	V	.F(¢½	&	&
Change in all positions: (when) VaN, (away) AVe, (will) ViL%, (swim) S:ViM, (we) Vi	W	V	&	&
No change	X	X	&	&
Strong "s" when spelled "s": (busy) BiS:i, (music) MY*u*S:iK, (was) V*o*S:, (his) H:iS:	Z	S:$s	&	&
AND change finally before unvoiced consonant: (froze to) FR:*o*S:T=*u*, (quiz kid) KVWiS:KiT=	Z	.S: (¢½	&	&
Change in all positions: (vision) V:Wi*S*AN, (measure) Ma*SeR*:, (confusion) KANFY*u*SAN	*z*	*S*	&	&

Key:

& as shown	% liquid sound	! excepting	*R* trilled R
$ spelled	. finally	(preceding	¢ consonant
: stronger	.. end of phrase	¼ dropped	¢: voiced "
	= interdental		¢½ un- " "

LITHUANIAN

Linguists might wonder why I have placed this chapter directly after the one on Russian, since Lithuanian is a Baltic rather than a Slavic language. But we are involved with dialects, not linguistics, and the Lithuanian dialect in America shows more common ties with Russian than even other Slavic dialects do. This could be due to proximity to Russia or to two centuries of Russian occupation.

As for Lithuanian settlement in the U.S., a large segment of it has been Jewish. Naturally, the dialect spoken by most of those immigrants was the Lithuanian form of Yiddish (see the chapter on Yiddish).

It was not until I moved to Sweden in 1958 that I came upon true Lithuanian dialects in English. Being just across the Baltic from Lithuania, Sweden has been a natural (and welcoming) haven for a large number of those who fled the Russian occupations of 1940 and 1944, and those who more recently have escaped to the West. During my stay in Sweden, I came to know several of these Lithuanian refugees, both in daily life and in my profession. I found them all, professors and secretaries, mechanics and businessmen, extremely adept at languages, and with an even greater command over English than the Swedes (which is quite an accomplishment!). But then again, the inventor of the world's only lasting international language, Esperanto, was a Lithuanian.

Vowel Changes

What immediately identifies a Lithuanian dialect is the shortening of American diphthong (double vowel) sounds—five out of six of them, in fact. Both the (A) of "fail" and the (O) of "foal" lose their second sound elements, while the (I) of "file," the (*o*E) of "foil" and the (U) of "fuel" each have their second elements drastically shortened.

Let's take these one at a time. (A) is made up of (e) and (E); when the Lithuanian dialect is done with it, all that is left is the (e)—so that "gate" and "main" sound like "get" and "men." The two vowel sounds of (O) are (*o*) and (*U*); with the second of these eliminated, the remaining (*o*) turns the sounds of "coat" and "no" into those of "caught" and "gnaw."

The diphthongs (*o*E) and (I)—the combination of (*A*) and (E)—both have (E) as their second element; and in both cases, this (E) of "feet" is weakened into the (i) of "fit." In other words, (*o*E) becomes (*o*i) and (I) becomes (*A*i). Finally, with (U), made up of (Y) and (*U*), again the second sound is shortened, so that the diphthong changes into (Y*u*).

As you might expect, all these shortened elements are also abbreviated when they stand by themselves. For example, the "oo" sound (*U*) of "wooed" and "Luke" comes to resemble the (*u*) in "would" and "look." So, if the amateur artist "drew poor fruit," a Lithuanian would say he:

(D=*R*:*u* P*uR*: F*R*:*u*T=).

Again (as when it was a second sound), the "ee" (E) of "seek" and "read," when by itself, converts into the (i) of "sick" and "rid." Thus if "we each received" raises at work, in this dialect:

(V:Wi i*C* *R*:iS:iV:WT=) raises.

However, at this point, compensation reversal (see page 28) pops up: having turned (E) into (i), the Lithuanian unconsciously tries to compensate by turning (i) into (E), so that "fill" and "sin" rhyme with "feel" and "scene." Thus, if the salesman "is a bit insistent," the Lithuanian-born would observe that he:

(ES:) a (BET= ENS:ES:T=*A*NT=).

But these aren't the only changes that the (E) and (i) sounds go through. The *rule of the Y-glide* applies to them both: in other words, either new sound is preceded by a (Y) when it follows D, L, N, T, *t*, or *T* in a word. So if a chemist "distills within" his lab, the Lithuanian says he:

(D=YES:T=YEL%S: V:WED=YEN) it.

And if you "need a teaching degree," as a Lithuanian, you:

(NYiD=) a (T=Yi*C*ENK D=Yi*GR*:i).

So far—with the exception of the shortening of the (I) sound—most of the vowel changes closely resemble the Russian dialect, especially in the Y-glide aspect. But in the next pair of sounds, affected by compensation reversal, the resemblance ends. For while Russian substitutes a broad "ah" (*A*) sound for (a), Lithuanian changes (a) to the even shorter (e), so that "sad" and "bat" come out sounding like "said" and "bet." So if you are to "act the madcap," being from Lithuania, you will have to:

(eKT=) the (MeD=KeP).

Reversing this, the (e) is made into (a) so that "wreck" and "dead" resemble "rack" and "Dad," and if the actor is learning how to "express dread," in Lithuanian dialect he will learn to:

(aXP*R*:aZ D=*R*:aD=).

Both of these sound substitutions are affected by a form of the Y-glide, but in this instance, only when they follow (L) or (N). Thus "lad" and "nap" are converted to (L%ieD=) and (NieP), while "let" and "neck" turn into (L%iaT=) and (NiaK).

Vowel changes that involve neither Y-glide nor reversals include what happens to (o). This is made into "aw" (*o*), so that "nod" and "tot" come to sound like "gnawed" and "taught"—and if you decided not to spend a fortune shining up your car, but "got common polish," being from Lithuania, you:

(G*o*T= K*o*MAN P*o*L%YES).

It's not that the Lithuanian can't manage the (o) sound. In fact, that's exactly what they substitute for (u)—making "nut" and "luck" sound more like "not" and "lock." So if the gardener gets a complaint about "uncut shrubs," to a Lithuanian, it is about:

(oNKoT= *SR*:oBS:).

The same (o) is used in place of "ah" (*A*), so if the trail guide warns us to "watch for large swamps," a Lithuanian would warn you to:

(V:Wo*C*) for (L%o*R*:*C* S:V:WoMPS:).

The last vowel change we'll examine here is the several forms that (*E*) takes. When this sound is spelled with an "e" as in "her nerve," the sound substituted is of "eh" (e), as in (¼e*R*: Ne*R*:V:W). When spelled "i" as in "first stir," the sound becomes "ee" (E) as in (FE*R*:S:T= S:T=YE*R*:). When spelled with an "o" and in the "word 'world'," the sound turns into "aw" (*o*) as in:

(V:W*oR*:D= V:W*oR*:L%T=);

and the same change takes place with a "u" spelling, so that to "nurse burns" converts into:

(N*oR*:S: B*oR*:NS:).

Consonant Changes

In all of the above, you've undoubtedly noted that every "r" gets strongly trilled (*R*¡). As we reviewed in the last chapter, to make this sound, place your tongue against the gum ridge behind the upper front teeth and then voice the sound so that the tongue vibrates—like a vocal imitation of a pneumatic drill or a machine gun. Thus a nature-lover may have a high "regard for rural parks," but if he's Lithuanian, he'll have a:

(*R*:iGo*R*:T= Fo*R*: *R*:u*R*:AL% Po*R*:KS:).

Yes, you're right: this is the Russian "r"—just as it was the Russian Y-glide. And as the rule of consonant agreement applies to Russian, it also applies to the Lithuanian dialect. Thus when a word ends in some unvoiced consonants (¢½)—P, T, or S—and the next word in the phrase begins with one of the voiced consonants (¢:)—such as B, D, G, V, or Z—then the unvoiced one changes to its voiced equivalent (P to B, T to D, or S to Z) to make the two consonants agree. The same applies when a word ends in certain voiced consonants—B, D, Z, or V—and the following word *in the same phrase* starts with one of the unvoiced ones: then again the final (in this case, voiced) consonant must change to agree with the one it precedes, a B changing to a P, a D to a T, a Z to an S, and a V to an F. For examples, please refer to the following *GUIDE PAGES*.

Those who have already played this game of "consonant agreement" with Russian, may have noted that the letter (F) was left out of the game this time around. This is because *any* final (F) in the Lithuanian dialect is changed to a (VW) sound. You'll remember, this is the sound you make when pursing your lips for a (W) while making a (V) sound. So, if the child complains that her mother gave her a "rough, stiff scarf," the Lithuanian child would complain of a:

(*R*:oVW S:T=YEVW S:Ko*R*:VW).

Keep this (VW) sound in mind, for the minute we get to a (Q), we convert that into a (KVW), and if a diet malted milk is a "quick liquid banquet," in our dialect it is a:

(KVWEK L%YEKVWED= BeNKVWET=).

Retaining the same mouth positions, but making a firm contact between upper teeth and lower lip, we come up with the sound (V:W), in which the (V) part is slightly stronger. This sound replaces *both* the (V) and the (W), so if people have an "involved view of why we would wait," if they were from Lithuania, they would have an:

(ENV:WoL%V:WD= V:WY*u* oV:W V:W*A*i V:Wi V:W*u*D= V:WeT=).

The majority of (Z) sounds we find in American English are written with an (S), for example: "has," "does," "his," "hers," "is," "was," and so forth. In the Lithuanian dialect, the sound substituted is (S:), or heavy, hissed (S). So, if we expect a bloodhound to "use his nose," in this dialect he'll have to:

(Y*u*S: ¼ES: NoS:).

Another change typical of the Lithuanian dialect is to substitute a (K) for *all* final (G)s. So if we want to buy a "big, long rug," as Lithuanians we'll want a:

(BEK, L%oNK *R*:oK).

Some American consonant sounds don't exist in Lithuanian. One of these is (J), which Lithuanians pronounce in the same place in the mouth but in the unvoiced form of "ch" (*C*). Thus if we should not be too quick to "judge an aging genius," being Lithuanians, we won't:

(*C*o*C*) an (e*C*ENK *C*iNYAS:).

Two more sounds that the Lithuanian-speaking lack in their language are both soft (*t*) and hard (*T*) "th"s. For the (*t*), they substitute an interdental "t" (T=)—and to speak of "three ruthless thieves," they would talk of:

(T=*R*:E *R*:*u*T=L%iaS: T=YiV:WS:).

The (*T*) on the other hand, is replaced by an interdental "d" (D=), and asking us to choose "either these or those," they will say:

(iD=e*R*: D=YiS:) or (D=oS:).

To review the interdental (=) position: the forward part of the tongue rests against the upper gum ridge *and* the back of the upper teeth, so that the tip of the tongue is *between* the teeth. This is how the Lithuanians form both their "d"s and their "t"s (as well as the letter substitutions just mentioned above). So if a Lithuanian wants to say an anthropologist "did good fieldwork," it would come out that she:

(D=YED= G*u*D= FiL%D=V:Wo*R*:K).

And if the "teacher taught straight facts," it would turn out that the:

(T=Yi*C*e*R*: T=*o*T= S:T=*R*:eT= FeKT=S:).

Finally, we come to the Lithuanian (L). Again, like the Russian one, it is "liquid" (L%), formed by arching the middle of the tongue firmly against the upper palate. For a more thorough explanation of this sound, see page 101. Since *all* Lithuanian (L)s become liquid (%), then a commentary that this session of the Congress had turned out "all brilliant laws," in Lithuanian dialect would become:

(oL% BR:EL%YANT= L%oS:).

In the following *GUIDE PAGES* you will find a number of exceptions to these rules among the subdialects. You will also find that the "lightest" of the Lithuanian dialects—the one closest to the American sounds—is designated as *Vilna, Educated*.

Music, Rhythm, and Pace

It is perhaps in the music that the Lithuanian dialect differs most from the Russian. First of all, it is only one to one-and-a-half tones lower than American English. The range is quite as wide as the American range, with the tone rising up to the subject of the sentence, and then falling off sharply at the end.

Though Lithuanian shares the Russian Y-glide and rolling "r," the "flowing" effect is much more like that of a sparkling stream than of the dark and brooding Volga. First, Lithuanian has a faster pace than Russian, being just slightly slower than American speech. Second, the combination of fewer "dark" vowel sounds and lighter stress of prefixes and suffixes (though stronger than American English), makes for a decidedly different Lithuanian music.

Observation and Notes

Unfortunately, aside from locating the Lithuanian societies and/or churches in your community, there is no source for observation of this dialect other than the accompanying tapes.

GENERAL LITHUANIAN - KLAIPEDA, BALTIC - VILNA EDUCATED LITHUANIAN

GUIDE PAGES		General Lith.	Klaipeda Baltic	Vilna Educated
CHANGE: (air) eR:, (pain) PeN, (baby) BeBi	A	e	&	
OR change: eiR:, PeiN, BeiBi	A			ei
BUT after L or N: (blame) BL%ieM, (snake) S:NieK, (nail) NieL%, (late) L%ieT=	A	ie)ln	&	
OR change: BL%ieiM, S:NieiK, NieiL%, L%ieiT=	A			iei)ln
CHANGE: (ear) iR:, (be) Bi, (see) S:i	E	i	&	&
BUT after D,L,N,T,t,T: (teach) T=YiC, (need) NYiD=, (theory) T=YieR:i, (believe) BiL%YiV:W	E	Yi)dL nTtT	&	&
CHANGE: (I'm) AiM, (side) S:AiD=, (my) MAi	I	Ai	&	&
CHANGE: (only) oNL%Yi, (no) No, (boat) BoT=	O	o	&	
OR change: ouNL%Yi, Nou, BouT=	O			ou
CHANGE: (cute) KYuT=, (use) YuS:, (few) FYu	U	Yu	&	&

		All 3
CHANGE: (bad) BeD=, (as) eS:, (angry) eNGR:i, (had) ¼eD=	a	e
BUT after L or N: (glad) GL%ieD=, (nap) NieP, (flat) FL%ieT=	a	ie)ln
CHANGE: (end) aNT=, (bed) BaD=, (wet) V:WaT=, (said) S:aD=	e	a
BUT after L or N: (let) L%iaT=, (neck) NiaK, (leg) L%iaK	e	ia)ln
CHANGE: (in) EN, (busy) BES:i, (bill) BEL%, (if) EF	i	E
BUT after D,L,N,T,t,T: (dig) D=YEG (lid) L%YED= (this) D=YES:	i	YE)dl
CHANGE: (not) NoT=, (lock) L%oK, (copy) KoPi, (odd) oD=	o	o
CHANGE: (love) L%oV:W, (but) BoT=, (was) V:WoS:, (up) oP	u	o
CHANGE: (calm) KoL%M, (watch) V:WoC, (are) oR:	A	o
If spelled ER: (were) V:WeR:, (her) ¼eR:, (refer) R:iFeR:	E	e$er
If " IR: (girl) GER:L%, (dirty) D=ER:T=i, (stir) S:T=ER:	E	E$ir
If " OR: (work) V:WoR:K, (word) V:WoR:T=, (worm) V:WoR:M	E	o$or
If " UR: (burn) BoR:N, (urge) oR:C, (turn) T=oR:N	E	o$ur
No change: (predict) PR:ID=EKT=, (propose) PR:IPoS:	I	I
No change: (count) KONT=, (doubt) D=OT=, (now) NO	O	O
CHANGE: (group) GR:uP, (soon) S:uN, (rule) R:uL%, (do) D=u	U	u
CHANGE: (dance) D=eNS:, (and) eNT=, (ask) eS:K	a	e
BUT after L or N: (laugh) L%ieVW, (nasty) NieS:T=i	a	ie)ln
When spelled IAL: (social) S:oSYAL%, (facial) FeSYAL%	e	YA$IAL
When spelled LE or EL: (apple) ePeL%, (level) L%iaV:WeL%	e	e$LEel
CHANGE: (above) ABoV:W, (family) FeMAL%Yi, (ago) AGo	i	A
Change before L: (call) KoL%, (false) FoL%S:, (halt) ¼oL%T=	o	o(l
No change: (could) KuD=, (put) PuT=, (book) BuK	u	u
CHANGE: (noise) NoiS:, (boy) Boi, (spoil) S:PoiL%	oE	oi

Change finally before unvoiced consonant: (grab for) GR:ePFoR:, (boob tube) BuPT=YuB	B	.P(¢½	&	
AND change at end of phrase: (robe.) R:oP., (tube.) T=YuP., (rib.) R:EP., (sob.) S:oP.	B	..P	&	
OR change: R:ouBP., T=YuBP., R:EBP., S:oBP.	B			..BP
No change: (church) CoR:C, (each) iC	C	C	&	&
Interdentalize: (day) D=e, (body) BoD=Yi	D	D=	&	&
AND change finally after consonant: (cold) KoL%T=, (mind) MAiNT=, (held) ¼aL%T=	D	.T=)¢	&	&
AND change finally before unvoiced consonant: (had for) ¼eT=FoR:, (bad cut) BeT=KoT=	D	.T= (¢½	&	
OR finally before vowel: (had it) H:eD=T=YET=	D			.D=T=(*

Key: & as shown; R trilled R; ¢ consonants; % liquid sound; ¼ drop; $ spelled; (preceding; ¢½ unvoiced"; . finally; * vowel; : stronger;) following; = interdental; .. " in sentn.

GENERAL LITHUANIAN - KLAIPEDA, BALTIC - VILNA EDUCATED LITHUANIAN

GUIDE PAGES		Genl.	Baltic	Vilna
CHANGE finally: (roof) R:uVW, (off) oVW, (laugh) L%ieVW, (safe) S:eVW, (life) L%AiVW	F	.VW	&	&
CHANGE finally: (big) BEK, (leg) L%iaK, (song) S:oNK, (bag) BeK, (fog) FoK	G	.K	&	
OR change: BEGK, L%iaGK, S:oNGK, BeGK, FoGK	G			.GK
DROP initally: (house) ¼OS:, (have) ¼eVW, (he) ¼i, (who) ¼u, (here) ¼iR:, (hope) ¼oP	H	-¼	&	
OR change all: H:OS:, H:eVW, H:i, H:u, H:iR: H:ouP, (somehow) S:oMH:O (behind) BiH:AiNT=				H:
Change in all positions: (judge) CoC, (joy) Coi, (page) PeC, (giant) CAieNT=	J	C	&	
OR change: zoz, zoi, Peiz, zAieNT=	J			z
No change: (ink) ENK, (ache) eK, (keep) KiP	K	K	&	&
LIQUID sound: (laugh) L%ieVW, (blue) BL%u, (told) T=oL%T=, (well) V:WaL%, (call) KoL%	L	L%	&	&
No change	M	M	&	&
No change	N	N	&	&
Change finally before voiced consonant: (stop gap) S:T=oBGeP (step down) S:T=aBD=ON	P	.B(¢:	&	
OR change: S:T=oBP:GeP, S:T=aBP:D=ON				.BP (¢:

		All 3
CHANGE all: (equal) iKVWeL%, (square) S:KVWeR:	Q	KVW
STRONG TRILL: (right) R:AiT=, (very) V:WaR:i, (are) oR:	R	R:

		Genl.	Baltic	Vilna
STRONGER: (say) S:e, (decide) D=iS:AiD=, (face) FeS:, (speak) S:PiK, (yes) YaS:	S	S:	&	&
AND change finally before voiced consonant: (face down) FeZD=ON, (nice boy) NAiABoi	S	.Z(¢:	&	
OR change: FeiS:ZD=ON, NAiS:ZBoi				.S:Z(¢:
Interdentalize: (tea) T=i, (tell) T=aL%, (trade) T=R:eD=, (title) T=AiT=eL%	T	T=	&	&
AND change finally before voiced consonant: (sit by) S:ED=BAi, (get back) GaD=BeK	T	.D= (¢:	&	
OR change: S:ED=T=BAi, GaD=T=BeK				.D=T=(¢:
Change in all positions: (through) T=R:u, (nothing) NoT=YENK, (bath) BeT=	t	T=	&	&
Change in all positions: (other) oD=eR:, (they) D=e, (smooth) S:MuD=, (this) D=YES:	T	D=	&	
OR change: oZeR:, Zei, S:MuZ, ZES:	T			Z
Change initially & medially: (voice) V:WoiS: (over) oV:WeR:, (view) V:WYu, (vow) V:WO	V	V:W	&	
OR no change: VoiS:, ouVeR:, VYu, VO	V			V
& change finally before unvoiced consonant: (of some) oFS:oM, (give to) GEFT=u	V	.F(¢½	&	&
Change in all positions: (when) V:WaN, (away) AV:We, (will) V:WEL%, (we) V:Wi	W	V:W	&	
OR change: VWaN, AVWei, VWEL%, VWi	W			VW

		All 3
When spelled S: (busy) BES:i, (music) MYuS:EK, (use) YuS:	Z	S:$s
& finaly before unvoiced consonant: (size ten) S:AiS:T=aN	Z	.S:(¢½

Key:

		C church	
& as shown	% liquid sound	(preceding	¢: voiced consonants
$ spelled	- initially	: stronger	¢½ un- " "
¼ dropped	. finally	R trilled R	= interdental

MASTER CATEGORY 10

IRISH

At the beginning of this book (page 11), I differentiated between dialects and varieties by pointing to the *intention* of the speaker. Whereas in a dialect the differences from American English are unintentional (as the speaker is trying to speak English correctly), in a variety the differences are *intentional*, because the speaker is speaking English as he or she learned it. At this point, someone might object that, since the Irish have a language of their own (Gaelic) that is quite unrelated to English, Irish is really a foreign dialect. But it fails the test of being a true dialect on three counts: 1) a person from Ireland *intends* to speak English exactly as he does, 2) the English spoken in Ireland is a native language taught in the schools along with Gaelic and spoken in everyday life among eighty percent of the people, and 3) the speaker of the Irish variety is *consistent* in every vowel and consonant change made, since *their* variety of English is what they are striving to produce, not American English.

The very fact of this consistency is what makes a variety harder to master; if you make an occasional slip in a dialect, it can always be attributed to the fact that your character "remembered" the American pronunciation. What all this means is that you're going to have to put more concentration into the learning, practice, and internalizing of Irish—especially since the Irish music is much more sharply differentiated from the American than any other variety in this book.

In Northern Ireland (Ulster), the ties with Great Britain are very strong among the Protestants, so that Gaelic (or Erse) is all but unknown to them. The Roman Catholics, on the other hand, often make it a point to have their children study "the mother tongue." Still, we haven't separated Ulster Irish from other subvarieties because there is no consistent rule; it varies from family to family. In the Irish Republic, however, geography plays a bigger role: in parts of Cork in the south, Kerry in the southwest, Galway in the west, and Donegal in the northwest, Gaelic is even spoken at home—but still not in the majority of households.

The eastern part of Ireland is greatly influenced by Dublin, which had been a British enclave on and off for hundreds of years. Very much like London, the city has its own varieties, delineated by the speaker's social position. "Outside the Pale"—as the area surrounding Dublin was known—the broadness of the varieties is so marked that there are seven vowel changes and six consonant changes that don't even occur in General Irish!

As mentioned earlier, I was fortunate enough to be brought up not too far from Chicago's West Side—at that time the salad bowl (Chicago was *never* a melting pot) of America. I heard every type of Irish variety, but the predominant one was Dublin Irish. I guess it's not too surprising that city dwellers should gather in a new city when they immigrate.

It was not until I served in the Armed Forces Radio Service in Germany that I was exposed to southern Irish on anything like a regular basis. In fact, it was daily; for six months I shared a room with an Irish boy, born and bred in County Cork—partly in Cork Township and partly in the countryside near Blarney Castle. Until then I had gone along with the naive notion that all Irish was (more or less) a musical language. I learned better: there is no way one can coax a musical sound out of the (a:*A*) of County Cork. This is the sound my friend made out of a simple "ah" (*A*), a vowel most Irishmen leave just as it is.

A former student of the Royal Academy of Dramatic Arts in London and a former member of the acting corps of the Bristol Old Vic, Peter O'Toole (shown here in a scene from Murphy's War, *1971) is best known for his British roles. However, when the role calls for it, Peter O'Toole can deliver his native Irish variety with all its gentle, lilting music.*

Vowel Changes

Not that the Irish are that easy on the rest of the vowels: for instance, every one of the diphthongs is converted into something else. Take (*o*E), made up of the "aw" (*o*) of "saw" and the "ee" (E) of "see." By moving the first part of this back in the mouth, the Irish come up with a completely new diphthong: (*i*E)—so that if we want to tell someone to "avoid spoiling the boy," in Irish it would come out:

(*i*V*i*ED SP*i*EL%*i*N::¼) the (B*i*E).

Interestingly enough, another totally different diphthong, (I)—made up of "ah" (*A*) and "ee" (E)—evolved into the same sound in Irish. So if "I like twilight time," being Irish I'd say:

(*i*E L%*i*EK T=W*i*EL%*i*ET= T=*i*EM).

In that last change, the first sound, "ah" (*A*), changes to "uh" (*i*). In the next diphthong, the same thing happens: Since the "ow" (*o*) of "brow" is composed of the "ah" (*A*) of "bra" and the "oo" (*U*) of "brew," "our outbound crowd" leaving on the luxury liner becomes:

(*iUR iU*T=B*iU*N::¼ K*R*i*U*D).

The next diphthong has to be handled very carefully, because not only is the sound widened into a triphthong but two of the three sounds in it are similar. What's more, they are right next to each other and can easily be merged, shortening the sound back into a diphthong. The triple vowel is "yoo" (U), which in Irish becomes (iY*u*). As you can see, the (i) and the (Y) could easily blend into one sound, but they must remain separate. That is not to say that they are made into two syllables—but nearly. You start with the (i) sound of "is," *followed* by arching your tongue to make the (Y) of (Y*u*). Avoid enunciating the (i) after the tongue is arched. So if the composer were asked to write some "amusing, humorous music," an Irishman doing the asking would request some:

(*i*MiY*u*Zi*N*::¼, HiY*uM*¼*R*iS MiY*u*Zi*K*).

Both of the remaining diphthongs undergo a form of shortening; the first to the point where it loses its final sound. This is the diphthong "ay" (A) as in "mate," a combination of the "eh" (e) in "met" and the "ee" (E) in "meet." In Irish the (E) is dropped entirely while the first vowel is stretched (:) into (e:). Remember, this is not the Irish trying to imitate the American "ay" (A) and failing; this is the *Irish* rendition of the sound. So if you have been studying a chapter a day and don't know whether you'll be "able to maintain this rate," in this variety you don't know if you're:

(e:B¼L%) to (Me:N::T=e:N::) this (*R*e:T=).

The last of the diphthongs is the "oh" (O) of "boat," made up of the "aw" (*o*) of "bought" and the "oo" (*U*) of "boot." Here the second sound is not eliminated, but merely shortened from the "oo" (*U*) of "fool" to the (*u*) of "full." Thus, if the government's concessions merely serve to "postpone" its "overthrow," for the Irish, they would merely:

(P*ou*ST=P*ou*N::) its (*ou*Ve*R*t*R**ou*).

Naturally enough, when the (*U*) stands by itself as in "shooed" and "kook," it too is abbreviated to (*u*), as in "should" and "cook." The Irish mechanic warning his apprentice that he will "lose loose tools," would say he would:

(L%*u*Z L%*u*S T=*u*L%Z).

In those words in which we encounter the (*u*) sound itself, this too is chopped down—into (*i*:)—so if we think our favorite candidate "should push her outlook," if from Ireland we'd say she:

(S*i*:D P*i*:S) her (*iU*T=L%*i*:K).

Two different simple vowels both end up with the same sound in Irish: the (o) of "mosque" and the (*a*) of "mask" both become "ahh" (*A*:). Thus, if at night the "shop got locked," to an Irishman the:

(S*A*:P G*A*:T= L%*A*:K¼T=).

And if the salsa is a "fast, athletic dance," for the Irish-born it would be a:

(F*A*:S¼, *A*:*t*I %eT=*i*K D*A*:N::S).

As you may have noticed from the (i) in "athletic" above, this too is weakened and becomes (*i*). So if the disgruntled diner complains of the contents of her creamer and "insists it's milk," in the Irish variety, she:

(*i*N::S*i*ST=S *i*T=S M*i*L%K).

Another shortened vowel is "ee" (E), which generally becomes "ii" (i:). So if, of all the animals in the zoo, only "these seem free," to the Irish only:

(*T*i:Z Si:M F*R*i:).

While conversion generally takes place, when the sound is spelled "ea," "ei," or "ere," it changes rather than shortens, and the "ee" (E) turns into "ayy" (A:). Thus, to "eat either here or there" becomes to:

(A:T= A:*TeR* HA:*R*) or there.

Nor is this the only vowel that is totally made over in Irish. For instance, "aw" (*o*) is changed to "ahh" (*A*:)—and if a Peace Party would urge us to "call off all wars," in Ireland it would urge that we:

(K*A*:L% *A*:F *A*:L% W*A*:*R*Z).

Another "changed" vowel is the (u) of "luck" and "stud," which is transformed into the (*u*) of "look" and "stood"—usually—so if we steam the sealed envelope till the flap "comes unstuck," to the Irish, it:

(K*u*MZ *u*N::ST=*u*K).

Yes, I did say "usually"; for when this (u) sound is spelled with an "a" and follows a "w" or "wh," the change is to (o). So if we ask "what was what?" in Irish we'd ask:

(H:WoT= WoZ H:WoT=).

Finally there is the vowel sound (*E*)—the third vowel that is made into some form of (*i*). So if we believe that "work earns returns," in this dialect we'd point out that:

(W*iR*iK *iR*N::Z *Ri*T=*iR*N::Z).

Consonant Changes

In the last sentence there are two forms of Irish "r"s: the (*Ri*) of (W*iRi*K) and the (*R*) of (*iR*N::Z). The latter is a simple trilled "r" (*R*). You may remember that this is made by putting your tongue loosely against the upper gum ridge, and voicing the sound so that the tongue vibrates (or flaps)—like an imitation of a pneumatic drill or a motorcycle motor. Most of the time this trilled (*R*) is found without embellishment—so that the question "right or wrong?" is turned into:

(*R*iET= *A*:*R* *RA*:N::G).

When the "r" ends a word and follows an (e:) or (*i*E) sound, however, it changes to (Y*iR*). So that a "rare chair" turns into a:

(*R*e:Y*iR* *C*e:Y*iR*)

and to "hire a choir" is made into:

(H*i*EY*iR*) a (KW*i*EY*iR*).

At the end of a word and following a (*u*) or (Y*u*) sound, the Irish "r" becomes (W*iR*)—and a "poor tour" changes to a:

(P*u*W*iR* T=*u*W*iR*)

and a "pure cure" to a:

(PiY*u*W*iR* KiY*u*W*iR*).

Two rules concerning "r" remain. First, when it precedes an F, G, K, L, or M, it changes to (*Ri*)—thus the "girl's dark scarf" in Irish comes out to be the:

(G*iRi*L%Z D*ARi*K SK*ARi*F).

Finally, when an "r" follows a (D) at the beginning of a word, it converts into (D*iR*). Thus a "drab dress" to someone from Ireland is a:

(D*iR*aB D*iR*eS).

From "girl's" above, you will see that the Irish "l" is "liquid" (L%). It is formed by arching the middle of the tongue firmly against the upper palate. Thus if the new miracle drug "will help millions," in this variety, it:

(W*i*L% HeL%P M*i*L%Y*i*N::Z).

The tongue also takes a new position for the Irish "t": the tip of it rests between the teeth, thus interdentalizing the letter: (T=). So if we've been "taught to take our time," to the Irish we've been:

(T=*A*:T= T=*u* T=e:K) our (T=*i*EM).

The only other two consonants that undergo important modifications in Irish are the (N) and the (W). The (N) is stressed a great deal (N::), pressing the tongue hard against the upper gum ridge—so that "only nine" changes to:

(*ou*N::L%i N::*i*EN::).

The (W) is affected when spelled "wh," so that a strong (H:W) results—thus if a reporter must know the "what, where, when, and why," in Irish, she must know the:

(H:WoT=, H:We:Y*iR*, H:WiN::), and (H:W*i*E).

Music, Rhythm, and Pace

In the GUIDE PAGES that follow this text, you will find half a dozen subvarieties. Of these, *Blarney* and *Cork Township* are major subvarieties, while *Trinity Graduate* is the lightest brogue.

However, even in the scantiest brogue, the music of the Irish comes through. If you are at all musically inclined, you'll remember the fame that Irish tenors once had—and it'll come as no surprise to you that Irish is spoken two tones higher than American English. This doesn't mean that the Irish are incapable of the lower tones; far from it. The *median* is two tones higher, but the *range* is so much greater than American speech that there may be a fair number of syllables in any given sentence that are lower. This is especially true of the final syllables of a phrase, since Irish has a tendency to start high and finish low. And the greater the intensity of emotion, the higher the point at which the phrase is started.

Since Irish uses a higher note to emphasize a word, there may also be a slight up-and-down or singsong effect in any emotional statement or question. Of course, stress (or hitting the word harder) is also used for emphasis—but never as a substitute for the raised tone.

Dublin-born Maureen O'Hara's English is so perfect (she won prizes in elocution at an early age) that we seldom identify her with the "Emerald Isle." A graduate of the Abbey Theatre School of Dublin and a former member of the Abbey's repertory acting corps, O'Hara is shown here in a scene from The Quiet Man *(Republic, 1952), one of the few roles to benefit from her Irish background.*

A scene from Ryan's Daughter, *(MGM, 1971): Two Englishmen, Suffolk-born John Mills on the left, Trevor Howard on the right, portraying two Irishmen. There always being a goodly number of native Irish in London, British actors have an enviable opportunity to study and master the variety and all its subvarieties.*

Two other factors differentiate Irish and make it more musical than American: it is spoken faster and it is spoken more flowingly. Periods, commas, question marks—none of the punctuation receives the full stops they do in American English. Nor do the Irish employ pauses as much to emphasize or underline the material that has gone before the pause (since they have both tone and stress for that job). Both of these factors—shorter stops and fewer pauses—contribute to the "flowing" effect of Irish.

Observation and Notes

For your variety models, there are the Irish roles played by Richard Harris, Maureen O'Hara, Dan O'Herlihy, and Peter O'Toole. (Note that I emphasize Irish roles, and not the ones in which they played Britons or Americans.)

You may wonder why I haven't included Barry Fitzgerald—supposedly the owner of the archetypal Irish brogue. Well, Fitzgerald's brogue wasn't his own. Fresh from Ireland, brimming with talent, he was

In the 40's Barry Fitzgerald's Irish brogue was his trademark, and the misleading model for a generation of dialecticians who thought Going My Way *(his breakthrough film) was* the *film to study. However, it was not until later films (such as* A Broth of a Boy, *shown here, Seven Arts, 1958) that Fitzgerald abandoned his constructed mélange of Irish subvarieties for the true lilt of his homeland.*

turned down for his first role—*because he didn't sound Irish enough*! In desperation, Fitzgerald turned to a dialects coach. Between this man and Barry's own memories of what he had heard in Ireland, Fitzgerald created a Dublin-Blarney-Kildare-Ulster-Galway brogue that had never been spoken by anyone other than himself (and perhaps his erstwhile coach). But it got him his first starring role.

Strangely enough, as he allowed his brogue to become truer, his roles became smaller and smaller. The impact of the man's acting ability had been so strong that the public's first impression of him was "Now there's a true Irishman," and any deviation, no matter how much more faithful to the real Irish sounds, was, to his fans, a watering down and a sad departure from authenticity.

Still, one thing survived the Irish hash of Fitzgerald's first roles: the music of the Irish variety. So, if you must see *Going My Way* for the sixteenth time, do so with an ear for the music, not the variety. For the combination of both, seek out the purer variety models suggested earlier and listen to the tapes.

GENERAL IRISH - DUBLIN CLERK, LESS EDUCATED - DUBLIN WORKER TRINITY GRADUATE

GUIDE PAGES	SOUND	General Irish	Dublin Clerk Less Educ.	Dublin Worker Irish	Trinity Graduate Irish
Change in all positions: (age) e:J, (baby) Be:Bi, (break) BRe:K, (say) Se:	A	e:	&	&	&
CHANGE: (be) Bi:, (we) Wi:, (he) Hi:, (these) Ti:Z, (meet) Mi:T=, (she) Si:	E	i:	&	&	&
BUT spelled EA,EI,ERE: (either) A:TiR, (heat) HA:T=, (here) HA:R, (each) A:C	E	A:$ea ei,er	&	&	&
AND in prefix, weak or final Y: (early) iRL%i, (believe) BiL%i:V, (emit) iMiT=	E	i { ½ or .y	&	&	&
Change in all positions: (like) L%iEK, (I'm) iEM, (nice) N::iES, (try) T=RiE	I	iE	&		&
OR change: L%oEK, oEM, N::oES, T=RoE	I			oE	
Change in all positions: (road) RouD, (own) ouN::, (slow) SL%ou, (no) N::ou	O	ou	&	&	&
Change in all positions: (cute) KiYuT=, (use) iYuZ, (humor) HiYuM¼R (few) FiYu	U	iYu	&	&	&
Change in all positions: (flat) FL%aT=, (bad) BaD, (happy) HaPi, (as) aZ	a				a
OR no change: FL%aT=, BaD, HaPi, aZ	a	a	&	&	
CHANGE before M,N,V: (memory) MiM¼Ri, (ever) iV¼R, (men) MiN::, (end) iN::¼	e	i(m,n or v	&	&	&
Change in all positions: (busy) BiZi, (in) iN::, (women) WiM¼N::, (it) iT=	i	i	&	&	&
Change in all positions: (clock) KL%A:K (on) A:N:: (copy) KA:Pi (not) N::A:T=	o	A:	&	&	&
Change in all positions: (blood) BL%uD, (up) uP (love) L%uV (bug) BuG, (us) uS	u	u	&	&	&
BUT spelled A after W: (what) H:WoT=, (was) WoZ, (whatnot) H:WoT=N::AT=	u	o$a)w	&	&	&
LONGER sound: (watch) WA:C, (far) FA:R, (calm) KA:L%M (car) KA:R (mark) MA:RK	A				A:
OR no change: WAC, FAR, KAL%M, MARK	A	A	&	&	
Change in all positions: (heard) HiRD, (were) WiR, (girl) GiRiL%, (word) WiRD	E	i	&	&	&
No change: (predict) PRIDiK¼	I	I	&	&	&
Change in all positions: (crowd) KRiUD, (out) iUT= (down) DiUN:: (loud) L%iUD	O	iU	&	&	&
Change in all positions: (group) GRuP, (soon) SuN::, (rule) RuL%, (true) T=Ru	U	u	&	&	&

		All 4
CHANGE: (laugh) L%A:F, (and) A:N::¼, (half) HA:F	a	A:
DROP: (simple) SiMP¼L%, (paper) Pe:P¼R, (reason) RA:Z¼N::	e	¼
No change: (family) FaMiL%i, (ago) iGou, (idea) iEDi:i	i	i
CHANGE: (floor) FL%A:R, (off) A:F, (all) A:L%	o	A:
CHANGE: (could) Ki:D, (pull) Pi:L%, (foot) Fi:T=	u	i:
CHANGE: (voice) ViES, (boy) BiE, (spoil) SPiEL%	oE	iE

Key:

S show	C church	R trilled R	% liquid sound
¼ drop	. final	(preceding	& as shown
½ weak	: longer	{ in prefix	$ spelled

GENERAL IRISH - DUBLIN CLERK, LESS EDUCATED - DUBLIN WORKER

TRINITY GRADUATE

GUIDE PAGES

GUIDE PAGES	SOUND	General Irish	Dublin Clerk Less Educ	Dublin Worker Irish	Trinity Graduate Irish
No change	B	B	&	&	&
Change initial DR: (dress) DiReS (drew) DiRu, (drain) DiRe:N::, (dream) DiRA:M	D	-DiR $dr	&	&	&
DROP finally after L or N: (mind) MAEN::¼, (and) A:N::¼, (cold) KouL%D	D	.¼)ln	&	&	
OR retain: MAEN::D, A:N::D, KouL%D	D				.D)ln
No change: (laugh) L%A:F (phrase) FRe:Z	F	F	&.	&	&
DROP fom ING suffix: (coming) KuMiN::¼ (singing) SiN::GiN::¼ (seeing) Si:iN::	G	ING}¼	&	&	&
No change	H	H	&	&	&
No change: (stage) ST=e:J, (judge) JuJ	J	J	&	&	&
DROP medially before consonant except R (accept) a¼SeP¼, (active) a¼T=iV	K			/¼(¢ !r	
AND drop finally after S: (ask) A:S¼, (desk) DeS¼ (task) T=A:S¼ (risk) RiS¼	K			.¼)s	
OR no change: aKSeP¼, A:SK, DeSK, RiSK	K	K	K		K
LIQUID sound: (lead) L%A:D (list) L%iS¼ (well) WeL% (silver) SiL%V¼R (ill) iL%	L	L%	&	&	&
No change	M	M	&	&	&
MUCH STRONGER: (name) N::e:M, (only) ouN::L%i, (in) iN::, (not) N::A:T=	N	N::	&	&	&
No change	P	P	&	&	&
No change	Q	Q	&	&	&
TRILL: (read) RA:D, (are) AR, (ready) ReDi, (very) VeRi, (wrote) RouT=	R	R	&	&	&
BUT change final after "e,e:,iE" sounds (fire) FiEYiR, (bare) Be:YiR	R	∘YiR) e e: iE	&	&	&
AND after "u,Yu" sounds: (poor) PuWiR (cure)KiYuWiR, (sure) SuWiR	R	∘WiR) u, Yu	&	&	&
AND before F,G,K,L,M: (park) PARiK, (girl) GiRiL%, (harm) HARiM	R	Ri(FG K,L,M	&	&	&
No change: (civil) SiViL%, (face) Fe:S	S	S	&	&	&
Interdentalize: (take) T=e:K, (it) iT= (battle) BaT=¼L%, (straight) ST=Re:T=	T	T=	&	&	&
BUT drop after consonant: (left) L%eF¼, (fact) FaK¼ (rest) ReS¼ (salt) SA:L%¼	T	.¼)¢	&	&	
OR retain: L%eFT=, FaKT=, ReST=	T				T=)¢
Interdentalize: (think) t=iN::K, (bath) BA:t=, (healthy) HeL%t=i, (death) Det=	t			t=	
OR no change: tiN::K, BA:t, HeL%ti, Det	t	t	t		t

		All 3
No change: (this) TiS, (other) uT¼R, (smooth) SMuT	T	T
No change	V	V
When spelled WH: (when) H:WiN::, (what) H:WA:T=	W	H:W$wh
No change: (zip) ZiP, (was) WuZ, (music) MiYuZiK	Z	Z

Key:

& as shown	% liquid sound	(preceding	S show, sure
$ spelled	- initially	) following	¢ consonants
4 for	/ medially	} in suffix	: stronger
¼ dropped	∘ finally	! excepting	R trilled R
			= interdental

BLARNEY IRISH - CORK TOWNSHIP IRISH - KILDARE RURAL IRISH

GUIDE PAGES	SOUND	Blarney Irish	Cork Township Irish	Kildare Rural Irish
Change in all positions: (age) e:J, (break) B*R*e:K, (baby) Be:Bi, (air) e:*R*, (way) We:	A	e:	&	&
CHANGE: (be) Bi:, (we) Wi:, (he) Hi:, (these) D=*T*i:Z, (meet) Mi:T=, (she) *S*i:, (eat) i:T=	E	i:	&	&
BUT spelled EA,EI,ERE: (either) A:D=*Ti R*, (heat) HA:T=, (each) A:*C*, (here) HA:*R*	E	A:$ea ei,er	&	&
AND final Y, weak or in prefix: (early) *iR*L%i (believe) BiL%i:V (emit) iM*i*T= (hurry) H*iR*i	E	i { ½ or .y	&	&
Change in all positions: (like) L%*o*EK, (nice) N::*o*ES, (I'm) *o*EM, (try) T=*Ro*E, (ice) *o*ES	I	*o*E	&	&
Change in all positions: (road) *RAUD*, (total) T=*AU*T=¼L% (own) *AU*N:: (grow) G*RAU* (no) N::*AU*	O	*AU*	&	
OR change: *Rou*D, T=*ou*T=¼L%, *ou*N::, N::*ou*	O			*ou*
Change in all positions: (cute) KiY*u*T=, (few) FiY*u*, (humor) HiY*u*M*iR*, (music) MiY*u*Z*i*K	U	iY*u*	&	&
Change in all positions: (happy) HA:Pi, (bad) BA:D, (flat) FL%A:T=, (as) A:Z, (sat) SA:T=	a	A:	&	
OR no change: HaPi, BaD, FL%aT=, aZ, SaT=	a			a
CHANGE before M,N,V: (memory) MiM¼*R*i, (ever) iV¼*R*, (men) MiN::, (end) iN::D, (gem) JiM	e	i(m,n or v	&	&
Change in all positions: (women) W*i*M¼N::, (in) *i*N::, (busy) B*i*Zi, (it) *i*T=, (is) *i*Z	i	*i*	&	&
Change in all positions: (clock) KL%A:K, (on) A:N::, (copy) KA:Pi, (not) N::A:T=, (odd) A:D	o	A:	&	&
CHANGE: (blood) BL%*o*D, (up) *o*P, (love) L%*o*V, (bug) B*o*G, (young) Y*o*N::G, (does) D*o*Z	u	*o*	&	
OR change: BL%*u*D, *u*P, L%*u*V, B*u*G, Y*u*N::G, D*u*Z	u			*u*
BUT when spelled A following a W: (what), H:WoT=, (was) WoZ, (whatever) H:WoT=iV¼*R*	u	o$a)w	&	&
Change in all positions: (watch) Wa:*AC*, (far) Fa:*AR*, (calm) Ka:*A*L%M, (mark) Ma:*A*RK	*A*	a:*A*	&	
OR longer: WA:*C*, FA:*R*, KA:L%M, MA:*R*K				A:
Change in all positions: (heard) H*iR*D, (were) W*iR*, (girl) G*iRi*L%, (word) W*iR*D, (her) H*iR*	*E*	*i*	&	&
No change: (predict) P*RI*D*i*KT=	*I*	*I*	&	&

		All 3
CHANGE all: (crowd) K*RiU*D, (out) *iU*T=, (down) D*iU*N::	*O*	*iU*
CHANGE all: (group) G*Ru*P, (soon) S*u*N::, (true) T=*Ru*	*U*	*u*
CHANGE all: (laugh) L%A:F, (and) A:N::D, (half) HA:F	*a*	A:
DROP: (simple) S*i*MP¼L%, (paper) Pe:P¼*R*, (reason) *R*A:Z¼N	*e*	¼
No change: (family) FA:M*i*Li, (system) S*i*ST=*i*M, (ago) *i*GA*U*	*i*	*i*
CHANGE all: (door) DA:*R* (off) A:F (all) A:L% (cause) KA:Z	*o*	A:
CHANGE ALL: (could) K*i*:D, (pull) P*i*:L%, (book) B*i*:K	*u*	*i*:

	SOUND	Blarney Irish	Cork Township Irish	Kildare Rural Irish
Change in all positions: (loyal) L%AE¼L%, (voice) VAES, (boy) BAE, (coin) KAEN::	*o*E	AE	&	
OR change: L%*i*E¼L%, V*i*ES, B*i*E, K*i*EN::	*o*E			*i*E

Key:

& as shown	*C* church	*T* this,with	*S* show,sure	: longer, stronger
$ spelled	% liquid sound	(preceding	*R* trilled R	
¼ dropped	= interdental	{ in prefix	. finally	½ weak
		) following		

BLARNEY IRISH - CORK TOWNSHIP IRISH - KILDARE RURAL IRISH

GUIDE PAGES	SOUND	Blarney Irish	Cork Township Irish	Kildare Rural Irish
No change	B	B	&	&
Change initial DR: (dress) DiReS (drew) DiRu (drain) DiRe:N:: (dream) DiRA:M (dry) DiRoE	D	-DiR $dr	&	&
OR drop finally after L or N: (and) A:N::¼, (cold) KouL%¼, (mind) MoEN::¼, (held) HeL%¼	D			.¼)ln
AND change before iY : (induce) iN::JiYuS, (dual) JiYu¼L%, (endure) iN::JiYuR	D	J(iYu	&	
AND change finally after consonant: (mind) MoEN::T=, (and) A:N::T=, (cold) KAUL%T=	D	.T=)¢	&	
AND change finally after weak vowel: (added) A:D¼T=, (minded) MoEN::D¼T=	D	.T=	&	
No change: (laugh) L%A:F, (phrase) FRe:Z	F	F	&	&
DROP from ING suffix: (coming) KoMiN::¼, (singing) SiN::GiN::¼, (seeing) Si:iN::¼	G	ING}¼	&	&
No change	H	H	&	&
No change: (judge) JoJ, (logic) L%A:JiK	J	J	&	&
No change: (keep) Ki:P, (ache) e:K	K	K	&	&
LIQUID sound: (lead) L%A:D, (list) L%iST=, (well) WeL%, (silver) SiL%V¼R, (all) A:L%	L	L%	&	&
No change	M	M	&	&
MUCH STRONGER: (name) N::e:M, (not) N::A:T=, (in) iN::, (only) AUN::L%i, (money) MoN::i	N	N::	&	&
No change	P	P	&	&
No change	Q	Q	&	&
TRILL: (read) RA:D, (ready) ReDi, (wrote) RAUT=, (very) VeRi, (are) a:AR, (dry) DiRoE	R	R	&	&
BUT change finally after "e, e: or E" sounds (fire) FoEYiR, (bare) Be:YiR, (hire) HoEYiR	R	.YiR) e e: E	&	&
AND after u or Yu sounds: (cure) KiYuWiR, (poor) PuWiR, (sure) SuWiR, (lure) L%YuWiR	R	.WiR) u, Yu	&	&
AND before F,G,K,L,M: (girl) GiRiL%, (park) Pa:ARiK, (harm) Ha:ARiM, (surf) SiRiF	R	Ri(FG K,L,M	&	&
Change initially before consonant: (sleep) SLi:P, (smile) SMoEL%, (speak) SPA:K	S	-S(¢		&
Interdentalize: (battle) BA:T=¼L%, (treat) T=RA:T=, (take) T=e:K, (it) iT=, (tea) T=A:	T	T=	&	&
OR drop after consonant: (left) L%eF¼, (fact) FaK¼ (rest) ReS¼ (salt) SA:L%¼ (dent) DeN::¼	T			¼)¢
Change in all positions: (think) T=tiN::K, (bath) BA:T=t (healthy) HeL%T=ti (death) DeT=t	t	T=t		&
Change in all positions: (other) oD=T¼R, (this) D=TiS (sooth) SuD=T (breathe) BRA:D=T	T	D=T		&
No change	V	V	&	&
When spelled WH: (when) H:WiN::, (where) H:We:YiR, (what) H:WoT=, (which) H:WiC	W	H:W $wh	&	&
No change: (zip) ZiP, (was) WoZ, (his) HiZ	Z	Z	&	&

Key:

C church	% liquid sound	- initially	(preceding
& as shown	= interdental	. finally	) following
$ spelled	¢ consonants	S show,sure	} in suffix
4 for	R trilled R	: stronger	¼ dropped

MASTER CATEGORY 11

SWEDISH & NORWEGIAN

The first time you glance at the *GUIDE PAGES* that follow, you may be struck by the number of Scandinavian subdialects, especially since Swedish and Norwegian are spoken only by about twelve million people—in Europe. However, the Scandinavian peninsula is fragmented geographically and, until recently, separated into isolated enclaves according to the main pursuits of the inhabitants: farming, logging, and mining. These are ideal conditions for producing half a dozen different languages, to say nothing of dialects, so it is no surprise that the people of Småland sound different from those of Norrland, who sound different from those of Skåne, and so forth.

In totaling up the number of people who speak Swedish or Norwegian, I have not included those in North America. A considerable percentage of these six million Scandinavian immigrants have kept the mother tongue alive.

Again, it was in Chicago that I first encountered the Swedish dialect, or rather its Småland variety. Småland, you see, had been the hardest hit of the Swedish provinces during the famine that drove so many Swedes to American shores. Together with immigrants from Norway and Finland, the Swedes settled in an area much like their homeland: the lake and forest country of Minnesota and Wisconsin. From there, many drifted down to the largest metropolis in the area, Chicago. And so the Småland dialect, with its singsong, up-and-down music, became "the Swedish dialect" to American ears. This was reinforced when new immigrants from Sweden learned *their* English from their Småland neighbors.

This was brought home to me after I grew up. I had married a girl from Norrland, not far from the Arctic Circle. In America, we visited her aunt in Chicago, a woman also brought up with the slow, monotonous drawl of Norrland. However, after twenty-five years in Chicago, the aunt spoke English with a decided Småland dialect.

The mass migration from Sweden included very few people from the iron-rich North (Norrland) or the crop-rich South (Skåne), which is why these two subdialects are not included in the *GUIDE PAGES*. There are, however, three types of Stockholm dialect; *Uppsala Graduate* is the lightest and the closest to American English. The inclusion of a southern (actually, south-central) Swedish and a rural Swedish from the same area is self-explanatory, but the section on *Finland Swedish* may surprise you.

Historically, Finland was a part of Sweden for four hundred years. Swedish is one of the two official languages of the country and is used as a daily language by a substantial minority in Finland. The sound of their Swedish is distinctive, however, and the music has a melody all its own.

Music is also one of the main factors in differentiating *Oslo, Norwegian* from General Swedish. Though many Norwegians may object that Norway has been a separate country for seventy-five years, and that Norwegian is a different language, the fact is that the Great Migration to America took place when Norway and Sweden were one nation. Even today the languages are mutually understood. In none of my trips to Norway did I speak anything but Swedish, yet the Norwegians and I had no trouble communicating clearly.

In addition, there are only a dozen or so changes in the Norwegian dialect that cannot be found in one or the other of the Swedish subdialects.

To some extent, Norwegian even shares the two characteristics that most surely identify the Swedish dialect: the handling of the American (J) sound, and the creation of diphthongs (two-sound vowels) from many simple and single vowels.

Vowel Changes

The fact that seven of these single sounds are made into diphthongs is due to: 1) the Swedish tendency to achieve emphasis by holding a vowel sound longer, and 2) the habit of making a music shift in the middle of a syllable, thus breaking up the vowel. The first example is the (E) of "seat," which has the (i) of "sit" appended *before* it. Thus, if "these seem easy," to a Swede:

(D±iES: S:iEM iES:iE).

The next instance is the (e) of "pet": this time the (i) of "pit" is added *after* it. So if our wish for our children is "let them excel," if we were from Sweden, it would be to:

(L±ei¼ D±eiM eiXeiL±).

Then, to the (u) sound of "come," a short (*A*½) like "calm" is affixed. Thus if the chef returned to find "one onion was uncut," the Swedish chef would find:

(Wu*A*½N u*A*½NYAN Wu*A*½S: u*A*½NKu*A*½T=½).

The simple (*A*) of "art," in this dialect, is supplemented with the (*i*) of "around"—so if you want to "watch the large swan," being Swedish you will want to:

(W*Ai*C) the (L±*AiR*½*S* S:W*Ai*N).

This same (*i*) is also added to the stretched (e:), (as in "best" to replace the (*E*) of "burst." Thus, if to catch up with a colleague, you had to review "her current work," as a Swede, you'd have to see:

(H:e:*iR*½ Ke:*iR*½*e*NT=½ We:*iR*½K).

Both the long (*U*) of "pool" and the short (*u*) of "pull" also get made into diphthongs in the Swedish dialect, *but only in the middle or at the end of a word*. To the (*U*) of "fool" is joined the (*u*) of "full"—so if the diner finds he has "two soup spoons," being from Sweden, he'd have:

(T=½*Uu* S:*Uu*P: S:P:*Uu*NS:).

In the second case, the (*i*) of "afoot" is added on in front of the (*u*) of the same "afoot." Thus, if my editor tried to make this a "good-looking book," a Swede would say she deserves credit for making it a:

(G*iu*D=L±*iu*KiiN¼ B½*iu*K).

Did you notice what happened to the (i) of "looking"? It got stretched to twice its American length. This extension effect also applies to the (I) of "isle" and the (*o*E) of "oil," turning them into (I:L±) and (*o*:EL±), respectively. Of course these latter two are not simple sounds in English; they are already diphthongs. But there is one diphthong that becomes so extended it is changed into a triphthong: the (U) of "fuel" becomes a compound of the (i) of "fill," the (*U*) of "fool" and the (*u*) of "full"—so if a shorter desert trip means we can "use fewer mules," being Swedish-speaking, we would:

(i*Uu*S: Fi*UueR*½ Mi*Uu*L±S:).

Oddly enough, there are three American diphthongs that become shorter: the (A) of "hay," the (O) of "hoe," and the (*O*) of "how." The first, a combination of the (e) of "met" and the (E) of "meet," settles down to a lengthened version of its initial sound: (e:). Thus, if the old tenant "may vacate today," a Swede will observe she:

(Me: Ve:Ke:T=½ T=½*Uu*D=e:).

The second, (O), made up of the (*o*) of "gnaw" and the (*U*) of "knew," has its final sound curtailed—so if the "old road slopes slowly," in the dialect the:

(*ou*L±D= *R*½*ou*D= S:L±*ou*P:S: S:L±*ou*L±iE).

The third, the (*O*) of "how," is composed of the (*A*) of "hah!" and the (*U*) of "who." In the middle or at the end of a word, the second sound is shortened again to the (*u*) of "hood." Thus, if the movies give us "loud surround-sound now," being Swedish-born we'd speak of:

(L±*Au*D= S:*AR*½*Au*ND= S:*Au*ND= N*Au*).

Back to the simple, single vowels. One, like the diphthongs just mentioned, is *shorter*—the (a) of "sat"—which becomes (a½).

The other two simple vowels are converted into new sounds. The (*a*) of "aunt" is flattened into the (a) of "at," so if you intend to meet "after the last dance," being from Sweden, you'd meet:
(aFT=½eR½) the (L±aS:T=½ D=aNS:).

The third vowel goes through two different kinds of changes, depending on circumstances and spelling. In most cases, the (*o*) of "saw" is turned into a lengthened version of the sound in "so" (O:). Thus, if we "all saw the broad door," the Swede will say we:

(O:L± S:O:) the (B½*R*½O:D= D=O:*R*½).

However, this same vowel, when spelled "a," "au," or "aw" in the middle of a word before a consonant, becomes (*oi*)—so that if mercenaries "swarm toward dwarf wars," in Swedish dialect, they:
(S:W*oiR*½M T=½*oiR*½D= D=W*oiR*½F W*oiR*½S:).

Consonant Changes

You've probably noticed that all the "r"s above were weak trills, or taps (*R*½). Actually, the "r" sound can differentiate between a number of Swedish *sub*dialects as effectively as different "r"s characterize major dialects. For example, the Uppsala Graduate (R) is the same as the American, simply because the educated Swede is among the few persons to whom English is not native who can handle the Anglo-American "r" sound. On the other hand, the Finland Swede rolls his "r"s as strongly as the Russian (*R*:). The Oslo and rural Norwegians do this too—except before (L), (N), or (T), when the "r" comes out exactly as the American (R). Finally, the western Norwegians (and the Skåne) use a uvular "r" (*r*)—which is discussed in Chapter 4 on the German dialect, page 54.

All the rest of the subdialect groups here, as well as General Swedish, use the soft trill (*R*½). For this sound, position your tongue to make a (D), but with the tongue forward enough and relaxed enough to "flap" or "tap." This is similar to the trilled "r" (*R*) of Italian (page 67), but with only one or two taps instead of a series. So, the mailman describing his "regular rural route," if Swedish-born will talk of his:

(*R*½eiGi*Uu*L±e*R*½*R*½*iuR*½eL± *R*½*AuT*=½).

Just as the tongue is in a different position from the American one to make this Swedish sound, so is it for the next three consonant changes: (L), (D), and (T). For the "l," the tongue moves forward until it touches the back of the upper front teeth; it becomes an "upperdental" (L±). Thus, if the head of the church bazaar wants to thank "all the helpful ladies," in this dialect, she will thank:

(O:L±) the (H:eiL±P:F*iu*L± L±e:D=iES:).

As you noticed in "ladies," Swedes "interdentalize" their "d"s (D=), too. They move their tongues forward until they are touching the backs of both the upper and lower teeth. So, since a morgue is a place full of "cold, dead bodies," if Swedish-speaking, we'd describe it as full of:

(K*ou*L±D= D=eiD= B½*A*D=iES:).

The "t" receives much the same handling in Swedish, except that it is never hit as hard as it is in English. The result is a weakened interdental (T=½)—thus, if I returned to the box office "to try to get better tickets," for the Swede, it would be:

(T=½*Uu* T=½*R*½I:T=½*Uu* GeiT=½ B½eiT=½e*R*½ T=½iiK*e*T=½S:).

Sometimes, studying dialects, one gets subtle hints that there may be such a thing as "racial memory." While almost every other dialect, when substituting "t" and "d" for soft "th" (*t*) and hard "TH" (*T*) respectively, use their particular "t" or "d," Swedish substitutes two new letters. Can it be that, somewhere, the memory lingers of the time when both (*t*) and (*T*) existed in Old Scandinavian? Old Scandinavian is the language that gave us our English words: their, they, them, thrift, thrive, and Thursday.

For whatever reason, the Swedes do not use their interdental forms of "t" and "d"; instead, they use "upperdental" forms (T± and D±), with the tongue touching the *upper* teeth only. So while "growth is a healthy thing," if Swedish, we would point out that:

(G*R*½*ou*T±) is a (H:eiL±T±iE T±iiNG).

And if we'd "rather bathe without clothes," as Swedes, we'd:

(*R*½aD±*eR*½ B½e:D± WiiD±*Au*T=½ KL±*ou*D±S:).

Of four other consonant sounds that do not exist in Swedish, the substitution for (Q) is the strangest. Swedes can handle the "w" sound—but when paired with the "k," as in (Q), it comes out (KV½). Thus a book may have "quite frequent quotes," but the Swedish-speaking will call them:

(KV½I:T=½F*R*½iEKV½*A*NT=½ KV½*ou*T=½S:).

As for the other three consonant sounds, (Z), (z), and (J), the Swedes hardly come close. The first, (Z), is always approximated by a hard-stressed (S:). So if your friend went to hear an ultra-modern composer and "was puzzled by his noisy music," then to a Swede she:

(Wu*A*½S: P:u*A*½S:*e*L±D=) by (H:iiS: N*o*:ES:iE Mi*UuS*:iiK).

The substitute for the (z), which also doesn't exist in Swedish, is even stranger: it

Greta Garbo's Stockholm-Swedish dialect gradually mellowed during her long and brilliant career in American films. By the time she made her last half-dozen films (such as Queen Christina, *MGM, 1933, shown here), it was bordering on "Continental"—except for the Swedish "music" that always marked her deliveries.*

is an (SY). Thus, while Turkey and Iran both have alphabets, "Persia's version is Asian." But if you were from Sweden, you'd point out that:

(P:e:*iR*½SY*A*S: Ve:*iR*½SY*A*N) is (e:SY*A*N).

The last of the consonant changes we'll look at is the most characteristic: what happens to the American (J). And what happens depends both on what part of the word it's found in and what part of Sweden the speaker is from. I do not say, "what part of Norway," because the Norwegians consistently turn (J) into (Y) *wherever* they find it. So remember, if you do this, you arc not speaking in a Swedish dialect, but a Norwegian one.

Now, the (Y) sound is made by arching the back of the tongue against the soft palate, the (J) sound by flattening the forward part of the tongue against the hard palate. Both start as voiced consonants and continue as fricatives (where the air is restricted but not stopped). The Swedish equivalent of an *initial* (J) starts with the back of the tongue and rolls forward, so that the result is (YJ).

So while my dog expresses glee with a "giant, joyful jump," the Swedish dialect would describe a:

(YJI:*A*NT = ½ YJ*o*:EF*iu*L ± YJu*A*½MP:).

When the (J) doesn't start the word, the Swedes resort to another fricative: "sh" (*S*), so that "badge" sounds more like "bash"—and if you "managed to dodge danger," being from Sweden, you'd tell how you:

(Ma½Nii*S*D =) to (D = *AS* D = e:N*SeR*½).

Music, Rhythm, and Pace

The music of the Swedish dialect is not quite what we've been led to believe by our contact with Smålander and Norwegians in the United States. Starting at a middle tone one-half to one note higher than American speech, the up-and-down variation does exist, but within much more rigid bounds than we may have thought. On page 14 you'll find an example of the so-called singsong quality and it's certainly worth repeating here. "Please tell me how to get to the rail-

When Anita Ekberg (shown here in Valerie, *United Artists/MGM, 1951) finally returned to Sweden for an extended visit, she had not only lost her Skåne (South Swedish) subdialect in her native language, but she had replaced it with a broad American accent.*

Ingrid Bergman (shown here with Charles Boyer in Gaslight, *MGM, 1944) spent so many years on the stage and in front of the cameras of so many countries, that she eventually developed a truly "Continental" dialect. Be on the lookout for her earlier films, such as* Intermezzo, For Whom the Bell Tolls *and* Casablanca, *to hear her Swedish dialect.*

road station," is a sentence of twelve syllables that could be played on the piano thus (underlined notes are held longer than the others):

F *E* *D* *rest*
(P:L±iES: T=½eiL± Mie

F *F* *E* *F* *F*
H:*Au* T=½*Uu* GeiT=½ T=½*Uu* D±*A*

E *D* *E* *D*
*R*½e:L± *R*½*ou*D= S:T=½e: SY*A*N).

This example also gives an idea of the rhythm of the Swedish dialect. Actually, the more educated the person, the less rhythmic the variation. The rhythm would sound almost American, except for two factors that make it "heavier," both in force and duration. First, though several syllables are stressed in one passage, their stress is uniform—and uniformly *heavy*. Second, except for prefixes—which are as unemphasized in Swedish as they are in English—the first syllable of a multisyllable word generally receives heavy emphasis, for example: "duration," "vanilla," or "suggestion."

With the exception of the lead in Hawaii, *Max Von Sydow's roles have given us the chance to hear a light "Uppsala Graduate" Swedish subdialect. When he dubbed in the English language version of* The Emigrants *(Warners, 1970, shown here), he allowed his dialect to become somewhat heavier, even adding a trace of "Växsjö, Southern Swedish" (Småland) so as not to sound appreciably different from his co-star, Liv Ullmann (above), who kept a good deal of her native Norwegian dialect. As both the Småland and Norwegian have a noticeable "sing-song" music, they were quite believable playing husband and wife.*

If it's urban, the pace of the Swedish dialect is quite similar to that of American English. If it's rural, it tends to be much slower.

Observation and Notes

For observation and study of Swedish dialects, there are the films of Greta Garbo, Ingrid Bergman, Bibi Andersson, and (when he doesn't portray an American) Max von Sydow—the greatest actor of the Swedish stage.

As for subdialect models, Anita Ekberg will do for Skåne and Liv Ullmann for Norway. Besides these, almost every community in the U.S. has its Swedish-American societies, Swedish Lutheran churches, and Swedish folk-dancing groups.

And, for television viewers who are curious about her, "Mrs. Olsen" of the Folger coffee commercials speaks English just as you and I—but on television her dialect is one hundred percent perfect, a goal we all can aim for.

GENERAL SWEDISH - STOCKHOLM, EDUCATED - UPPSALA GRADUATE

STOCKHOLM, LESS EDUCATED

GUIDE PAGES	SOUND	General Swedish	Stockholm Educated Swed.	Uppsala Graduate Swed.	Stockholm Less Educated
CHANGE: (make) Me:K, (name) Ne:M	A	e:	&		&
OR longer: MA:K, NA:M, MA:N, KA:M	A			A:	
Change in all positions: (feel) FiEL±, (mean) MiEN (seem) S:iEM (weep) WiEP:	E	iE	&		&
OR longer: FE:L±, ME:N, S:E:M, WE:P:	E			E:	
LONGER SOUND: (wife) WI:F, (my) MI:, (by) B½I:, (kind) KI:ND=, (lie) L±I:	I	I:	&		
OR change: WAE:F, MAE:, B½AE:, KAE:ND=	I			AE:	
OR change: VuEF, MuE, B½uE, KuENT=½	I				uE
Change in all positions: (old) *ou*L±D= (solo) S:*ou*L±*ou*, (smoke) S:M*ou*K	O	*ou*	&	&	
OR change: *Eu*L±T=½, S:*Eu*L±*Eu*, S:M*Eu*K	O				*Eu*
Change in all positions: (use) i*Uu*S:, (mule) Mi*Uu*L±, (few) Fi*Uu*, (new) Ni*Uu*	U	i*Uu*	&		
OR no change: UZ, MUL±, FU, NU	U			U	
OR change: YE*U*:S:, MYE*U*:L±, FYE*U*:, NYE*U*:	U				YE*U*:
SHORTER: (add) a½D=, (at) a½T=½, (man) Ma½N (knapsack) Na½P:S:a½K (as) a½S:	a	a½	&	&	&
Change in all positions: (end) eiND=, (excel) eiXeiL±, (said) S:eiD=	e	ei	&		
OR no change: eND=, eXeL±, S:eD=	e			e	
OR change: A:ND=, A:XA:L±, S:A:D=	e				A:
DOUBLY LONG: (if) iiF, (milk) MiiL±K, (distinct) D=iiS:T=½iiNKT=½ (is) iiS:	i	ii	&	&	&
Change in all positions: (on) AN (fog) FAG (topnotch) T=½AP:NAC (got) GAT=½	o	*A*	&	&	&
Change in all positions: (love) L±uA½V (numskull) NuA½S:KuA½L±, (up) uA½P:	u	uA½	&	&	
OR change: E*U*P:, NE*U*:MS:KE*U*:L±, L±E*U*:V	u				E*U*:
Change in all positions: (watch) WA*i*C, (gala) GA*i*L±A*i*, (swan) S:WA*i*N	A	A*i*	&	&	
OR change: Vu:S, Gu:L±u:, S:Vu:N	A				u:
Change in all positions: (earn) e:*iR*½N (work) We:*iR*½K, (first) Fe:*iR*½S:T=½	*E*	e:*i*	&		
OR change: eRN, WeRK, FeRS:T=½	*E*			e	
OR DROP "r": *E*½N, V*E*¼K, F*E*¼S:T=½	*E*				*E*¼
NO change: (prevent) P:*R*½*I*VeiNT=½	*I*	*I*	&	&	&
NO change initially: (ounce) *O*NS:, (out) *O*T=½, (hour) *O*R½, (owl) *O*L±	*O*	-*O*	&	&	
BUT change in middle and end: (loud) L±*Au*D=, (sound) S:*Au*ND=, (now) N*Au*	*O*	/.*Au*	&	&	
OR change all: A*U*NS:, L±A*U*D=, A*U*R½, NA*U*	*O*				A*U*
No change at start or end of phrase:	*U*	- .. *U*	&	&	
Change medially & finally: (too) T=½*Uu* (fool) F*Uu*L±, (moon) M*Uu*N, (do) D=*Uu*	*U*	/ . *Uu*	&	&	
OR change all: T=½E:*U*, FE:*U*L±, ME:*U*N	*U*				E:*U*

Key:

& as shown	/ medially	: stronger	C church
¼ dropped	. finally	½ weakened	= interdental
- initial	.." in sentn.	*R* trilled R	± upperdental

GENERAL SWEDISH - STOCKHOLM, EDUCATED - UPPSALA GRADUATE

STOCKHOLM, LESS EDUCATED *GUIDE PAGES*	SOUND	General Swedish	Stockholm Educated Swed.	Uppsala Graduate Swed.	Stockholm Less Educated
CHANGE: (ask) aS:K, (bath) B½aT±	a	a		&	
OR change: A:S:K, B½A:T±, P:L±A:NT=½	a		A:		A:
No change: (level) L±eiVeL±	e	e	&	&	&
Change in all positions: (ago) AGou,	i	A	&		&
(family) Fa½MAL±iE, (mama) MAiMA					
OR no change: iGou, Fa½MiL±E:, MAiMi	i			i	
Change when spelled A: (all) O:L±,	o	O:$a	&		&
(saw) S:O: (awful) O:FiuL± (law) L±O:		au aw			
BUT medially before a consonant: (call)	o	/oi½	&	&	&
Koi½L±, (talk) T=½oi½K, (war) Woi½R½		$a(¢			
AND no change initially when spelled	o	-o$o	&	&	&
O: (off) oF, (order) oR½D=eR½		ou oo			
BUT change otherwise: (cough) KO:F,	o	O:$o	&		&
(door) D=O:R½, (loss) L±O:S:					
OR no change: KoF, D=oR½, L±oS:, oF	o			o$o	
NO change initially: (umlaut) uML±AuT=½	u	-u	&		
BUT change otherwise: (book) B½iuK,	u	iu	&		
(put) P:iuT=½, (good) GiuD=					
OR no change: B½uK, P:uT=½, GuD=	u			u	
OR change all: EU:ML±AUT=½, B½EU:K	u				EU:
NO change initially: (oil) oEL±	oE	-oE	&	&	&
BUT change otherwise: (coin) Ko:EN,	o	/.o:E	&	&	&
(voice) Vo:ES:, (boy) B½o:E					
WEAKER: (baby) B½e:B½iE, (bob) B½AB½,	B	B½	&	&	&
(suburb) S:uA½B½e:iR½B½, (bib) B½iiB½					
Change in all positions: (chin) SiiN	C				S
(church) SE¼S, (much) MEU:S					
OR no change: CiiN, Ce:iR½C, MuA½C	C	C	&	&	
Between teeth: (did) D=iiD=, (dread)	D	D=	&	&	&!.
D=R½eiD= (added) a½D=eD= (deed) D=iED=					
OR change finally: D=iiT=½, D=R½A:T=½	D				.T=½
No change: (fifteen) FiiFT=½iEN	F	F	&	&	&
DROP from "ing" suffix: (going) GouiiN¼	G	¼ing)	&		&
(coming) KuA½MiiN¼ (living) L±iiViiN¼					
STRONGER initially: (house) H:AuS:,	H	-H:	&	&	&
(here) H:iER½ (has) H:a½S: (he) H:iE					
Change initially: (jump) YJuA½MP:,	J	-YJ	&		
(giant) YJI:eNT=½, (joy) YJo:E					
OR change: YEU:MP:, YuEeNT=½, Yo:E	J				-Y
OR no change: JuA½MP:, JAE:eNT=½, Jo:E	J			-J	
AND change medially & finally: (major)	J	/.S	&		&
Me:SeR½, (edge) eiS, (stage) S:T=½e:S					
OR change; MA:YJeR½, eYJ, S:T=½A:YJ	J			/.YJ	
No change: (character) Ka½R½eKT=½eR½	K	K	&	&	&
Touching upper teeth: (lull) L±uA½L±,	L	L±	&	&	&
(skillful) S:KiiL±FiuL±, (well) WeiL±					

Key:

& as shown — - initial — : stronger — = interdental — ! excepting

$ spelled — / medial — ½ weakened — ± upperdental — S show, sure

. finally —) suffix — R trilled R — ¢ consonants

GENERAL SWEDISH - STOCKHOLM EDUC. - UPPSALA GRAD - STHM.LESS EDUC.

GUIDE PAGES	SOUND	General Swedish	Stockholm Educated	Uppsala Graduate	Sthm. Less Educated
No change: (humdrum) H:uA½MD*R*½uA½M	M	M	§	§	§
No change: (condition) KuA½ND=iiSYuA½N	N	N	§	§	§
STRONGER: (paper) P:e:P:*e*R½, (pipe) P:I:P:, (people) P:iEP:*e*L±	P	P:	§	§	§
Change in all positions: (quick) KV½iiK (equal) iEKV½*e*L±, (quite) KV½I:T=½	Q	KV½	§	§	
OR change: KViiK, iEKV*e*L±, KVuET=½	Q				KV
Light trill: (rare) *R*½e:*R*½, (regular) *R*½eiGi*U*uL±*e**R*½, (rural) *R*½*U*u*R*½*e*L±	R	*R*½	§		§
OR no change: RA:R, ReGUL±*e*R, R*U*uR*e*L±	R			R	
STRONGER: (cease) S:iES:, (say) S:e: (space) S:P:e:S: (stress) S:T=½*R*½eiS:	S	S:	§	§	§
NO change when spelled SH: (shush) *S*uA½*S*, (wish) Wii*S*, (show) *Sou*	*S*	*S*$sh	§	§	§
BUT change when spelled S medially: (sensual) S:eiNSY*Uue*L±	*S*	/SY$s	§		§
OR change finally: WiiS:, *S*uA½S:	*S*				.S:
OR no change: S:eNS*Ue*L±	*S*			*S*	
LIGHTLY between teeth: (get) GeiT=½, (test) T=½eiS:T=½, (into) iiNT=½*Uu*	T	T=½!	§	§	§
BUT drop finally before D, T, *t* or *T*: (get done) Gei¼D=uA½N, (got thin) GA¼T±iiN, (sit there) S:ii¼D±e:*R*½	T	.¼(d, t,*t*,*T*	§	§	§
Tongue against upper teeth: (healthy) H:eiL±T±iE, (thing) T±iiNG	*t*	T±	§	§	§!
OR drop finally before D, T, *t* or *T*: (death defying) D=ei¼D=iEFI:iiN¼, (health tonic) H:A:L±¼T=½ANiiK	*t*				.¼(d, t,*t*,*T*
Change in all positions: (this) D±iiS: (other) uA½D±*eR*½	*T*	D±	§		§!
OR drop finally before D, T, *t* or *T*: (smooth taste) S:ME*U*:¼T=½e:S:T=½, (with thought) Vii¼T±O:T=½	*T*				.¼(d, t,*t*,*T*
OR no change: *T*iiS:, S:M*Uu**T* T=½A:S:T=½	*T*			*T*	
No change: (involve) iiNVAL±V	V	V	§	§	§
Change in all positions: (we) ViE, (away) AVe:, (why) VuE, (will) ViiL±	W				V
OR no change: WiE, AWe:, WI:, WiiL±	W	W	§	§	
No change: (six) S:iiX (taxi) T=½a½XiE	X	X	§	§	§
Change in all positions: (yet) YJeiT=½ (young) YJuA½NG, (years) YJiE*R*½S:	Y		YJ		YJ
OR no change: YeiT=½, YuA½NG, YiE*R*½S:	Y	Y		§	
Change in all positions: (zone) S:*ou*N (busy) B½iiS:iE, (please) P:L±iES:	Z	S:	§		§
OR no change: Z*ou*N, B½iiZE:, P:L±E:Z	Z			Z	
Change in all positions: (Asia) e:SYA (measure) MeiSYe:*iR*½ (vision) ViiSY*e*N	z	SY	§	§	§

Key:

§ as shown	/ medially	: stronger	= interdental
$ spelled	ₒ finally	½ weakened	± upperdental
¼ dropped	(before	! excepting	*R* trilled R

VÄXSJÖ, SOUTH SWEDISH - ÅSEDA, RURAL - VASA, FINLAND SWEDISH

GUIDE PAGES	SOUND	Växsjö Southern Swedish	Aseda Rural Swedish	Vasa Finland Swedish
Change in all positions: (make) Me:K, (name)	A	e:	&	
Ne:M, (base) B½e:S:, (fade) Fe:D=, (may) Me:				
OR change: MeiK, NeiM, B½EIS:, FeiD, Mei				ei
Change in all positions: (feel) Fe:L± (mean)	E	e:		
Me:N, (seem) S:e:M, (weep) We;P:, (he) H:e:				
OR change: FA:L±, MA:N, S:A:M, VA:P, H:A:	E		A:	
OR shorter: Fi:L, Mi:N, S:i:M, Wi:P, Hi:	E			i:
LONGER SOUND: (wife) WI:F (my) MI: (by) B½I:	I	I:		
(kind) KI:ND=, (lie) L±I:, (hide) H:I:D=				
OR change: VuEF, MuE, B½uE, KuENT=½, L±uE	I		uE	
OR change: WAiF, MAi, B½Ai, KAiND, LAi, HAiD	I			Ai
Change in all positions: (old) *o*:L±D= (solo)	O	*o*:	&	&
S:*o*:L±*o*:, (smoke) S:M*o*:K, (pose) P:*o*:S:				
Change in all positions: (use) i*Uu*S: (mule)	U	i*Uu*		&
Mi*Uu*L± (few) Fi*Uu* (new) Ni*Uu* (cute) Ki*Uu*T=½				
OR change: YE*U*:S:, MYE*U*:L±, FYE*U*:, KYE*U*:T=½	U		YE*U*:	
Change in all positions: (as) e:S: (man) Me:N	a	e:	&	&
(add) e:D= (knapsack) Ne:P:S:e:K (at) e:T=½				
Change in all positions: (end) *a*ND= (excel)	e	*a*	&	
*a*X*a*L±, (said) S:*a*D=, (extend) *a*XT=½*a*ND=				
OR longer: e:ND, e:Xe:L, S:e:D, e:XTe:ND	e			e:
DOUBLY LONG: (if) iiF (milk) MiiL±K (critic)	i	ii	&	
K*R*½iiT=½iiK (distinct) D=iiS:T=½iiNKT=½				
OR change: EF, MELK, K*R*:ETEK, DES:TENKT	i			E
Change in all positions: (on) *o*:N, (fog)	o	*o*:	&	
F*o*:G, (topnotch) T=½*o*:PN*o*:*S*, (got) G*o*:T=½				
OR change: *A*N, F*A*G, T*A*PN*A*S, G*A*T				*A*
Change in all positions: (up) uA½P:, (love)	u	uA½	&	
L±uA½V (numskull) NuA½MS:KuA½L± (us) uA½S:				
OR change: *o*:P, L*o*:V, N*o*:MS:K*o*:L, *o*:S:	u			*o*:
Change in all positions: (gala) G*a*l±*a*, (far)	A	*a*	&	
F*aR*½, (swan) S:W*a*N (watch) W*aS* (art) *aR*½T=½				
OR longer: GA:LA:, FA:*R*:, S:WA:N, WA:*S*, A:*R*:T	A			A:
Change in all positions: (earn) e:*iR*½N (work)	*E*	e:*i*		&
We:*iR*½K (first) Fe:*iR*½S:T=½ (burn) B½e:*iR*½N				
OR DROP "r": *E*¼N, V*E*¼K, F*E*¼S:T=½, B½*E*¼N	*E*		*E*¼	
No change: (prevent) P:*R*½*I*V*a*NT=½	*I*	*I*	&	&
Change in all positions: (out) a*U*T=½ (ounce)	*O*	a*U*	&	
a*U*NS: (sound) S:a*U*ND= (loud) L±a*U*D= (now) Na*U*				
OR no change initially: *O*T, *O*NS: (hour) *OR*:	*O*			- *O*
AND change otherwise: S:*A*uND, L*A*uD, N*A*u				/ . *A*u
No change initially or at end of phrase.	*U*	- .. *U*		&
Change medially & finally: (fool) F*Uu*L± (do)	*U*	/ . *Uu*		&
D=*Uu* (moon) M*Uu*N (too) T=½*Uu* (lose) L±*Uu*S:				
OR change all: FE*U*:L±, D=E*U*:, ME*U*:N, T=½E*U*:	*U*		E*U*:	

Key:

& as shown	/ medially	: stronger	*S* show, sure
¼ dropped	. finally	½ weakened	= interdental
- initial	.. " in sentn.		± upperdental
			R trilled R

VÄXSJÖ, SOUTH SWEDISH - ÅSEDA, RURAL - VASA, FINLAND-SWEDISH

GUIDE PAGES	SOUND	Växsjö Southern Swedish	Aseda Rural Swedish	Vasa Finland Swedish
Change in all positions: (ask) e:S:K, (bath) B½e:T±, (plant) P:L±e:NT=½, (dance) D=e:NS:	*a*	e:	&	
OR change: A:S:K, B½A:T, PLA:NT, DA:NS:	*a*			A:
No change: (level) L±*a*V*e*L±, (often) *o*F*e*N	*e*	*e*	&	&
Change in all positions: (ago) *A*G*o*: (family) Fe:MAL±e:, (mama) M*a*M*A*, (opinion) AP:iiNYAN	*i*	*A*	&	&
Change when spelled A,AW,AU: (all) O:L± (saw) S:O:, (awful) O:F*iu*L±, (autumn) O:T=½AM	*o*	O:$a aw au	&	&
BUT medially before consonants: (call) K*oi*½L± (talk) T=½*oi*½K (war) W*oi*½*R*½ (cause) K*oi*½S:	*o*	/ *oi*½ (¢	&	&
AND no change initially when spelled O,OU: (off) *o*F, (order) *oR*½D=*eR*½, (ought) *o*T=½	*o*	-*o* $o ou	&	&
BUT change otherwise: (cough) KO:F, (door) D=O:*R*½, (loss) L±O:S:, (wrong) *R*½O:NG	*o*	/.O:$o ou oo	&	&
NO change initially: (umlaut) *u*ML±*aU*T=½	*u*	-*u*		
BUT change otherwise: (book) B½*iu*K, (put) P:*iu*T=½, (woman) W*iu*MAN, (good) G*iu*D=	*u*	/.*iu*		
OR change all: E*U*:ML±*aU*T=½, B½E*U*:K, VE*U*:MAN	*u*		E*U*:	
OR longer: *u*:MLA*u*T, B½*u*:K, W*u*:MAN, P*u*:T	*u*			*u*:
NO change initially: (oily) *o*EL±e:	*o*E	-*o*E	&	
BUT change otherwise: (coin) K*o*:EN, (boy) B½*o*:E, (voice) V*o*:ES:, (avoid) AV*o*:ED=	*o*E	/.*o*:E	&	
OR change: *o*iLi:, K*o*iN, B½*o*i, V*o*iS:, AV*o*iD	*o*E			*o*i
WEAKER: (baby) B½e:B½e:, (bob) B½*o*B½, (bib) B½iiB½, (suburb) S:u*A*½B½e:*iR*½B½	B	B½	&	&
Change in all positions: (chin) *S*iiN, (much) Mu*A*½*S*, (church) *S*e:*iR*½*S*, (speech) S:P:e:*S*	C	*S*	&	&
Between the teeth: (did) D=iiD= (made) Me:D= (dread) D=*R*½*a*D= (added) e:D=*e*D= (deed) D=e:D=	D	D=	&!	
OR change finally: D=iiT=½, Me:T=½, D*R*½*a*T=½	D		.T=½	
OR no change: DED, MeiD, D*R*:e:D, e:D*e*D, Di:D	D			D
No change: (fifteen) FiiFT=½e:N, (fife) FI:F	F	F	&	&
DROP from "ing" suffix: (going) G*o*:iiN¼, (coming) Ku*A*½MiiN¼, (living) L±iiViiN¼	G	¼ing)	&	&
STRONGER initially: (house) H:a*U*S: (he) H:e: (here) H:e:*R*½, (has) H:e:S:, (hand) H:e:ND=	H	-H:	&	
OR no change: HA*u*S:, Hi:, Hi:*R*:, He:S:	H			H
Change initially: (jump) YJu*A*½MP:, (general) YJ*a*N*eR*½AL±, (joy) YJ*o*:E, (giant) YJI:*e*NT=½	J	-YJ		&
OR change: Yu*A*½MP:, Y*a*N*eR*½AL±, Y*o*:E, YuE*e*NT=½	J		-Y	
AND change otherwise: (major) Me:*SeR*½, (edge) *aS*, (stage) S:T=½e:*S*, (gradual) G*R*½e:*SUu*L±	J	/.*S*	&	&
No change: (character) Ke:*R*½*e*KT=½*eR*½	K	K	&	&
Touching upper teeth: (lull) L±u*A*½L±, (low) L±*o*:, (well) W*a*L±, (skillful) S:KiiL±F*iu*L±	L	L±	&	
OR no change: L*o*:L, L*o*:, We:L, S:KELF*u*:L	L			L

Key:

& as shown	- initial	: stronger	= interdental	*S* show, sure
$ spelled	/ medial	½ weakened	± upperdental	! excepting
	. final	) suffix	*R* trilled R	¢ consonants

GUIDE PAGES	SOUND	Växsjö Southern Swedish	Aseda Rural Swedish	Vasa Finland Swedish
No change: (humdrum) H:uA½MD=R½uA½M	M	M	&	&
No change: (condition) KuA½ND=iiSYuA½N	N	N	&	&
STRONGER: (paper) P:e:P:eR½, (pipe) P:I:P:, (people) P:e:P:eL±, (stop) S:T=½o:P: OR no change: PeiPeR:, PAiP, Pi:PeL, S:TAP	P P	P:	&	 P
Change in all positions: (quick) KV½iiK, (equal) e:KV½eL±, (quite) KV½I:T=½ OR change: KViiK, A:KVeL±, KVuET=½	Q Q	KV½	 KV	&
Light trill: (rare) R½e:R½, (roar) R½O:R½, (rural) R½UuR½eL±, (regular) R½aGiUuL±eR½ OR heavy trill: R:eiR:, R:O:R:, R:UuR:eL	R R	R½	&	 R:
STRONGER: (cease) S:e:S:, (space) S:P:e:S:, (say) S:e:, (stress) S:T=½R½aS:, (yes) YJaS:	S	S:	&	&
No change when spelled SH: (shush) SuA½S, (wish) WiiS, (show) So:, (smash) S:Me:S BUT change medially when spelled S: (sensual) S:aNSYUueL±, (issue) iiSYUu OR change finally: So:S:, WES:, S:MA:S:	S S S	Ssh /SYs	& &	 .S:
LIGHTLY between teeth: (tight) T=½I:T=½, (get) GaT=½ (into) iiNT=½Uu (test) T=½aS:T=½ BUT drop finally before D,T,t or T: (get done) Ga¼D=uA½N, (got thin) Go:¼T±iiN OR no change: Te:S:T, Ge:T Do:N, ENTUu, TAiT	T T T	T=½ .¼(d, t,t,T	& &	 T
Tongue against upper teeth: (bath) B½e:T±, (thing) T±iiNG, (healthy) H:aL±T±e: BUT drop finally before D, T, t or T: (death defying) D=a¼D=e:FI:iiN¼ OR change all: TENG, B½A:T, He:LTi:, De:T	t t t	T±! .¼(d, t,t,T	&	 T
Tongue against upper teeth: (this) D±iiS:, (other) uA½D±eR½, (breathe) B½R½e:D± OR drop finally before D, T, t or T: (smooth taste) S:MEU:¼T=½e:S:T=½ OR change all: DES:, o:DeR:, B½R:i:D, S:MUuD	T T T	D±	&! .¼(d, t,t,T	 D
No change: (involve) iiNVo:L±V	V	V	&	&
Change in all positions: (will) ViiL± (away) AVe: (why) VuE (we) VA: (twist) T=½ViiS:T=½ OR no change: WiiL±, AWe:, WI:, We:	W W	 W	V	 &
No change: (six) S:iiX, (taxi) T=½e:Xe:	X	X	&	&
Change in all positions: (young) YJuA½NG, (yet) YJaT=½, (years) YJe:R½S:, (yes) YJaS: OR no change: Yo:NG, Ye:T, Yi:R:S:, Ye:S:	Y Y	YJ	&	 Y
Change in all positions: (zone) S:o:N (busy) B½iiS:e:, (please) P:L±e:S:, (was) WuA½S:	Z	S:	&	&
Change in all positions: (Asia) e:SYA, (vision) ViiSYeN, (measure) MaSYe:iR½ OR no change: eizA, VEzeN, Me:ze:iR:	z z	SY	&	 z

Key:

& as shown	/ medially	: stronger	= interdental
$ spelled	. finally	½ weakened	± upperdental
¼ dropped	(before	! except	R trilled R

OSLO NORWEGIAN - MOSS, RURAL NORWEGIAN - BERGEN, WESTERN NORWAY

GUIDE PAGES	SOUND	Oslo Norwegian	Moss Rural Norwegian	Bergen Western Norway
Change in all positions: (make) Me:K, (name) Ne:M, (base) Be:S:, (fade) Fe:D, (may) Me:	A	e:	&	&
Change in all positions: (feel) Fi:L±, (he) Hi:, (mean) Mi:N, (seem) S:i:M, (weep) Vi:P	E			i:
OR no change: FEL±, HE, MEN, S:EM, VEP	E	E	&	
LONGER SOUND: (wife) VI:F, (kind) KI:ND, (my) MI:, (by) BI:, (hide) HI:D, (lie) L±I:	I	I:	&	&
Change in all positions: (old) EuL±D, (pose) PEuS:, (smoke) S:MEuK, (solo) S:EuL±Eu	O	Eu	&	&
Change in all positions: (use) YEUS:, (mule) MYEUL±, (cute) KYEUT, (few) FYEU, (new)NYEU	U	YEU	&	&
Change in all positions: (add) AD, (as) AS:, (man) MAN, (knapsack) NAPS:AK, (back) BAK	a	A	&	&
Change in all positions: (end) aND, (excel) aXaL±, (said) S:aD, (bed) BaD, (tell) TaL±	e	a	&	&
DOUBLY LONG: (if) iiF (milk) MiiL±K (critic) KR:iiTiiK (distinct) DiiS:TiiNKT (is) iiS:	i		ii	
OR no change: iF, MiL±K, KR:iTiK, DiS:TiNKT	i	i		&
Change in all positions: (on) *o*N (topnotch) T*o*PN*o*C, (fog) F*o*G½, (got) G*o*T, (stop) S:T*o*P	o	*o*		&
OR change: *o*:N, T*o*:PN*o*:C, F*o*:G½, G *o*:T, S:T*o*:P	o		*o*:	
Change in all positions: (up) EP, (us) ES:, (numskull) NEMS:KEL± (love) L±EV (cut) KET	u	E	&	
OR change: *o*P, *o*S:, N*o*MS:K*o*L±, L±*o*V, K*o*T	u			*o*
No change: (gala) GAL±A, (watch) VAC	A	A	&	&
DROP the "r": (earn) E¼N, (merger) ME¼YE¼, (work) VE¼K, (burn) BE¼N, (first) FE¼S:T	E	E¼	&	&
No change: (prevent) PR:*I*VaNT	*I*	*I*	&	&
Change in all positions: (out) *o*UT, (ounce) *o*UNS:, (loud) L±*o*UD, (now) N*o*U, (hour) *o*UR:	*O*	*o*U	&	&
Change in all positions: (fool) FEUL±, (do) DE , (moon) MEUN, (lose) L±EUS:, (too) TEU	*U*	EU	&	&
No change: (ask) *a*S:K, (dance) D*a*NS:	*a*	*a*	&	&
No change: (level) L±aV*e*L±, (often) *o*F*e*N	*e*	*e*	&	&
Change in all positions: (ago) AGEu (family) FAMAL±E, (mama) MAMA, (opinion) APiNYAN	*i*	A	&	&
No change: (all) *o*L±, (off) *o*F, (caught) K*o*T	*o*	*o*	&	&
Change in all positions: (book) BEUK (woman) VEUMAN (put) PEUT (good) GEUD (pull) PEUL±	*u*	EU	&	&
No change: (oil) *o*EL± (coin) K*o*EN (boy) B*o*E	*o*E	*o*E	&	&

CHANGE before S or T: (bobsled) B*o*PS:L±aD, (club tie) KL±EP TI: (curb side) KE¼P S:I:D	B	P(s,t	&	&
No change: (church) CE¼C, (much) MEC	C	C	&	&

Key:

& as shown
¼ dropped
。 finally
(preceding
: stronger
½ weakened
R trilled R
± upperdental

OSLO NORWEGIAN - MOSS, RURAL NORWEGIAN - BERGEN, WESTERN NORWAY

GUIDE PAGES	SOUND	Oslo Norwegian	Moss Rural Norwegian	Bergen Western Norway
CHANGE before S or T: (had some) HAT SEM, (did to) DiiT TEU, (bad scene) BAT S:EN	D	T(s,t		&
OR drop finally before consonants: HA¼SEM	D		.¼(¢	
No change: (fifteen) FiFTEN, (fife) FI:F	F	F	&	&
CHANGE before S or T: (pig sty) PiK S:TI:	G	K(s,t	&	&
& change finally: (big) BiG½, (hug) HEG½	G	.G½	&	&
No change: (hothouse) HoTHoUS:, (has) HAS:	H	H	&	&
Change in all positions: (general) YaNeR:AL± (jump) YEMP, (just) YES:T, (giant) YI:eNT	J	Y	&	&
No change: (character) KAR½eKTeR:	K	K	&	&
Touching upper teeth: (lull) L±EL± (well) VaL±, (skillful) S:KiL±FEUL±, (low) L±Eu	L	L±	&	&
No change: (humdrum) HEMDR:EM	M	M	&	&
No change: (condition) KENDiSEN	N	N	&	&
No change: (paper) Pe:PeR:, (pipe) PI:P	P	P	&	&
Change in all positions: (equal) EKV½eL±, (quick) KV½iK, (quite) KV½I:T, (quit) KV½iT	Q	KV½		
OR change: EKVeL±, KViiK, KVI:T, KViiT	Q		KV	KV
STRONG TRILL: (rare) R:e:R:, (rear) R:ER:, (rural) R:EUR:eL±, (regular) R:aGYEUL±eR:	R	R:!	&	
BUT no change before L, N or T: (barn) BARN, (poorly) PEURL±E, (sport) S:PoRT	R	R(l,n or t	&	
OR change all: *r*e:*r*, *r*E*r*, BA*r*N, *r*EU*r*eL±	R			*r*
STRONGER: (cease) S:ES:, (space) S:Pe:S, (say) S:e:, (stress) S:TR:aS:, (yes) YJaS:	S	S:	&	&
No change: (shush) *SES*, (sure) *SEUR:*	*S*	*S*	&	&
No change: (test) TaS:T, (tight) TI:T	T	T	&	&
Change in all positions: (healthy) HaL±TE, (bath) BAT, (mouth) MoUT, (thing) TiNG½	*t*	T	&!	&
OR drop finally before D, T, *t* or *T*: (death defying) Da¼ DEFI:iiNG½	*t*		.¼(d, t,*t*,*T*	
Tongue against upper teeth: (other) ED±eR:, (this) D=iS:, (breathe) BR:ED±, (that) D±AT	*T*	D±	&	
OR change: EZe*r*, ZiS:, BRi:Z, ZAT	*T*			Z
Change before S or T: (have said) HAF S:aD, (love to) L±EF TEU, (give some) GiF S:EM	V	F(s,t	&	&
Change in all positions: (twist) TViS:T, (will) ViL±, (why) VI:, (away) AVe:, (we) VE	W	V	&	&
No change: (six) S:iX, (taxi) TAXE	X	X	&	&
Change in all positions: (young) YJENG½, (yet) YJaT, (years) YJER:S:, (yes) YJaS:	Y	YJ	&	&
Change in all positions: (zone) S:EuN, (was) VES: (busy) BiS:E (please) PL±ES: (is) iS:	Z	S:	&	&
No change: (vision) VizeN, (measure) MazE¼	z	z	&	&

Key:

& as shown	(preceding	R trilled R	± upperdental
¼ dropped	: stronger	*r* uvular R	¢ consonants
. finally	½ weakened	! excepting	

MASTER CATEGORY 12

SCOTTISH

Scottish and Irish were once the same language, the Scots having come over to the isle of Britain from Ireland. Once there, however, they mingled with the native Celts (Picts and Britons). The first Kingdom of Scotland (1034 A.D.) even included the Germanic-speaking Angles. Topography and the pursuit of livelihoods eventually divided the people into Highland (rural) speakers and Lowland (more urban) ones, a division reflected in the *GUIDE PAGES* that follow. Also reflected is the strong English influence in the university town of Edinburgh, where the Scottish burr comes closest to the speech of the educated Englishman.

Despite the long separation from the Irish, and the fact that Gaelic fell into disuse in Scotland, the similarities between the two varieties are so great that there is a strong danger of confusing them if we try to learn them by observation alone. And since Irish and Scottish are both varieties of English, each must be consistent within itself to be believable and accurate.

The three main differences between them are: 1) the more strongly trilled "r" (*R*:) in Scottish; 2) the Scottish use of the glottal stop (@); 3) the generally "broader flavor," because the Scottish vowel sounds are not shortened as much as the Irish.

The first distinction is easy to remember: the Irish speak with a brogue (one "r"), the Scottish with a burr (two "r"s).

Vowel Changes

The differentiation of vowel sounds calls for careful examination, since the differences are often small and subtle. Take the change in the diphthong (*O*) as in "how"—in American English, a combination of the (*A*) of "hah!" and the (*U*) of "who." The Irish merely shorten the first element, (*A*), into the (*i*) of "ago"; the Scottish both *shorten* the first sound and *lengthen* the second one. So, if the young politician "found out about power," being from Scotland, we'd say he:

(F*iU*:ND *iU*:@ iB*iU*:@ P*iU*:*eR*:).

This is the only diphthong that goes through a double change; the other five alter only one element each. For example, the (*o*E) of "oil" is composed of the (*o*) of "all" and the (E) of "eel." The Scottish retains the long second sound but abbreviates the first into the (*i*) of "normal." Thus, while we might say of rowdy young sailors that the "boys enjoyed a noisy voyage," if Scottish, we would say the:

(B*i*EZ i:NJ*i*ED) a (N*i*EZi: V*i*E*i*J).

The (I) of "wine" is made up of the (*A*) of "wan" and the (E) of "wean." Again, the second long sound is preserved while the first is abridged, this time to the (u) of "one"—so that if "dry ice might be fine" to keep the sherbet cold, a Scot might suggest that:

(D*R*:uE uES MuE@) be (FuEN).

Incidentally, while the dictionary suggests that the odd, nonphonetic spelling of "one" comes from the Anglo-Saxon *an*, it is just as likely to have come from the Scottish *ane* (which in turn descended from the Norse *eyn*). While in Sweden, I discovered that the centuries-long Scandinavian settlements in Scotland had left Scottish with a number of words similar to modern-day Swedish. "Ane" is an example, a cognate of the Swedish *en*, which means number "one." Then there's the Scottish *bairn* for "child," like the Swedish *barn*; *braw* for "good," like the Swedish *bra*; *nieve* for "fist," which in Swedish is *näve*—and many others.

But back to the diphthongs: the (A) of "wait" consists of the (e) of "wet" and the (E) of "wheat"; this last is reduced to the (i) of "wit"—so that if the secretary found that since she "ate cake daily, she became overweight," if Scottish-born, she would find that since she:

(ei@ KeiK½ DeiLi:) she (Bi:KeiM *o*Ve*R*:Wei@).

Did you notice how the (O) in "overweight" changed? In American English, this diphthong is a combination of the (*o*) in "bought" and the (*U*) in "boot." In Scottish, the second vowel sound is lost entirely, so that "pose" and "low" come to sound like "pause" and "law." Thus, if the local tour guide might "know most old roads," to a Scot, he would:

(N*o* M*o*ST *o*LD *R*:*o*DZ).

Another diphthong containing the "oo" sound is the (U) of "fuel," combining (Y) and (*U*) as in "fool." In this case, the (*U*) is shortened to the (*u*) of "full." So that, if the developer has enough land left to add a "few, new huge units," if Scottish, we would speak of a:

(FY*u* NY*u* HY*u*J Y*u*N*i*TS).

When the (*U*) is found by itself, naturally a similar substitution takes place, so that "pool" and "luke" sound like "pull" and "look." So if we wanted to say that the "tour group soon moved on," in Scottish variety we would remark that the:

(T*uR*: G*R*:*u*P S*u*N M*u*VD) on.

However, at this point we run into our first "compensation reversal" (page 28), with the substitutions working in the *other* direction, so that "could" and "soot" are pronounced like "cooed" and "suit." And if we believe that by smiling more, every "woman would look good," then being Scottish, our proposition would come out that every:

(W*U*M¼N W*U*D L*U*K½ G*U*D).

There is another case of reversal in Scottish: the (o) of "rot" and "sot" becomes the (*o*) of "wrought" and "sought"—*and vice versa*. Thus, if the owner complained to his help that there was "not a polished pot in the shop," as a Scot, he'd observe that there was:

(N*o*@) a (P*o*L*i*SD P*o*@) in the (*So*P).

And if the sawmill hand thinks a big "log ought" to make "broad boards," then in this variety he would tell you how a big:

(L*o*G *o*@) to make (B*R*:oD B*uR*:DZ).

"Aha!" you're saying, "that last 'aw' in 'boards' didn't turn into (o)." Quite right, for one of the characteristic changes in the Scottish variety is that the "aw" (*o*) sound, when spelled "oa," "o," "oo," or "ou" coming before an "r" turns into the (*u*) of "look." So if the paralegal is seeking a "form for a court order," if Scottish-speaking, she will ask for a:

(F*uR*:M F*uR*:) a (K*uR*:@ *uR*:D*eR*:).

This same sound substitutes in the second characteristic change, wherein the (u) of "buck" and "stud" becomes the (*u*) of "book" and "stood." Thus if the bulldog "was young but ugly," for the Scot he:

(W*u*Z Y*u*NG B*u*@ *u*GLi:).

We have now reached the point where we should stop talking about characteristic changes and start investigating characteristic vowel substitutes. As you saw above, (*u*) is one of these, replacing two different vowel sounds. The next substitute also replaces two other vowels. In the first case, (o) replaces (*a*), so that "mask" sounds like "mosque"—and if a little too much wine makes us feel as though we'd "rather laugh and dance," if we were Scottish, we'd:

(*R*:o*TeR*: LoF oND DoNS).

As you probably noted, the (a) of "and" *also* changed into (o); this means that "add" and "hat" rhyme with "odd" and "hot." So that if I "am a happy man," being Scottish-born, I'd admit that I:

(oM) a (HoPi: MoN).

The phonetics of "happy" above give us our clue to our next pair of replaced vowels, for they both are supplanted by a long (i:). In the instance above, the (E) of "seat" is trimmed down to a stretched version of the (i) of "sit." So if "she seemed so free and easy" to us, as Scots, we would say:

(Si: Si:MD) so (F*R*:i:) and (i:Zi:).

The second replaced vowel is the (e) of "ten." It changes to a longer reading of the (i) in "tin" when it comes before a "g," "l," "m," "n," or "v." Therefore, if the accountants triple-checked their figures in order to "exempt themselves from error," if from Scotland, they did it to:

(i:GZi:MT *T*i:MSi:LVZ) from (*iR*:*eR*:).

In another characteristic vowel replacement, the "e" (e) in "error" becomes the (*i*) of "ago" rather than (i:); this is because it precedes an "r."

There are three more examples of the (*i*) standing in for another vowel. The first occurs when the (i) of "limp" comes before two *separate* consonant sounds. Thus, if it's true that Lowlands Scottish has a "distinct English imprint," the Scot will talk of a:

(D*i*ST*i*NKT *i*NGLi:*S* *i*MP*R*:*i*NT).

Another such case is where the (*i*) replaces the "ah" (*A*) of "palm"—so if the reviewing general "calmly watched the armies march by," being Scottish, we'd describe how he: (K*i*LMLi: W*i*CD) the (*iR*:Mi:Z M*iR*:*C*) by.

The third instance is where the ubiquitous (*i*) usurps the (*E*) of "urge." Thus, if the crowd had to quiet down before the "girl's first word was heard," the Scot would speak of before the:

(G*iR*:LZ F*iR*:ST W*iR*:D) was (HA*R*:D)

You noticed the A in "heard"? That is another vowel substitution: when (*E*) at the beginning or the middle of a word is spelled "e" or "ea," the (*E*) of "stir" turns into the (A) of "stare." So if the diligent philosophy student refuses to "learn perverse concerns," the Scottish-born would point out he'd refused to:

(LA*R*:N PA*R*:VA*R*:S K*i*NSA*R*:NZ).

Consonant Changes

You may have observed that, unlike Irish—Scottish has only one form of the "r," the strongly trilled one (*R*:) and it is consistent. This trill, you may remember, is made by placing the tongue against the back of the upper gum ridge and voicing the sound strongly to produce a rapid vibration (or flapping) similar to an imitation of a pneumatic drill or a motorcycle. Thus, if "our amateur author friend wrote very poor stories," a Scot would observe that:

(*iU*:*R*: oM*i*C*eR*: o½*te**R*: F*R*:*i*ND *R*:*o*@ V*iR*i: *PuR*: ST*uR*:i:Z).

The Scottish version of the "t" in "wrote" leads us to the most characteristic of the consonant substitutions: the glottal stop (@). The glottis is the opening between the vocal chords in the larynx: to "stop" the sound there is quite easy. First, take a breath and then let it out through your mouth. Unless you added sound, this should have been silent. Now pronounce the word "hot," paying special attention to where the "h" originates; did you notice how this fricative consonant was made by narrowing an opening in the throat? If not, pronounce the word again until you locate that narrowed opening. That place is the glottis, and the glottal stop (@) is made by cutting off the air (and the sound it carries) *at* the glottis: closing the glottis instead of merely narrowing it. Use the word "hot" to practice this new sound, substituting the glottal stop (@) for the "t." That is one of the places where the Scot employs the glottal stop: at the end of a word, directly after a vowel. Thus, the admonition to "sit tight," in Scottish variety becomes:

(Si:@ TuE@).

The (@) is also used instead of a double "t" in the middle of a word. So if an after-dinner drink makes the food "settle a little better," for a Scot it would make it:

(Se@*e*L) a (L*i*@*e*L Be@*eR*:).

The third and fourth substitutions of the (@) for the "t" both come after an "r." One of them comes at the end of a word—thus a "short skirt" is made into a (*SuR*:@ SK*iR*:@). The other comes in the middle of a word, before a vowel sound—so if the university was "starting thirty important proj-

One has to dig hard to unearth a film in which David Niven did his native Scottish "burr." Generally, we're most familiar with his impeccable British English in such films as United Artists' 1956 Around the World in 80 Days *(shown here with his co-star, Cantinflas of Mexico). When the role called for it, Niven could slip into the so-called "Atlantic English" (a stage blend of British and American) since he had worked in a Canadian lumber camp and in various newspaper-connected jobs in the U.S. before becoming a film star.*

ects," being Scottish-born, we would talk of:

(St*iR*:@*i*NG *tiR*:@i: *i*MP*uR*:@*i*NT) projects.

You probably saw that the "t" at the end of "important" did *not* turn into a glottal stop (@); it is essential *not* to use the glottal stop (@) as an indiscriminate replacement for "t."

Remember: 1) you never use the glottal stop at the beginning of a word; 2) you only use it in the middle of a word to replace a double "t" or a "t" that follows an "r" and precedes a vowel; 3) it only substitutes for a final "t" after a vowel or an "r."

Finally, where the word "not" would be contracted into "n't" in English, instead of pronouncing it (No@), the Scots render it (N*i*). Thus "can't," "wasn't," "won't," "isn't," "hasn't," and "aren't" are converted into:

(KoNN*i*), (W*u*ZN*i*), (W*i*LN*i*), (*i*ZN*i*), (HoZN*i*), and (*iR*:N*i*).

When the verb to be contracted ends in a "d," that "d" is made into an "n," so that "didn't," "hadn't," "couldn't," "wouldn't," and "shouldn't" are changed into:

(Di:NN*i*), (HoNN*i*), (K*U*NN*i*), (W*U*NN*i*) and (*SU*NN*i*).

The last consonant conversion of any consequence happens to the "wh" in the

In most of his film roles (including that of James Bond), Sean Connery's British English is modified by the Scottish "rolled" (or trilled) R. Finally, in The Man Who Would Be King *(Columbia/Allied Artists, 1975, shown here), he allowed himself the luxury of speaking with the true Scottish variety which his ear had been used to hearing when he was growing up in Scotland.*

Scottish variety: it is changed to a strong (H:W). Thus, if a reporter were sent to cover "what, when, where, and why," to a Scot, this would be:

(H:W*u*@, H:Wi:N, H:Wei*R*:), and (H:WuE).

Music, Rhythm, and Pace

The Scottish music is similar to the American in many ways. The placement is the same, though the range is smaller. The inflection is the same, while the variation is less. Rhythmically, however, the strongly rolled "r" (*R*:) and the glottal stop (@) tend to make the Scottish variety heavier and more staccato than American speech. As to stress, the location of the emphasized syllables and the force of their stress is generally the same.

Observation and Notes

The Scots "burr" is well delivered by Sean Connery, Deborah Kerr, David Niven, and David McCallum, when they are playing Scottish roles. Remember, Scottish is a variety, so you'll need to study the *GUIDE PAGES* with special diligence. If you have the accompanying tapes, you may want to spend more time than usual with them, as well.

GENERAL SCOTTISH - EDINBURGH, EDUCATED - BRAEMAR, HIGHLAND

GUIDE PAGES	SOUND	General Scottish	Edinburgh Educated Scots	Braemar Highland Scots
Change in all positions: (aim) eiM, (maintain) MeiNTeiN, (cake) KeiK½, (day) Dei, (ate) ei@	A	ei	&	&
SHORTEN all: (easy) i:Zi:, (seem) Si:M, (he) Hi:, (east) i:ST, (believe) Bi:Li:V	E	i:	&	&
Change in all positions: (die) DuE, (likewise) LuEKWuEZ, (I'll) uEL, (nice) NuES, (side) SuED	I	uE	&	&
Change in all positions: (own) *o*N, (old) *o*LD, (boat) B*o*@, (potato) P*o*TeiT*o*, (snow) SN*o*	O	*o*	&	
OR change: AN, ALD, BA@, PATeiTA, SNA	O			A
SHORTEN all: (you) Y*u*, (mule) MY*u*L, (few) FY*u* (use) Y*u*Z, (music) MY*u*Zi:K½, (value) VoLY*u*	U	Y*u*	&	&
Change in all positions: (as) oZ, (bad) BoD, (am) oM, (knapsack) NoPSoK½, (flat) FLo@	a	o	&	&
CHANGE before G,L,M,N,V: (every) i:V*iR*:i:, (end) i:ND (leg) Li:G (bell) Bi:L (them) *T*i:M	e	i:(gLmNv	&	&
AND change before R: (error) *iR*:*iR*:	e	*i*(r	&	&
LONGER preceding consonant + vowel: (busy) Bi:Zi:, (visit) Vi:Zi:@, (within) Wi:*T*i:N	i	i:(¢*	&	&
AND longer before final consonant: (if) i:F, (critic) K*R*:i:Ti:K½, (in) i:N, (bit) Bi:@	i	i:(.¢	&	&
BUT change before two consonants: (lift) L*i*FT, (insist) *i*NS*i*ST, (print) P*R*:*i*NT	i	*i*(¢¢	&	&
Change in all positions: (odd) *o*D, (hopscotch) H*o*PSK*oC*, (clock) KL*o*K½, (drop) D*R*:*o*P, (fog) F*o*G	o	*o*	&	
OR change: *i*D, H*i*PSK*iC*, KL*i*¼, D*R*:*i*P, F*i*G	o			*i*
Change in all positions: (touch) T*uC*, (love) L*u*V, (up) *u*P, (does) D*u*Z, (was) W*u*Z	u	*u*	&	&
Change in all positions: (calm) K*i*LM, (spa) SP*i*, (watch) W*iC*, (gala) G*i*L*i*, (swan) SW*i*N	*A*	*i*	&	&
OR before R: (far) FA*R*:, (star) STA*R*:	*A*			A(r
CHANGE: (burn) B*iR*:N, (girl) G*iR*:L, (word) W*iR*:D, (first) F*iR*:ST, (were) W*iR*:	*E*	*i*	&	&
BUT when initial or medial ER or EAR: (earn) A*R*:N, (nerve) NA*R*:V, (heard) HA*R*:D	*E*	-/A$ erEAR	&	&
No change: (predict) P*R*:*I*D*i*KT	*I*	*I*		
Change in all positions: (about) *i*B*iU*:@, (how) H*iU*:, (found) F*iU*:ND, (ounce) *iU*:NS, (now) N*iU*:	*O*	*iU*:	&	&
SHORTEN all: (too) T*u*, (lose) L*u*Z, (rule) *R*:*u*L, (soup) S*u*P, (blue) BL*u*, (shoe) *Su*, (flew) FL*u*	*U*	*u*		&
OR no change: T*U*, L*U*Z, *R*:*U*L, S*U*P, BL*U*, *SU*, FL*U*	*U*		*U*	
Change in all positions: (ask) oSK½, (laugh) LoF, (plant) PLoNT, (and) oND, (bath) Bo*t*	*a*	o	&	&
No change: (title) TuET*e*L, (dozen) DuZ*e*N	*e*	*e*	&	&
DROP when weak: (family) FoM¼Li:, (system) S*i*ST¼M, (women) Wi:M¼N, (pajama) P¼J*i*M*i*	*i*	¼"½	&	&

Key:

" when	- initially	*C* church	: stronger	*S* show, sure
& as shown	/ medially	(preceding	½ weak(er)	*t* thin, bath
$ spelled	. finally	¢ consonant	@ glottal stop	*T* them, with
* vowel(s)		*R* trilled R		¼ dropped

GENERAL SCOTTISH - EDINBURGH, EDUCATED - BRAEMAR, HIGHLAND

GUIDE PAGES	SOUND	General Scottish	Edinburgh Educated Scots	Braemar Highland Scots
SHORTEN if spelled A,AU,AW: (all) o½L, (saw) So½, (caught), Ko½@, (talk) To½K½, (cause) Ko½Z	o	o½$a au aw	&	&
BUT change if spelled O,OA,OU (except before R): (off) oF, (broad) BR:oD, (ought) o@	o	o$oOA ou!(r	&	&
BUT before R if spelled O,OO,OU,OA: (door) DuR:, (form) FuR:M, (court) KuR:@, (board) BuR:D	o	u$oOO oaOU(r	&	&
LONGER sound: (book) BUK½, (full) FUL, (put) PU@, (would) WUD, (good) GUD, (wolf) WULF	u	U	&	&
Change in all positions: (noise) NiEZ, (toy) TiE, (point) PiENT, (oil) iEL, (boy) BiE	oE	iE	&	&

No change	B	B	&	&
No change: (church) CiR:C, (future) FYuCiR:	C	C	&	&
No change	DFGHJ	D F G H J		
Weaker finally: (cake) KeiK½, (ink) iNK½, (neck) Ni:K½, (risk) R:iSK½, (thank) toNK½	K	.K½	&	
OR drop finally: Kei¼, i:N¼, Ni:¼, R:i:S¼	K			.¼
DROP finally after AW,OO,YOO: (cool) Ku¼, (small) SMo½¼; (fuel) FYu¼, (tall) To½¼	L			.¼)o, U or U
OR no change: KuL, SMo½L, FYuL, To½L	L	L	&	
No change	MNPQ	M N P Q		
STRONG TRILL: (rear) R:i:R:, (very) ViR:i:, (dry) DR:uE, (alright) o½LR:uE@, (for) FuR:	R	R:	&	&
No change	S	S	&	&
No change: (show) So, (sure) SuR:	S	S	&	&
No change: (outset) iU:se@, (waits) Weis	s	s	&	&
GLOTTAL STOP if spelled TT: (little) Li@eL, (bottle) Bo@eL, (better) Be@eR:	T	/@$tt	&	&
" " finally after vowel: (sit) Si:@, (tight) TuE@, (street) STR:i:@	T	.@)*	&	&
" " " after R: (court) KuR:@, (skirt) SKiR:@, (part) PiR:@	T	.@)r	&	&
" " medially before vowel after R: (important) iMPuR:@iNT, (turtle) TiR:@eL	T	/@(*)r	&	&
No change: (thing) tiNG, (north) NuR:t	t	t	&	&
DROP from WITH: Wi¼	T			¼with
OR no change: Wi:T, (other) uTiR:, (they) Tei	T	T	&	
DROP finally: (involve) iNViL¼, (give) Gi¼, (have) Ho¼, (of) u¼, (five) FuE¼, (wave) Wei¼	V			.¼
OR no change: iNVoLV, Gi:V, HoV, uV, FuEV	V	V	&	
CHANGE when spelled WH: (nowhere) NoH:WiR:, (when) H:Wi:N, (what) H:Wu@, (why) H:WuE	W	H:W $ wh	&	&
No change	X	X	&	&
No change: (zoo) Zu, (busy) Bi:Zi:, (his) Hi:Z	Z	Z	&	&
No change: (measure) MeziR:, (vision) VíziN	z	z	&	&

Key:
& as shown ¼ dropped ! excepting : stronger @ glottal stop
$ spelled / medially (preceding ½ weakened R trilled R
. finally) following * vowel(s)

MASTER CATEGORY 13

FRENCH

One of the first dialects I remember hearing as a child was that of Jeanette, the wife of our family friend, Claude Richards. To this day I can hear her, a slight tinge of exasperation in her voice, saying "Cloh-d." And since I became an adult, I have numbered native-born French people among my closest friends, in North and South America, in Europe, and during numerous stays in the south of France.

It was there I learned to listen for the Italian influence that underlies the *Nice, Southern* subdialect. From my Belgian friends in Stockholm I spotted the Germanic influence that shapes the *Bruxelles, Belgian* subdialect—and from my many stays in Geneva, I came to recognize the internationally influenced *Geneva, Educated Swiss* subdialect—which is the "lightest" dialect and closest to American English.

Knowing the history of the French language, it's surprising that there are so few real subdialects. After all, French started as a mixture of Latin and Gallic, then added Frankish and Norse. But as France became a dominant military and cultural force, one single French language took precedence not only at home but as an international language. Some forms of French are still spoken in the western hemisphere: in Quebec, Louisiana, Haiti, Martinique, and French Guiana.

Vowel Changes

The characteristic features of the dialect are its longer vowel sounds and nasalization. The nasalization is caused by sounding the vowels through the nasal passages, instead of through the mouth. Actually, this is not a vowel function per se, but the influence of the consonant that follows the subject vowel. As an illustration, pronounce "ran," "rank," and "rang." Notice how the position of the tongue forms the "n" farther and farther back in the mouth until, on the last word, the air escapes through the nose. Now try "sin," "sink," and "sing": the metamorphosis of the "n" becomes so clear that you can understand how the last sound, "ng," rates its own special symbol in the International Phonetic Alphabet. Nasalization is no more complicated than that: the closing of the oral passage while shaping an "m" or "n" so that the preceding vowel comes out through the nose.

Of course this is not exclusively French; Portuguese has it too, but the dialects are easily distinguishable as French has twice as much nasalization. Let's examine some vowels to see where we find it.

There is only one *compensation reversal* in French, and this is between the (O) of "so" and the (*o*) of "saw." The French change "low" and "close" to "law" and "clause"—so if we saw her "smoky gold coat," and we were from France, we'd describe the:

(SM*o*KE: G*o*L¼ K*o*T).

Since there is a reversal involved here, the (*o*) in turn becomes a shortened version of the "oh" (O½), and "raw" and "bought" end up sounding close to "row" and "boat." Thus if you object to rash international accusations because that "sort of talk causes war," then as a Frenchman, you'll object that that:

(SO½*r*½ ¼) of (TO½K KO½Z*e*Z *i*WO½*r*½).

Now when those sounds come before a nasalized "m" or "n," (see rules of nasalization, page 152) both the (O) sound and the (*o*) are altered into a nasalized "oh" (Ǫ). So if this is his "only home," for the French it will be his:

(ǪN̦LE: ¼ǪM̦).

And if she sang a "haunting song," being French-speaking, we'd call it a:

(¼QNTE:N¼ SQNG).

The nasalized "oh" (Q) is encountered rather often. Besides substituting for the two vowels above, it stands in for three more when they are nasalized: the (o) of "bond," the (u) of "bunk," and the (*i*) of "banana." In the first case, it occurs when the (o) is spelled "o" and precedes a nasalized "m" or "n." Thus an impatient motorist's "prompt honk" is made into her:

(P*r*½QMP¼ ¼QNK).

When the (o) is in other positions, it turns into "aw" (*o*)—so that the discovery that "everybody's not honest" is converted into:

(#aV¼*r*½E:B*o*D=E:S N*o*T *o*N#aS¼).

The (u) of "but" goes through the same two modifications. Normally, it is transformed into (*o*)—thus the question "What does love come from?" becomes:

(*i*W*o*T D=*o*Z L*o*V K*o*M F*r*½QM?).

As you saw in "from," the (u) sound when spelled "o" also shifts to (Q) when nasalized. So that if the things she hadn't finished could be called "among the undone," in French dialect they'd be:

(*A*MQNG) the (uND=QN).

Take a look at the "u" in "undone." When this sound is spelled "u" before a nasalized "m" or "n," it is modified into (u). Thus the soccer player's complaint against an "unjust umpire," to a Frenchman would be against an:

(uN*zo*S¼ uMP*A*E:*r*½).

One more vowel change results in a nasal "oh" (Q). It takes place when the (*i*) of "ago" is spelled "o" before a nasalized "m" or "n"—which means that if he polled his "companions' combined opinions" as to where they'd eat, in this dialect we'd report that he polled his:

(KQMP*A*½NYQNZ KQMP*A*E:NT *A*PE:NYQNS).

As you can see from the "o" in "opinion," a non-nasalized (*i*) is changed into "ah" (*A*)—so our observation that environmentalists want to "connect the political with the natural" comes out in French dialect as:

(K*A*N#aK¼) the (P*A*LE:TE:K*e*L) with the (N*A*½TU*r*½*A*L).

In the word "natural," we find that (a) is turned into a short "ah" (*A*½) in the French dialect. Thus if she "had ransacked his knapsack," the French-born would remark that she:

(¼*A*½D=*r*½*A*NS*A*½KT) his (N*A*½PS*A*½K).

As you can see from "ransacked," the (a) before a nasalized "m" or "n" *when spelled* "a" changes into a nasal "ah" (*A*)—so the "man's angry red bandana" becomes the:

(M*A*NS *A*NG*r*½E:) red (B*A*ND=*A*½N*A*).

There are four other vowel sounds that are made into the nasal "ah" (*A*) before a nasalized "m" or "n"; the others include the (*a*) of "aunt," the (*A*) of "want," the (A) of "paint," and the (e) of "went."

The nasal "ah" (*A*) substitutes for (*a*) when it is spelled "a"—thus the young tree-climber who "can't advance past the slanted branch" would be described by a Frenchman as one who:

(K*A*NT *A*½D=V*A*NS P*A*½S¼) the (SL*A*NT*e*D=B*r*½*A*N*S*:).

From the French version of "past," you can tell what happens to the (*a*) in other positions: it alters into short "ah" (*A*½). So that if the high school coach wanted to "gather the fastest athletes in the class," being from France, he would say he wanted to:

(G*A*½Z*er*½) the (F*A*½ST*e*S¼*A*½SLE:TS) in the (KL*A*½S).

The same transformations happen to "ah" (*A*). Thus, if the doctor advises the overweight man to "start watching his heart," being French-born, the doctor will tell him to:

(ST*A*½*r*½¼ *i*W*A*½*S*:E:N¼) his (¼*A*½*r*½¼).

Again, if spelled "a" before a nasalized "m"

or "n," the "ah" (*A*) shifts to nasal (*A̧*)—so that if the Florida landscaper "wants quantities of palms by the swamp," as a Frenchwoman, she:

(*i*WA̧ŅTS QA̧ŅTE:TE:S) of (PA̧ M̧S) by the (S*i*WA̧M̧P).

As mentioned, a similar substitution takes place with "ay" (A) when spelled "a" before a nasalized "m" or "n." Thus, if de Sade's family had the Marquis imprisoned because their "shameful namesake was insane," for the French this would be because their:

(*S*A̧M̧FAL NA̧M̧SeK) was (ȩŅSA̧Ņ).

The second "a" in "namesake" shows what happens to a non-nasalized "ay" (A): it is shortened to the (e) of "bet"—so that if "they may be late today," being French we'd guess:

(Ze Me) be (LeT *T*UD=̧e).

The (e) of "bet" also is reshaped: into an "open" (#) version of the (a) of "bat." This very French (#a) is made by pronouncing the (a) with a more open throat. Try it: say "bat" and feel the positions of your tongue and throat. Now repeat "bat" with the tongue more depressed and the throat more open for the "a." Thus, if the teacher hadn't finished the lesson because he didn't "expect the bell yet," being French-speaking we'd say it was because he didn't:

(#aXP#aK¼) the (B#aL Y#aT).

However, when this (e) is spelled "e" before a nasalized "m" or "n," it too is transformed into a nasal "ah" (*A̧*). So that if the wording of *Finnegan's Wake* can lead us into "tempting mental benders," the dialect will express it as:

(TA̧M̧PTE:N¼ MA̧ŅTeL BA̧ŅD=̧er½S).

By now you may have the impression that *all* vowels turn into (Q̧) or (*A̧*) when nasalized, but remember that (u) becomes (ų). Another vowel that makes the same change is the "ow" (*O*) of "sound" when spelled "ou." Thus the furniture shopper who sought "out a bouncy rounded lounge," being French-born, would say she sought:

(*A*T) a (BųŅSE: *r*½ųŅD=̧*e*D=̧ LųŅ*z*).

Did you notice what happened to the (*O*) in "out"? Because it didn't precede the "m" or "n," it turned into "ah" (*A*). So if the new campus rules can't "allow loud, shouting crowds now," if we were from France, we'd say they couldn't:

(*A*L*A* L*A*D=̧ *S*ATE:N¼ K*r*½*A*D=̧S N*A*).

One unique nasalization remains: this is what happens to the (i) of "sink" when it is spelled "i" and precedes a nasalized "m" or "n"; it becomes a nasal "eh" (ȩ). Thus, if the Darwinian "insists our instincts are imprinted by time," in the French dialect, he:

(ȩŅSE:STS) our (ȩŅSTȩŅKTS) are (ȩM̧P*r*½ȩŅT*e*D=̧) by time.

In all other positions, the (i) gets lengthened into "eee" (E:) since there are no regular (E)s in French. So if I have to call the newspaper back to see "if the music critic's still busy," as a Frenchman, it would be to see:

(E:F) the (MUZE:K K*r*½E:TE:KS STE:L BE:ZE:).

This lengthening effect applies to "ee" (E) and both diphthongs that are formed with (E): (I), which is (*A*) plus (E), and the "oy" (*o*E) of "boy." These three become respectively, (E:), (*A*E:), and (*o*E:).

Another vowel sound that doesn't exist in French is the (*u*) of "stood." The French replace it with the (*E*) sound of "stirred," making "pull" and "look" sound more like "pearl" and "lurk." Thus, if the fascinated "woman couldn't put the book down," a French person will tell how the:

(*i*W*E*MAN K*E*D=̧N¼ P*E*T) the (B*E*K) down.

Rules of Nasalization

Since it is the nasalization of the "m" and "n" that affects the vowels that come before, let's examine the rules that govern nasalization. There are only two: 1) when an "m" or "n" comes at the end of a phrase and 2) when an "m" or "n" precedes any consonant *except* "m" or "n," either in the middle or at the end of a word. So if the council passes a number of regulations on environment because they expect the "sum total to improve them," the French-speaking would say they expect the:

(SuM ToTeL) to (eMPr½UV ZAM).

And if the psychiatrist was ready to release the patient because he now "enjoyed a sane condition," then a French psychiatrist would do so because his patient now:

(ANzoE:T) a (SAN KOND=E:SYON).

Consonant Changes

You can see that the "c" of "condition" affects the preceding "n" of "sane": this is the result of *liaison*. (We've already encountered this interaction in Russian and a couple of other dialects, but we'll review it here.) Liaison connects the words of a phrase so that the end of one word and the beginning of the next one affect each other. For example, the French pronounce (B) exactly as we do *except* when it precedes a vowel in the middle or at the end of a word; then it is converted into (P). Thus if it was the "baby's habit to grab at things," it becomes the:

(BePE:Z ¼APE:T) to (Gr½A½P A½T) things.

Similarly, the consonant (F) shifts to a (V) when it comes at the end of a word and the following word starts with a vowel. So a lumberjack at a society dinner might watch the other guests to see "if any laugh at his rough edges," but if French-born, it would be to see:

(E:V #aNE: LA½V A½T) his (r½oV #azeS).

Likewise, a final (G) before a vowel is made into a (K). Thus if we say that an elephant has a "leg as big as a tree," as French people we would say it has a:

(L#aK A½S BE:K A½Z) a tree.

A final (D) in the same position becomes a (T)—so if the officer designed an obstacle course and "said he made it as bad as he could," being from France, he:

(S#aT ¼E: MeT E:T) as (BA½T A½Z ¼E: KED=).

The final "d" in "could" shows how to sound the "d" in any other circumstances: it becomes a lowerdental "d" (D=), where the tip of the tongue touches the back of the lower front teeth, and the (D=) is formed by the forward part of the tongue touching the upper gum ridge. Thus if you went to a tax expert because you "needed added deductions," in this dialect you went because you:

(NE:D=eT A½D=eD= D=E: D=oKSYONS).

Other consonant alterations are likely to be more radical because the specific American consonant sound does not exist in French. For example, "ch" (*C*) for the French is a strong "sh" (*S*:). So if the circuit preacher travels from town to town to "preach at each church," a French person would say:

(Pr½E:S:) at (E:S: S:Er½S:).

From the "r"s in "preach" and "church," you can see that the French have no equivalent for the American (R). Instead they use a light variant of the uvular "r" (*r*½). This uvular "r" (*r*), you'll remember, is formed in German like a soft gargling sound, the back of the tongue vibrating against the soft lobe (the uvula) hanging above it. The French (*r*½), however, is less a vibrating sound than a fricative one; in other words, though produced in the same place, it is made by the friction of the air passing through a narrow opening between the back of the tongue and the uvula. A little vibration accompanying the sound, is almost unavoidable—and is still correct French. Thus, if the poetry teacher ignored the doggerel turned in by some students because he felt he could "really disregard poorly written poetry," being French-speaking, he might explain that he felt he could:

(r½E:LE: D=E:Sr½GA½r½¼ PUr½LE: r½E:TeN Po#aTr½E:).

(H) is another sound that doesn't exist in French. Therefore, most French-speaking people treat it as they would in their own language: as a silent letter. So, if the amateur botanist "had her hothouse here,"

being French we'd relate how she:
(¼*A*½T ¼*Er*½ ¼*o*T¼*AZ* ¼E:*r*½).

(J) also has a different pronunciation in French, and this is carried over into the dialect, transforming the (J) of "vegetable" into the (*z*) of "vision." Thus, if seventeen is the minimum age for entry into the services because by then a person is of an "age to judge the stages of danger," in the dialect, one would be of an:
(e*z*) to (*zoz*) the (STe*z*eZ) of (D=ANzer½).

Neither "th" sounds exist in French, so substitutes must be used. The soft "th" (*t*) of "thin" is reshaped into (S)—so if a wise person "thought both paths through" before acting, a Frenchwoman would say they:
(SO½T B*o*S P*A*½S S*r*½*U*).

The hard "TH" is transformed into (Z)—thus, if you'd "rather bathe in smoother weather," the French would say you'd:
(*r*½*A*½*Zer*½ BeZ) in (SM*UZer*½ *i*W#a*Zer*½).

Finally, the French approximation of the "w" in "weather" above shows their inability to make that sound without a little help-vowel to start them off. So if in growing up our choice "was always between wants and whims," being French-born, we'd say it:
(*i*W*o*Z O½L*i*WeS BE:T*i*WE:N *i*WANTZ) and (*i*WE:MS).

(Left) Fortunately for students of the French dialect, there are many readily available dialect models on the screen. Few, however, have been as durable as Yves Montand (shown here in On a Clear Day You Can See Forever, *Paramount, 1970). He and his wife, Simone Signoret, have each appeared in English-speaking roles since the early days of their long film careers. (Right) Alain Delon (shown here in United Artists' 1972* Scorpio*) has portrayed several different nationalities in his many roles in English-speaking films. However, like Montand, he was allowed to retain his French dialect for* Is Paris Burning?, *a film full of authentic dialect and variety role examples, which is often aired on TV.*

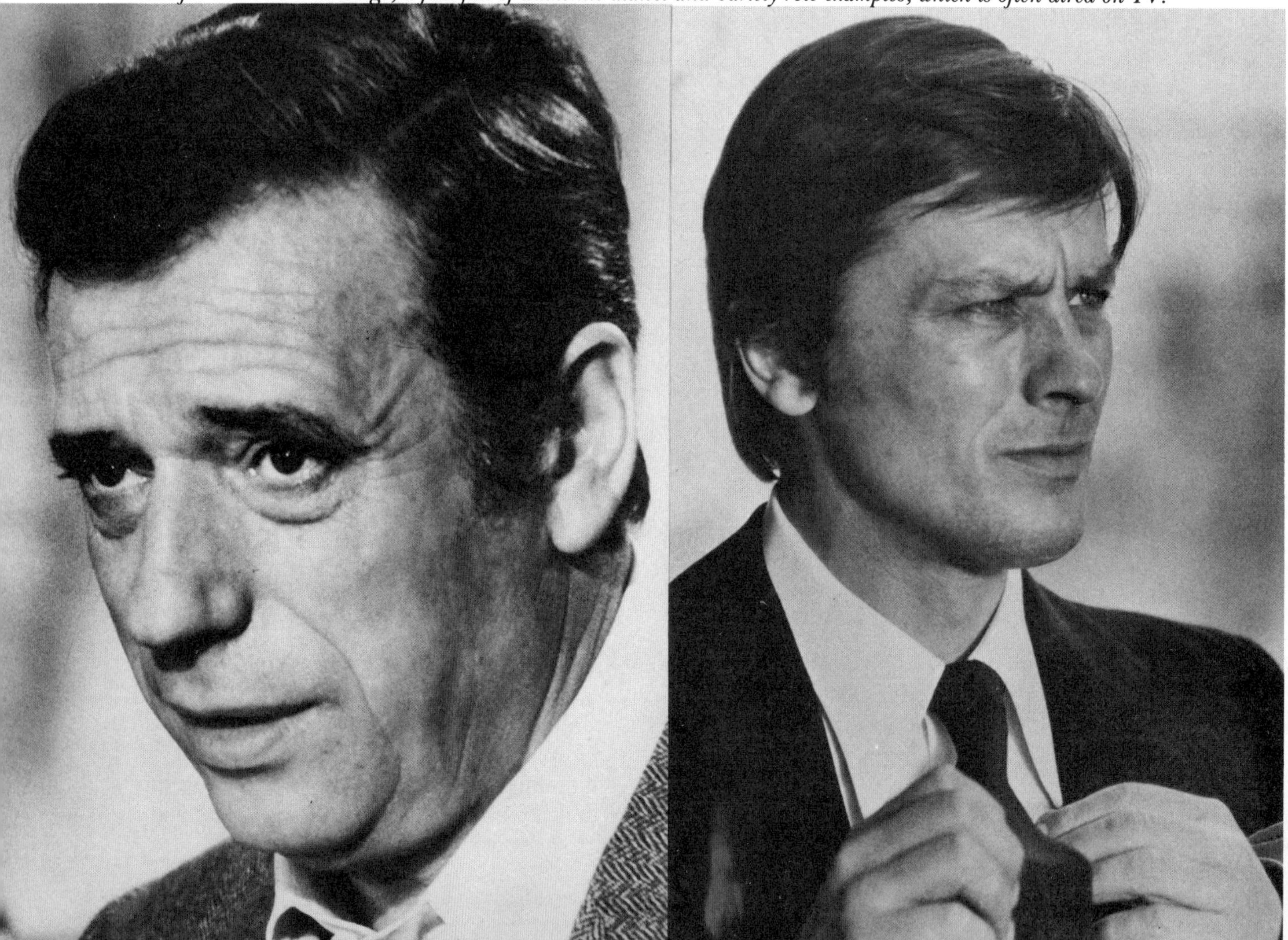

Other variations in vowel and consonant being minor, you can consult the *GUIDE PAGES* for them. Right now, it is more important that we move on to the *music* of the French dialect.

Music, Rhythm, and Pace

First, the dialect is spoken from one-half to one tone higher than American English. Second, its range is rather wider; and, third, it has more up-and-down variety.

Though the liaison makes the music flowing and liquid, at the same time it is heavier because of the French stress. Always stronger than our own, the emphasis usually lights on only one syllable in each polysyllable. In a word of two syllables, it is the final one that is likely to be stressed; for example, where we say English, Swedish, natural, and soldier, the French say *Anglais, Suédois, naturel,* and *soldat*.

As for pace, the dialect is always spoken more rapidly than American English—especially the Parisian subdialect.

Observation and Notes

As for dialect models, there are many: Anouk Aimée, Jean-Paul Belmondo, Charles Boyer, Robert Clary (of *Hogan's Heroes*), Jean-Pierre Aumont, Corinne Calvet, Simone Signoret, Alain Delon, Jeanne Moreau, Yves Montand, and Catherine Deneuve. And for an authentic south-of-France dialect, when playing someone from his own native Marseilles, there is Louis Jourdan.

Louis Jourdan carried off his roles with such élan and suavity that it is easy to identify his speech with that of a Parisian aristocrat. Yet, whether in Streets of Montmartre, Made in Paris *or* Gigi *(MGM, 1958, as seen here with Paris-born Leslie Caron), whenever his roles called for anger or excitement of any kind, his native Marseilles-Nice subdialect shows through.*

GENERAL FRENCH - PARIS - TOULON, RURAL - NICE, SOUTHERN

GUIDE PAGES		General French	Paris French	Toulon Rural	Nice, Southern
CHANGE: (vacate) VeKeT, (made) MeD=̦, (say) Se, (nail) NeL, (ache) eK	A	e	&		
OR change: VaKaT, MaD=̦. Sa, NaL, aK	A			a	
OR change: Ve:GK:e:T, Me:D=̦, Se:, Ne:L	A				e:
AND change before nasalized M or N if spelled A: (name.) NA̦M̦., (sane.) SA̦N̦.	A	A̦$a (M̦,N̦	&	&	&
LONGER sound: (easy) E:ZE:, (believe) BE:LE:V, (see) SE:, (steel) STE:L	E	E:	&	&	&
LONGER sound: (I'll) AE:L, (by) BAE:, (side) SAE:D=̦, (likewise) LAE:K*i*WAE:S	I	AE:		&	&
OR change: Ai:L, BAi:, SAi:D=̦	I		Ai:		
CHANGE: (boat) B*o*T, (smoke) SM*o*K, (old) *o*L¼, (solo) S*o*L*o*, (know) N*o*	O	*o*	&	&	&
AND change before nasalized M or N if spelled O: (only) O̦N̦LE:, (home) ¼O̦M̦	O	O̦$o (M̦,N̦	&	&	&
Change in all positions: (few) FYE*u*, (mule) MYE*u*L, (music) MYE*u*ZE:K	U			YE*u*	
OR no change: FU, MUL, MUZE:K	U	U	&		&
CHANGE: (flag) FLA½G, (had) ¼A½D=̦, (as) A½S, (bad) BA½D=̦, (madcap) MA½D=̦KA½P	a	A½			&
OR change: FL*a*G, ¼*a*D=̦, *a*S, B*a*D=̦	a		*a*		
OR change: FLeG, ¼eD=̦, eS, BeD=̦	a			e	
AND change before nasalized M or N if spelled A: (damp) D=̦A̦M̦P, (man.) MA̦N̦.	a	A̦$a (M̦,N̦	&	&	&
CHANGE: (expect) #aKSP#aK¼, (said) S#aD=̦, (let) L#aT, (dead) D=̦#aD=̦	e	#a	&		
OR change: #AKSP#AK¼, S#AD=̦, L#AT	e			#A	
OR change: *a*GK:SBP:*a*GK:¼, S*a*D=̦, L*a*T	e				*a*
AND change before nasalized M or N if spelled E: (tempt) TA̦M̦P¼, (end.) A̦N̦¼.	e	A̦$e (M̦,N̦	&	&	&

		All 4
CHANGE: (women) *i*WE:MeN, (if) E:F, (busy) BE:ZE:	i	E:
AND change before nasalized M or N when spelled I: (in.) e̦N̦, (imprint.) e̦M̦P*r*½e̦N̦¼. (instinct) e̦N̦STe̦N̦K¼	i	e̦$i (M̦,N̦
CHANGE: (body) B*o*D=̦E:, (clock) KL*o*K, (not) N*o*T	o	*o*
AND change before nasalized M or N if spelled O: (on.) O̦N̦., (prompt)P*r*½O̦M̦P¼, (bronze)B*r*½O̦N̦Z, (honk) ¼O̦N̦K	o	O̦$o (M̦,N̦

		General French	Paris French	Toulon Rural	Nice, Southern
CHANGE: (ugly) *o*GLE:, (hubbub) ¼*o*B*o*B, (love) L*o*V, (blood) BL*o*D=̦, (does) D=̦*o*Z	u	*o*			&
OR change: *E*GLE:, ¼*E*B*E*B, L*E*V, BL*E*D=̦	u		*E*	&	
AND change before nasalized M or N if spelled U: (uncut) U̦N̦K*o*T, (gum.) GU̦M̦.	u	U̦$u (M̦,N̦	&	&	&
AND change before nasalized M or N if spelled O: (among) AMO̦NG, (ton.) TO̦N̦.	u	O̦$o (M̦,N̦	&	&	&
SHORTEN: (car) KA½*r*½ (watch) *i*WA½*C*, (mark) MA½*r*½K (gala) GA½LA½, (spa) SPA½	A	A½			&
OR change: K*ar*½,*i*W*aC*, M*ar*½K,G*a*L*a*, SP*a*	A		*a*	&	
AND change before nasalized M or N if spelled A: (swamp) S*i*WA̦M̦P (wan.) *i*WA̦N̦.	A	A̦$a (M̦,N̦	&	&	&

Key:

C church	& as shown	(preceding	=̦ lower dental
$ spelled	: stronger	*r* uvular R	, nasalized
¼ dropped	½ weakened	*R* trilled R	# open sound

GENERAL FRENCH - PARIS - TOULON, RURAL - NICE, SOUTHERN

GUIDE PAGES		General French	Paris French	Toulon Rural	Nice, Southern
RETAIN with R sound: (merger) M*Er*z*Er*½, (girl) G*Er*½L (work) *i*W*Er*½K (hurl) ¼*Er*½L	*E*	*Er*½	&		
OR retain: MERzER, GERL, *i*WERK, ¼ERL	*E*			*R*	&
No change: (predict)P*r*½*I*D╤E:K¼	*I*	*I*	&	&	&
CHANGE: (out) AT, (how) ¼A, (owl) AL, (loud) LAD╤, (now) NA, (hour) A*r*½	*O*	A	&	&	&
AND change before nasalized M or N if spelled OU: (found.) FųN̦¼. (ounce) ųN̦S	*O*	ų$ou (M̦,N̦	&	&	&
Change in all positions: (boot) BE*u*T, (lose) LE*u*Z, (do) D╤E*u*, (drew) D╤RE*u*	*U*			E*u*	
OR no change: B*U*T, L*U*Z, D╤*U*, D╤*r*½	*U*	*U*	&		&
CHANGE: (after) A½FT*Er*½ (brass) B*r*½A½S, (rather) *r*½A½Z*Er*½, (half) ¼A½F	*a*	A½	&	&	
OR change: AFT*E*R, B:RAS, RAD╤*E*R, ¼AF	*a*				A
AND change before nasalized M or N if spelled A: (dance) D╤ĄN̦S, (and.) ĄN̦¼.	*a*	Ą$a (M̦,N̦	&	&	&
CHANGE in final LE: (apple) A½PL*i*, (muscle) M*o*SL*i*, (simple) SȩM̦PL*i*	*e*	.L*i* $1e	&	&	&
CHANGE: (ago) AG*o*, (machine) MASE:N, (above) AB*o*V, (idea) AE:D╤E:A	*i*	A	&	&	&
OR drop when weak: (pajama) P¼z*a*MA, (system) SE:ST¼M, (family) FeM¼LE:	*i*			¼"½	
AND change before nasalized M or N if spelled O: (combine) KǪM̦BAE:N	*i*	Ǫ$o (M̦,N̦	&	&	&
CHANGE: (all) O½L, (off) O½F, (saw) SO½ (board) BO½*r*½¼ (cause) KO½S (war)*i*WO½*r*½	*o*	O½	&		
OR change: OL, OF, SO, BOR¼, KOS, *i*WOR	*o*			O	&
AND change before nasalized M or N if spelled O: (long) LǪN̦G, (wrong) *r*½ǪN̦G	*o*	Ǫ$o (M̦,N̦	&	&	&
Change in all positions: (book) BEK, (put) PET, (could) KED╤, (woman) *i*WEMAN	*u*	E	&	&	
OR change: B:*U*GK:, BP:*U*T, GK:*U*D╤	*u*				*U*
Change in all positions: (toy) T*o*E:, (choice) *S*:*o*E:S, (boy) B*o*E:	*o*E	*o*E:	&	&	&

STRONGER: (baby) B:e:B:E, (but) B:*o*T, (because) B:E:GK:OZ, (blab) B:LA½B:	B				B:
OR change final & medial before vowel: BePE:, (rub out) *r*½*o*PAT (habit) ¼A½PE:T	B	/.P(*	&	&	
Change in all positions: (cheap) *S*:E:P, (each) E:*S*:, (church) *S*:E*r*½*S*:	C	*S*:	&	&	
OR no change: CE:BP:, E:C, CERC	C				*C*

		All 4
LOWER DENTALIZE: (did) D╤E:D╤, (added) A½D╤*e*D╤, (day) D╤e	D	D╤
BUT drop finally after a consonant: (mind) MAE:N¼, (bird) BE*r*½¼ (cold) K*o*L¼, (send) S#aN¼, (card) KA½*r*½¼	D	.¼)¢
AND change finally before a vowel: (died out) D╤AE:TAT, (bid on) BE:TO½N, (made up) MeT*o*P, (said it) S#aTE:T	D	.T(*
CHANGE finally before vowel: (off of) O½V*o*V	F	.V(*

Key:

& as shown	$ spelled	*R* trilled R	" when	/ medial	╤ lower dental
: stronger	z measure	*S* show,sure	# open	. final	
½ weakened	*r* uvular R	(preceding	¼ drop	* vowels	, nasalized

GENERAL FRENCH - PARIS - TOULON, RURAL - NICE, SOUTHERN

GUIDE PAGES		General French	Paris French	Toulon Rural	Nice, Southern
CHANGE finally before vowel: (big as) BE:K*A*½S, (leg iron) L#aK*A*E:*Er*½N	G	.K(*	&	&	
OR stronger finally: B:E:G:, L*a*G:	G				.G:
AND drop from ING suffix: (living) LE:VE:N¼, (meeting) ME:TE:N¼	G	¼ing)	&	&	&
					All 4
DROP: (hothouse) ¼*o*T¼*A*S, (here) ¼E:*r*½ (had) ¼*A*½Dǂ	H				¼
CHANGE: (judge) z*o*z, (age) ez, (gradual) G*r*½*A*½zU*e*L	J				z
Change in all positions: (ache) e:GK:, (kick) GK:E:GK:, (clock) GK:L*o*GK:	K				GK:
OR no change: eK, KE:K, KL*o*K	K	K	&	&	
					All 4
No change	L				L
NASALIZE medially & finally before consonant except M,N: (sum total) Su̦M̦T*o*T*e*L, (improve) e̦M̦P*r*½*U*V (empty) A̦M̦PTE:	M				/.M̦(¢ ! M N
AND at end of phrase: (flame.) FLA̦M̦., (home.) ¼Q̦M̦.	M				..M̦
NASALIZE medially & finally before consonant except M,N: (tin type) Te̦N̦T*A*E:P, (onto) Q̦N̦T*U*, (until) u̦N̦TE:L	N				/.N̦(¢ ! M N
AND at end of phrase: (noun.) Nu̦N̦., (none.) NQ̦N̦.	N				..N̦
Change in all positions: (pep) BP:*a*BP:, (play) BP:Le:, (up) *o*BP:, (put) BP:*U*T	P				BP:
OR no change: P#aP, Ple, *o*P, P*E*T	P	P	&	&	
No change	Q	Q	&	&	&
ALL are lightly uvular: (rare) *r*½e*r*½, (read) *r*½E:Dǂ (for) FO½*r*½ (dry) Dǂ*r*½*A*E:	R	*r*½	&		
OR TRILL: *R*e*R*, *R*E:Dǂ, FO½*R*, Dǂ*R*AE:	R			*R*	&
					All 4
Change between vowels: (decide) DǂE:Z*A*E:Dǂ (basic) BeZE:K	S				Z/*
Change medially before silent I: (conscious) KQ̦N̦SY*o*S	*S*				/SY(¼i
DROP finally after consonant: (left) L#aF¼, (rest) *r*½#aS¼	T				.¼)¢
Change in all positions: (bath) B*A*½S, (thought) SO½T, (south) SAS, (thin) SE:N	*t*	S	&	&	
OR change: B:*A*Tǂ, TǂOT, SATǂ, TǂE:N	*t*				Tǂ
Change in all positions: (those) Z*o*S, (other) *o*Z*Er*½ (that) Z*A*½T, (with) *i*WE:Z	*T*	Z	&	&	
OR change: Dǂ*o*Z, *o*Dǂ*E*R, Dǂ*A*½T, *i*WE:Dǂ	*T*				Dǂ
No change: (vote) V*o*T, (of) *o*V	V	V	&	&	&
Add "*i*" sound: (was) *i*W*o*S, (which) *i*WE:S: (always) O½L*i*WeS, (between) BE:T*i*WE:N	W	*i*W	&		&
OR change: V*E*S, VE:*C*, OLVaS, BE:TVE:N	W			V	
"KSY" for KS sound: (complexion.) KQ̦MPL#aKSYQ̦N̦., (luxury) L*o*KSY*Er*½E:	X	KSY 4 k*S*	&	&	&
Final S when spelled S: (please) PLE:S, (does) Dǂ*o*S, (use) US, (theirs) Ze*r*½S	Z	.S$s	&	&	
OR no change: BP:LE:Z, Dǂ*o*Z, UZ, Dǂe:*R*Z	Z				Z
ZY if spelled Z or SI: (azure) *A*½ZU*r*½, (illusion.) E:L*U*ZYQ̦N̦. (vision) VE:ZY*o*N	z	ZY$z or si	&	&	&

Key:

& as shown	4 for	/ medially	! excepting	¢ consonant
: stronger	# open	. finally	(preceding	*r* uvular R
* vowels	½ weak	.. " in senten.	) following	*R* trilled R
/* between"	¼ drop	ǂ lowerdental	) in suffix	, nasalized

FRENCH: MARSEILLES, LESS EDUCATED - BRUXELLES, BELGIAN - GENEVA, EDUCATED SWISS

GUIDE PAGES

	SOUND	Marseilles Less Educated	Bruxelles Belgian French	Geneva Educated Swiss French
CHANGE: (ache) eK, (say) Se, (vacate) VeKeT,	A	e	&	
(nail) NeL, (waylay) *i*WeLe, (maybe) MeB:E:				
OR change: eiK, Sei, VeiKeiT, *i*WeiLei	A			ei
AND change before nasalized M or N if spell-	A	A̦$a	&	
ed A: (name.) NA̦M̦. (paint) PA̦N̦T (came.) KA̦M̦.		(M̦,N̦		
LONGER sound: (easy) E:Z:, (steel) STE:L,	E	E:	&	
(teach) TE:C, (believe) B:E:LE:V				
OR no change: EZE, STEL, TEC, B:ELEV	E			E
LONGER sound: (I'll) AE:L, (by) B:AE:, (side)	I	AE:	&	
SAE:D╤, (likewise) LAE:K*i*WAE:Z (try) Tʀ½AE:				
OR change: Ai:L, B:Ai:, SAi:D╤, LAi:K*i*WAi:Z	I			Ai:
SHORTER sound: (smoke) SMO½K, (know) NO½,	O	O½	&	&
(solo) SO½LO½, (old) O½L¼, (below) B:E:L)½				
AND change before nasalized M or N if spelled	O	O̦$o	&	&
O: (only) O̦N̦LE:, (home.) H:O̦M̦., (own.) O̦N̦.		(M̦,N̦		
No change: (use) UZ, (cute) KUT, (few) FU	U	U	&	&
CHANGE: (as) A½Z, (madcap) MA½D╤KA½P,	a	A½	&	
(knapsack) N ½PS ½K, (bad) B: ½D╤				
OR change: *a*Z, M*a*D╤K*a*P, N*a*PS*a*K, B:*a*D╤	a			*a*
AND change before nasalized M or N if spelled	a	A̦$a	&	&
A: (man.) MA̦N̦., (am.) A̦M̦., (stamp) STA̦M̦P		(M̦,N̦		
CHANGE: (let) L#aT, (expect) #aKSP#aKT, (said)	e	#a		
S#aD╤, (bedstead) B:#aD╤ST#aD╤, (smell) SM#aL				
OR longer: Le:T, e:GK:SBP:e:GK:T, Se:D╤	e		e:	&
AND change before nasalized M or N if spelled	e	A̦$e	&	
E: (sent) SA̦N̦T, (tempt) TA̦M̦PT, (end.) A̦N̦¼.		(M̦,N̦		
OR change: Se̦NT, Te̦MPT, e̦N̦D╤	e			e̦$e(M̦,N̦
OPEN sound: (if) #iF, (dig) D╤#iG, (critic)	i	#i	&	&
Kʀ½#iT#iK (busy) B:#iZE:, (visit) V#iZ#iT				
AND change before nasalized M or N if spelled	i	e̦$i	&	
I: (imprint) e̦MPʀ½e̦NT, (infringe) e̦NFʀ½e̦N̦z		(M̦,N̦		
CHANGE: (clock) KL*o*½K, (hobnob) H:*o*½B:N*o*½B:,	o	*o*½		&
(not) N*o*½T, (stop) ST*o*½P, (fog) F*o*½G				
OR change: GK:L*o*GK:, H:*o*BN*o*B, N*o*T, ST*o*BP:	o		*o*	
AND change before nasalized M or N if spelled	o	O̦$o	&	&
O: (on.) O̦N̦., (prompt) Pʀ½O̦MPT (honk) H:O̦N̦K		(M̦,N̦		

		All 3
CHANGE: (up) *o*P, (love) L*o*V, (was) *i*W*o*Z, (does) D╤*o*Z	u	*o*
AND change before nasalized M or N if spelled U: (uncut)	u	u̦$u
u̦N̦K*o*T, (pump) Pu̦MP, (hunt) H:u̦N̦T, (sum.) Su̦M̦.		(M̦,N̦
AND change before nasalized M or N if spelled O: (among)	u	O̦$o
AMO̦N̦G, (front) Fʀ½O̦N̦T (son.) SO̦N̦.		(M̦,N̦
SHORTEN: (car) KA½ʀ½ (watch) *i*WA½C, (spa) SPA½ (are) A½ʀ½	A	A½
AND change before nasalized M or N if spelled A: (wand.)	A	,$a
*i*WA̦N̦¼., (swamp) S*i*WA̦M̦P, (swan.) S*i*WA̦N̦.		(M̦,N̦
RETAIN with R sound: (merger) MEʀ½zEʀ½(girl) GEʀ½L	E	Eʀ½

Key:

C church	& as shown	z measure	╤ lowerdental
# open	: stronger	$ spelled	(preceding
. final	½ weakened	¼ dropped	ʀ uvular R
			, nasalized

FRENCH: MARSEILLES, LESS EDUCATED - BRUXELLES, BELGIAN - GENEVA, EDUCATED SWISS

GUIDE PAGES	SOUND	Marseilles Less Educated	Bruxelles Belgian French	Geneva Educated Swiss French
No change: (predict)P*ʀ*½*I*Dǂ#iKT	*I*	*I*	&	&
No change: (out) *O*T, (how) H:*O* (cloud) KL*O*Dǂ	*O*	*O*	&	&
BUT change before nasalized M or N if spelled OU: (found.) Fu̦N̦¼., (mountain) Mu̦N̦TAN	*O*	u̦$ou (M̦,N̦	&	&
No change: (boot) B:*U*T, (do) Dǂ*U*, (drew) Dǂ*ʀU*	*U*	*U*	&	&
CHANGE: (after) A½FT*Eʀ*½ (rather)*ʀ*½A½Dǂ*Eʀ*½ (ask) A½SK, (brass) B:*ʀ*½A½S (half) H:A½F	*a*	A½	&	&
AND change before nasalized M or N if spelled A: (can't) KA̦N̦T, (dance) DǂA̦N̦S, (lamp) LA̦M̦P	*a*	A̦$a (M̦,N̦	&	&
CHANGE in final LE: (muscle) M*o*SL*i*, (apple) A½PL*i*, (simple) Se̦M̦PL*i*, (title) TAE:TL*i*	*e*	.L*i* $le	&	
OR no change: M*o*S*e*L, *a*P*e*L, S#iMP*e*L, TAi:T*e*L	*e*			*e*
CHANGE: (above) AB:*o*V (idea) AE:DǂE:A (extra) #aXT*ʀ*A, (pajama) PAzA½MA, (family) FA½MALE:	*i*	A	&	
OR change: *E*B:*o*V, Ai:DǂE:*E*, eXT*ʀE*, P*E*zA½ME	*i*			*E*
AND change before nasalized M or N if spelled O: (combine) KO̦M̦B:AE:N, (action.) A½KSYO̦N̦.	*i*	O̦$o (M̦,N̦	&	
SHORTEN: (all) *o*½L, (off) *o*½F, (war) *i*W*o*½*ʀ*½ (cause) K*o*½Z, (board) B:*o*½*ʀ*½¼ (saw) S*o*½	*o*	*o*½	&	&
AND change before nasalized M or N if spelled O: (song) SO̦N̦G, (long) LO̦N̦G, (wrong)*ʀ*½O̦N̦G	*o*	O̦$o (M̦,N̦	&	
CHANGE: (woman) *i*W*E*MAN, (book) B:*E*K, (put) P*E*T, (could) K*E*Dǂ, (good) G*E*Dǂ, (pull) P*E*L	*u*	*E*		&
OR change: V*U*MAN, B:*U*GK:, BP:*U*T, GK:*U*Dǂ	*u*		*U*	
LONGER: (choice) *Co*E:S, (boy) B:*o*E:, (oil) *o*E:L, (avoid) AV*o*E:Dǂ, (enjoy) A̦N̦z*o*E:	*o*E	*o*E:	&	&

STRONGER: (baby) B:eB:E:, (but) B:*o*T, (bob) B:*o*½B:, (because) B:E:K*o*½Z, (bulb) B:*o*LB:	B	B:		&
OR change finally & medially before a vowel: BePE:, (rub out)*ʀ*½*o*P*O*T, (habit) H:A½P#iT	B		/.P(*	
No change: (church) *CEʀ*½*C* (future) FU*CEʀ*½	C	C	&	&
LOWER DENTALIZE: (did) Dǂ#iDǂ, (good) G*E*Dǂ, (added) A½Dǂ*e*Dǂ, (credit)K*ʀ*½#aDǂ#iT	D	Dǂ	&	&
BUT drop finally after consonant: (mind) MAE:N¼, (bird) B:*Eʀ*½¼ (cold) KO½L¼	D	.¼)¢	&	
OR change finally before vowel: (died out) DǂAE:T*O*T (bid on) B#iT*o*N, (did up) Dǂ#iT*o*BP:	D		.T(*	
CHANGE finally before a vowel: (laugh at) LA½VA½T, (off of) *o*½V*o*V, (if any) #iV#aNE:	F	.V(*		&
OR no change: LA½FA½T, *o*½F*o*FV:, #iFe:NE:	F		F	
CHANGE finally before a vowel: (big as) B:#iKA½Z, (leg iron) L#aKAE:*Eʀ*½N	G	.K(*	&	
OR stronger finally: Le:G:, B:#iG:	G			.G:
AND drop from ING suffix: (coming) K*o*M#iN¼, (meeting) ME:T#iN¼, (living) L#iV#iN¼	G	¼ing}		

Key:

4 for	(preceding	z measure	, nasalized	& as shown
# open	) following	$ spelled	¢ consonants	: stronger
¼ drop	} in suffix	/ medial	ǂ lowerdental	½ weakened
* vowels		. finally		*ʀ* uvular R

FRENCH: MARSEILLES, LESS EDUCATED - BRUXELLES, BELGIAN - GENEVA, EDUCATED SWISS

GUIDE PAGES

	SOUND	Marseilles Less Educated	Bruxelles Belgian French	Geneva Educated Swiss French
		All 3		
STRONGER: (hothouse) H:A½TH:*O*S, (behind) B:E:H:AE:N¼	H	H:		
CHANGE: (judge) *zoz*, (gradual) Gʀ½A½zUeL, (age) ez	J	z		
Change in all positions: (ache) eGK:, (kick) GK:#iGK:, (clock) GK:L*o*GK:, (cake) GK:eGK:	K		GK:	
OR no change: eK, K#iK, KL*o*½K, KeK	K	K		&
No change:	L	L	&	&
NASALIZE medially & finally before consonant except M or N: (sum total) SųM̦TO½TeL (empty) A̧M̦PTE:, (improve) ȩM̦Pʀ½*U*V (humble) H:ųM̦B:L*i*	M	/.M̦(¢ ! M N	&	&
AND NASALIZE at end of phrase: (same.) SA̧M̦., (home.) H:Q̧M̦., (them.) D=̦A̧M̦., (slim.) SLȩM̦.	M	..M̦	&	&
NASALIZE medially & finally before consonant except M or N: (tin type) TȩN̦TAE:P, (until) ųN̦T#iL, (onto) Q̧N̦T*U*, (only) Q̧N̦LE:	N	/.N̦(¢ ! M N	&	&
AND NASALIZE at end of phrase: (noun.) NųN̦., (run.) ʀ½ųN̦. (pen.) PA̧N̦., (none.) NQ̧N̦.	N	..N̦	&	&
Change in all positions: (pep) BP:e:BP:, (play) BP:Le, (up) *o*BP:, (put) BP:*U*T	P		BP:	
OR no change: P#aP, PLe, *o*P, P*E*T	P	P		&
		All 3		
No change	Q	Q		
Lightly uvular: (rare) ʀ½eʀ½, (read) ʀ½E:D=̦, (try) Tʀ½AE:	R	ʀ½		
Change between vowels: (decide) D=̦E:ZAE:D=̦ (basic) B:eZ#iK	S	Zǂ		
Change medially before I: (motion.) MO½SYQ̧N̦.	*S*	/SY(i		
DROP finally between consonants: (left hand) L#aF¼H:A½N¼	T	.¼₵		
Change in all positions: (thought) T=̦*o*½T, (bath) B:A½T=̦, (thin) T=̦#iN, (south) S*O*T=̦	*t*	T=̦	&	
OR change: T=*o*½T, B:A½T=, T=#iN, S*O*T=	*t*			T=
Change in all positions: (those) D=̦O½Z, (other) *o*D=̦*E*ʀ½ (that) D=̦A½T, (with) *i*W#iD=̦	*T*	D=̦	&	
OR change: D=O½Z, *o*D=*E*ʀ½, D=*a*T, *i*W#iD=	*T*			D=
Change in all positions: (vote) FV:O½T, (of) *o*FV:, (involve) ȩN̦FV:*o*LFV:, (over) O½FV:*E*ʀ½	V		FV:	
OR no change: VO½T, *o*V, ȩN̦V*o*½LV, O½V*E*ʀ½	V	V		&
ADD "*i*" sound: (was) *i*W*o*Z, (which) *i*W#iC, (always) *o*½L*i*WeZ, (between) B:E:T*i*WE:N	W	*i*W		&
OR change: V*o*S, V#iC, *o*½LVeS, BE:TVE:N	W		V	
KSY for "k*S*" sound: (luxury) L*o*KSY*E*ʀ½E:, (complexion) KQ̧M̦PL#aKSY*o*N	X	KSY 4k*S*	&	&
Final S when spelled S: (please) BP:LE:S, (does) D=̦*o*S, (use) US, (theirs) D=̦e:ʀ½S	Z		.S$s	
OR no change: PLE:Z, D=̦*o*Z, UZ, D=̦#aʀ½Z	Z	Z		&
ZY if spelled Z or SI: (azure) A½ZUʀ½, (illusion.) #iL*U*ZYQ̧N̦., (vision.) V#iZYQ̧N̦.	z	ZY$z or si	&	
OR no change: *a*zUʀ½, #iL*U*zQ̧N̦., V#izQ̧N̦.	z			z

Key:

C church	& as shown	= interdental	! excepting	¢ consonants
4 for	$ spelled	=̦ lowerdental	(preceding	₵ between "
# open	: stronger	.. end of phrase	ʀ uvular R	/ medially
¼ drop	½ weakened	ǂ between vowels	, nasalized	. finally

The Beatles not only made Liverpool Cockney "a sound heard round the world," but they also raised the speaking of it to a fad for two generations of young Britons. Coming to dominate British speech increasingly, it now stands almost shoulder-to-shoulder with "proper" British English, and has gained such acceptance that it may well emerge as the dominant variety spoken in England.

MASTER CATEGORY 14

COCKNEY

Can you imagine anyone writing a world-class, record-breaking musical about a girl who comes up in the world by losing her Brooklyn accent? Of course not. And therein lies the difference between Flatbush and Cockney, for Henry Higgins's point in *My Fair Lady* was that the economic caste system of the time defined Londoners by how they spoke—with Cockney at the bottom of the pile.

Although George Bernard Shaw, the author of *Pygmalion*, on which *My Fair Lady* is based, was making a social comment, the device he chose to illustrate the point was a variety then barely over a hundred years old. Since then the Cockney variety (generally confined to those born within the sound of the bells of St. Mary-le-Bow Church) has infiltrated New York, Australia, New Zealand, and lately "proper" London speech itself.

As Professor Higgins observed in the play, the subvarieties of Cockney are so distinct that he could often identify even the *street* on which a particular speaker was raised. In the *GUIDE PAGES* that follow, we'll be looking at three forms (or degrees) of Cockney. General Cockney is both the main variety and the median form; *Cockney Worker* represents the most extreme degree of the variety. You'll find several instances where I have given *both* General and *Worker Cockney*, for the differences between the two can be so great as to make them nearly two distinct varieties.

Finally, there is *Liverpool Cockney*, the lightest form and the one that (through the Beatles and other rock groups) has infiltrated "proper" British speech. This "Liverpool" form is the result of Cockney workers migrating from London to Liverpool and taking their speech patterns with them. A similar thing happened during the Second World War, when southern California was flooded with defense workers from Oklahoma and Arkansas. Consequently, within a mere twenty years, that area's (and eventually the whole nation's) concept of "proper" American speech was transformed.

There is still a similarity between Cockney and Australian, but we'll investigate the Anzac dialect in its own chapter. Here we'll concentrate on the "earmarks" of Cockney. In the area of consonants, these include the use of the glottal stop (@), the handling of the "l" sound, the "h," and the "hard TH" (*T*). However, the truest yardstick of Cockney uniqueness is found in its vowels.

Vowel Changes

Three-quarters of the vowel sounds in Cockney are different from American English; forty percent are longer. This elongation applies especially to the diphthongs, one of which is even stretched into a triphthong.

This sound is the one that triggers the *My Fair Lady* number, "Why Can't the English?" with Eliza Doolittle's version of "Oh!" Our (O)—part "aw" (*o*), part "oo" (*U*)—becomes a really remarkable sound in Cockney Worker, made up of the (a) of "an," the "ah" (*A*) of "swan," and the "oo" (*Ū*) of "swoon." Thus, if our friend lives on the river and points out his houseboat as the "only old boat I own," in his Cockney Worker dialect he'd say it's the:

(HaONL*i*E HaOL¼ BaO@ *o*E HaON).

On the other hand, General Cockney makes (O) into a combination of the (u) of "fund" and the (*O*) of "found," changing the above statement into the:

(u*O*NL*i*E u*O*L½D Bu*O*@ *oA* u*O*N).

As you can see, another diphthong that gives us two widely different readings is (I), consisting of "ah" (*A*) and "ee" (E). For the Cockney Worker, this sound turns into the double vowel (*o*E), as in "boy." Thus, if they say 'sunset,' "they likewise might say 'twilight'," becomes:

(D*A*:E L*o*EKW*o*EZ M*o*E@ S*A*:E TW*o*EL*o*E@).

However, in General Cockney it becomes:

(VuE L*oA*KW*oA*Z M*oA*@ SuE TW*oA*L*oA*@),

since General Cockney makes (I) into "aw" plus "ah" (*oA*).

"They" and "say" as just given in Worker and General Cockney are our first examples of diphthong "half changes." (A) is actually the (e) of "bet" joined with the (E) of "beat." Both General and Worker Cockney retain the second sound, (E), while altering the first one. General Cockney replaces the (e) with (u) as in "but"—so that if the trip "may take you eight days," in the main variety, the trip:

(MuE TuEK iY*i*U uE@ DuEZ).

The Worker subvariety, however, substitutes a long "ah" (*A*:) for the (e), so that for them the trip:

(M*A*:E T*A*:EK iYi*U* *A*:E@ D*A*:EZ).

The word "you" above provides us with a new approach to the diphthong. Neither of the original sounds (Y) and (*U*) are changed, but both are *preceded* with the (i) of "sit." Thus, when listening to the radio, very "few tune out beautiful music," in Cockney is transformed into very:

(FiYi*U* TiYi*U*N *Ai*@ BiYi*U*T*e*F*u*L MiYi*U*Zi@).

The "ow" (*O*) sound of "out" above consists of "ah" (*A*) and "oo" (*U*). This double vowel also goes through a half change—but which half changes depends on what you're speaking. If it is General Cockney, the *second* half alters into the (*i*) of "ago"—so that if you returned after ten years and "found our town crowded now," the main variety would say that you:

(F*Ai*ND *Ai*¼ T*Ai*N KR*Ai*D*e*D N*Ai*).

The Worker's subvariety alters the *first* half of the diphthong into the (a) sound of "at." Thus the same phrase would tell us you:

(Fa*U*N¼ a*U*¼ Ta*U*N KRa*U*D*e*D Na*U*).

In the Cockney variety, even simple single vowels can be transformed into diphthongs. For example, "ee" (E) gets introduced by (i)—so that if "he seemed to believe me," the Cockney would observe that:

(¼*i*E S*i*EM*e*D Tu*U* B*i*EL*i*EV M*i*E).

The "to" in that phrase illustrates a second case: the prefacing of "oo" (*U*) with the (u) of "but." Thus, if our guide briefed us so that we "soon knew whose tour group was to move first," in Cockney we would report that we:

(Su*U*N Nu*U* ¼uUZ Tu*U*¼ GRu*U*P) was (Tu*U* Mu*U*V) first.

While the previous two vowels merely *added on* sounds, several simple vowels are altered completely. The (a) of "bad," for example, shifts into (e) as in "bed." So that if "Iran had acted mad at Baghdad," a Cockney would describe how:

(iReN ¼eD eKT*e*D MeD e@ BeGDeD).

Another example is the conversion of the (*i*) of "ago" into the (*E*) sound of "urge." Thus, if the zoo keeper gave the monkey an "extra banana," the Cockney observation would be that he gave him an:

(e½XTR*E* B*E*NeN*E*).

The next two vowels, (u) and (*a*), are both modified into the same sound: "ah" (*A*). Thus "won" turns into "wan"—and if the censor approved of *Blue Lagoon* because she didn't think "young love was ugly," being Cockney, she wouldn't think:

(Y*A*NG L*A*V W*A*Z *A*GL*i*E).

As with other British subvarieties, the (*a*) of

"aunt" also broadens—so if the shy sophomore's partner lags behind the beat because he "can't ask the lass to dance faster," the Cockney would explain that the boy:

(KANT ASK) the (LAS) to (DANS FASTe¼).

Strangely enough, the "ah" sound itself changes too, into a long "aww" (*o*:). Thus, if the groundkeeper warns that the "garden harbors a large squad of wasps," if he's a Cockney, he would tell us that the:

(G*o*:¼DeN ¼*o*:¼Be¼Z) a (L*o*:J SKW*o*:D) of (W*o*:SPS).

The (o) of "cot" is also transformed into a long version of the (*o*) of "caught." So that, if after all their work they still had "not gotten a topnotch, solid operation," then the Cockney variety would comment that they had:

(N*o*:@ G*o*:TeN) a (T*o*:PN*o*:*C*, S*o*:LiD *o*:PeRuES*E*N).

Not surprisingly, the (*o*) itself is generally lengthened into (*o*:)—so that if the barrister argued that by "law, the court ought to order a halt," being a Cockney, he would argue that by:

(L*o*:) the (K*o*:¼@ *o*:@) to (*o*:¼De¼) a (¼*o**U*L½@).

What happened to that last "aw" in "halt" came about because it was affected by the weak "l" (L½) that followed it and therefore had an "oo" (*U*) appended to it. Thus, if you think that "false talk always causes trouble," being a Cockney, you would point out that:

(F*o**U*L½S T*o**U*L½K *o**U*L½¼uEZ K*o*:Z*e*Z TRAB*U*L½).

Consonant Changes

As you can tell from "trouble," a final "le" is also influenced by the "l" being weak, with the result that when it follows a consonant, it is transformed into (*U*L½). So if the king always used an alias on archeological trips because his "title might rattle simple people," a Cockney would suggest he used the alias because his:

(T*o**A*@*U*L½) might (Re@*U*L½ SiMP*U*L½P:EP*U*L½).

There are other occasions when the "l" is weak: in the Worker subvariety, *all* final "l"s are weak (L½). Thus the statement, "if I feel ill I will tell you" becomes:

if I (F*i*EL½ HiL½) I (WiL½ TiL½) you.

When an "l" follows a vowel and precedes a consonant, it becomes weak in all Cockney varieties. So that if reading a certain book can "help build self-worth," the Cockney would advise that it could:

(¼e½L½P BiL½D Se½L½F W*E*¼*t*).

The rendering of "r" in "worth" above illustrates how it too is affected by following a vowel and preceding a consonant; it is simply dropped (¼). Thus, if no one "cares to earn harsh words," the Cockney would remark that no one:

(KuE¼Z) to (*E*¼N ¼*o*:¼*S* W*E*¼DZ).

The phenomenon of *liaison* (linking the final letter of one word to the beginning of the next word) insures that whenever an "r" ends a word, unless the next word starts with a vowel, the "r" is omitted. So if the psychologist can offer his patient a "sure cure for her fear," if he were Cockney, he'd talk of a:

(*S*u*U*¼ KiYi*U*¼ F*o*:R ¼*E*¼ F*i*E¼).

Liaison is at work in the rules for three other conversions: the first is that a final "d" before an initial "y" turns it into a "j." Thus the quote: "I asked, 'Did you have a bad year?' and he said, 'Yes.'" comes out:

I asked, (DiJiYi*U*) have a (BeJ*i*ER?) and he (Se½Je½S).

The second conversion affects the final "k," which shifts into a glottal stop (@) *except* after a consonant or before a vowel. A glottal stop, you'll remember, is a sharp cutting off of air and sound by closing the throat (for a more thorough explanation, see page 145). To illustrate this rule: if we have to have sympathy for a "weak bloke like Mac," a Cockney will say we should feel sorry for a:

(W*i*E@ BLu*O*@ LuE@ Me@).

The third letter affected by liaison is the final "t" when it follows a "k," "p," or "s" and does not precede a vowel. In those cases, the "t" is eliminated (¼). Thus, if a lack of time were to "interrupt the reporters' last fact-gathering fest," for the Cockney, it would:

(iNT*E*RAP¼) the reporters' (L*A*S¼ FeK¼) gathering (Fe½S¼).

Except for that instance, a final "t" *always* becomes a glottal stop (@) in Cockney. So if our friend asked of a certain matter "that we let that sit tight," in the Cockney variety, she would ask:

(Ve@) we (Le½@ Ve@ Si@ To*A*@).

This replacement can also take place in the middle of a word: 1) before an "le" or 2) before a weak vowel and an "l." Thus, if the lovers fought a "subtle little battle," it would be a:

(S*A*@*U*L½ Li@*U*L½ Be@*U*L½),

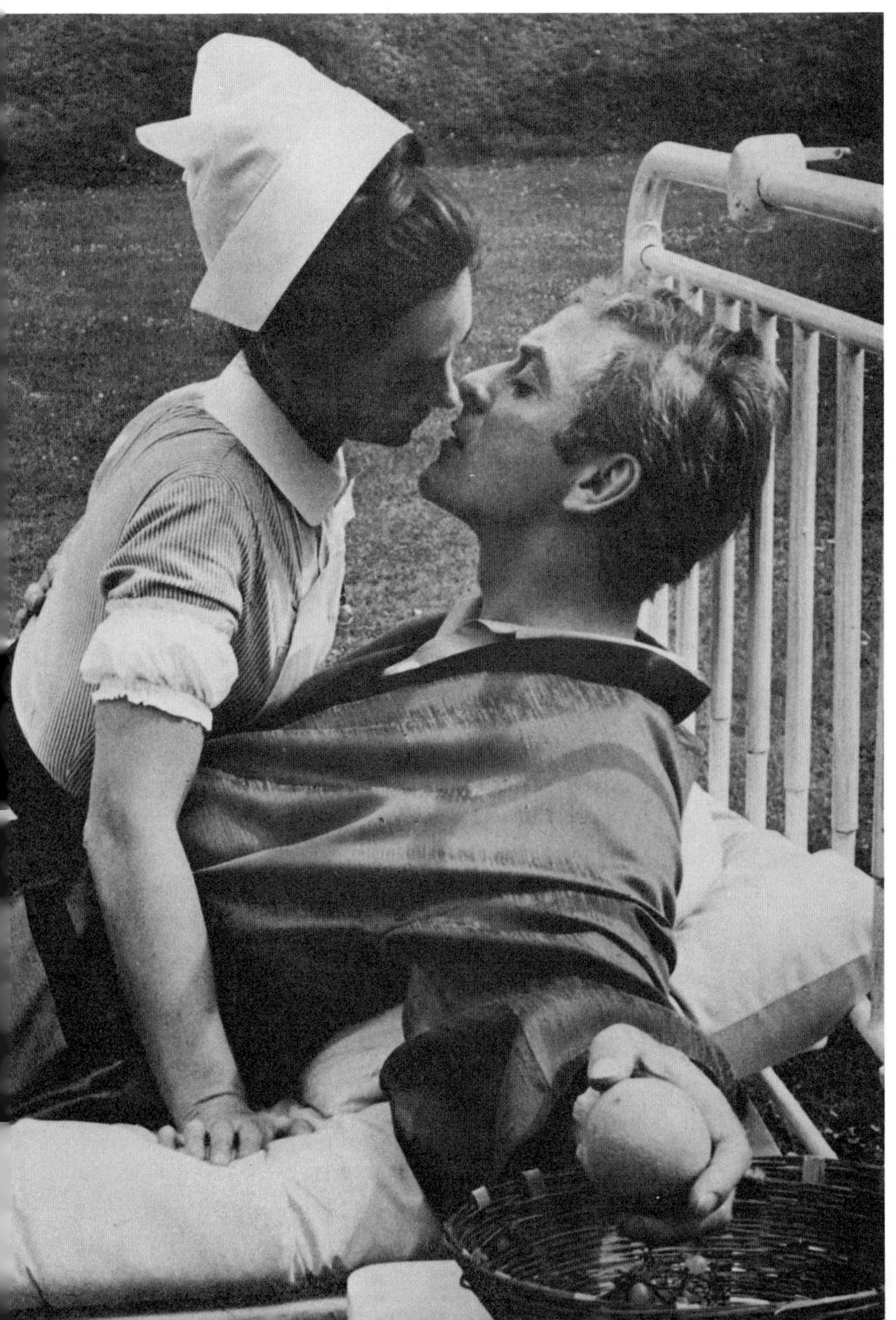

Though Michael Caine's first big screen role was that of a dapper, English officer-aristocrat (in Zulu*), it was a Cockney role in* The Ipcress File *which elevated him to fame. He parlayed this success and his ease with the Cockney variety into his second smash hit,* Alfie *(Paramount/Sheldrake, 1966, shown here). After 21 more film leads, many lightly tinged with Cockney, he again used the variety to full effectiveness in* The Man Who Would Be King.

and if we feel uranium is a "totally fatal metal," it is translated into a:

(Tu*O*@*e*L*i*E FuE@*e*L Me½@*e*L).

In two cases, consonants are dropped following another consonant in the middle of a word. The first is "w"—so that if the direction of life tends "always somewhat upward," in Cockney it tends:

(*oU*L½¼uEZ SAM¼*A*@ *A*P¼*E*¼D).

The other is "h." Thus, if we suspect that "perhaps she overheard somehow," as Cockneys, we'd suspect that:

(P*E*R¼ePS) she (u*O*VeR¼*E*¼D SAM¼*Ai*).

Most people are aware that it is a Cockney habit to drop initial "h"s. So if we say of the foster child that "he has always hated his home here," for a Cockney it turns out that:

(¼*i*E ¼eZ *o*UL½¼uEZ ¼uETeD ¼iZ ¼u*O*M ¼*i*E¼).

As for adding "h"s, this is restricted to the Cockney Worker subvariety, and then only under very specific conditions. The first is when a vowel starts a phrase, such as "Aim," "Old," or "Out," which at the beginning of a sentence are made into:

(H*A*:EM), (Ha*O*L¼), and (Ha*U*@).

The second "h" addition is to a word that starts with a vowel and follows a weak consonant. Thus, if "he will ask you to tell all of it," in Cockney Worker we must suppose that:

(¼*i*E WiL½ HASK) you to (Til½ H*oU*L½ HAV i@).

Finally, when an initial vowel sound follows a "y" or another vowel, it too gets an "h." So the question, "How is it you are so easy on her?" is reshaped into:

(¼a*U* HiZ i@ iYi*U* H*o*:¼) so (H*i*EZ*i*E H*o*:N ¼*E*¼?).

Consonant changes that are dependent on spelling are the same as in British English: 1—the "ch" (*C*) sound when spelled "tu" becomes (TY). Thus, to "get the future picture" evolves into:

get the (FiYi*U*TY*E*¼ PiKTY*E*¼).

2—a medial "f" sound when spelled "ph" is transformed into (V)—so that her "nephew's symphony" turns into:

her (Ne½ViYi*U*Z SiMV*E*N*i*E).

The "sh" (*S*) sound changes to (Syi) when spelled "su"—thus an extra "sensual issue" of a magazine is transformed into an extra:

(Se½NSYi*U*L iSYi*U*).

Two more consonant alterations remain to be considered, both regarding "th" sounds. The first has the "hard TH" (*T*) reshaped into a (V) in General Cockney; the second transforms it into a (D) in Worker Cockney, while the "soft th" (*t*) becomes (F). So if "this has nothing to do with those other things," in General Cockney we would find that:

(ViS) has (N*A**t*iN¼) to do (WiV Vu*O*Z *A*V*e*¼ *t*iNGZ),

while in Worker Cockney we would say that:

(DiS) has (N*A*FiN¼) to do (WiD Da*O*Z *A*D*e*¼ FiNGZ).

Music, Rhythm, and Pace

As does British English, Cockney has a large musical range and more variation than American English; however, it is only one to one-and-a-half tones higher. Also, Cockney is not "clipped"; rather it is combination of staccato (because of the glottal stops) and *flowing* music (due to the liaison factor). Stress, as with British, is generally only on one syllable per word. The pace at which Cockney is spoken is faster than American speech but slower than British.

Observation and Notes

As to observation, listen to recordings of G. B. Shaw's *Pygmalion* and *My Fair Lady*. When the *Late Show* telecasts *Alfie*, catch (and take notes on) Michael Caine's Cockney. Late night TV is also useful for viewing and monitoring the films of Cary Grant, whose "touch of 'Bow bells' " rings throughout almost every role he ever played. For the Liverpool subvariety, there are the films and recordings of the Beatles. Finally, the tapes made to accompany this book can provide you with recorded examples of all the changes cited in this chapter.

While Cary Grant's long career seldom called for the use of hs native Bristol-Liverpool variety, he never really lost the sound—even when playing a highly educated archaeologist in Bringing Up Baby *(RKO, 1938, shown here with Katharine Hepburn). Interesting to note: the first film he made which became a permanent cinema classic,* Gunga Din, *gave him a role in which he could—and* did*—stress the Cockney rather than suppress it.*

GENERAL COCKNEY - COCKNEY WORKER - LIVERPOOL COCKNEY

GUIDE PAGES	SOUND	General Cockney	Cockney Worker	Liverpool Cockney
Change in all positions: (aim) uEM, (say) SuE, (maybe) MuEBiE, (maintain) MuENTuEN	A	uE		&
OR change: HA:EM, SA:E, MAE:BiE, MAE:NTA:EN	A		A:E	
CHANGE: (easy) iEZiE, (believe) BiELiEV, (we) WiE, (seem) SiEM, (release) RiELiES, (me) MiE	E	iE	&	
OR shorten: E½ZE½, BE½LE½V, WE½, SE½M, ME½	E			E½
AND change before final R: (we're all) WiYEROUL, (earache) iYERuE@, (cheer up) CiYERAP, (sneer at) SNiYERe@	E	iYE (.r	&	&
Change in all positions: (I'm) oAM, (try) TRoA, (pipe) PoAP, (likewise) LoAKWoAZ	I	oA		
OR change: HoEM, TRoE, PoEP, LoEKWoEZ	I		oE	
OR change: AM, TRA, PAP, LAKWAZ	I			A
Change: (old) uOL½D, (postpone) PuOSTPuON, (slow) SLuO, (road) RuOD, (solo) SuOLuO	O	uO		&
OR change: HaOL¼, PaOSTPaON, SLaO, RaOD	O		aO	
AND change final OW in polysyllable: (fellow) Fe½LE, (tomorrow) TEMo:RE, (pillow) PiLE	O	.E$ow ?:	&	
Change in all positions: (you) iYiU, (few) FiYiU, (music) MiYiUZi@, (fuel) FiYiUL	U	iYiU	&	&

Change in all positions: (am) eM, (map) MeP, (glad) GLeD, (as) ez, (pan) PeN, (magic) MeJi@	a	e	&	&
SHORTEN: (expense) e½XPe½NS, (leg) Le½G, (dead) De½D, (men) Me½N, (said) Se½D	e	e½		&
OR change: iXPiNS, LiG, DiD, MiN, SiD	e		i	
CHANGE in polysyllable when strong: (critic) KRETi@, (imprint) EMPRiNT, (insist) iNSES¼	i		E?:":	
OR no change: KRiTi@, iMPRiNT, iNSiS¼	i	i		&
CHANGE: (on) o:N, (hobnob) ¼o:BNo:B, (fog) Fo:G, (topnotch) To:PNo:C, (solid) So:LiD	o	o:	&	
OR change: o½N, ¼o½BNo½B, Fo½G, To½PNo½C	o			o½
AND drop medially when weak: (combine) K¼MBoAN, (concoct) K¼NKo:K¼	o	/¼"½	&	&
Change in all positions: (ugly) AGLiE, (was) WAZ, (love) LAV, (up) AP, (does) DAZ	u	A	&	&

Change in all positions: (watch) Wo:C, (swamp) SWo:MP, (large) Lo:¼J, (car) Ko:¼	A	o:	&	
OR lengthen: WA:C, SWA:MP, LA:¼J, KA:¼	A			A:
No change: (burn) BE¼N, (her) ¼E¼, (word) WE¼D	E	E	&	&
No change: (predict) PRIDiK¼	I	I	&	&
Change in all positions: (ounce) AiNS, (how) ¼Ai, (down) DAiN, (loud) LAiD, (allow) ELAi	O	Ai		&
OR change: HaUNS, ¼aU, DaUN, LaUD, ELaU	O		aU	

Key:

C church	& as shown	: stronger	" when
$ spelled	/ medially	½ weakened	(preceding
¼ dropped	. finally	! excepting	?: polysyllable
			@ glottal stop

GENERAL COCKNEY - COCKNEY WORKER - LIVERPOOL COCKNEY

GUIDE PAGES	SOUND	General Cockney	Cockney Worker	Liverpool Cockney
Change in all positions: (fool) FuUL, (lose) LuUZ, (true) TRuU, (drew) DRuU, (soup) SuUP	U	uU		
OR change: FiUL½, LiUZ, TRiU, DRiU, SiUP	U		iU	&
Change in all positions: (rather) RAVE¼, (bath) BAt, (dance) DANS, (half) ¼AF	a	A	&	&
Change final LE after consonant: (simple) SiMPUL½, (trouble) TRABUL½, (apple) ePUL½	e	.UL½)¢	&	&
Change in all positions: (above) EBAV, (ago) EGuO, (family) FeMELiE, (extra) e½XTRE	i	E	&	&
LONGER sound: (off) o:F, (broad) BRo:D, (war) Wo:¼, (cause) Ko:Z, (door) Do:¼, (long) Lo:NG	o	o:	&	&
AND change before L: (call) Ko:UL½ (tall) To:UL½ (always) o:UL½¼uEZ (fall) Fo:UL½	o	o:U(L	&	
OR add R when final: (law) LoR, (saw) SoR, (draw) DRoR, (jaw) JoR, (raw) RoR	o		oR".	
OR longer: Ko:L, o:L½WuEZ, Lo:, So:, DRo:	o			o:
No change: (put) Pu@, (good) GuD, (could) KuD	u	u	&	&
Change in all positions: (choice) Co:ES, (toy) To:E, (noise) No:EZ, (employ) e½MPLo:E	oE	o:E	&	
OR change: CoiS, Toi, NoiZ, e½MPLoi	oE			oi

No change:	B	B	&	&
CHANGE to TY when spelled TU: (picture) PiKTYE¼, (future) FiYiUTYE¼	C	TY$tu	&	&
CHANGE finally before Y: (did you) DiJiYiU, (said yes) Se½Je½S, (bad year) BeJiE¼	D	.J(Y	&	&
OR drop finally after L or N: (and) HAN¼, (build) BiL¼, (mind) MoEN¼, (cold) KaOL¼	D		.¼)ln	
CHANGE medially when spelled PH: (nephew) Ne½ViYiU, (symphony) SiMVENiE	F	/V$ph	&	&
DROP from ING suffix: (coming) KAMiN¼, (singing) SiNGiN¼, (living) LiViN¼	G	¼ing)		&
OR change: KAMiNK, SENGiNK, LEViNK	G		King)	
DROP INITIALLY: (he) ¼iE, (had) ¼eD, (hot) ¼o:@, (whole) ¼uOL, (half) ¼AF, (his) ¼iZ	H	-¼	&	&
DROP medially after consonant: (forehead) Fo:R¼e½D, (somehow) SAM¼Ai, (perhaps) PER¼ePS	H	/¼)¢	&	&
OR add to vowel at start of phrase: (Easy) HiEZiE, (aim) HA:EM, (old) HaOL½¼, (as) HeZ	H		-- +H (*	
OR add to initial vowel after vowel or Y: (you are) iYiUHo:¼, (easy as) HiEZiEHeZ, (say it) SA:EHiT, (how is) ¼aUHiZ	H		-+H(*)* or Y	
OR add to initial vowel after weak consonant: (all of) oUL½HAV, (tell it) TiL½Hi@, (call up) KoUL½HAP, (will ask) WiL½HASK	H		-+H(*)½¢	

Key:

+ add to	- initially	(preceding	& as shown	t bath, thin
¼ drop	-- " in phrase	) following	: stronger	¢ consonants
* vowels	/ medially	) in suffix	½ weakened	@ glottal stop
$ spelled	. finally			

GENERAL COCKNEY - COCKNEY WORKER - LIVERPOOL COCKNEY

GUIDE PAGES	SOUND	General Cockney	Cockney Worker	Liverpool Cockney
No change: (judge) JAJ, (age) uEJ	J	J	&	&
FINAL GLOTTAL STOP except after consonant or before vowel: (cake) KuE@, (back) Be@, (oak) uO@, (like) LuE@, (week) WiE@, (bloke) BLuO@	K	.@!)¢ ! (*	&	
OR no change: KuEK, BeK, uOK, LAK, WE½K	K			K
WEAK MEDIALLY after vowel before consonant: (build) BiUL½D, (self) Se½UL½F, (calm) Ko:UL½M	L	/ L½)*(¢	&	&
OR weaken finally, too: (will) WiL½, (tell) TiL½, (feel) FiEL½, (skull) SKAL½	L		.L½	
OR no final change: WiL, Te½L, FiEL, SKAL	L	.L		&
No change	M	M	&	&
No change	N	N	&	&
No change	P	P	&	&
No change	Q	Q	&	&
DROP after vowel before consonant: (cares) KuE¼Z, (harm) ¼o:¼M, (word) WE¼D, (fork) Fo:¼K	R	¼)*(¢	&	&
DROP finally except before vowel: (her.) ¼E¼., (roar.) Ro:¼., (fire.) FoA¼., (cure.) KiYiU¼.	R	.¼!(*	&	&
No change: (yes) Ye½S, (nice) NoAS	S	S	&	&
Medial SYi when spelled SU: (sensual) Se½NSYiUL, (issue) iSYiU, (tissue) TiSYiU	S	/SYi $su	&	&
MEDIAL GLOTTAL STOP before LE: (battle) Be@UL½, (little) Li@UL½, (kettle) Ke½@UL½	T	/@(le	&	&
MEDIAL GLOTTAL STOP before weak vowel and L: (metal) Me½@eL, (fatal) FuE@eL, (total) TuO@eL	T	/@ (½*1	&	&
DROP finally after K,, P or S, except before vowel: (fact) FeK¼, (interrupt) iNTERAP¼, (last) LAS¼, (direct) DERe½K¼, (rest) Re½S¼	T	.¼)k Ps!(*	&	&
FINAL GLOTTAL STOP except as above: (treat) TRiE@, (taught) To:@, (sit) Si@, (get) Ge½@	T	.@!	&	&
OR add to final CE in "once" and "twice": WANST, TWoEST	T		+.CEin number	
Change in all positions: (nothing) NAFiNK, (mouth) MaUF, (through) FRiYiU, (three) FRiE	t		F	
OR no change: NAtiN¼, MAit, tRiYuU, tRiE	t	t		&
Change in all positions: (that) Ve@, (other) AVE¼, (with) WiV, (those) VuOZ, (this) ViS	T	V		
OR change: De@, ADE¼, WiD, DaOZ, DiS	T		D	
OR no change: Te@, ATE¼, WiT, TuOZ, TiS	T			T
No change	V	V	&	&
DROP after consonant when weak: (somewhat) SAM¼A@, (always) oUL½¼uEZ, (upward) AP¼E¼D	W	¼)¢"½	&	
OR no change: SAMWA@, o:L½WuEZ, APWE¼D	W			W
No change	X	X	&	&
No change	Z	Z	&	&
No change: (measure) Me½zE¼, (vision) VizEN	z	z	&	&

Key:

& as shown	@ glottal stop	! excepting	$ spelled	/ medial
: stronger	¢ consonant(s)	(preceding	+ add to	. finally
½ weakened	* vowel(s)	) following	¼ dropped	" when

Rod Taylor (shown here with Maggie Smith in The VIPs, *MGM, 1963) was part of that generation of Australians so embarrassed by their native variety that they went to great trouble to lose their identifying accent. Like Taylor, many travelled to England in their teens, as much to perfect "proper" British speech as to study in their particular fields. Often, as mentioned before, they found a large contingent of Canadians already there for the same purpose.*

MASTER CATEGORY 15

AUSTRALIA & NEW ZEALAND ANZAC

The term ANZAC stands for the Australia and New Zealand Army Corps or a soldier from that group. For our purposes, it identifies a variety spoken by two young and vigorous nations whose speech is heard more and more on TV and in films.

Just as the English language is the result of the combination of elements from many languages, so the Anzac variety is the end product of several varieties: British, Scottish, Irish, American, and Cockney. To the untrained ear, the Cockney influence seems so strong that Anzac is indistinguishable from it. Yet in actuality only thirty percent of Anzac sounds bear a strong resemblance to Cockney; the main influence is clearly British English.

The differences between the Australian subvarieties and those between Australian and New Zealand subvarieties have their roots in geographical separation and social and national heritages. One glance at the map points up the differences: over a thousand miles of ocean lie between Australia and New Zealand, and hundreds of miles separate Sydney, Melbourne, Brisbane, and Perth.

Historically, Australia was first settled as a penal colony to which England transported convicted criminals and Irish political offenders—a use to which the mother country could no longer put the American colonies after 1776. New Zealand, on the other hand, was populated by free men and women from the British Isles—and later, to some extent, by freed settlers from Australia.

The American influence on the Anzac variety came with the Americans who sought gold in Australia in the 1850s. They, together with a large influx of Scottish sheep drovers, completed the mixture that was to be Anzac. The result follows British English in a great number of its diphthong versions, most of its consonant modifications, and some of its pronunciations of simple vowels. While many of those vowels show strong Cockney influences, new and original Anzac forms are just as frequent. As for the New Zealand subvarieties, the easiest change to pinpoint is the substitution of the (u) of "nut" for *both* the (O) of "note" and the (o) of "not."

Vowel Changes

In General Anzac, because of the Scottish influence, the (o) is part of the only compensation reversal we find. In this case, the (o) and the (*o*) change places so that "cot" and "body" sound like "caught" and "bawdy"—and vice versa. Thus, "the hock shop was not locked" becomes:

the (HoK SoP) was (N*o*T LoKT)

and "in autumn, long walks are in order" turns into:

in (oT¼M, LoNG WoKS) are in (*o*:¼D*e*¼).

Note that, in the last word, "order," the "aw" (*o*) becomes *longer* (:) rather than changing; this happens with any (*o*) sound that precedes a dropped (¼) "r," making "war" into (W*o*:¼).

Two other vowels that are lengthened both follow the British pattern. Thus "ah" as in "calm" is drawn out into "ahh" (*A*:), while "ay" (A) as in "mate"—consisting of the (e) of "met" and the (E) of "meet"—is stretched out into "ehh-ee" (e:E). Among the less educated and the rural population, this diphthong is converted into a more typical "Aussie" form. In these two subvarieties the Cockney influence still hangs on, and the (A) is transformed into a combination of the (u) sound of "but" and the (i) sound of "bit." Thus the phrase "I may take eight days" evolves into:

(oi Mui TuiK uiT DuiZ).

Also, in these subvarieties you'll notice that (I), made up of "ah" (*A*) and "ee" (E), is transformed into (oi), a joining of (o) as in "hot" and (i) as in "hit"—making the admonition, you mind your business, and "I'll likewise mind mine" into:

(oiL LoiKWoiZ MoiN¼ MoiN).

In General Anzac, however, (I) is merely shortened (again like the British) into (*A*i), and the admonition ends:

(*A*iL L*A*iKW*A*iZ M*A*iN¼ M*A*iN).

Another double vowel that embodies the British "clipped" effect is the (*o*E) of "boy." Again the (E) is shortened into (i), resulting in an (*o*i) sound. So that, if the way Texans "exploited oil coin annoyed him," the Anzac would say that the way they:

(e½XPL*o*iTeD *o*iL K*o*iN *i*N*o*iD) him.

The British influence emerges not only in lengthenings and shortenings but also in outright changes. The (*u*) of "put," for instance, is moved *forward* (;) in the mouth, so that "the woman took a good look" is reshaped into:

the (W*u*;M¼N T*u*;K) a G*u*;D L*u*;K).

Again, as in British, the "yoo" sound—(Y) + (*U*) = (U)—expands into a triphthong (Yi*U*). Thus, if the deacon was "immune to lewd humor," for the Anzac, he was:

(*i*MYi*U*N) to (LYi*UD* HYi*U*M*e*¼).

Another diphthong following the British pattern is the "oh" (O) of "coat." Here the first half "aw" (*o*) is altered into "eh" (e), giving us an (e*U*)—so that if they had to "postpone the boat show," in Anzac we would explain that they had to:

(Pe*U*S¼Pe*U*N) the (Be*U*T Se*U*).

Among the rural and less educated Anzacs, however, the Cockney influence again appears, transforming the same double vowel into (u*u*) using the (u) of "but" and the (*u*) of "put"—so that they too had to:

(Pu*u*S¼Pu*u*N) the (Bu*u*T S*u*u).

The Anzac also drops the (*i*) sound as in "ago" whenever it is weak between consonants, as do the British. Thus, if one views absolute monarchy as a sort of "family political system," as an Anzac, one would call it a:

(FaeM¼L*i*E½ P*i*LiTiK¼L SiST¼M).

The next vowel modification is not found in all British English but just the London Executive subvariety. This is the metamorphosis of "ow" (*O*)—"ah" (*A*) + "oo" (*U*)—into (e*U*) or "eh" + "oo." So if the tailor asks, "How about brown trousers?," if from down under he'll ask:

(He*U* *i*Be*U*T BRe*U*N TRe*U*Z*e*¼Z?).

Of course, Anzac branches off from British in many instances. Where the British pronounce the (u) of "cut" as "ah" (*A*), the Anzac follows the American pronunciation. The same is true of the (*a*) in "path," which for the Australian-born—as for many Americans—shifts into the (a) of "pat." Thus, if he'd "rather ask his aunt to dance," in this variety he'd:

(Ra*Te*¼ aSK) his (aNT) to (DaNS).

Finally, as with many Americans and almost all Cockneys, the Anzac shortens the (e) of "bet" to half as long (e½).

Naturally, some changes in this variety are purely Anzac. The (*I*) of "predict," "pretend," and "prevent," for example, evolves into the (e) of "predator," giving us (PReDiKT), (PReTe½ND), and (PReVe½NT). In some cases, the pure Anzac flavor turns simple vowel sounds into diphthongs, such as when the (a) of "sat" adds on the (e) of "set" to become (ae). So that if he was a "man who had his plans mapped out," our Anzac would say he was a:

(MaeN) who (HaeD) his (PlaeNZ MaePT) out.

Another vowel made into a diphthong is "oo" (*U*) as in "boot"; here the (*i*) of "ago" is added on at the beginning of the sound, while the "oo" itself is cut in half, giving us (*iU*½). Thus, if in chess it is a mistake "to move too soon," in the Australia/New Zealand variety, it's a mistake:

(T*iU*½ M*iU*½V T*iU*½ S*iU*½N).

Next, there are three cases in which (i) as in "big" is transformed into (*i*) as in "ago." The first is when it is spelled "i" and found in a weak (unstressed) position. So if we "insisted the critic was English," as Anzacs, we:

(*i*NSiSTeD) the (KRiT*i*K) was (iNGL*iS*).

The second is in "es" plurals and in the third person—thus, if he buys the platter because "it matches his dishes," for an Anzac:

(*i*T MaeC*i*Z HiZ DiS*i*Z).

The final example is found in the suffixes "ate," "ed," "ess," "est," "less," "let," "ness," and "ity." So that if the actor's portrayal had the "quality of desperate, heedless rashness," the Anzac reviewer would speak of a:

(KW*A*:L*i*T*i*E½) of (De½SP¼R*i*T, H*ii*:DL*i*S RaeSN*i*S).

It is, however, in the handling of the "ee" (E) sound of "feet" that this variety is most unique. In ordinary cases, this (E) is made into a diphthong combining (*i*) as in "afoot" with a longer (:) version of (i) as in "fit," giving us (*i*i:). So if we are going over the instructor's posts that are open, and "these three need teaching degrees," being from Australia, we would observe that:

(*T*ii:Z *t*R*i*i: N*i*i:D T*i*i:*C*iNG D*i*E½GR*i*i:Z).

Did you notice what happened to the first (E) in "degree"? It became just a trifle longer than the others: a combination of the (*i*) with a short "ee" (E½). This is the change that takes place with the (E) sound when found in the prefixes "be," "de," "e," "re," or "se." It also occurs in any final "y." Thus, if what we have "here's merely a very easy theory," in this variety, what we have:

(Hi:¼Z Mi:¼L*i*E½) a (Ve½*R*½*i*E½*i*i:Z*i*E½ *t*ii:*R*½*i*E½).

Take a close look at the words "here's" and "merely" because you'll find the last change in the (E) sound there. The (E) that comes before a dropped (¼) "r" is weakened into a long (i:), thus reshaping "earlobe," "cheerful," and "fearless" into:

(i:¼Le*UB*), (*C*i:¼F¼L), and (Fi:¼L*i*S).

Consonant Changes

In the paragraph above, we see two handlings of the "r." The first is in the words "very" and "theory," where a short trill (*R*½) is substituted (the tongue taps once against the upper gum ridge; see page 21). As in British English, this happens only in the middle of a word between two vowels. So, if we should talk of a "rural story's moral," the Anzac would convert that into a:

(R*u*;*R*½*i*L STo*R*½*i*E½Z Mo*R*½*i*L).

The other Anzac (and British) treatment of "r" is to eliminate it under certain circumstances. One case is when the "r" follows a vowel and precedes a consonant—thus, if the bandmaster explains that the "march's first part is short," if he were Australian, he would point out that the:

(M*A*:¼*C*e*Z* F*E*¼ST P*A*:¼T) is (*S*o:¼T).

The second situation in which the "r" is omitted is when it comes at the end of a word and is not followed by a vowel. So if they spotted a "fire near the far door," being Australian-born, they would report a:

(F*A*i¼ Ni:¼) the (F*A*¼ Do:¼).

As with Cockney and British English, the remaining three consonant changes have to do with spelling and position. In American English a medial "tu" is sometimes pronounced "ch" (*C*). Not so in Anzac; it is pronounced (TY). Thus, a professor tempting his class with a promise of a "future lecture with pictures," if Anzac would promise a:

(FYi*U*TY*u*;¼ Le½KTY*u*;¼) with (PiKTY*u*;¼Z).

Again, in American speech a medial "su" is sometimes articulated as "sh" (*S*); in Anzac it is (SYi). And if it can be said of a magazine that this month's "issue was sensual," our Anzac friends would remark that the:

(iSYi*U*) was (Se½NSYi*U*L).

Although she has cultivated an almost country-western American variety in her singing, Olivia Newton-John's native Anzac often emerges when she speaks "normally," as on television talk shows and in the spoken introductions to her songs during live film concerts. Here she is in her first big film role, Grease *(Paramount, 1978), in which a few lines of dialogue established the reason she didn't sound like the rest of her American high school friends.*

Finally, a medial "ph" is always pronounced (V), rather than (F) as in American English. So if we refer to her "nephew's symphony," if we were Anzacs, we'd talk of her:

(Ne½VYi*U*Z SiMV*i*N*i*E½).

Besides sound changes, there are four words that receive unique treatments in Australia/New Zealand: "basic," "forehead," "electric," and "comrade." In rural and less educated sections of Australia and in most of New Zealand, "basic" is pronounced (BaSiK) to rhyme with "classic." In all of Australia, "forehead" is pronounced (Fo*R*½¼e½D), while in New Zealand it's (Fu*R*½¼e½D). "Electric" comes out (eLe½¼TRiK) in rural and less educated Australian speech, while "comrade" emerges variously as (KoMRiD) in General and more educated Australian; (KoMRAD) to rhyme with "Tom prayed" in rural and less educated Australian; and (KumRAD) to rhyme with "some paid" in New Zealand. Of course, "comrade" is used much less often among most Anzacs than the truly typical "mate," which is pronounced diversely: (Me:ET) in most of Australia and educated New Zealand; (MuiT) in rural Australia and New Zealand; and (MeiT) in uneducated New Zealand speech.

Music, Rhythm, and Pace

The Anzac music is the one element in this variety that has the most in common with Cockney. It is spoken one-and-a-half tones higher than American English and has a somewhat larger range and variety. Then too, it combines a flowing feeling with a staccato flavor, the result of the Anzac

The definitive film of Anzac varieties is appropriately about the group that brought the term "Anzac" into the dictionary: the Australian-New Zealand Army Corps. Here, shown in that picture, Gallipoli *(Paramount, 1982), are Mark Lee and Mel Gibson. Gibson has gone on to several more starring roles, and his international acceptance has made Australians more proud than self-conscious about their native speech. As Liverpool Cockney threatens to topple British English in England, so Anzac may soon be accepted as "Educated English" among even the most snobbish Australians and New Zealanders.*

marriage between Cockney *liaison* and British crispness.

It is in pace that we encounter the greatest difference between Australia and New Zealand. The New Zealand varieties are spoken almost as fast as British English; Australian, however, is spoken even more slowly than General American.

Observation and Notes

Now most TV audiences can see Anzac-originated programs and films in their own living rooms. For those of us who are studying dialects, this provides a rich source for observation. No longer do we have to depend on the occasional Anzac sports star, opera singer, or ballet dancer. Now the Anzac variety can be heard almost any night of the week. One hint: we currently receive many TV series and television movies from Australia/New Zealand. Keep an eye out for them, and plan your viewing so that you can have a cassette recorder at hand. By strict attention and careful selection, you should be able to build up your own Anzac variety library in a very short time.

GENERAL ANZAC-AUSTRALIAN, EDUCATED-AUSTRALIAN, LESS EDUCATED (SYDNEY) BRISBANE, RURAL

GUIDE PAGES	SOUND	General ANZAC	Aust. Educated	Aust. Less Edu. (in Syd.)	Brisbane, Rural
CHANGE: (age) e:EJ, (vacate) Ve:EKe:ET, (maintain) Me:ENTe:EN, (weigh) We:E	A	e:E	&		
OR change: uiJ, VuiKuiT, MuiNTuiN, Wui	A			ui	&
AND change before dropped R: (hairpin) He:¼PiN, (care) Ke:¼, (barely) Be:¼L*i*E½	A	e:(¼r	&	&	&
OR change in "basic": BaSiK	A			BaSiK	&
CHANGE: (eat) *i*i:T, (seem) S*i*i:M, (he) H*i*i:, (each) *i*i:*C*, (these) *T**i*i:Z	E	*i*i:	&		
OR change: *i*ET, S*i*EM, H*i*E, *i*E*C*, *T**i*EZ	E			*i*E	
OR change: *i*iT, S*i*iM, H*i*i, *i*i*C*, *T**i*iZ	E				*i*i
AND change before dropped R: (earlobe) i:¼Le*U*B, (here) Hi:¼, (merely) Mi:¼L*i*E½	E	i:(¼r	&	&	&
AND change in prefixes BE,DE,E,RE,SE: (believe) B*i*E½L*i*i:V, (emit) *i*E½MiT	E	*i*E½{e be de		&	
OR change: BE½L*i*EV, E½MiT	E		E½{be		
OR change: B*i*iL*i*iV, *i*iMiT	E				*i*i{be
AND change final Y: (easy) *i*i:Z*i*E½, (greasy) GR*i*i:S*i*E½, (theory) *t**i*i:*i**R*½*i*E½	E	.*i*E½ $y		&	
OR change: *i*EZE½, GR*i*ESE½, *t**i*E*i**R*½E½	E		.E½$y		
OR change: *i*iZ*i*i, GR*i*iS*i*i, *t**i*i*i**R*½*i*i	E				.*i*i$y
OR change in "electric": eLe½¼TRiK	E			eLe½¼TRiK	
SHORTER: (ice) AiS, (night) NAiT, (try) TRAi, (likewise) LAiKWAiZ, (my) MAi	I	Ai	&		
OR change: oiS, NoiT, TRoi, LoiKWoiZ	I			oi	&
Change in all positions: (own) e*U*N, (road) Re*U*D, (solo) Se*U*Le*U*, (no) Ne*U*	O	e*U*	&		
OR change: u*u*N, Ru*u*D, Su*u*Lu*u*, Nu*u*	O			u*u*	&
Change in all positions: (use) Yi*U*Z, (mule) MYi*U*L, (few) FYi*U*, (cute) KYi*U*T	U	Yi*U*	&	&	&
Change in all positions: (as) aeZ, (at) aeT, (ransack) RaeNSaeK, (glad) GLaeD	a	ae	&	&	&
OR change in "comrade": KoMRiD	a	KoMRiD	&		
OR " " " : KoMRAD				KoMRAD	&

		All 4
SHORTER: (end) e½ND, (well) We½L, (said) Se½D, (dead) De½D	e	e½
Change if spelled I in weak position: (insist) *i*NSiST	i	*i*$i"½
AND change in ES plurals and 3rd person: (sizes) SAiZ*i*Z, (his) H*i*Z, (matches) Mae*C**i*Z, (it) *i*T, (dishes) Di*S**i*Z	i	*i*"es) his
AND change in suffixes ATE,ED,ESS,EST,LESS,LET,NESS,ITY: (charity) Cae*R*½*i*T*i*E½, (useless) Yi*U*SL*i*S (omelet) *o*½M¼L*i*T	i	*i*)ity less
CHANGE: (on) *o*½N, (drop) DR*o*½P, (odd) *o*½D, (not) N*o*½T	o	*o*
BUT drop medially if weak: (combine) K¼MBAiN, (concoct) K¼NK*o*½KT, (compose) K¼MPe*U*Z, (confess) K¼NFe½S	o	/¼"½
No change: (up) uP, (does) DuZ, (was) WuZ, (love) LuV	u	u
LONGER: (far) FA:¼, (watch) WA:*C*, (swamp) SWA:MP	*A*	*A*:
No change: (girl) G*E*¼L, (work) W*E*¼K, (turn) T*E*¼N	*E*	*E*

Key:

C church	& as shown	(preceding	*t* thin, both	" when
/ medial	$ spelled	{ in prefix	*T* that, with	*S* sure, she
. final	¼ dropped	} in suffix	*R* trilled R	: stronger
				½ weakened

GENERAL ANZAC-AUSTRALIAN, EDUCATED-AUSTRALIAN, LESS EDUCATED (SYDNEY) BRISBANE, RURAL

GUIDE PAGES

	SOUND	General ANZAC	Aust. Educated	Aust. Less Edu. (in Syd.)	Brisbane, Rural
CHANGE in PRE prefix: (predict) PReDiKT (pretend) PReTe½ND, (prevent) PReVe½NT	*I*	{ PRe		&	
OR change: PRE½DiKT, PRE½Te½ND	*I*		{PRE½		
OR change: PR*i*iDiKT, PR*i*iTe½ND	*I*				{PR*i*i
Change in all positions: (down) De*U*N, (out) e*U*T, (how) He*U*, (loud) Le*U*D	*O*	e*U*	&	&	
OR change: Da*u*N, a*u*T, Ha*u*, La*u*D	*O*				a*u*
CHANGE: (soon) S*iU*½N, (rule) R*iU*½L, (do) D*iU*½, (true) TR*iU*½, (fool) F*iU*½L	*U*	*iU*½		&	
OR change: S*iU*N, R*iU*L, D*iU*, TR*iU*, F*iU*L	*U*		*iU*		
OR change: S*iu*N, R*iu*L, D*iu*, TR*iu*, F*iu*L	*U*				*iu*
BUT spelled U,UI,UE,EU,EW except after J,R,T,W or CH: (blue) BLYi*U*, (flew) FLYi*U*, (knew) NYi*U*, (glue) GLYi*U*	*U*	Yi*U*$u ew!)j rTwCH	&	&	&

		All 4
SHORTER: (after) aFT*E*¼, (dance) DaNS, (ask) aSK	*a*	a
No change: (apple) aeP*e*L, (dozen) DuZ*e*N	*e*	*e*
DROP between consonants when weak: (family) FaeM¼L*i*E½, (system) SiST¼M, (banana) B¼NaN*i*, (combine) K¼MBAiN	*i*	¼₵"½
CHANGE: (all) oL, (cough) KoF, (cause) KoZ, (off) oF	*o*	o
BUT longer before dropped R: (order) *o*:¼De¼, (war) W*o*:¼, (door) D*o*:¼, (board) B*o*:¼D, (court) K*o*:¼T, (for) F*o*:¼	*o*	*o*:(¼r
FORWARD placement: (book) B*u*;K, (put) P*u*;T, (could) K*u*;D	*u*	*u*;
SHORTER: (oil) *o*iL, (boy) B*o*i, (choice) C*o*iS, (toy) T*o*i	*o*E	*o*i

		General ANZAC	Aust. Educated	Aust. Less Edu. (in Syd.)	Brisbane, Rural
No change	B	B (all 4)			
CHANGE if spelled TU: (picture) PiKTY*E*¼ (future) FYi*U*TY*E*¼	C	TY$tu (all 4)			
DROP finally before consonant: (made for) Me:E¼F*o*:¼	D	.¼(¢ (all 4)			
CHANGE medially when spelled PH: (nephew) Ne½VYi*U*	F	/V$ph (all 4)			
No change	G	G (all 4)			
DROP in "forehead": Fo*R*½¼e½D	H	F o *R* ½ ¼ e ½ D			
No change: (judge) JuJ, (age) e:EJ	J	J	&	&	&
Drop medially in "electrik": eLe½¼TRiK	K			eLe½¼TRiK	
DROP if weak after vowel & before consonant: (calm) K*A*:¼M, (bulb) Bu¼B	L				¼)* (¢"½
OR no change: K*A*:LM, BuLB	L	L	&	&	
No change	MNPQ	M	N	P	Q

		All 4
DROP after vowel before consonant: (cares) Ke:¼Z, (work) W*E*¼K	R	¼)*(¢
LIGHT TAP medially between vowels: (very) Ve½*R*½*i*E½	R	/*R*½*̸
DROP finally except before vowel: (roar) R*o*:¼, (fire) FAi¼	R	.¼!(*

		General ANZAC	Aust. Educated	Aust. Less Edu. (in Syd.)	Brisbane, Rural
No change: (yes) Ye½S, (nice) NAiS	S	S	&	&	&
Medial SYi if spelled SU: (sensual) Se½NSYi*U*L, (tissue) TiSYi*U*	*S*	/SYi $su	&	&	&
No change:	T*t*TVWXZz	T *t* *T* V W X Z z			

Key:

		" when	$ spelled	& as shown
; forward	: stronger	(preceding	*R* trilled R	¢ consonants
/ medial	½ weakened	{ in prefix	* vowels	₵ between "
. finally	¼ dropped	) following	*̸ between "	! excepting

NEW ZEALAND: CHRISTCHURCH, RURAL - AUCKLAND, EDUCATED - DUNEDIN, LESS EDUCATED

GUIDE PAGES		Christ church	Auck-land	Dun-edin
CHANGE: (age) uiJ, (vacate) VuiKuiT, (way) Wui, (maintain) MuiNTuiN, (take) TuiK	A	ui		
OR change: e:EJ, Ve:EKe:ET, We:E, Me:ENTe:EN	A		e:E	
OR change: eiJ, VeiKeiT, Wei, MeiNTeiN, Tei@	A			ei
AND change in "basic": BaSiK	A	BaSiK	&	BaSi@
CHANGE: (eat) *i*i:T, (seem) S*i*i:M, (he) H*i*i:, (each) *i*i:*C*, (these) *T**i*i:Z, (we) W*i*i:	E		*i*i:	&
OR change: *i*iT, S*i*iM, H*i*i, *i*iC, *T**i*iZ, W*i*i	E	*i*i		
AND change before R: (earache) E*ER*½uiK, (hearing) HE*ER*½iNG, (weary) WE*ER*½*i*i	E	E*E*(r	&	&
OR change in prefixes BE, DE, E, RE, SE: (believe) B*i*E½L*i*i:V, (release) R*i*E½L*i*i:S	E		*i*E½{e be de	
OR change final Y: (easy) *i*i:Z*i*E½, (theory) *t**i*i:*iR*½*i*E½, (greasy) GR*i*i:S*i*E½	E		.*i*E½ $y	
Change in all positions: (ice) oiS, (my) Moi, (likewise) LoiKWoiZ, (night) NoiT, (try) TRoi	I	oi		
OR change: AiS, MAi, LAiKWAiZ, NAiT, TRAi	I		Ai	
OR change: *i*ES, M*i*E, L*i*EKW*i*EZ, N*i*ET, TR*i*E	I			*i*E
Change in all positions: (own) u½N, (road) Ru½D, (solo) Su½Lu½, (no) Nu½, (old) u½LD	O	u½		&
OR change: o½N, Ro½D, So½Lo½, No½, o½LD	O		o½	

		All 3
CHANGE: (use) Yi*U*Z, (mule) MYi*U*L, (few) FYi*U* (cute) KYi*UT*	U	Yi*U*
CHANGE: (as) aeZ, (ransack) RaeNSaeK, (at) aeT (map) MaeP	a	ae
AND change in "comrade": KuMRAD	a	KuMRAD
SHORTER: (end) e½ND, (expect) e½XPe½KT, (said) Se½D	e	e½
Change if spelled I in weak positions: (insist) *i*NSiST	i	*i*$i"½
AND change in ES plurals and 3rd person: (sizes) SoiZ*i*Z, (his) H*i*Z, (matches) Mae*C**i*Z, (it) *i*T, (dishes) Di*S**i*Z	i	*i*"es) his
AND change in suffixes ATE,ED,ESS,EST,LESS,LET,NESS,ITY: (charity) Cae*R*½*i**T**i*i, (useless) Yi*U*SL*i*S, (omelet) uM¼L*i*T	i	)ity less
OR change in weak 2nd syllable: (English) iNGLu*S*, (habit) HaeBuT, (delicate) De½LuK*i*T, (mystic) MiSTuK	i	u"½2nd syllab

		Christ church	Auck-land	Dun-edin
Change in all positions: (on) uN, (topnotch) TuPNuC, (not) NuT, (drop) DRuP, (clock) KLuK	o	u	&	
OR change: *o*½N, *To*½PN*o*½*C*, N*o*½T, DR*o*½P, KL*o*½K	o			*o*½
Change before L: (numskull) NuMSKoL, (ulcer) oLS*E*¼, (dull) DoL, (gull) GoL, (lull) LoL	u	o(l	&	&
LONGER: (far) FA:¼, (watch) WA:*C*, (spa) SPA:, (swamp) SWA:MP, (are) A:¼, (start) STA:¼T	A	A:	&	
OR shorter: FA½¼, WA½C, SPA½, SWA½MP, A½¼	A			A½
No change: (girl) G*E*¼L, (work) W*E*¼K, (her) H*E*¼	*E*	*E*	&	&
CHANGE in PRE prefix: (pretend) PR*i*iTe½ND, (prevent) PR*i*iVe½NT, (predict) PR*i*iDiKT	*I*	{PR*i*i		&
OR change: PReTe½ND, PReVe½NT, PReDiKT	*I*		{ PRe	
Change in all positions: (out) auT, (down) DauN, (how) Hau, (loud) LauD, (sound) SauND	*O*	au		
OR change: e*U*T, De*U*N, He*U*, Le*U*D, Se*U*ND	*O*		e*U*	
OR change: *iU*:T, D*iU*:N, H*iU*:, L*iU*:D, S*iU*:ND	*O*			*iU*:

Key:

		t thin,both		
C church	& as shown	*T* that,with	(preceding	$ spelled
¼ drop	: stronger	*S* sure,show	{ in prefix	@ glottal stop
. final	½ weakened	*R* trilled R	) in suffix	

NEW ZEALAND: CHRISTCHURCH, RURAL - AUCKLAND, EDUCATED - DUNEDIN, LESS EDUCATED

GUIDE PAGES

		Christchurch	Auckland	Dunedin
CHANGE: (soon) SiuN, (rule) RiuL, (true) TRiu (fool) FiuL, (do) Diu, (wound) WiuND	U	iu		&
OR change: SiU½N, RiU½L, TRiU½, FiU½L, DiU½	U		iU½	
BUT spelled U,UI,UE,EU,EW except after J,R,T W or CH: (blue) BLYiU, (flew) FLYiU, (knew) NYiU, (glue) GLYiU, (suit) SYiUT	U	YiU$ue ew!)jR T W CH	&	
		All 3		
SHORTER: (after) aFTE¼, (dance) DaNS, (laugh) LaF	a	a		
No change: (apple) aePeL, (dozen) DuZeN	e	e		
DROP between consonants when weak: (family) FaeM¼Li	i	¼₵"½		
CHANGE: (all) u½L, (cough) Ku½F, (saw) Su½, (cause) Ku½Z, (off) u½F, (broad) BRu½D	o	u½		
OR change: o½L, Ko½F, So½, Ko½Z, o½F, BRo½D	o		o½	
OR change: *o*½L, K*o*½F, S*o*½, K*o*½Z, *o*½F, BR*o*½D	*o*			*o*½
BUT longer before dropped R: (door) D*o*:¼, (order) *o*:De¼, (war) W*o*:¼, (board) B*o*:¼D	*o*	*o*:(¼r	&	&
		All 3		
FORWARD placement: (book) Bu;K, (put) Pu;T, (could) Ku;D	u	u;		
SHORTER: (oil) *o*iL, (boy) B*o*i, (choice) C*o*iS, (toy) T*o*i	*o*E	*o*i		
No change	B	B		
CHANGE if spelled TU: (picture) PiKTYE¼ (future) FYiUTYE¼	C	TY$tu		
DROP finally before consonant: (made for) Mui¼F*o*:¼	D	.¼(¢		
CHANGE medially when spelled PH: (nephew) Ne½VYiU	F	/V$ph		
No change	G	G		
DROP in "forehead": FuR½¼e½D	H	F u R ½ ¼ e ½ D		
No change: (judge) JuJ, (age) uiJ	J	J	&	&
GLOTTAL STOP finally except before a vowel: (kick) Ki@, (wreck) Re½@, (pack) Pae@	K			.@!(*
OR no change: KiK, Re½K, PaeK	K	K	&	
DROP when weak after a vowel and before a consonant: (calm) KA:¼M, (bulb) Bu¼B	L	¼"½)* (¢		&
No change	MNPQ	M	N P	Q
LIGHT TAP medially between vowels: (story) STu½R½ii, (very) Ve½R½ii, (hearing) HEER½iNG	R	/R½*̸	&	
OR TRILL: ST*o*½Rii:, Ve½Rii:, HEERiNG	R			R
		All 3		
DROP after vowel before consonant: (cares) Kui¼Z, (work) WE¼K	R	¼)*(¢		
DROP finally except before vowel: (roar) R*o*:¼, (fire) Foi¼	R	.¼!(*		
No change: (yes) Ye½S, (nice) NoiS	S	S		
Medial SY if spelled SU: (issue) iSYiU, (sensual) Se½NSYiUL, (tissue) TiSYiU	S	/SYi $su	&	&
MEDIAL GLOTTAL STOP before LE: (battle) Bae@eL, (little) Li@eL, (kettle) Ke½@eL	T			/@(le
MEDIAL GLOTTAL STOP before weak vowel and L: (metal) Me½@eL (fatal) Fei@eL (total) Tu½@eL	T			/@ (½*1
OR no change: BaeTeL, LiTeL, Me½TeL, FuiTeL	T	T	&	
No change	tTVWXZz	t T V W X Z z		

Key:

		$ spelled	& as shown	
; forward	: stronger	! excepting	R trilled R	¢ consonants
/ medial	½ weakened	(preceding	* vowels	₵ between "
. finally	¼ dropped	) following	*̸ between "	@ glottal stop

MASTER CATEGORY 16

CZECHOSLOVAKIAN

The Czecho-Slovak dialect is spoken by two different peoples, each with its own language, religion, and history. From the tenth century to the sixteenth, the land of the Czechs (known as Bohemia) was a strong and independent political power in Central Europe. In contrast, Slovakia was ruled by Hungary throughout most of its existence.

At the end of World War I, Bohemia and Slovakia joined with Moravia and Ruthenia to form Czechoslovakia. The little country's fierce dedication to democracy and independence was cut short after only twenty years (1918–38) when the Western powers used Czechoslovakia in a futile attempt to appease the voracious appetite of Adolf Hitler. Then in 1948 it became a Russian satellite.

Naturally, this long history of foreign oppression and domination has brought many Czechoslovak refugees to the U.S.—and with them, their dialects. A glance at the *GUIDE PAGES* will show four subdialects: *Prague, Educated* and *Nitra, Slovakia*, which differ from General Czechoslovakian in their handling of consonants; *Brno, Bohemia* and *Kladno, Rural*, which differ in the vowels.

As Slavic languages, Czech and Slovak share several characteristics with Russian and Polish: with Russian, the rules for consonant agreement (pages 101–102) and the treatment of "v," "w," and "r"; with Polish, the Y-glide (pages 78–80) and the shortening of almost all diphthong sounds.

Vowel Changes

In the latter connection, "eh-ee," (A) as in "bay" is abridged to (ei)—a combination of the (e) of "rest" and the (i) of "wrist." Thus, if "they ate late today," a Czech might report that:

(D=ei eiT= L%ieiT= T=*U*D=ei).

Note that after the "L" in "late," the sound gets the Polish Y-glide treatment, becoming "iei"; this occurs after both "l" and "n," so that "name" comes out (NieiM).

"Ah-ee"—(I) as in "buy"—is another double vowel where the (E) is reduced to (i). So if she's a girl who could "idolize the right kind of guy," someone born in Czechoslovakia would observe that she could:

(*A*iD=*A*L%*A*iZ) the (*R*:*A*iT= K*A*iN¼) of (K*A*i).

Finally, "aw-ee"—(*o*E) as in "boy"—also has the (E) curtailed to an (i). Thus, if the doting father "enjoys spoiling his boy with toys," if he were from Czechoslovakia, he would say he:

(aNC*o*iS SP*o*iL%YEN¼) his (B*o*i) with (T=*o*iS).

The remaining two diphthongs lose their second sound—the (*U*) of "boot"—entirely. In the first instance, "aw-oo"—the (O) of "boat"—is left with only the "aw" of "bought." So if he ran the "whole boat show solo," the Czech-speaking would point out that he ran the:

(H*o*L% B*o*T= *So* S*o*L%*o*).

In the second case, "ah-oo"—the (*O*) of "bout"—retains only the "ah" (*A*), so that "brow" and "crouch" come to resemble "bra" and "crotch." And if we "proudly ask: 'now, how about our town?'," as Czechoslovaks we would:

(P*R*:*A*D=L%Yi) ask: (N*A*, H*A* *A*B*A*T= *AR*: T=*A*N?).

You saw that the (*i*) of "about" is also

transformed into "ah" (*A*), the characteristic vowel of this dialect. So the observation that a paranoid government suspects even "normal, natural ideas and opinions" is modified into their suspecting even:

(N*o*:¼MAL%, NA*C*e*R*:AL% *A*iD=Yi:AS) and (APENYANS).

The (a) in "natural" is another vowel that turns into "ah" (*A*). Thus, if the "man had on a ragged bandana," for the Czech, the:

(MAN HAD=) on a (*R*:*A*K*e*D= BAND=ANA).

(*A*) also takes the place of the (u) sound of "won" and "what," transforming them into "wan" and "watt." So if "young love touches all of us," being from Czechoslovakia, we would comment that:

(YANK L%AF T=*AC*e*S) all (AV:W AS).

Finally, the (*a*) of "aunt" also becomes "ah" (*A*). Thus, if the hosts of the masked ball "ask that we unmask after this dance," in Czechoslovak dialect they would:

(ASG) that (V:Wi: *A*NMASK *A*FT=*eR*:) this (D=ANS).

Oddly enough, (*A*) itself doesn't retain its form but is one of the vowels that is shortened (or flattened); it is reduced to (o) as in "stop." So that if the winner of the contest was the one who "swallowed the largest quantities of waffles," being Czechs, we would announce it was the one who:

(SV:WoL%*o*D=) the (L%o¼*CAST*= KVoNT=YET=Yi:S) of (V:WoFeL%S).

Another such case is the "eh" (e) sound of "head" and "shell," which is flattened till those words rhyme with "had" and "shall." Thus, if she "said to expect them next Wednesday," if Czech-born, she:

(SaT=) to (aGZPaK¼ D=aM NiaGZ¼ V:WaNS¼ei).

Note the Y-glide effect on "next"; this is because the (e) replacement followed an "n." The same applies when it follows an "l," turning "left leg" into:

(L%iaFT= L%iaK).

Other consonants that take a Y-glide when followed by certain vowels are "d," "t," and both "hard TH" (*T*) and "soft th" (*t*). The additional vowels are the (i) of "lip" and the (E) of "leap." In the first instance, (i) is converted into "yee" (YE), so that if one speaks of "this inquisitive English mystic," if Czech-born one might talk of:

(D=YES ENKVESA*T*=YEV:W ENKL%YE*S* MEST=YEK).

You can also see that where (i) *doesn't* turn into (YE) it becomes "ee" (E) ("inquisitive English mystic"). As a sort of compensation, almost the reverse is true of the "ee" (E) sound, making it into a long (i:). Thus, if an instructor complains that it's not "easy to teach these people theories," being Czech-born, he must find that it's not:

(i:Si:) to (T=Yi:*C* D=Yi:S Pi:PeL% T=Yi:*AR*:i:S).

Of course you noted the Y-glides in "teach," "these," and "theories."

Another example of "compensation reversal" takes place between (o) and (*o*). In the first case, (o) as in "cot" and "hock" ends up sounding like (*o*) as in "caught" and "hawk." So that if the editor tells his reporter to "stop concocting odd, shocking copy," in this dialect, he'd tell her to:

(ST=*o*P KANK*o*KT=YEN¼ *o*T=, S*o*KEN¼ K*o*Pi:).

The opposite takes place when the "aw" (*o*) sound comes before an "l," so that the same editor might describe his reporter as one whose "tall talk's all false," pronouncing it:

(T=oL% T=*o*:KS oL% FoL%S).

Note that when (*o*) *doesn't* come before "l" it is merely lengthened ("talk," with the "l" silent).

The (*u*) of "put" is also drawn out, to the point where it becomes another sound: (*U*)—so that "soot" and "full" sound like "suit" and "fool." Thus, if the decorator said the "cushion would look good in wool," if from Czechoslovakia, she would suggest that the:

(K*U*SAN V:W*U*D= L%*U*K K*U*T=) in (V:W*U*L%).

Our last look at vowels are the two instances in which the (*E*) of "fur" changes. In the first case, when this sound (*E*) is *spelled* "e," it evolves into "eh" (e). So that if our decorator's stockbroker said that a "certain merger concerned her," if a Czech, he'd explain that a:

(Se¼T=¼N Me¼*C*e*R*: KANSe¼N¼ He*R*:).

In the second case, (*E*) is altered into "aw" (*o*) when it is spelled "o." Thus, if Martin Luther King, Jr. won the Nobel Prize because the "world took comfort from his work," the Czech-speaking would say the:

(V:Wo¼L%¼) took (K*A*MFo¼T=) from his (V:Wo¼K).

Consonant Changes

Note how all the "r"s disappeared. This is because each of them came before another consonant in the middle of a word, and so were dropped (¼). In any other case, the "r" is strongly trilled (*R*:). The tongue is placed against the gum ridge behind the upper front teeth and vibrated till the sound is like an imitation of a motorcycle, a machine gun, or a pneumatic drill (for a more complete description, see page 12). So if this "year we are very sure of a dry spring," as Czechoslovakians, this:

(Yi:*R*:) we (o*R*: V:Wa*R*:i: *SUR*:) of a (D=*R*:*A*i SP*R*:ENK).

We first met the rule of consonant agreement on page 101 in the chapter on Russian; it applies here as well. Thus, the *unvoiced* consonants "f," "k," "p," and "s" become, respectively, (V), (G), (B), and (Z) at the end of a word, before any *voiced* consonant (B, D, L, *R*:, *T*, V:W, and Z). In the reverse application, the *voiced* consonants "b," "v," "z," and "*T*" emerge as (P), (F), (S), and (T=), respectively, when they are final and precede any *unvoiced* consonant (F, *C*, K, P, Q, S, *S*, and T=). Finally, the (B) becomes a (P) whenever it ends a phrase or sentence.

Certain American consonant sounds do not exist in Czech or Slovak. Neither the "d" nor the "t," for instance, are formed with the tongue against the upper gum ridge but rather with the tongue between the teeth (=). Thus, if you "had good days and bad days," in the Czech dialect, you would remark that you:

(HAD= K*U*D= D=eiS *A*N¼ BAD= D=eiS).

Did you notice that the "d" in "and" was omitted entirely? This occurs both in the middle and at the end of a word when the "d" follows another consonant.

What happens to the "t" is illustrated when a Czech or Slovak tells someone "that it's important to stick strictly to the facts," saying:

(D=*A*T= E¼S EMPo:¼T=ANT= T=*U* ST=YEK S¼*R*:EK¼L%YI: T=*U*) the (F*A*K¼S).

As we can see from "it's," "strictly," and "facts," when the "t" precedes another consonant in the middle of a word, it is eliminated (¼).

(L) is also articulated in the Russian manner: (L%). This *liquid* (%) "l" is made by arching the middle of the tongue against the upper palate (for a more complete description, see page 101). So if one can be "lulled by those lilting, lyrical lines" in a poem, the Czechoslovakian would be:

(L%*A*L%D=) by (D=*o*Z L%YEL%T=YEN¼, L%Yi:*R*:EK*e*L% L%*A*iNS).

As you can see from "those," Czechs can't even approximate some American sounds. The "hard TH" (*T*) of "those" is one of them, which is why it becomes an *interdental* "d" (D=). Thus, if we know the airline gave someone else our luggage because ours was filled "with other clothes than these," if we were Czech, we would complain that they were filled:

(V:WED= *A*D=*e*R: KL%*o*D=Z D=*A*N D=Yi:S).

The "soft th" (*t*) is also replaced, this time with an *interdental* "t" (T=), so that if you maintain that exercise makes one "both healthy and thin," being Czech-speaking, you would say that it makes one:

(B*o*T= HaL%T=Yi:) and (T=YEN).

Another substitution is the unvoiced (K) of "kilt" for the voiced "hard g" of "guilt." Thus the admonition that "if you keep guzzling, you're going to get groggy" becomes:

if you keep (KAZL%YEN¼) you're (K*o*EN¼) to (KaT= K*R*:*o*Ki:).

Note that the "g" is *dropped* (¼) from all "ing" suffixes ("guzzling," "going"). The voiced "j" of "joke" is another sound that the Czech replaces with its unvoiced counterpart, in this case "ch" (*C*) as in "choke." So if the "judge awarded major damages," the Czech-born will report that the:

(*CAC*) awarded (Mei*CoR*: D=*AMeCe*S).

The handling of "v" and "w" is typically Slavic: make the sound by pursing the lips for a "w," pushing the lower lip up to touch the edge of the upper teeth, and *voicing* the

Most of Herbert Lom's roles have been too restrained for his native Czechoslovakian (Prague) dialect to emerge as more than a Continental lilt. However, starting with A Shot in the Dark, *Lom created a character, Chief Inspector Dreyfus, which called for total madness. In this and every other film that pitted his character against Peter Sellers's Inspector Clouseau (such as* The Pink Panther Strikes Again, *United Artists, 1976, shown here) Lom's dialect sallies forth in mad scene after mad scene.*

result. Thus, the sentence: "They must vow never to involve private views, because that's when we will walk away," changes into:

They must (V:WA NiaV:WeR:) to (ENV:WoL%F PR:AiV:WET= V:WUS) because that's (V:WaN V:Wi: V:WEL% V:Wo:K AV:Wei).

In contrast, the "w" part of the Czech substitute for the American (Q) is so subtle that the result sounds like a (KV). So if the cassette player is brought in for repairs with the "request that they quiet the squeaking and squealing" of the mechanism, the Czechoslovakian would:

(R:i:KVaST=) that they (KVAieT=) the (SKVi:KEN¼) and (SKVi:L%YEN¼).

Music, Rhythm, and Pace

As for the music of this dialect, it is spoken two tones lower than American English, has a much larger range, and more up-and-down variation. The principal stress is on the first syllable, but the other syllables are never slurred. For the most part, it is clear and a bit staccato, colored only by the Y-glide and by the effects of consonant agreement. Appropriately, the fully orchestrated version of Smetana's *The Moldau* bears a distinct resemblance to the patterns of Czechoslovak speech (and therefore to the dialect). The stately slowness of that work is also characteristic of the pace of the dialect.

Observation and Notes

Besides Czechoslovak literature, it is hard to say where we can observe the authentic characteristics of these people, who have always adapted quickly to American ideas and ways. However, the dialect itself can be heard at various local Czech and Slovak societies and churches—and sometimes in the speech of character actor Herbert Lom (especially when his role calls for intensity or excitement).

GENERAL CZECHOSLOVAKIAN - PRAGUE, EDUCATED - NITRA, SLOVAKIA - BRNO, BOHEMIA - KLADNO, RURAL

GUIDE PAGES		Generl Czech	Prague Educ.	Nitra Slovak	Brno, Bohem	Kladno Rural
						All 5
CHANGE: (main) Mein, (say) Sei, (heyday) HeiD=ei	A					ei
BUT after L or N: (name) NieiM, (lane) L%ieiN	A					iei)ln
CHANGE: (each) i:C, (me) Mi:, (seem) Si:M, (be) Bi:, (he) Hi:	E	i:	&	&	&	
BUT after D,L,N,T,t,T: (teach) TYi:C, (lean) L%Yi:N, (knee) NYi:	E	Yi:)d lNttT	&	&	&	
OR change: iC, Mi, SiM, TiC, Ni	E					i
						All 5
SHORTEN: (ice) AiS, (line) L%AiN, (my) MAi, (I'm) AiM	I					Ai
CHANGE: (own) oN, (solo) SoL%o, (whole) HoL%, (no) No	O					o
No change: (you) U, (few) FU, (use) US, (cute) KUT=	U					U
CHANGE: (am) AM, (man) MAN, (ran) R:AN, (lamb) L%AM, (catch) KAC	a	A	&	&		&
OR change: eM, MeN, R:eN, KeC	a				e	
OR after L,N: L%ieM, (nap) NieP	a				ie)ln	
						All 5
CHANGE: (edge) aC, (bell) BaL%, (them) D=aM, (men) MaN	e					a
BUT after L or N: (ledge) L%iaC, (neck) NiaK, (let) L%iaT=	e					ia)ln
CHANGE: (in) EN, (bill) BEL%, (him) HEM, (chin) CEN	i					E
BUT after D,L,N,T,t,T: (dim) D=YEM, (lit) L%YET=, (knit) NYET=, (til) T=YEL%, (thick) T=YEK, (this) D=YES	i					YE)d lNttT
CHANGE: (on) oN, (stop) ST=oP, (not) NoT=, (clock) KL%oK	o					o
CHANGE: (run) R:AN, (touch) T=AC, (does) D=AS, (up) AP	u					A
CHANGE: (calm) KoL%M, (large) L%o¼C, (watch) V:WoC	A					o
CHANGE if spelled ER: (her) HeR:, (were) V:WeR:	E					e$er
AND " " " OR: (worm) V:Wo¼M, (worse) V:Wo¼S	E					o$or
No change: (predict) PR:ID=EK¼, (propose) PR:IPoS	I					I
CHANGE: (hour) AR:, (brown) BR:AN, (now) NA, (out) AT=	O					A
No change: (room) R:UM, (do) D=U, (true) T=R:U	U					U
CHANGE: (and) AN¼, (dance) D=ANS, (laugh) L%AF	a					A
No change: (simple) SEMPeL%, (dozen) D=AZeN	e					e
CHANGE: (ago) AGo, (sofa) SoFA, (pajama) PACoMA, (above) ABAV:W	i	A	&	&	&	
OR change initially: AGo, ABAV:W	i					-A
						All 5
LONGER: (door) D=o:R:, (form) Fo:¼M, (law) L%o:	o					o:
BUT before L: (all) oL%, (call) KoL%, (fall) FoL%	o					o(l
CHANGE: (bush) BUS, (full) FUL%, (could) KUD=, (put) PUT=	u					U
SHORTER: (oil) oiL%, (join) CoiN, (boy) Boi, (noise) NoiS	oE					oi

CHANGE at end of phrase: (bob.) BoP., (club.) KL%AP.	B	..P
AND final before unvoiced consonant: (grab for) GR:AP Fo:R:	B	.P(¢½
No change: (much) MAC, (future) FUCER:, (which) V:WEC	C	C
INTERDENTAL: (day) D=ei, (did) D=YED=, (dumb) D=AM	D	D=
BUT DROP medially and finally after a consonant: (endure) aN¼UR:, (childhood) CAiL%¼HUD=, (and) AN¼, (cold) KoL%¼	D	/.¼)¢
AND change finally before unvoiced consonant: (did so) D=YET=So, (bad for) BAT=Fo:R:, (had come) HAT=KAM	D	.T=(¢½

Key:

$ spelled	: stronger	. finally	S show, sure	= interdental
¼ dropped	& as shown	.. " at end of phrase	R trilled R	¢ consonants
% liquid	- initial		(preceding	¢½ unvoiced "
	/ medially		) following	

GENERAL CZECHOSLOVAKIAN - PRAGUE, EDUCATED - NITRA, SLOVAKIA - BRNO, BOHEMIA - KLADNO, RURAL

GUIDE PAGES		Generl Czech	Prague Educ.	Nitra Slovak	Brno, Bohem	Kladno Rural
						All 5
Change finally before voiced consonant: (off base) o:V BeiS, (if this) EV D=YES, (safe bet) SeiV BaT=	F					.V(¢:
CHANGE: (go) Ko, (big) BEK, (grain) KR:eiN, (again) AKaN	G					K
AND DROP from ING suffix: (going) KoEN¼ (moving) MUV:WEN¼	G					¼ing)
No change	H					H
CHANGE: (judge) CAC, (age) eiC, (major) MeiCoR:, (damage) D=AMAC	J	C	&		&	&
OR change: D=ZAD=Z, eiD=Z	J			D=Z		
						All 5
Change finally before a voiced consonant: (make do) MeiG D=U, (stick by) ST=YEG BAi, (think that) T=YENG D=AT=	K					.G(¢:
LIQUID SOUND: (lull) L%AL%, (law) L%o:, (will) V:WEL%	L					L%
No change	MN					M N
CHANGE finally: (ink) ENG, (sunk) SANG, (thank) T=ANG	n					.NG
Change finally before a voiced consonant: (step down) STaB D=AN, (stop them) SToB D=aM (soap dish) SoB D=YES	P					.B(¢:
CHANGE: (equal) i:KVAL%, (square) SKVeiR:, (quit) KVET=	Q					KV
STRONG TRILL: (rear) R:i:R:, (very) V:WaR:i:, (are) oR:	R					R:
BUT DROP medially before a consonant: (art) o¼T=, (burn) BE¼N, (farm) Fo¼M, (dark) D=o¼K, (curl) KE¼L%	R					/¼(¢
Change finally before a voiced consonant: (face down) FeiZ D=AN, (nice boy) NAiZ Boi, (miss them) MEZ D=aM	S					.Z(¢:
No change: (shush) SAS, (sure) SUR:, (motion) MoSAN	S					S
INTERDENTAL: (tell) T=aL%, (ten) T=aN, (team) T=Yi:M, (but) BAT=	T	T=	&	&	&	&
BUT DROP medially before a consonant: (strictly) S¼R:EK¼L%Yi:	T	/¼(¢	&	&	&	&
CHANGE: (thin) T=YEN, (both) BoT= (healthy) HaL%T=Yi: (three) T=R:i:	t	T=		&	&	&
OR change: SEN, BoS, HaL%Si:	t		S			
CHANGE: (then) D=aN, (that) D=AT= (with) V:WED=, (other) AD=eR:	T	D=		&	&	&
OR change: ZaN, ZAT=, V:WEZ	T		Z			
CHANGE: (view) V:WU, (vow) V:WA, (ever) aV:WeR:, (oven) AV:WeN	V	V:W	&		&	&
OR no change: VU, VA, aVeR:, AVeN	V			V		
BUT change finally before unvoiced consonant: (of some) AF SAM	V	.F(¢½	&	&	&	&
						All 5
CHANGE: (water) V:Wo:T=eR:, (away) AV:Wei, (when) V:WaN	W					V:W
CHANGE KS sound: (taxi) TAGZi:, (box) BoGZ, (next) NaGZT=	X					GZ4ks
CHANGE if spelled S: (busy) BESi:, (music) MUSEK, (his) HES, (prison) PR:ESeN, (was) V:WAS, (result) R:i:SAL%T=	Z					S$s
AND change finally before an unvoiced consonant: (size ten) SAiS: T=aN, (jazz combo) CAS: KoMBo	Z					.S: (¢½
No change: (pleasure) PLazER:, (vision) V:WEzAN	z					z

Key:

		& as shown		
C church	$ spelled	: stronger	¢ consonants	R trilled R
¼ drop	/ medial	(preceding	¢: voiced "	= interdental
4 for	. finally	) in suffix	¢½ un- " "	% liquid sound

MASTER CATEGORY 17

YUGOSLAVIAN

Yugoslavia is a sort of Balkan "UN" where respectably sizable groups speak, variously, Slovene, Albanian, Hungarian, Turkish, Slovak, Italian, Romany, Bulgarian, and even German. Linguistically, however, the "land of the southern Slavs" is dominated by the Serbs and the Croats. Although these two people communicate in two dialects of the *same* language, there are vast differences in their religions, cultures, histories, and even their alphabets. The Serbs have enjoyed military and political power, as well as nationhood; they are overwhelmingly Eastern Orthodox, and use the Cyrillic alphabet. The Croats have seldom had either political independence or power, are predominantly Roman Catholic, and use the Roman alphabet. Despite these differences, the one subdialect that stands out the most in the GUIDE PAGES is the *Zagreb, Educated*, because General Yugoslavian is such a "broad" dialect.

It isn't the Slavic liquid "l," the strongly trilled "r," or consonant agreement that makes this dialect so broad; Czechoslovak has all of these. It is the shortening of most of the simple vowels—and *all* of the diphthongs—that takes it so far from American English sounds.

Vowel Changes

For example, the "oo" (*U*) part of "yoo" (U) as in "unit" is reduced till it sounds like the vowel of "full" rather than that of "fool." Thus, if the music teacher understands the "value of a few pure tunes to beautiful music," if she's from Yugoslavia, she'll see the:
(VeL%Y*u*) of a (FY*u* PY*uR*: T=Y*u*NS) to
(BY*u*T=*A*F*u*L% MY*u*SEK).

That same (*U*) element makes up the second part of (*O* = *AU*) as in "cow," and again it is shortened. So that if we have a friendship so solid that we "cannot now allow doubt about our vows," as Yugoslavs, we cannot:
(N*Au* AL%*Au* D=*Au*T= AB*Au*T=
AuR: V*Au*S).

The next diphthong (I = *A*E), as in "bite," also retains the (*A*) while abbreviating the second sound, this time to the (i) of "bit." Thus, "I might try iodine" becomes:
(*A*i M*A*iT= T=*R*:*A*i *A*i*A*T=*A*iN).

The (E) element is also weakened to (i) in the double vowel (*o*E) as in "boy." So if a jealous earl "employed poison to destroy the royal choice," being Yugoslav we would say that he:
(eMPL%*o*iT= P*o*iS¼N) to
(D=YES¼*R*:*o*i) the (*R*:*o*ieL% C*o*iZ).

The (E) part of (A = eE) as in "bay" doesn't survive the shortening process at all: "main" and "waste" come out sounding like "men" and "vest"—and "they say most pain fades away" changes into:
(D=e Se) most (PeN FeT=S *A*Ve).

Similarly, the second element of the diphthong (O = *oU*) as in "boat" is completely lost, making "so" and "pose" sound like "saw" and "pause," and if the musician "knows the whole oboe solo," our Yugoslav would report that she:
(N*o*S) the (*h*oL% *o*B*o* S*o*L%*o*).

Even some simple vowels are abridged. The (*U*) of "wooed" and "Luke," for instance, is transformed into the sound in "would" and "look." Thus, if his "blue moods soon ruined their honeymoon," the Yugoslav-born would explain that his:
(BL%*u* M*u*T=S S*u*N *R*:*u*EN¼) their
(*h*oNiM*u*N).

Another abbreviated vowel is "ah" (*A*) as in "heart." It is transformed into the (o) of "hot"—so if "we want to watch the Guard squad march by," being Yugoslav-speaking, we might announce:

(Vi VoN¼) to (Vo*C*) the (Go¼T= SKVoD= Mo¼*C*) by.

You noticed that the (E) of "we" was chopped down; this results in "eat" and "seen" coming to resemble "it" and "sin." Thus, if "he and she both believe in weird theories," the Yugoslav would find that:

(*h*i) and (*S*i) both (BiL%iF EN Vi¼T= T=i*AR*:iS).

You can see from what happens to the (i) of "in" that a *reverse conversion* takes place. So if we try the number again to see "if it is still busy," being Yugoslav-born, we would talk of seeing:

(EF ET= ES *S*T=YEL% BESi).

In "still" we observe our first case of the Y-glide; that initial Y is added after D=, L%, N, or T=. Thus, if he found that mice "didn't live in this thin niche," a Yugoslav would advise that they:

(D=YEN¼ L%YEF EN D=YES T=YEN NYE*C*).

The only other instance of the Y-glide is when the (e) of "said" follows either an L or an N. So if the conservatives are determined that they will "never let the Left into the next election," if Yugoslav-speaking, you could say that they will:

(NieV*eR*: L%ieD=) the (L%ieF¼) into the (NieX¼ iL%ieKS*A*N).

In two cases vowels are actually *lengthened*. The "aw" (*o*) of "fall" becomes "aww" (*o*:), and the (*i*) of "ago" is extended to "ah" (*A*). Thus, "pajamas on the family sofa" become:

(P*AC*oM*A*S) on the (FeM*A*L%i SoF*A*).

Note how the (a) is altered in "family"; this is one of several vowels whose sounds are completely changed by the Yugoslav-speaking. In this instance, the (a) of "bad" and "ham" turns into the (e) of "bed" and "hem." Thus, "he was glad he had packed a bandana" becomes:

he was (GL%eT=) he (*h*eT= PeKT=) a (BeNT=eN*A*).

Another total conversion happens to the (u) of "nut" and "suck," making it into the (o) of "not" and "sock." So if their "love of justice has undone the government," if Yugoslavian you would comment that their:

(L%oF oF *C*oS¼EZ) has (oNT=oN) the (GoV*u*¼NM*A*N¼).

Another transformation is made in the (*a*) of "aunt," which becomes the uniquely Yugoslav diphthong (*A*e)—consisting of the (*A*) of "watt" and the (e) of "wet." Thus, if he finished that "last flask rather fast," being from Yugoslavia, you might observe that he finished that:

(L%*A*eS¼ FL%*A*eSK *R*:*A*eD=*eR*: F*A*eS¼).

The (*E*) of "her" undergoes two changes. In most cases, it is reshaped into the (*u*) of "book," so that "pert" and "word" turn out to be similar to "put" and "wood," and if she "worked to earn her return," to a Yugoslav she:

(V*u*¼KT=) to (*u*¼N *hu*R: *R*:iT=*u*¼N).

However, when spelled "a," the (*E*) shifts into "ah" (*A*), and a "separate collar" becomes a:

(SeP*AR*:ET= KoL%*AR*:).

Consonant Changes

You saw the R handled in two ways in the last phrases. In the middle of a word and before another consonant, it is dropped (¼)—so if we wondered what "part of the world the girl was born in," in this dialect we would wonder what:

(Po¼T=) of the (V*u*¼L%¼) the (G*u*¼L%) was (B*o*:¼N) in.

In all other positions, the R receives the strong Slavic trill (*R*:). For this, press the tip of the tongue against the upper gum ridge and voice the sound until the tongue vibrates, producing a sound like the imitation of a pneumatic drill (for more on this, see page 12). Thus, if in Hollywood it's not "very rare to find writers for hire," if Yugoslav-born we would point out that it's not:

(Ve*R*:i *R*:e*R*:) to find (*R*:*A*iT=e¼S Fo:*R*: h*A*i*R*:).

A second typically Slavic handling is the liquid "l" (L%), made by arching the middle of the tongue against the upper palate (further description on page 101). So if the fund "will help all brilliant, skillful lads," for the Yugoslav, the fund:

(VEL% *h*eL%P *o*:L% B*R*:EL%*YA*N¼, SKEL%F*u*L% L%eT=S).

Slavic consonant agreement is another characteristic of this dialect. The unvoiced consonants F, K, P, and T change into their voiced counterparts (V, G, B, and D=) when they are final and precede a *voiced* consonant (B, D=, G, V, or Z) in the same phrase. Contrariwise, the voiced consonants Z, D, and B turn into their unvoiced counterparts (S, T=, and P) when they are final and precede an *unvoiced* consonant (*C*, F, K, P, Q, S, *S*, or T=) in the same phrase.

This same shift takes place when B or D comes at the end of a phrase. Thus "bulb.," "rob.," and "bribe." become (BoL%P.), (*R*:oP.), and (B*R*:*A*iP.), while "did.," "had.," and "made." change into (D=YET=.), (*h*eT=.), and (MeT=.). F and S both alter *whenever* they are final—thus, to "conceive of love" becomes to:

(K*A*NSiF oF L%oF).

And our request to "lease us a nice place" evolves into:

(L%iZ oZ) a (N*A*iZ PL%eZ).

Z becomes S whenever it is *spelled* "s," so that "his nose was pleased by flowers" emerges as:

(*h*ES NoS VoS PL%iSD=) by (FL%*Aue*¼S).

Finally, J and "zh" (*z*) both shift to the unvoiced mode *at all times*. Thus, "we can't manage to judge such strange urges" transforms into:

we can't (MeNE*C*) to (*C*o*C*) such (*S*T=*R*:eN*C* *u*¼*C*e*S*)

and "the confusion between delusions, visions, and illusions causes divisions" changes into:

the (K*A*NFY*u*S*A*N) between (D=YEL%*u*S*A*NS, VE*S*ANS) and (EL%*u*S*A*NS) causes (D=*A*VE*S*ANS).

The Yugoslav handling of D and T rates separate study. Both consonants are pronounced interdentally (=): with the tongue touching the edge of the upper front teeth rather than the upper gum ridge. Thus, if the parrot "said 'Good day,' distinctly," for a Yugoslav she:

(SeD= G*u*D= D=e D=YES¼ENK¼L%i)

and if she was "taught to tell the truth," being from Yugoslavia we would remark that she was:

(T=*o*:T= T=*u* T=eL%) the (T=*R*:*u*T=).

When D or T follow a consonant at the end of a word, the sound is dropped (¼). So if he didn't "mind a cold hand," the Yugoslav would suggest that he didn't:

(M*A*iN¼) a (KoL%¼ *h*eN¼)

and if she "couldn't rest till the guilt left," if born in Yugoslavia, you would say that she:

(K*u*T=N¼ *R*:eS¼) till the (GEL%¼ L%ieF¼).

You noted what happened to the D in "couldn't"; that occurs whenever it is in the middle of a word. Thus, "support was needed under the middle of her body" becomes:

support was (NiT=*e*D= oNT=*eR*:) the (MET=*e*L%) of her (BoT=i).

On the other hand, T is *dropped* (¼) from the middle of a word, before *or* after another consonant. So that if the committee "itself was mostly into their fact-finding stage," a Yugoslav should say that the committee:

(E¼SeL%V) was (MoS¼L%i EN¼u D=eR: FeK¼FAiNT=YEN¼) stage.

As you saw, the "hard TH" (T) of "their" is one of the half-dozen consonant sounds that can't be articulated by Yugoslavs; in this case, they turn it into an interdental "d" (D=). Thus, if we never took a trip "other than with them," if Yugoslav-speaking, we would say:

(oD=eR: D=eN VED= D=eM).

Since the "soft th" is modified into another interdental (T=), "economists thought of nothing but health through growth," turns into:

economists (T=o:T=) of (NoT=YENG) but (heL%T= T=R:u GR:oT=).

W is another consonant Yugoslavs can't handle: they convert it into V. So if we promised "we would wave farewell when we went away," if Yugoslav-born, we might admit we promised:

(Vi VuD= VeF FeR:VeL% VeN Vi VeN¼ AVe).

This also affects Q, so that "it became quite quiet since it quit squeaking" comes out:

it became (KVAiT= KVAieT=) since it (KVET= SKViKEN¼).

From "squeaking" you can see that an initial S evolves into an "sh" (S) when it precedes another consonant. So the admonition: "stop speaking sneaky slanders," becomes:

(ST=oP SPiKEN¼ SNiKi SL%EN¼e¼S).

Finally, when faced with the American "h," Yugoslavs transform it into a heavy "h" (H:) in the middle of a word, and a (h) at the start of a word. This last is formed where we normally produce K and G, except that instead of shutting off the air entirely, we leave a narrow opening to let it hiss through (for more, see page 12). So, if "he had hotheads in his household," we'd say:

(hi heT= ho¼H:eT=S) in (hES hAuSH:oL%¼).

Music, Rhythm, and Pace

All of these modifications are fitted into a Yugoslav music that is spoken three tones lower than American English and enjoys a wider range and a greater up-and-down variation. The dialect is flowing, slower than American speech, and marked by clear vowel sounds. Unfortunately, the stress is inconsistent, since the Yugoslav can single out a prefix, a suffix, or an ending to receive the greatest emphasis.

Observation and Notes

As holds true for many other Slavic peoples in the U.S., your best bet for hearing the dialect is in the churches (Serbian Orthodox and Croatian Catholic) and the ethnic societies. In larger American cities, however, there is one other delightful possibility: the Yugoslav folk-dance centers. Like the Greeks, the Yugoslavs are devoted to their native dances, anxious to teach outsiders, and ready to befriend anyone who shows an interest in their culture. If you have this opportunity, don't let it get away!

GENERAL YUGOSLAV - BEOGRAD, SERBIAN - LJUBLJANA, SLOVENE

ZAGREB, EDUCATED *GUIDE PAGES*	SOUND	General Yugoslav	Beograd Serbian Yugo.	Ljubljana Slovene Yugo.	Zagreb Educated Yugo.
Change in all positions: (aim) eM, (air) e*R*: (maybe) MeBi (nail) NeL% (say) Se	A	e	&	&	
OR change: eiM, ei*R*:, MeiBi:, NeiL%	A				ei
Change in all positions: (tree) T=*R*:i, (each) i*C* (here) *h*i*R*: (reveal) *R*:iViL%	E	i	&	&	
OR change: T=*R*:i:, i:*C*, H:i:*R*:	E				i:
Change in all positions: (I'm) *A*iM (by) B*A*i (line) L%*A*iN (try) T=*R*:*A*i (my) M*A*i	I	*A*i	&	&	&
Change in all positions: (home) *ho*M, (only) *o*NL%i (solo) S*o*L%*o* (show) *So*	O	*o*	&	&	
OR change: H:*ou*M, *ou*NL%i:, S*ou*L%*ou*, *Sou*	O				*ou*
Change in all positions: (you'll) Y*u*L%, (few) FY*u*, (pure) PY*uR*:, (mule) MY*u*L%	U	Y*u*	&	&	&
Change in all positions: (am) eM (man) MeN, (angry) eNG*R*:i, (happy) *h*ePi	a	e	&	&	
OR no change: aM, MaN, aNG*R*:i:, H:aPi:	a				a
CHANGE after L or N: (next) NieKS½, (let) L%ieT= (neck) NieK (leg) L%ieG	e	ie)ln	&	&	&
CHANGE: (pin) PEN, (fish) FE*S*, (him) *h*EM, (chill) *C*EL%, (in) EN, (it) ET=	i	E			&
OR no change: PiN, Fi*S*, H:iM, *C*iL%, iN	i		i	&	
BUT after D,L,N,T,*t*,*T*: (dim) D=YEM, (till) T=YEL%, (English) ENGL%YE*S*	i	YE)dL nT*tT*			&
OR change: D=YiM, T=YiL%, iNGL%Yi*S*	i		Yi)dL	&	

		All 4
No change: (on) oN, (hopscotch) *h*oPSKo*C*, (stop) ST=oP	o	o
CHANGE: (up) oP, (come) KoM, (was) VoS, (does) D=oS	u	o
CHANGE: (are) o*R*:, (swan) SVoN, (far) Fo*R*:, (calm) KoL%M	*A*	o
CHANGE: (girl) G*u*¼L%, (were) V*uR*:, (work) V*u*¼K	*E*	*u*
BUT if spelled AR: (separate) SePA*R*:*e*T=, (collar) KoL%A*R*:	*E*	A$ar
No change: (predict) P*R*:*I*D=EK¼, (propose) P*R*:*I*P*o*S	*I*	*I*

CHANGE: (out) *A*uT=, (down) D=*A*uN	*O*	*Au*		&	&
OR change: *A*T=, D=*A*N, (now) N*A*	*O*		A		
Change in all positions: (do) D=*u*, (soon) S*u*N, (room) *R*:*u*M, (true) T=*R*:*u*	*U*	*u*	&	&	
OR change: D=*u*:, S*u*:N, *R*:*u*:M, T=*R*:*u*:	*U*				*u*:
Change in all positions: (dance) D=AeNZ, (ask) AeSK (bath) BAeT= (laugh) L%AeF	*a*	Ae			&
OR change: D=ANZ, AS:K, BAT=, L%AF	*a*		A		
OR change: D=eNZ, eZK, BeT=, L%eF	*a*			e	

		All 4
No change: (apple) ePeL%, (dozen) D=oZ*e*N, (often) *o*:F*e*N	*e*	*e*
CHANGE: (sofa) S*o*FA, (ago) AG*o*, (family) FeMAL%i	*i*	A
LONGER: (door) D=*o*:*R*:, (all) *o*:L%, (cause) K*o*:S	*o*	*o*:
No change: (push) Pu*S*, (good) GuD=, (would) VuD=	*u*	*u*
CHANGE: (boy) B*o*i, (oil) *o*iL%, (noise) N*o*iS (join) *C*oiN	*o*E	*o*i

Key:

			t thin, both
C church	*h* loch, ich	*S* show, sure	*T* then, with
¼ dropped	& as shown	*R* trilled R	= interdental
$ spelled	: stronger	) following	% liquid sound

GENERAL YUGOSLAV - BEOGRAD, SERBIAN - LJUBLJANA, SLOVENE ZAGREB, EDUCATED

GUIDE PAGES		Gen. Yugo.	Beograd Serb.	Ljublj Sloven	Zagreb Educ.
Change finally before unvoiced consonant:	B	.P(¢½	&	&	&
(grab for) GR:ePFo:R: (hub cap) hoPKeP					
AND change at end of phrase: (sob.) SoP.,	B	..P	&	&	
(rub.) R:oP., (web.) VeP., (fib.) FEP.					
OR change: SoBP., R:oBP., VWeBP., FEBP.	B				..BP
No change: (much) MoC, (future) FYuCuR:	C	C	&	&	&
INTERDENTAL: (day) D=e, (drop) D=R:oP,	D	D=	&	&	&
(done) D=oN, (dream) D=R:iM, (do) D=u					
BUT change medially: (body) BoT=i,	D	/T=	&	&	
(under) oNT=eR:, (middle) MET=eL%					
OR change: BoD=T=i:, oND=T=eR:	D				/D=T=
AND drop finally after consonant: (land)	D	.¼)¢	&	&	&
L%AeN¼, (cold) KoL%¼, (send) SeN¼					
& change final before unvoiced consonant:	D	.T=	&	&	&
(did for) D=YET=Fo:R: (had some) heT=SoM		(¢½			
AND change at end of phrase: (had.) heT=.,	D	..T=	&	&	
(died.) D=AiT=., (bed.,) BeT=.					
OR change: H:aD=T=., D=AiD=T=., BeD=T=.	D				..D=T=
Change finally before voiced consonant:	F	.V(¢:	&	&	
(off base) o:VBeS, (half done) hAeVD=oN					
OR change: o:VFBeiS, H:AeVFD=oN	F				.VF(¢:
DROP from ING suffix: (going) GoEN¼,	G	¼ing)	&	&	&
(coming) KoMEN¼, (getting) GeT=EN¼					
Change initially: (him) hEM, (how) hAu,	H	-h		&	
(here) hiR:, (have) hAeF, (high) hAi					
OR stronger: H:EM, H:Au, H:i:R:, H:AeVF	H		-H:		&
AND stronger medially: (household)	H	/H:	&	&	&
hAuSH:oL%¼, (perhaps) PuR:H:ePS					
CHANGE: (judge) CoC, (gradual) GR:eCueL%	J	C	&	&	
OR change: zoz, GR:azueL%	J				z
Change finally before voiced consonant:	K	.G(¢:	&	&	
(make do) MeGD=u, (back door) BeGD=o:R:					
OR change: MeiGKD=u:, BaGKD=o:R:	K				.GK(¢:
LIQUID SOUND: (lull) L%oL% (let) L%ieT=	L	L%	&	&	&
No change	MN	MN	&	&	&
Change finally: (ink) ENG, (sunk) SoNG,	n	.NG	&	&	
(chunk) CoNG, (thank) T=eNG, (pink) PENG					
OR change: ENGK, SoNGK, CoNGK, T=aNGK	n				.NGK
Change finally before voiced consonant:	P	.B(¢:	&	&	
(step down) ST=eBD=AuN (pop gun) PoBGoN					
OR change: ST=eBPD=AuN, PoBPGoN	P				.BP(¢:
Change in all positions: (quick)	Q	KV		&	
KVEK, (equal) iKVeL%, (square) SKVeR:					
OR change: KVWEK, i:KVWeL%, SKVWeiR:	Q		KVW		&
STRONG TRILL: (rear) R:iR:, (unrest)	R	R:	&	&	&
oNR:eS¼, (very) VeR:i, (dry) D=R:Ai					
BUT drop medially before consonant:	R	/¼(¢	&	&	
(park) Po¼K, (born) Bo:¼N, (girl) Gu¼L%					
OR retain: PoR:K, Bo:R:N, GuR:L%	R				/R:(¢

Key:
h loch, ich - initially z pleasure ¢ consonants
(preceding ¼ dropped / medially S show, sure ¢: voiced "
) following & as shown . finally R trilled R ¢½ un- " "
) in suffix : stronger .. " in phrase % liquid = interdental

GENERAL YUGOSLAV - BEOGRAD, SERBIAN - LJUBLJANA, SLOVENE

ZAGREB, EDUCATED

GUIDE PAGES	SOUND	General Yugoslav	Beograd Serbian Yugo.	Ljubljana Slovene Yugo.	Zagreb Educated Yugo.
Change initially before a consonant: (stop) *S*T=oP, (sleep) *S*L%iP, (snow) *S*N*o*	S	-*S*(¢			&
OR no change: ST=oP, SL%iP, SN*o*	S			-S(¢	
OR change medially: (useful) Y*u*ZF*u*L%, (decide) D=YiZAiD=, (insect) InZeK¼	S			/Z	
OR no change: Y*u*SF*u*L%, D=YESAiD=, ENSeK¼	S	/S			&
OR stronger: S:T=oP, Y*u*S:F*u*L%, iNS:eK¼	S		-/S:		
AND change finally: (cease) SiZ, (yes) YeZ (nice) NAiZ (less) L%ieZ (us) oZ	S	.Z	&	&	
OR change: Si:SZ, YeSZ, NAiSZ, L%ieSZ	S		.		.SZ
No change: (show) *So*, (sure) *SuR*:	*S*	*S*	&	&	&
INTERDENTAL: (take) T=eK, (tell) T=eL%, (tie) T=Ai, (trade) T=*R*:eD=, (toe) T=*o*	T	T=	&	&	&
BUT drop medially before or after consonant: (into) EN¼*u*, (itself) E¼SeL%F	T	/¼Ɪ¢	&	&	
OR retain: ENT=*u*, ET=SeL%F	T				/T=
BUT drop finally after a consonant: (apt) eP¼, (fact) FeK¼, (rest) *R*:eS¼	T	.¼)¢	&	&	&
& change finally before voiced consonant: (sit back) SED=BeK, (get down) GeD=A*u*N	T	.D= (¢:	&	&	
OR change: SED=T=BaK, GeD=T=D=A*u*N	T				.D=T=(¢:
Change in all positions: (thin) T=YEN, (nothing) NoT=YEN¼, (mouth) MA*u*T=	*t*	T=	&	&	&
Change in all positions: (other) oD=*eR*:, (them) D=eM (with) VED= (that) D=eT=	*T*	D=	&	&	&
Change medially: (over) *o*V:W*eR*: (never) NeV:W*eR*:, (advertise) eD=V:W*u*¼T=AiS	V		/V:W	&	
OR no medial change: *o*V*eR*:, NeV*eR*:	V	/V			&
BUT change finally: (involve) ENVoL%F, (revive) *R*:iVAiF (give) GEF (love) L%oF	V	.F	&	&	
OR change: ENVoL%VF, *R*:i:VAiVF, GEVF	V				.VF
Change in all positions: (where) Ve*R*:, (away) AVe, (why) VAi, (swim) SVEM	W	V	&		
OR change: V:We*R*:. AV:We, V:WAi, SV:WEM	W			V:W	
OR change: VWei*R*:, AVWei, VWAi, SVWEM	W				VW
No change	X	X	&	&	&
Change when spelled S: (busy) BESi (is) ES (please) PL%iS (was) VoS (use) Y*u*S	Z	S$s		&	&
OR change: BiS:i, iS:, PL%iS:, VoS:	Z		S:$s		
& change final before unvoiced consonant: (size ten) SAiST=eN (jazz combo) CeSKoMB*o*	Z	.S(¢½		&	
OR change: S:AiS:T=eN, CeS:KoMB*o*	Z		.S:(¢½		
OR change: SAiZST=eN, zaZSKoMB*ou*	Z				.ZS(¢½
Change in all positions: (vision) VE*S*AN (measure) Me*SuR*: (confusion) KANFY*uS*AN	z	*S*	&	&	
OR no change: VEzAN, Mez*u*R:, KANFY*u*zAN	z				z

Key:
¼ dropped ¢ consonants - initial (preceding = interdental
$ spelled ¢: voiced " / medial Ɪ before/after *R* trilled R
& as shown ¢½ un- " " . finally) following :stronger

MASTER CATEGORY 18

HUNGARIAN

The Hungarian dialect is one that has dogged my steps through twenty-nine countries and four continents, till I am halfway convinced that, no matter what remote corner of the world I might find myself in, somehow an English-speaking Hungarian will pop up and become one of my closest friends.

While the pressures of foreign domination and domestic tyranny have scattered Hungarians over the face of the earth, they have solidly united those who remained on the Magyar Plain (which they have occupied for the last thousand years). Thus, we find much less fragmentation and differences among the subdialects. Naturally, the subdialect closest to American English is *Budapest, Educated*. Bearing no resemblance to the parodied "Dracula" dialect, *Budapest, Educated* is often mistaken for General Central European—or even that most general of dialects, the Continental accent.

Unlike the languages of most of the rest of Europe, Hungarian is neither Slavic, Germanic, nor Romance; its "closest relative" is Finnish. At one time, the two were grouped as the Finno-Ugric branch; but present-day Finnish bears about as much relation to Hungarian as Persian does to English. Both languages however, have retained the same music, which makes for a strong similarity in the dialects; we'll explore the differences in the following chapter on Finnish.

Vowel Changes

The most identifiable characteristics of the Hungarian dialect are its handling of final consonants, of simple vowels, and of diphthongs. Seventy percent of all final consonant sounds are followed by a barely voiced (*e*½). This is an even shorter, less-voiced vowel than the one that we saw serving a parallel function in Italian. Parallel rather than the same function, since the Italian add-on is a substitute for the vowel with which most Italians words end while this one is the result of Hungarian clarity and consequent overemphasis.

The difference in vowel treatment is twofold: most simple vowels are changed; all diphthongs are shortened. These double vowels number six in American English. Three of them have "ee" (E) for a second sound: "ay" (A) as in "bay" = eE, (I) as in "buy" = *A*E, and (*o*E) as in "boy." In these three, the (E) is reduced to the (i) of "fill." So if the furniture refinishers are phoning and "they say they will take the table away today," if we were from Hungary, we would report that:

(Dei Sei Dei) will (TeiK*e*½) the (TeiBeL*e*½ *A*Vei T*u*Dei).

Then if I want to suggest that you "might like my fried rice," as a Hungarian, I would say that you:

(M*A*iT*e*½ L*A*iK*e*½ M*A*i F*R*: :*A*iD*e*½ *R*: : *A*iZ*e*½).

In the last of this trio, "oy," not only is the second sound reduced but the first is changed from "aw" (*o*) to "ah" (*A*). Thus, if the "boy's annoying voice spoiled the voyage," a Hungarian might complain that the:

(B*A*iS *A*N*A*iiNG*e*½ V*A*iZ*e*½ SP*A*iLD*e*½) the (V*A*iiJ*e*½).

The other three diphthongs have "oo" as a second sound: "oh" (O) as in "foal" = *oU*, "yoo" (U) as in "fuel" = Y*u*, and "ow" (*O*) as in "foul" = *AU*. We must approach each one individually. In the "yoo" (U) of "use," the (*U*) is cut down to the (*u*) of "put." Thus, if you think very "few value the mule as beautiful or cute," and you are Hungarian-speaking, you must observe that:

(F*Yu* VeL*Yu*) the (M*Yu*L*e*½) as
(B*Yu*TeF*u*L*e*½) or (K*Yu*T*e*½).

On the other hand, the (O) of "phone" and "close" loses its (*U*) part entirely, making those words sound like "fawn" and "clause." So if he "rode his own polo ponies," in the Hungarian dialect, you would say that he:

(*R*:: oD*e*½) his (oN*e*½ PoLo PoNES).

Finally, in the (*O*) of "now," not only is the "oo" (*U*) eliminated, but the "ah" (*A*) is drawn out (:). Thus, if you want to exclaim "how about those downtown crowds!" being Hungarian-born, you would comment:

(H*A*: *A*B*A*:T*e*½) those (D*A*:NT*A*:N*e*½
K*R*::*A*:DS!).

Considering their roles in the diphthongs, it's not surprising that "ee" (E) and "oo" (*U*) are often abbreviated when found as simple vowels. The final "y" sound, for instance, is weakened to the (i) of "pit," and a "happy, healthy country" becomes a:

(HePi, HeL*t*i K*A*NT*R*::i).

The (*U*) of "fool" and "wooed" also suffers reduction: to the (*u*) of "full" and "wood." And if the whole "school group soon knew," in this dialect, we'd remark that the whole:

(SK*u*L*e*½ G*R*::*u*P*e*½ S*u*N*e*½ N*u*).

Most simple vowels are modified in other ways. The (u) of "buck" and "stud," for example, is transformed into the (*u*) of "book" and "stood" whenever it is spelled "u." So if you wanted to say that this "numbskull loves guns," being Hungarian, you would say that this:

(N*u*MSK*u*L*e*½ L*A*VS G*u*NS).

You can see from "loves" what happens when the (u) sound is *not* spelled with a "u": it is broadened to an "ah" (*A*). So the secret "of what was done among governments" becomes the secret:

(*A*V*e*½ V*A*T*e*½ V*A*S D*A*N*e*½ *A*M*A*NG*e*½
G*A*Vo*R*::NMeNTZ*e*½).

Two additional simple vowels shift into (*A*) in this dialect: the (o) of "lot" and the (*i*) of "ago." Thus, it "got hot on top" for the Hungarian-born comes out:

it (G*A*T*e*½ H*A*T*e*½ *A*N*e*½ T*A*P*e*½),

and "mature, balanced opinions" emerges as:

(M*A*C*uR*::, BeL*A*NSD*e*½ *A*PiNY*A*NS).

The "eh" (e) sound accounts for two other American vowels. The (a) of "bad" and "man" turns into the (e) of "bed" and "men." So if the police "had ransacked the man's knapsack," the Hungarian-speaking would talk of how they:

(HeD*e*½ *R*::eNSeKD*e*½) the (MeNS
NePSeK*e*½).

The second vowel affected is the (*a*) of "laughed" and "vast," which is converted to the (e) of "left" and "vest." So if she "grasped the answer rather fast," we'd say she:

(G*R*::eSPD*e*½) the (eNS*eR*:: *R*::eD*eR*::
FeST*e*½).

One totally Hungarian transformation is that of the "aw" (*o*) of "sought" into the (*u*) of "soot" whenever it is spelled "o," "ou," "oa," or "oo." Thus, if the architect "fought strongly for more broad doors" in his building, being from Hungary, he might tell how he:

(F*u*T*e*½ ST*R*::*u*NGLi F*uR*:: M*uR*::
B*R*::*u*D*e*½ D*uR*::S).

Finally, the (*E*) of "bird" and "fur" evolves into the "aw" (*o*) of "board" and "four," and if the "girl's work earned her high returns," to a Hungarian the:

(G*oR*::LS V*oR*::K *e*½ *oR*:: ND*e*½ H*oR*::)
high (*R*::iT*oR*::NS).

Consonant Changes

Most of the consonant alterations we encounter occur because the American sounds do not exist in Hungarian. As you've seen the only "r" sound the Hungarian knows is the very strongly trilled "r" (*R*::), made by pressing the tip of the tongue against the upper gum ridge and voicing the "r" until it resembles a machine gun (for more, see page 12). Thus, "regardless if our rules are right or wrong," becomes:

(*R*::iG*AR*::DLiZ*e*½) if (*A*:*R*:: *R*::*u*LS *AR*:: *R*::AiTe½ *uR*:: *R*::*u*NG*e*½).

For the same reasons, all (W)s become (V)s in General Hungarian. So that if we wanted to say "meanwhile, we were swimming away westward," it would end up as:

(MENV*A*iL*e*½, VE V*oR*:: SViMiNG*e*½ *A*Vei VeSTV*oR*::D*e*½).

If you consult the following *GUIDE PAGES*, you can see how your character's pronunciation of this letter will tell much about his education and background.

Naturally, the inability to produce a (W) sound influences the way the (Q = KW) is handled. But somehow—perhaps because there's an unvoiced consonant to start the sequence—at least a partial (W) emerges as (KVW), and "the sides of a square are quite equal" becomes:

the sides of a (SKVWei*R*::) are (KVW*A*iT*e*½ EKVW*A*L*e*½).

For a more detailed description of the (VW), see page 13.

Since Hungarian has neither a "hard TH" (*T*) nor a "soft th" (*t*), both are reshaped. At the beginning and in the middle of a word, soft th (*t*) changes to (T), hard TH (*T*) to (D); at the end of a word, they become (T*e*½) and (D*e*½), respectively. Thus, "through both thick and thin" comes out:

(T*R*:: *u* BoT*e*½ TiK*e*½) and (TiN*e*½),

while "they loathe those others" emerges as:

(Dei LoD*e*½ DoS *A*D*eR*::S).

The reason for the difference at the end of a word is that Hungarians "hit" final consonants so hard that it almost seems as though a vowel is being added. Just how this (*e*½) sound is used is described at the beginning of the chapter, but if you consult the *GUIDE PAGES*, you'll find that the (*e*½) is added to *almost* every consonant when it stands in a final position.

This final placement influences (Z) and (S) differently: (Z) alters to (S) and (S) to (Z*e*½). So "he was his father's size" shifts into:

he (V*A*S HiS F*A*D*eR*::S S*A*iS),

and "across this space" alters to:

(*A*K*R*:: *u*Z*e*½ DiZ*e*½ SPeiZ*e*½).

Even being in the middle of a word can affect a sound; thus a medial (X) becomes (GZ) before another consonant. So if we decide to "exclude the next expert," if Hungarian-born, we could decide to:

(eGZKL*u*D*e*½) the (NeGZT*e*½ eGZP*oR*::T*e*½).

Music, Rhythm, and Pace

None of the sound changes that we've looked at set this dialect apart half as much as does its distinctive music. Both its rhythm and its up-and-down variety make it unique—and these are largely dictated by the special style of Hungarian emphasis. The normal pace is fairly rapid, but whenever a word is to be emphasized, the stressed syllable of that word (always the first syllable) is drawn out to three or four times its regular length. In a polysyllable, all syllables following the stressed one are also slightly slower than normal.

This rhythmic emphasis is accompanied by a tonal one, the subject syllable being raised two full tones over normal, with the inflection dropping off sharply. Besides giving the dialect much more up-and-down variety, this gives its pace a specific "stop-and-go" (or "pause-and-proceed") quality.

In other respects, the Hungarian dialect has a slightly smaller range than American English, is spoken one tone higher, is lighter, and has a falling inflection at the end of a sentence.

Observation and Notes

Besides the Gabors, Eva and Zsa Zsa, the only model for the Hungarian dialect that comes to mind can be heard on the late night screenings of Bela Lugosi movies.

Of course, a great number of Hungarian-born scientists, economists, and sociologists can be heard on talk-show TV, and, in addition, there are also Hungarian ethnic centers, clubs, and churches, if you live in an urban center. If not, and you have the accompanying tapes, use them to full advantage—and expand your repertoire!

Bela Lugosi—in the created-for-America film (and perpetuated in later sequels) Dracula. *Though only one of a number of Hungarian actors in Hollywood at that time, his character's particular Transylvanian drawl (a slow Debrecen subdialect) became identified with the Hungarian dialect for millions of viewers. Later Hungarian stars, such as Eva Bartok and the Gabor sisters, with their light Budapest-Continental dialects, did nothing to change the aural image that Lugosi had established.*

GENERAL HUNGARIAN - DEBRECEN, LESS EDUCATED - BUDAPEST, EDUCATED HAJOS, RURAL

GUIDE PAGES		General	Debrecen	Budapest	Hajos Rural
Change in all positions: (say) Sei, (age) eiJe½, (maintain) MeiNTeiNe½	A	ei	&	&	
OR change: Sei:, ei:Je½, Mei:NDei:Ne½	A				ei:
Change final Y: (easy) EZi, (happy) HePi, (greasy) GR::ESi, (theory) tEAR::i	E	.i$y	&	&	&
Change in all positions: (I'll) AiLe½, (likewise) LAiKVAiS, (try) TR::Ai	I	Ai	&	&	
OR change: Ai:Le½, LAi:KV:WAi:S, TR::Ai:	I				Ai:
Change in all positions: (solo) SoLo, (old) oLDe½, (no) No, (roll) R::oLe½	O	o	&		
OR change: SouLou, ouLDe½, Nou, R:ouLe½	O			ou	
OR change: So:Lo:, o:LDe½, No:, R::o:Le½	O				o:
Change in all positions: (your) YuR::, (cute) KYuTe½, (few) FYu, (mule) MYuLe½	U	Yu	&	&	
OR change: Yu:R::, KYu:Te½, FYu:	U				Yu:
Change in all positions: (at) eTe½, (am) eMe½, (ransack) R::eNSeKe½, (man) MeNe½	a	e	&		
OR change: a:Te½, a:Me½, R:a:NSa:Ke½	a			a:	
OR change: e:Te½, e:Me½, R::e:NSe:Ke½	a				e:
LONGER: (let) Le:Te½, (tell) Te:Le½	e				e:
OR no change: LeTe½, TeLe½	e	e	&	&	
LONGER: (it) i:Te½, (fill) Fi:Le½	i				i:
OR no change: iTe½, FiLe½	i	i	&	&	
Change in all positions: (on) ANe½, (got) GATe½, (topnotch) TAPNACe½	o	A	&	&	
OR change: A:Ne½, GA:Te½, TA:PNA:Ce½	o				A:

		All 4
CHANGE: (does) DAS, (what) VATe½, (love) LAVe½, (was) VAS	u	A
BUT if spelled U: (up) uPe½, (cut) KuTe½, (us) uZe½	u	u$u

		General	Debrecen	Budapest	Hajos Rural
LONGER: (calm) KA:LMe½, (mark) MA:R::Ke½	A				A:
OR no change: KALMe½, MAR::Ke½	A	A	&	&	
CHANGE: (earn) oR::Ne½, (girl) GoR::Le½ (work) VoR::Ke½, (turn) ToR::Ne½	E	o	&	&	&
No change: (predict) PR::IDiKTe½	I	I	&	&	&
Change in all positions: (now) NA:, (out) A:Te½, (down) DA:Ne½, (how) HA:	O	A:	&		&
OR change: NAu, AuTe½, DAuNe½, HAu	O			Au	
Change in all positions: (do) Du, (fool) FuLe½, (soon) SuNe½, (knew) Nu	U	u	&	&	
OR change: Du:, Fu:Le½, Su:Ne½, Nu:	U				u:
Change in all positions: (and) eNDe½, (past) PeSTe½, (laugh) LeFe½, (path) Pet	a	e	&		&
OR change: e½NDe½, Pe½STe½, Le½Fe½	a			e½	
No change: (simple) SiMPeLe½	e	e	&	&	&
CHANGE: (ago) AGo, (family) FeMALi	i	A	&		&
OR no change: iGou, Fa:MiLi	i			i	
CHANGE if spelled O: (off) uFe½, (door) DuR::, (cough) KuFe½, (broad) BR::uDe½	o	u$o	&		
OR change: u:Fe½, Du:R::, Ku:Fe½	o				u:$o
OR no change: oFe½, DoR:, KuFe½	o			o$o	
AND no change if spelled A: (all) oLe½	o	o$a	&	&	&

Key:

: stronger	$ spelled	t thin,both	C church
½ weakened	. finally	R trilled R	& as shown

GENERAL HUNGARIAN - DEBRECEN, LESS EDUCATED - BUDAPEST, EDUCATED

HAJOS, RURAL *GUIDE PAGES*		General	Debrecen	Budapest	Hajos Rural
LONGER: (push) P*u*:*S*, (took) T*u*:Ke½	*u*				*u*:
OR no change: P*u*S, T*u*Ke½	*u*	*u*	&	&	
Change in all positions: (oil) AiLe½, (point) PAiNTe½, (boy) BAi, (joy) JAi	*o*E	Ai	&		&
OR change: *o*iLe½, P*o*iNTe½, B*o*i, J*o*i	*o*E			*o*i	
Change finally: (bob) BABe½, (bib) BiBe½	B	.Be½	&	&	&
Change finally: (church) *Co**R*::*C*e½	C	.Ce½	&	&	&
Change finally: (did) DiDe½ (dead) DeDe½	D	.De½	&	&	&
Change finally: (fluff) FL*u*Fe½	F	.Fe½	&	&	&
Change finally: (gag) GeGe½, (big) BiGe½	G	.Ge½	&	&	&
STRONGER: (has) H:e:S, (here) H:E*R*::	H				H:
OR no change: HeS, HE*R*::	H	H	&	&	
Change finally: (judge) J*u*Je½ (age) eiJe½	J	.Je½	&	&	&
Change finally: (kick) KiKe½ (cake) KeiKe½	K	.Ke½	&	&	&
Change finally: (lull) L*u*Le½, (til) TiLe½	L	.Le½	&	&	&
Change finally: (mum) M*u*Me½, (him) HiMe½	M	.Me½	&	&	&
Change finally: (none) NANe½, (in) iNe½	N	.Ne½	&	&	&
Change finally: (pep) PePe½, (pop) PAPe½	P	.Pe½	&	&	&
Change in all positions: (quit) KVWiTe½, (equal) EKVWeLe½, (square) SKVWei*R*::	Q	KVW	&		
OR change: KVW:iTe½, EKVW:eLe½	Q			KVW:	
OR change: KV:Wi:Te½, EKV:WeLe½	Q				KV:W
VERY STRONG TRILL: (rear) *R*::E*R*::, (are) A*R*::, (very) Ve*R*::i, (true) T*R*:: *u*	R	*R*::	&		&
OR STRONG TRILL: *R*:E*R*:, A*R*:, Ve*R*:i	R			*R*:	
Change finally: (cease) SEZe½ (yes) YeZe½	S	.Ze½	&		&
OR no change finally: SES, YeS	S			.S	
OR change medially before consonant: (ask) eZKe½, (dismiss) DiZMiZe½, (last) LeZTe½	S		/Z(¢		&
OR no change: eSKe½, DiSMiZe½, LeSTe½	S	/S(¢		&	
No change: (show) *S**o*, (sure) *S**u**R*::	*S*	*S*	&	&	&
Change finally: (get) GeTe½, (sit) SiTe½	T	.Te½	&	&	&
OR change medially after a consonant: (into) iND*u*, (empty) eMPDi	T		/D)¢		&
OR no change medially: iNT*u*, eMPTi	T	/T)¢		&	
No change: (thin) *t*iNe½, (both) B*o**t*	*t*	*t*	&	&	&
Change initial & medial: (they) Dei, (other) AD*o**R*::, (that) DeTe½	*T*	-/D	&	&	&
AND change finally: (smooth) SM*u*De½	*T*	.De½	&	&	&
Change finally: (involve) iNVALVe½	V	.Ve½	&	&	&
Change in all positions: (was) VAS, (away) AVei, (swim) SViMe½, (we) VE	W	V			
OR change: VWAS, AVWei, SVWiMe½, VWE	W		VW		
OR change: VW:AS, *i*VW:ei, SVW:iMe½	W			VW:	
OR change: V:WAS, AV:Wei:, SV:WiMe½	W				V:W
Change medially before a consonant: (expert) eGZP*o**R*::Te½, (next) NeGZTe½	X	/GZ(¢	&	&	&
Change finally: (was) VAS, (size) SAiS	Z	.S	&	&	&
Change finally: (rouge) *R*::*u**z*e½	*z*	.*z*e½	&	&	&

Key:

: stronger	(preceding	$ spelled	¢ consonants	/ medial
½ weakened	) following	& as shown	- initially	. final

MASTER CATEGORY 19

FINNISH

During the year I lived in Finland, I was exposed to the Finnish dialect only about half the time. This was because I lived in Vaasa where almost half the population is Swedish-speaking—a heritage from the long period (1155–1809) when Finland was part of Sweden. Though there are pockets of Swedish-speaking communities scattered throughout the country, ninety-five percent of the population has Finnish (or "Suomi") as its everyday language. Naturally, this is the dialect you will hear from the overwhelming majority of Finns.

If they are from the capital, Helsinki, the likelihood is that their accent in American English may be lighter; if from the country (*Kuopio, Rural* in the *GUIDE PAGES*), the dialect tends to be broader.

Vowel Changes

In its transcription, the Finnish language frequently uses doubled vowels to indicate a lengthening of a simple vowel. This vowel elongation constitutes an important difference between the Finnish and Hungarian dialects, since the tendency in Hungarian is to change rather than draw out simple vowel sounds. Note this distinction: the similarity in their *music* makes for confusion between the two dialects.

Another resemblance to the Hungarian accent is in the way Finns shorten all American diphthongs. As an example, the "oo" part of the double vowel (U) as in "fuel" is cut down till it resembles a long (:) version of the (*u*) in "full," resulting in a (Y*u*:) sound. So if the rental complex has a "few cute units," being Finnish, we'd say it had a:

(VWY*u*: KY*u*:T Y*u*:Ni:TZ).

Another case in point is the "eh-ee" (A) in "gaze." The second part of this sound, the (E) of "feel," is abridged to (i) as in "fill," giving us (ei), and if "they say they waited eight days," the Finn would report that:

(Dei Sei Dei VWeiT*e*D eiT DeiS).

A similar thing happens to the (I = *A*E) of "guys": it is shortened to (*A*i). So that if "I like my wife by my side," in Finnish dialect I might declare that:

(*A*i L*A*iK M*A*i VW*A*iVW B*A*i M*A*i S*A*iD).

In a final instance, the (*o*E) in "boy" is pared down to (*o*i). Thus, if they "avoid toil like poison," being born in Finland, you might remark that they:

(eV*o*iD T*o*iL) like (P*o*iZ*e*N).

Whenever the second element of a diphthong is totally eliminated, the first element is prolonged (:). For example, the "aw-oo" (O) of "hole" is reduced to "aw-w," and if one would "totally overthrow the old coalition," being Finnish-speaking we can point out that they want to:

(T*o*:T*e*Li: *o*:V*eR*TR*o*:) the (*o*:LD K*o*:eli:SeN).

Likewise, the "ah-oo" (*O*) of "howl" is chopped down to "ah-h." So if we will "now count out loud," in this dialect the announcement is that we will:

(N*A*: K*A*:NT *A*:T L*A*:D).

The most common doubled-vowel we encounter in written Finnish is "aa" (as in "Vaasa")—so we can understand how Finns come to broaden some simple vowels into "ah-h" (*A*:). Naturally, the (*A*) of "lark" is lengthened in this manner, but so is the (o) of "lock." Thus, if the millionaire real estate developer wants to "hobnob with topnotch jocks," for a Finnish-born person, he wants to:

(H*A*:PN*A*:P) with (T*A*:PN*A*:*s* DZ*A*:KZ).

Finally, the (*a*) of "aunt" is also drawn out to (*A*:). So that if the "dancer had a rather plastic laugh," if you were Finnish you would find that the (D*A*:NSe*R*) had a:

(*RA*:De*R* PL*A*:STi:K L*A*:VW).

The other three vowels that are stretched out (:) are the (*u*) in "put," the (e) in "pet," and the (i) in "pit." These become, respectively (*u*:), (e:), and (i:).

Two of our American vowel sounds are contracted by the Finnish. The first of these is "ee," contracted till the (E) of "feel" sounds more like the (i) of "fill." Thus, if "we see these seats seem to be free," a Finn will observe that:

(VWi: Si: Di:S Si:TZ Si:M) to (Pi: VW*R*i:).

The second sound is the "oo" (*U*) in "fool," cut down till it is closer to a long (:) version of the (*u*) in "full." So that if you'd like "to move to the cool, blue room," in this dialect you'd want:

(T*u*: M*u*:V T*u*:) the (K*u*:L, Pl*u*: *Ru*:M).

The Finns also use this same (*u*:) to replace the "aw" (*o*) of "call." Thus, if everyone "ought to halt all this war talk," a Finnish speaker would point out that they: (*u*:T) to (H*u*:LT *u*:L) this (VW*u*:*R* T*u*:K).

Another characteristic substitution is of the "eh" (e) of "Kelly" for the (*i*) of "practical." So when his "ideas balanced his companions' opinions," if Finnish-born you would describe how his:

(*A*iDi:eS Be:LeNST) his (KeMPe:NYeNS ePi:NYeNS).

Notice that the (a) sound in both "balanced" and "companions" was replaced by a long "eh-h" (e:). The same applies wherever this sound is found. Thus, if the "man's as mad as a hatter," our Finn might express it as:

the (Me:NS e:S Me:D e:S) a (He:Te*R*).

Still another transformation occurs when the Finns encounter the (u) of "cut"; they change this to a long (:) version of the "aw" (*o*) in "caught." So if we want to ask "what was that sudden hubbub?" in the Finnish dialect we have to inquire:

(VW*o*:T VW*o*:S) that (S*o*:DeN H*o*:P*o*:P?).

One last vowel conversion to consider is that of the (*E*) in "fur"; this shifts into a drawled (:) "ah-h" as in "far." Thus, if in the mayor's press conference, "her first words referred to current concerns," being Finnish you would report that:

(H*A*:*R* VW*A*:*R*ST VW*A*:*R*DS *R*i:VW*A*:*R*D) to (K*A*:*R*eNT KeNS*A*:*R*NS).

Consonant Changes

You surely noticed the trilled R (*R*) substituting for all American r sounds. This (*R*) is made by pressing the tip of the tongue against the upper gum ridge and voicing the sound until the resulting tongue vibration resembles the child's impression of a machine gun or a motorcycle.

(*R*) is common to most European tongues, but where other dialects merely modify many American consonants, Finnish tends to change them. Of course, the Germanic and Romance languages are the ancestors of English, while Finnish is no kin at all. A characteristic example of the Finnish tendency is with the (B) sound; here it turns into P. So if "after her bubble bath she grabbed her husband's robe," if Finnish-speaking you'd tell how:

after her (Po:PeL P*A*:T) she (G*R*e:PT) her (H*o*:ZPeNDS *Ro*:P).

Another typical alteration is from the (*C*) of "pitch" to the (*s*) of "pits." Thus, if the "research listed each church which changed preachers," our Finn would comment that the:

(*R*i:S*A*:*Rs*) listed (i:*s* *sA*:*Rs* VWi:*s* *s*eiNDZD P*R*i:*s*e*R*S).

Note how the (J) sound in "changed" came out as (DZ); this means that if "judge Jack George enjoys bridge," a Finn would say:

(DZ*o*:DZ DZe:K DZ*u*:*R*DZ eNDZ*o*iS P*R*i:DZ).

Of course if there are many (J)s in your dialogue, you might help the cause of clarity by using the *Helsinki, Educated* (Dz)—a combination of D with the (*z*) of "vision." You may also find it necessary to use the Helsinki subdialect if the "sh" (*S*) of "shed" comes up often in your lines, since this becomes the (S) of "said" for the Finnish-speaking in general. That means that "the chauffeur motioned the chef to 'shush', " degenerates into:

the (S*o*:VWe*R* M*o*:SeND) the (Se:VW) to (S*o*:S).

A more familiar change is the Finnish shift of the (*t*) of "thigh" into the (T) sound of "tie." Thus, if "both athletes thought wealth worthless," being Finnish-born, you would explain that:

(P*o*:T *A*:TLi:TZ T*u*:T VWe:LT VW*A*:*R*TLi:Z).

A second recognizable conversion is from the (*T*) in "there" to the (D) in "dare," making "they breathe with their mouths" into:

(Dei P*R*i:D VWi:D Dei*R* M*A*:DS).

In the Slavic dialects, we investigated the (VW) sound, made by pursing the lips for a (W), bringing the lower lip back and up until it touches the edge of the upper front teeth, and then voicing the result. This sound pops up in three different cases in Finnish dialect. First, it substitutes for (F). So when we want to know "if the fifteen orphans feel safe," as Finns we might ask:

(i:VW) the (VWi:VWTi:N *u*:*R*VWe*N*S VWi:*L* Sei*VW*).

The second substitution is for (W)—so that if "work on the walkway was a week away," to the Finn:

(VW*A*:*R*K) on the (VW*u*:KVWei VW*o*:S) a (VWi:K eVWei).

Naturally, this change affects our (Q) as well, and if "all sides of a square are quite equal," in our dialect:

all sides of a (SK*e*½VWei*R*) are (K*e*½VW*A*iT i:K*e*½VWeL).

The last consonant change we'll examine is actually a reversal. First, whenever an (S) sound ends a word, it becomes a (Z). Thus, if you saw the "stress lines cross its face," if you were from Finland, you would talk of seeing:

(ST*R*e:Z L*A*iNS K*Ru*:Z i:TZ VWeiZ).

Next, as shown in "lines," the opposite transformation takes place when a final (Z) sound is involved. So if "the model says 'his phrase was please pose', " for a Finn:

the model (Se:S Hi:S VW*R*eiS VW*o*:S PLi:S P*o*:S).

Music, Rhythm, and Pace

As noted at the beginning of this chapter, Finnish music is almost identical to that of Hungarian: the rhythm and variety are dictated by the manner of stress. The first syllable of any emphasized word is drawn out to two or three times "normal" (the Finnish normal being much slower than either Hungarian or American speech). In polysyllables, all syllables following the first one are also pronounced a bit slower. A tonal stress accompanies this phenomenon: the emphasized syllable is raised two full tones over normal, and then the inflection drops off sharply. Thus, though the Finnish pace is slower than Hungarian and its pitch is lower (as low as American English), it has the same "pause-and-proceed" quality as Hungarian.

Observation and Notes

I wish I could offer more assistance in directing you toward useful dialect models, but a scarcity of Finnish actors in American media (their own theatrical climate is far better) makes this virtually impossible. All I can suggest is a trip or two to your local Finnish ethnic society, to a Finnish Lutheran or Finnish Eastern Orthodox church, or to your cassette player with the accompanying tape.

GENERAL FINNISH - TURKU, LESS EDUCATED - KUOPIO, RURAL

HELSINKI, EDUCATED

GUIDE PAGES

	SOUND	General Finnish	Turku Less Educated Finn	Kuopio Rural Finnish	Helsinki Educated Finn
Change in all positions: (say) Sei, (take) TeiK, (came) KeiM, (late) LeiT	A	ei	&		&
OR change: Se:, Te:K, Ke:M, Le:T	A			e:	
		All 4			
CHANGE: (mean) Mi:N, (eat) i:T, (see) Si:, (deal) Di:L	E	i:			
CHANGE: (I'll) AiL, (kind) KAiND, (my) MAi, (like) LAiK	I	Ai			
Change in all positions: (note) N*o*:T, (only) *o*:NLi:, (solo) S*o*:L*o*:, (so) S*o*:	O	*o*:	&		
OR change: N*o*::T, *o*::NLi:, S*o*::L*o*::	O			*o*::	
OR change: N*ou*T, *ou*NLi:, S*ou*L*ou*, S*ou*	O				*ou*
Change in all positions: (you) Y*u*:, (cute) KY*u*:T, (few) VW*u*:, (mule) MY*u*:L	U	Y*u*:	&	&	
OR change: Y*u*, KY*u*T, F:VY*u*, MY*u*L	U				Y*u*
Change in all positions: (glad) GLe:D, (fact) VWe:KT, (at) e:T, (am) e:M	a	e:	&		
OR change: GLeiD, VWeiKT, eiT, eiM	a			ei	
OR change: GLeD, F:VeKT, eT, eM	a				e
LONGER: (let) Le:T, (tell) Te:L	e	e:	&	&	&
LONGER: (in) i:N, (till) Ti:L, (it) i:T	i	i:	&	&	&
Change in all positions: (on) A:N, (stop) STA:P, (got) GA:T, (not) NA:T	o	A:	&	&	&
Change in all positions: (up) *o*:P, (gun) G*o*:N, (love) L*o*:V, (does) D*o*:S	u	*o*:	&		
OR change: *o*::P, G*o*::N, L*o*::V, D*o*::S	u			*o*::	
OR change: o:P, Go:N, Lo:V, Do:S	u				o:
LONGER: (are) A:*R*, (calm) KA:LM	A	A:	&	&	&
Change in all positions: (girl) GA:*R*L, (earn) A:*R*N, (word) VWA:*R*D, (her) HA:*R*	*E*	A:	&		
OR change: GA::*R*:L, A::*R*:N, V:WA::*R*:D	*E*			A::	
OR change: G*i*:*R*½L, *i*:*R*½N, VW:*i*:*R*½D	*E*				*i*:
No change: (predict) PR*I*Di:KT	*I*	*I*	&	&	&
Change in all positions: (out) A:T, (down) DA:N, (now) NA:, (loud) LA:D	*O*	A:	&	&	
OR change: A*u*T, DA*u*N, NA*u*, LA*u*D	*O*				A*u*
Change in all positions: (do) D*u*:, (soon) S*u*:N, (lose) L*u*:S, (knew) N*u*:	*U*	*u*:	&	&	
OR change: D*u*, S*u*N, L*u*S, N*u*	*U*				*u*
Change in all positions: (ask) A:SK, (last) LA:ST, (and) A:ND, (dance) DA:NS	*a*	A:	&	&	&
No change: (apple) e:P*e*L, (dozen) D*o*:Z*e*N	*e*	*e*	&	&	&
Change in all positions: (ago) eG*o*:, (family) VWe:MeLi:, (extra) e:XT*R*e	*i*	e	&	&	
OR change: *E*G*ou*, F:VeM*E*Li:, e:XT*R*½*E*	*i*				*E*
Change in all positions: (talk) T*u*:K, (cause) K*u*:S, (saw) S*u*:, (war) VW*u*:*R*	*o*	*u*:	&	&	&!$o
OR if spelled O: (dog) D*ou*G, (off) *ou*F:V	*o*				*ou*$o
LONGER: (pull) P*u*:L, (took) T*u*:K	*u*	*u*:	&	&	
OR no change: P*u*L, T*u*K	*u*				*u*

Key: ! excepting

$ spelled & as shown : stronger ½ weakened *R* trilled R

GENERAL FINNISH - TURKU, LESS EDUCATED - KUOPIO, RURAL HELSINKI, EDUCATED

GUIDE PAGES		General	Turku Less	Kuopio	Helsinki
Change in all positions: (toy) Toi, (point) PoiNT, (oil) oiL, (voice) VoiZ	oE	oi	&		&
OR change: To:i, Po:iNT, o:iL, Vo:iZ	oE			o:i	
Change in all positions: (bulb) Po:LP, (baby) PeiPi:, (husband) Ho:ZPeND	B	P		&	
OR change: BPo:LBP, BPeiBPi:, Ho:ZBPeND	B		BP		
OR change: B:Po:LB:P, B:PeiB:Pi:	B				B:P
Change in all positions: (chin) si:N, (cheap) si:P, (each) i:s, (much) Mo:s	C	s	&		
OR change: s:i:N, s:i:P, i:s:, Mo::s:	C			s:	
OR change: DJi:N, DJi:P, i:DJ, Mo:DJ	C				DJ
No change	D	D	&	&	&
Change in all positions: (fine) VWAiN, (if) i:VW, (few) VWYu:, (laugh) LA:VW	F	VW		&	
OR change: V:WAiN, i:V:W, V:WYu:, LA:V:W	F		V:W		
OR change: F:VAiN, i:F:V, F:VYu, LA:F:V	F				F:V
No change	GH	G H	&	&	&
Change in all positions: (judge) DZo:DZ, (logic) LA:DZi:K, (gradual) GRe:DZu:eL	J	DZ	&	&	
OR change: Dzo:Dz, LA:Dzi:K, GR½eDzueL	J				Dz
No change	KLMNP	K	L M	N	P
Change in all positions: (quit) Ke½VWi:T, (equal) i:Ke½VWeL, (square) SKe½VWeiR	Q	Ke½VW			
OR change: Ke½VW:i:T, i:Ke½VW:eL	Q		Ke½VW:		
OR change: Ke½V:Wi:T, i:Ke½V:WeL	Q			Ke½V:W	
OR change: KVW:i:T, i:KVW:eL, SKVW:eiR½	Q				KVW:
TRILL: (rear) Ri:R, (art) A:RT, (dry) DRAi, (very) Ve:Ri:, (for) VWu:R	R	R	&		
OR STRONG TRILL: R:i:R:, A:R:T, DR:Ai	R			R:	
OR TAP: R½i:R½, A:R½T, DR½Ai, Ve:R½i:	R				R½
Change finally: (cease) Si:Z, (yes) Ye:Z	S	.Z	&	&	
OR change finally: Si:ZS, Ye:ZS	S				.ZS
Change in all positions: (shush) So:S, (show) So:, (sure) Su:R, (motion) Mo:SeN	S	S		&	
OR change: S:So:S:S, S:So:, S:Su:R	S		S:S		
OR change: SS:o:SS:, SS:ou, SS:uR½	S				SS:
					All 4
No change	T				T
CHANGE: (both) Po:T, (thing) Ti:NG, (healthy) He:LTi:	t				T
CHANGE: (there) DeiR, (other) o:DeR, (with) VWi:D	T				D
No change: (give) Gi:V, (of) o:V	V				V
Change in all positions: (week) VWi:K, (away) eVWei, (swim) SVWi:M, (was) VWo:S	W	VW	&		
OR change: V:Wi:K, eV:We:, SV:Wi:M	W			V:W	
OR change: VW:i:K, EVW:ei, SVW:i:M	W				VW:
No change	X	X	&	&	&
Change finally: (size) SAiS, (his) Hi:S	Z	.S	&	&	&
No change: (vision) Vi:zeN	z	z	&	&	&

Key:

: stronger ½ weakened s waits, its R trilled R & as shown . final

GREEK

Here is a dialect to which you may have easy access. In urban centers throughout the English-speaking world, there are Greek communities; Greek restaurants still abound; Greek folk-dancing halls are to be found in nearly every large city (and they welcome non-Greeks). I have learned more of the Greek dialect in America than I did in Greece (where it is overlaid on British English).

However, with a couple of unnotable exceptions, the subdialects in our *GUIDE PAGES* are related to how much education the speaker has in American English rather than to regional variations. The General Greek in those pages is what is spoken by most of those coming here from Greece.

With Greek we are really starting from scratch: there are no other dialects we can refer to. The Greek alphabet differs from all others (despite resemblances to some Slavic ones). This difference accounts for at least three of the consonant changes we will deal with, and causes no little confusion for Greeks when they encounter apparently similar vowel characters in English.

Vowel Changes

As an example, the diphthong "eh-ee" (A) is shortened, leaving only the "eh" (e) sound. This results in "main" and "lace" sounding more like "men" and "less," and "they say they aided eight ailing waifs" is made into:

(D=e S:e D=e eD=*e*D= eT= eLiN¼ BVeFS:).

Strangely enough, "eh" (e) itself is modified into flat (a), so that "bed" and "pen" come to resemble "bad" and "pan." Thus, "Never mind the expense, let's send them express!" emerges as:

(NaBV*uoR*) mind the (a*h*SPaNS:, LaT=S: S:aN¼ *T*aM a*h*SP*R*aS:!).

However, the (a) isn't left alone either: the Greek sound for this letter being "ah" (*A*), that's what it becomes in this dialect. So if the hiker was "glad she had snacks in her backpack," to a Greek, she was:

(G*h*L*A*D=) she (*h*AD= S:N*Ah*S:) in her (B*A*KP*A*K).

This same (*A*) replaces the (*a*) of "aunt." Thus, when the teacher "gathers the class can't grasp his last answer," he'll say that he:

(G*hĀTuo*R*S*:) the (KLAS: KANT= G*hR*AS:P) his (L*A*S:T= *A*NS:*uoR*).

Finally, the same substitution of the ubiquitous (*A*) occurs when a Greek encounters the (*i*) sound of "ago." Thus, if the psychiatric worker asked her to "abandon her abnormal opinions about pajamas," if he were Greek, he'd request that she:

(*A*BAND=*A*N) her (*A*BN*uoR*M*A*L *A*PiNY*A*NS: *A*B*uo*T= P*AzA*M*A*S:).

Despite these examples, there is a strong tendency in the Greek dialect to *shorten* American vowel sounds. The "oo" (*U*) of "suit" and "pool," for instance, is abridged to the (*u*) of "soot" and "pull," and so if we "soon knew whose proofs moved the jury," in this dialect, we:

(S:*u*N N*u hu*S: P*Ru*FS: M*u*BV¼) the (*zuR*i).

This same transformation takes place with the "oo" part of the diphthong "y-oo" (U). So if advertising "uses our illusion that youth is beauty to delude us," being Greek-speaking, we would find that advertising: (YuS:eS:) our (iLYuSYAN) that (Yut:) is (BYuT=i) to (D=iLYuD=) us.

Another abridgment is that of the "ee" (E) in "feel" and "deep" into the (i) in "fill" and "dip." Thus, if "he dreamed he'd seen a speakeasy here," for a Greek: (hi D=RiMD= hiD= S:iN) a (S:PiKiS:i hiR).

Naturally, this reduction also applies to the "ee" part of the double vowel "ah-ee" (I), and if "I'd like to buy some wild rice," if I were from Greece, I would explain that: (AiD= LAiK) to (BVAi) some (BVAiL¼ RAiS:).

The most common and most characteristic Greek vowel substitute is the sound (*uo*), made up of (*u*) as in "full" and "aw" (*o*) as in "fall," both run together as a single diphthong. Even the "aw" sound in "fall" is transformed into this (*uo*). Thus "he can't afford any more court costs at all" shifts into:
he can't (AF*uo*R¼) any (M*uo*R K*uo*RT= K*uo*S:T=S:) at (*uo*L).

This same "aw" is an element of the diphthong "aw-ee" (*o*E), so naturally what results is (*uo*E)—and if she "employed her voice to spoil his enjoyment," the Greek-born would observe that she:
(aMBL*uo*ED=) her (BV*uo*ES:) to (S:P*uo*EL) his (aN*zuo*EMANT=)

Note: this is the *only* double vowel that undergoes such a metamorphosis.

The diphthong "aw-oo" (O) simply changes into (*uo*). So if it were their "goal to overthrow both old rogues," then our Greek would say that it was their:
(Gh*uo*L) to (*uo*BV*uo*Rt:R*uo* B*uo*t: *uo*L¼ R*uo*GhS:).

Likewise, the double vowel "ah-oo" (*O*) becomes (*uo*). Thus, "she allows her spouse to lounge around the house" is reshaped into:
she (AL*uo*S:) her (S:P*uo*S:) to (L*uo*Nz AR*uo*N¼) the (h*uo*S:).

If by now you can't tell how truly indispensable this (*uo*) is to the Greek dialect, then be informed that it also replaces four other simple vowel sounds. The first is the (o) in "hot," and if they "got stopped on Operation Hopscotch," a Greek would point out that they:
(Gh*uo*T= S:T=*uo*PT= *uo*N *uo*P*uo*ReS:*uo*N h*uo*PS:K*uo*s).

Next is the (u) of "hut": thus, "such unjust governments must cover up much blundering" is converted to:
(S:*uos* *uo*N*zuo*S:T= Gh*uo*BV*uo*RNMANT=S: M*uo*S:T= K*uo*BV*uo*R *uo*P M*uos* BL*uo*MD=*uo*RiN¼).

As you just saw, the third case is the (*e*) sound of "governments" and "cover." So, "paper" turns into (PeP*uo*R), "apple" into (AP*ou*L), "gorgeous" into (Gh*uo*R*zuo*S:), "nation" into (NeS:*uo*N) and so on. Finally, (*uo*) also takes the place of (*E*) as in "hurt." So if the music critic "heard the solo's first third with a perverse smirk on his face," as Greeks we would say that he:
(h*uo*R¼) the solo's (F*uo*RS:T= t:*uo*R¼) with a (P*uo*RBV*uo*RS: S:M*uo*RK) on his face.

Consonant Changes

Note that all the "R"s in the sentences above were trilled (*R*). This sound is produced by pressing the tip of your tongue against the upper gum ridge and voicing the consonant until the tongue vibrates. Thus, if the "preacher misread 'For richer, for poorer'," to the Greek, the:
(PRis*uo*R MiS:RaD= F*uo*R Ris*uo*R, F*uo*R PuR*uo*R).

At the end of a word, the (G) is dropped completely from "ing" and "ong," so if she's "becoming a strong, growing, gangling girl," if you were Greek-born, you would speak of her:
(BiK*uo*MiN¼) a (S:T=R*uo*N¼, GhR*uo*iN¼, GhANGhLiN¼ Gh*uo*RL).

As you may have noticed, every time we've met up with a (G) in this chapter—except before "ee" (E) or "eh" (e)—the Greeks transformed it into (G*h*). This fricative is produced where we make our (G)s, but a small opening is left between the tongue and soft palate, and air is forced through this opening at the same time the (G*h*) is sounded. This *voicing* distinguishes (G*h*) from the other fricative (*h*).

The unvoiced fricative we mention, (*h*), is used by the Greeks in two different situations. First, it replaces all (H)s, and "he hates her high-handed, heartless behavior" is altered to:

(*h*i *h*eT=S: *h*uoR *h*Ai*h*AND=eD=, *h*ART=LaS: Bi*h*eBVY*uo*R).

Second, Greeks use it when they encounter the letter "X," which in their alphabet is pronounced (*h*). Not surprisingly then, (*h*S) takes the place of the "KS" sound of (X), and "the text mixed sex and Marxism" comes out:

the (T=a*h*ST= Mi*h*ST= S:a*h*S) and (MAR*h*SiS:M).

Oddly enough, the Greeks have a considerably easier time with the "GZ" sound of (X) and merely modify this into (GS). So if the "executives examined existing examples," being born in Greece, we would report that the:

(aGSaKY*u*T=iBVS: aGSAMiN¼ aGSiS:T=iN¼ aGSAMB*uo*LS:).

As you saw from "executives" and "examples," if a (Z) sound is *spelled* "S," the Greek uses a long hissed (S:). Thus, "pleasantly surprising music" ends up as:

(PlaS:ANT=Li S:*uo*RPRAiS:iN¼ MY*u*S:iK).

Greeks also exchange this (S:) for our "sh" (*S*). Thus, her "flashy showmanship evoked emotional reactions" shifts into her:

(FLAS:i S:*uo*MANS:iP) evoked (iM*uo*S:ANAL RiAKS:ANS:).

Look back at "hates," "heartless," "sex," and "surprising"; you'll see that all "normal" (S)s are also lengthened into (S:). Similarly, the Greeks draw out the (*t*) of "think" because their own letter, theta, is articulated as (*t*:) in Greek.

Tau and delta are two other characters of the Greek alphabet, but they are not handled like our (T) and (D); rather, they are interdental. This means that instead of the tongue touching the upper gum ridge, it touches the lower edge of the upper front teeth. Thus, "it's important to get the best ticket" evolves into:

(iT=S: iMP*uo*RT=ANT= T=*u* GaT=) the (BaS:T= T=iKeT=),

and "she dreaded being dependent on her dad" into:

she (D=RaD=eD=) being (D=iPaND=ANT=) on her (D=AD=).

However, at the end of a word following a consonant, the Greeks lose all their (D)s. Thus, "told they'd find him old and blind" is transformed into:

(T=*uo*L¼ TeD= FAiN¼) him (*uo*L¼ AN¼ BLAiN¼).

(W) is also eliminated at times: whenever it follows (*u*) in the middle of a word. Thus, "aiming toward a two-way thruway" turns into:

aiming (T=*u*¼*uo*R¼) a (T=*u*¼e *t*:R*u*¼e).

In all other instances, (W) is replaced by (BV). Thus, if you want to know "why we were always wishy-washy," ask:

(BVAi BVi BV*uo*R *uo*LBVeS: BViS:i-BVAS:i).

This (BV) sound can be found in the Spanish dialect as well (page 31). The Spanish (BV) is made by almost bringing the lips together for a "B." However, for the Greek version you can let the lower edge of your upper front teeth lightly touch your lower lip. The resulting (BV) pops up in three other places. All (Q)s, for example, become (KBV)s, and a "request that he quickly quell his frequent misquotes" is made into a:

(RiKBVaS:T=) that he (KBViKLi KBVaL) his (FRiKBVANT= MiS:KBV*uo*T=S:).

(BV) also changes places with (V), so that whatever "involves reviving the love of bravery," for the Greek:

(iNBVuoLBVS: *R*iBV*A*iBViN¼) the (*L*uoBV *uo*BV B*R*eBV*eR*i).

The uneducated will convert even the "b" of "bravery" into (BV), making it into (BV*R*eBVuo*R*i), and the "slumbering suburbs" into the:

(S:*Luo*MBV*uoR*iN¼ S:*uo*MBV*uoR*BVS:).

Note that an (M) is interpolated before the (BV) in "suburbs"; this happens wherever a "b" comes between vowels, but only among those uneducated in English.

Our last four consonant substitutions all stem from the peculiarities of modern Greek. First: when "p" follows a medial "m" sound it is replaced by (B). Thus, "to compare sample employer impressions," to a Greek would be:

to (K*A*MBe*R* S:*A*MB*uo*L aMB*L*uoE*uoR* iMB*R*aS:*A*NS:).

Second, the (*C*) of "rich" is reshaped into the (*s*) of "ritz," and if her "church chose a rich bachelor as future preacher," then in this dialect, her:

(*suoRs suo*S:) a (*R*is BA*s*L*uoR*) as (FY*usuoR* P*R*i*suoR*).

Third, the (J) of "virgin" changes into the (*z*) of "version," and "judging the general genealogy of language" emerges as:

(*zuoz*iN¼) the (*z*aN*R*uoL *z*iNi*uo*L*Az*i) of (LANG*h*BVi*z*).

As well-known producer A.C. Lyles noted, Irene Papas (pictured here in Iphigenia*) has an "earthy, womanly charm in person" which she brings to her screen roles, making each portrayal vivid in its reality. Her dialect, too, reflects her Greek-village background, and is an excellent example of non-Athenian Greek.*

Oddly, the (*z*) sound itself is transformed into (SY), so if we took "pleasure in the disclosure of a decision to measure television's confusion," being Greek, we took:
(PLaSY*uo*R) in the (D=iS:KL*uo*SY*uo*R) of a (D=iS:iSY*A*N) to (MaSY*uo*R T=aL*A*BViSY*A*NS: K*A*NFY*u*SYAN).

Music, Rhythm, and Pace

The Greek dialect, like the Greek language, is spoken two to three tones higher than American English. A greater excitability among the speakers produces a greater range, much more up-and-down variety, a faster pace, and a heavier rhythm than American speech. The Greek method of emphasizing words adds to the uniqueness of its music. If the accented syllable is on a high note, it is followed by a *falling* inflection; if on a low note, by a *rising* inflection.

Observation and Notes

It is difficult to point out dialect models for Greek; even Aristotle (Telly) Savalas was born in New York City. In fact, so few Greek-born actors play in English-language films that Greek roles are frequently portrayed by others. For example, *Zorba the Greek* had only one Greek star: Irene Papas; the other major roles went to a Mexican-born American (Anthony Quinn) and a Russian-born French actress (Lila Kedrova). One true model does stand out: Melina Mercouri, whose first English-language role in *Never on Sunday* established her as an international star. Unfortunately for her film fans, Mercouri has devoted more and more of her time to Greek politics.

For purposes of observation and study, there are the Greek restaurants and folk-dancing centers mentioned at the beginning of the chapter. Not a bad alternative; this could be your most enjoyable dialect-learning experience of all. Have fun—but don't forget to take along your cassette recorder!

Melina Mercouri captured audiences all over the world with her portrayal of a life-loving prostitute in Never on Sunday. *Born, schooled and trained in Athens, she brings her native "Athens, Educated" subdialect to every role, including* Gaily, Gaily *(United Artists/MGM, 1969, shown here).*

GENERAL GREEK - SALONIKA, LESS EDUCATED - PIRAEUS, UNEDUCATED ATHENS, EDUCATED

GUIDE PAGES	SOUND	General Greek	Salonika Less Educated	Piraeus Uneducated	Athens Educated Greek
Change in all positions: (fail) FeL, (ache) eK, (maintain) MeNT=eN, (pay) Pe	A	e	&	&	
OR change: FeiL, eiK, MeiNT=eiN, Pei	A				ei
Change in all positions: (seem) S:iM, (eat) iT=, (me) Mi, (easy) iS:i, (be) Bi	E	i	&	&	
OR change: S:i:M, i:T=, Mi:, i:S:i:, Bi:	E				i:
Change in all positions: (like) LAiK, (I'm) AiM, (side) S:AiD=, (die) D=Ai	I	Ai	&	&	&
Change in all positions: (note) N*uo*T=, (only) *uo*NLi, (no) N*uo*, (solo) S:*uo*L*uo*	O	*uo*	&	&	
OR change: N*u*OT, *u*ONLi:, N*u*O, S:*u*OL*u*O	O				*u*O

		All 4
CHANGE: (fuel) FY*u*L, (use) Y*u*S:, (music) MY*u*S:iK	U	Y*u*
CHANGE: (flat) FL*A*T=, (am) *A*M, (mad) M*A*D=, (as) *A*S:	a	*A*
CHANGE: (said) S:aD=, (bell) BaL, (dead) D=aD=, (end) aN¼	e	a

	SOUND	General Greek	Salonika Less Educated	Piraeus Uneducated	Athens Educated Greek
DOUBLY LONG: (it) iiT=, (till) T=iiL, (in) iiN, (if) iiF, (critic) KRiiT=iiK	i			ii	
OR no change: iT=, T=iL, iN, iF	i	i	&		&
Change in all positions: (on) *uo*N, (clock) KL*uo*K, (not) N*uo*T=, (odd) *uo*D=	o	*uo*	&	&	
OR change: *o*N, KL*o*K, N*o*T=, *o*D=	o				*o*
Change in all positions: (cut) K*uo*T=, (blood) BL*uo*D=, (does) D=*uo*S:	u	*uo*	&	&	
OR change: K*ui*T=, BL*ui*D=, D=*ui*S:	u				*ui*
No change: (calm) KALM, (are) *A*R	A	*A*	&	&	&
Change in all positions: (earn) *uo*RN, (first) F*uo*RS:T=, (burn) B*uo*RN	*E*	*uo*	&	&	
OR change: *u*RN, F*u*RS:T=, B*u*RN	*E*				*u*
No change: (predict) PRID=iKT=	*I*	*I*	&	&	&
Change in all positions: (now) N*uo*, (down) D=*uo*N, (out) *uo*T=, (loud) L*uo*D=	*O*	*uo*	&	&	
OR change: NA, D=AN, AT=, LAD=	*O*				A

		All 4
CHANGE: (do) D=*u*, (soon) S:*u*N, (fruit) FR*u*T=, (lose) L*u*S:	*U*	*u*
CHANGE: (dance) D=*A*NS:, (ask) *A*S:K, (laugh) L*A*F	*a*	*A*
IF spelled OR: (labor) LeB*uo*R, (glamor) G*h*LAM*uo*R	*e*	*uo*$or
IF " ER: (paper) PeP*uo*R, (over) *uo*BV*uo*R, (ever) aBV*uo*R	*e*	*uo*$er
IF " OUS: (precious) PRaS:*uo*S:, (gorgeous) G*huo*Rz*uo*S:	*e*	*uo*$ous
IF " ION: (nation) NeS:*uo*N, (station) S:T=eS:*uo*N	*e*	*uo*$ion
IF " LE: (apple) *A*P*uo*L, (simple) S:iMB*uo*L	*e*	*uo*$le
IF " EL: (level) LaBV*uo*L, (channel) *s*AN*uo*L	*e*	*uo*$el

	SOUND	General Greek	Salonika Less Educated	Piraeus Uneducated	Athens Educated Greek
Change in all positions: (sofa) S:*uo*FA, (attack) AT=AK, (family) FAMALi	*i*	A	&	&	&
Change when spelled A,AW,AU: (law) L*u*o, (all) *u*oL, (cause) K*u*oS:, (talk) T=*u*oK	*o*	*uo*$au a aw	&	&	
OR change: Lo, oL, KoS:, T=oK	*o*				o$a
AND change when spelled O,OO,OU,OA: (or) *uo*R, (loss) L*uo*S:, (door) D=*uo*R	*o*	*uo*$oo o ou	&	&	&

Key: z measure ¼ dropped *s* waits,its *h* loch,ich
$ spelled & as shown : stronger *R* trilled R = interdental

GENERAL GREEK - SALONIKA, LESS EDUCATED - PIRAEUS, UNEDUCATED ATHENS, EDUCATED

GUIDE PAGES	SOUND	General Greek	Salonika Less Educated	Piraeus Uneducated	Athens Educated Greek
No change: (book) B*u*K, (full) F*u*L	*u*	*u*	&	&	&
Change in all positions: (coin) K*uo*EN, (oil) *uo*EL, (boy) B*uo*E, (noise) N*uo*ES:	*o*E	*uo*E	&	&	&
Change in all positions: (bob) B:V*uo*B:V, (maybe) MeB:Vi, (by) B:VAi, (rub) *R*uoB:V	B		B:V		
OR change: BV*uo*BV, BVAi, *R*uoBV	B			BV	
BUT between vowels, add **M**: MeMBVi	B			+M(b‡	
OR no change: B*uo*B, MeBi, BAi, *R*uoB	B	B			&
CHANGE: (much) M*uo*ꞩ, (church) ꞩ*uo*Rꞩ	C	ꞩ	&	&	
OR no change: M*ui*C, C*u*RC	C				C
DROP final after consonant: (land) LAN¼ (cold) K*uo*L¼, (bird) B*uoR*¼, (mind) MAiN¼	D	.¼)¢	&	&	
OTHERWISE INTERDENTALIZE: (dead) D=aD=, (body) B*uo*D=i, (food) F*u*D=, (do) D=*u*	D	D=	&	&	
OR no change: LAND, MAiND, DaD, B*o*Di:	D				D
OR change finally before vowel: (did it) D=ii*R*iiT=, (read all) *R*a*Ru*oL	D			.*R*(*	
DROP medially before a consonant: (after) A¼T=*uoR*, (fifteen) Fii¼T=iN	F			/¼(¢	
OR no change: AFT=*uoR*, FiFT=iN	F	F	&		&
DROP finally from ING or ONG: (coming) K*uo*MiN¼, (along) AL*uo*N¼, (bring) B*R*iN¼	G	.¼ing .¼ong	&	&	&
CHANGE except before E or e: (glass) G*h*LAS:, (go) G*huo*, (angry) ANG*hR*i	G	G*h*! (E e		G*h*!(¢ or(Ee	
OR change before consonant: *h*LAS:, AN*hR*ii	G			*h*(¢	
OR no change: G*u*O, GLAS:, ANG*R*i:	G				G
CHANGE: (ahead) A*h*aD=, (household) *huo*S:*huo*L¼, (had) *h*AD=, (here) *h*i*R*	H	*h*	&	/*h*	
OR stronger: AH::aD=, H::AS:H::*u*OLD	H				H::
OR drop initially: ¼*uo*S:*huo*L¼, ¼AD=	H			-¼	
Change in all positions: (judge) z*uo*z, (procedure) P*R*IS:iz*uoR*, (giant) zAiANT=	J	z			&
OR change: Dz*uo*Dz, P*R*IS:iDz*uoR*, DzAiANT=	J		Dz		
OR change: DZ*uo*DZ, P*R*IS:iDZ*uoR*, DZAiANT=	J			DZ	
Change when spelled CH: (ache) e*h*, (chorus) *huo*RAS:, (stomach) S:T=*uo*Mi*h*	K		*h*$ch		
OR change before *uo*,*uo*,A: (cap) *h*AP, (cause) *huo*S:, (cut) *huo*T=, (car) *h*A*R*	K			*h*(*uo* *uo* A	
OR no change: K*uo*RAS:, KAP, K*uo*S:, K*uo*T=	K	K			K
No change	LMN	LMN	&	&	&
Change following M: (simple) S:iMB*uo*L, (compare) KAMBe*R*, (lamp) LAMB, (imp) iMB	P	B)m	&	&	&
OR add M between vowels: (paper) PeMP*uoR*, (stopping) S:T=*uo*MPiiN¼	P			+M(p‡	

Key:

z vision	*h* loch,ich	ꞩ its,waits	! excepting	= interdental
+ add to	- initial	*R* trilled R	(preceding	* vowels
¼ dropped	/ medially	& as shown	) following	‡ between "
$ spelled	. finally	: stronger		¢ consonants

GENERAL GREEK - SALONIKA, LESS EDUCATED - PIRAEUS, UNEDUCATED ATHENS, EDUCATED

GUIDE PAGES	SOUND	General Greek	Salonika Less Educated	Piraeus Uneducated	Athens Educated Greek
Change in all positions: (quit) KBViT=, (equal) iKBVAL, (frequent) FRiKBVANT=	Q	KBV		&	
OR change: KBV:iT=, iKBV:AL, FRiKBV:ANT=	Q		KBV:		
OR change following a consonant: (square) S:GBVeR, (inquire) iNGBVAiR	Q		GBV)¢	&	
OR change: KuWiT=, i:KuWAL, S:KuWeiR	Q				KuW
TRILLED: (rear) RiR, (alright) uoLRAiT= (very) BVaRi, (are) AR, (spring) S:PRiN¼	R	R	&	&	&
STRONGER: (cease) S:iS:, (stop) S:T=uoP (decide) D=iS:AiD=, (nice) NAiS:	S	S:	&	&	&
Change in all positions: (shush) S:uoS:, (sure) S:uR, (motion) MuoS:uoN	*S*	S:	&	&	
OR change: SS:uiSS:, SS:uR, MuOSS:uoN	*S*				SS:
INTERDENTALIZE: (tight) T=AiT=, (to) T=u, (detail) D=iT=eL, (treat) T=RiT=	T	T=	&	&	&
OR change medially when spelled TT: (better) BaRuoR, (little) LiRuoL	T		/R$tt	&	
OR drop medially after consonant, before vowel: (empty) aMP¼i, (into) iN¼u	T		/¼)¢	&	
OR change finally between vowels: (it is) iRiS:, (at all) ARuoL, (out of) uoRouBV	T		.Rƒ	&	
STRONGER: (think) t:iNK, (both) Buot:, (nothing) Nuot:iN¼, (faithful) Fet:F L	t	t:	&	&	&
No change: (them) TaM, (other) uoTuoR	*T*	*T*	&	&	&
Change in all positions: (vote) BVuoT=, (involve) iNBVuoLBV, (never) NaBVuoR	V	BV		&	
OR change: BV:uoT=, iNBV:uoLBV:, NaBV:uoR	V		BV:		
OR no change: VuOT=, iNVoLV, NaVuoR	V				V
CHANGE: (was) BVuoS:, (always) uoLBVeS:, (between) BiT=BViN, (why) BVAi, (we) BVi	W	BV		&	
OR change: uoLBV:eS:, BiT=BV:iN, BV:Ai	W		BV:		
BUT drop medially after u: (toward) T=u¼uoR¼, (thruway) t:Ru¼e	W	/¼)u	&	&	
OR change: uWuiS:, oLuWeiS:, T=uWo D=	W				uW
CHANGE GZ sound: (example) aGSAMBuoL, (exact) aGSAKT=, (anxiety) ANGSAiiT=i	X	GS4gz	&	&	
OR change GZ: ahZAMBuoL, ANhZAiiT=i	X				hZ4gz
OR change KS sound: (expert) ahSPuoRT=, (taxi) T=AhSi, (sex) S:ahS, (mix) MihS	X	hS4ks			&
Change if spelled S: (music) MYuS:iK, (does) D=uoS:, (busy) BiS:i, (is) iS:	Z	S:$s	&	&	&
Change in all positions: (television) T=aLABViSYuoN, (pleasure) PLaSYuoR	z	SY	&	&	
OR no change: T=aLAVizuoN, PLazuoR	z				z

Key:

4 for	h loch,ich	R trilled R	= interdental	* vowels
/ medial	& as shown	(preceding	$ spelled	ƒ between "
. final	: stronger	) following	¢ consonants	¼ dropped

MASTER CATEGORY 21

INDIAN

There are eighteen instances of *exact* correspondence between General Indian and General British West Indian, so it is quite easy for the untrained ear to confuse them. To point up the differences between them, the two chapters adjoin one another.

The most important distinction is that General British West Indian is a *variety* of English that most of its speakers use in their daily lives, while General Indian is a *dialect* and not the native language of those who speak it. What they *do* speak depends on where they live in India: this populous subcontinent has 782 languages and dialects, of which seventy are each spoken by at least 100,000 people. This fragmentation, however, is not strongly reflected in the subdialects in the following *GUIDE PAGES*, because only *one* Indian English is taught throughout the country.

Indian English is much closer to British than to American English. Generally, the subdialect that is lightest is *New Delhi, Educated*, but you'll come across exceptions due to regionalisms.

One of the major reasons that this dialect is so distinctive is the number of complete sound changes it entails: seven consonants and ten vowels are not merely modified but radically affected.

Vowel Changes

As an example, the (a) of "tan" and "bat" becomes the (e) of "ten" and "bet," and if a "man had backpacked from Baghdad to Afghanistan," and we were from India, we would say the:

(MeN HeD BeKPeKT) from (BeGDeD) to (eFGeNAZTeN).

The same (e) is all that is left of the double vowel "eh-ee" (A) when the Indian gets done with it. Thus, "we'll be able to take a great vacation if payday's not too late," becomes:

we'll be (eBuL) to (TeK) a (GReT VWeKeSAN) if (PeDeS) not too (LeT).

Another diphthong that the Indian shortens is the "aw-oo" (O) sound of "coat" and "bowl." Chopping off the "oo," this dialect leaves only the (*o*) of "caught" and "ball." So that if "both old fellows rode slowly homeward," the native of India would observe that:

(BoT oLD FeLoS RoD SLoLE HoMVWARD).

The double vowel "Y-oo" (U) is merely shortened, so that the "oo" element one finds in "fool" shrinks to the (*u*) in "full"—and "new, pure fuel assumes huge value" comes out:

(NYu, PYuR FYuL AZYuMS HYuC VWeLYu).

This same shrinkage affects "oo" (*U*) when it is found by itself. Thus, if nothing could lift the "losing schoolroom's gloomy mood," being born in India you would refer to the:

(LuSEN¼ SKuLRuMS GLuME MuD).

There *is* one case in which a vowel sound is lengthened: (i) as in "did" and "lick" is stretched into "ee" (E) as in "deed" and "leak." Thus, "it didn't inhibit his inquisitive instincts" emerges as:

(ET DENT ENHEBET HES ENKVESATEVW ENZTENKTS:).

These are all the modifications you will find in Indian vowels; all the rest are outright changes. For example, the "eh" (e) sound of "bed," when found in a prefix is changed into the "ee" (E) of "bead." Thus, if Congress is "expected to enact extensive exemptions," being from India, you would say they were:

(EXPeKTeD) to (ENeKT EXTenZEVW EXeMSANS).

We meet another change in the diphthong "ow" (O) as in "now." This is converted into (Ou), which is made up of the "oh" of "no" and the (u) of "nook." Thus, to tell "how our proud spouting aroused the crowd's outraged shouts," as Indians we would have to explain:

(HOu OuR PROuD SPOuTEN¼ AROuSD) the (KROuDS OuTReCD SOuTS:).

A less complicated transformation is that of the (o) of "cot" into the (o) of "caught." So if we know that her usual "honest, solid job has not gotten sloppy," if we were Indian, we might reassure her boss that her usual:

(oNEST, SoLED JoB) has (NoT GoTN SLoPE).

Oddly enough, the (o) sound itself shifts into "ah" (A) in Indian dialect, so that "court" comes to resemble "cart"—and if the pet sweater was "the right sort for long, short, broad, or tall dogs," we would describe it as:

the right (SART FAR LANG, SART, BRAD AR TAL DAGS).

Alone or as part of a diphthong, this (A) dominates many of the vowel changes. To illustrate, "aw-ee" (oE) alters into "ah-ee" (AE), and an "adroit employment of royal poise" becomes an:

(ADRAET EMPLAEMANT) of (RAEAL PAES).

Another case is (u) as in "one," which turns into (A) as in "wan." Thus, if "some rough, unjust sons come from unloving mothers," an Indian would point out that:

(SAM RAF, ANJAST SANS KAM FRAM ANLAVWEN¼ MAD¼RS).

As with many former parts of the British Empire, India also broadens the (a) of "aunt" into (A). So if he is tired "after that last, fast, half-athletic dance," our Indian must express his fatigue:

(AFT¼R) that (LAZT, FAZT, HAFATLeTEK DANS:).

With one, small exception, the (i) sound of "ago" is also made into (A), and if "his political companions had alarming opinions," in Indian dialect you would remark that:

his (PALETEKAL KAMPeNYANS) had (ALARMEN¼ APENYANS).

The exception applies *only* to Bombay and Jaipur. These subdialects reshape any (i) found in a *second* syllable into "ay" (A) as in "say." Thus a "scientific, balanced family system" ends up as a:

(SIANTi:Fi:K, BeLANZT FeMALi SI:ZTAM).

The next two conversions into (A) have multiple exceptions. The (e) sound becomes (A) when spelled "al" but when the spelling is "el" or "le" it is pronounced (u) as in "pull." So while we may speak of a "vital, natural metal ore" as being a:

(VWITAL, NeC¼RAL MeTAL) ore,

we must talk of "trouble over a simple little title" as:

(TRABuL oVW¼R) a (SEMPuL LETuL TITuL).

As you can see from the pronunciation of "natural" and "over," the (e) sound is simply dropped (¼) from (eR) combinations, and if he hired an "abler paper cover maker," an Indian would put it that he hired an:

(eBL¼R PeP¼R KAVW¼R MeK¼R).

The final vowel changes we'll consider happen to the (E) of "fur." When spelled "ir," "ear," or "ar," we substitute (A) as in "far." Thus, if I "heard the first girl returned early, dirty, and thirsty," in this dialect I would report that I:

(HARD) the (FARZT GARL RETiRND ARLE, DARTE), and (TARZTE).

As you see from "returned," if this sound is spelled "ur" we replace the (*E*) with (*i*). So that "the curvy nurse spurned his urgent pursuit," to an Indian is:

the (K*iR*VWE N*iR*S: SP*iR*ND) his (*iRC*ANT P*iR*Z*u*T).

If an Indian comes across an (*E*) spelled "or," he exchanges it for the (*u*) in "full," and "at worst his work was worth kind words" comes out as:

at (VW*uR*ST) his (VW*uR*K) was (VW*uR*T) kind (VW*uR*DS).

When (*E*) is spelled "er," and it is weak (as in "butter"), it is dropped (¼). Otherwise, "eh" (e) takes its place, and "her nervous concerns over germs were perverse" emerges as:

(He*R* Ne*R*VW*A*S: K*A*NZe*R*NS *o*VW¼*R* *C*e*R*MS VWe*R* Pe*R*VWe*R*S:).

Consonant Changes

All the "r"s in that last sentence illustrate the usual Indian handling of the "r": it is trilled. The tongue is pressed against the front upper gum ridge and the (*R*) is vibrated, sounding like a child's version of a machine gun or a mortorcycle. When the "r" is final and precedes a consonant, it is dropped (¼), but otherwise all "r"s are trilled. Thus, if accountants "are forced to reread more dry records every March," if you were born in India, you might say that they:

(*A*¼ F*AR*ZD) to (*R*E*R*ED M*A*¼ D*R*I *R*eK*AR*DS eVW*R*E M*ARC*).

Indians are quite careful with consonants: the only other one they drop is the (G) from the "ing" ending. So if we hope "we're not going to be regretting the coming meeting," being Indian we would wish that:

we're not (G*o*EN¼) to be (*R*EG*R*eTEN¼) the (K*A*MEN¼ METEN¼).

In two instances, an unvoiced consonant is voiced. At the end of a word, the "p" sound of "cup" is altered into the "b" sound of "cub." So if the Broadway critic is surprised at how a "ripe pinup can pep up a limp flop," in our dialect he'd report how:

(*R*IB PEN*A*B) can (PeB *A*B) a (LEMB FL*o*B).

In the other case in point, the medial (S) in "muscle" is transformed into the (Z) in "muzzle." Thus, if "his bossy sister dismissed his best classes as useless," an Indian-born student would complain that:

(HES B*A*ZE SEZT¼*R* DEZMEZED HES BeZT KL*A*Z*e*S eS Y*u*ZLeS:).

That last sentence also shows that a voiced consonant is sometimes unvoiced. As you can see from "his," "classes," and "as," a final (Z) gets shaped into an (S) if it is spelled "s." In the *middle* of a word and between vowels, this conversion takes place no matter how the original (Z) sound is spelled. So if "the busy prison supervisor rises easily, not lazily," if you were Indian, you would say that the:

(BESE P*R*ES*A*N S*u*P*e**R*VWIS¼*R* *R*ISeS ES*A*LE,) not (LeS*A*LE).

A similar shift affects (*z*) in words like "intrusion" turning it into (*S*) as in "revolution." Thus a "leisurely, luxurious pleasure excursion" ends up as a:

(LeS*iR*LE, L*A*GS*uR*E*A*S: PLeS*iR* eXK*iR*S*A*N).

The last example of this kind of consonant switch is the (J) of "ridge." It is made into the "ch" (*C*) of "rich" whenever it is spelled with a "g" or a "dg." So if the "large, ginger-haired genius was generally logical," for an Indian, the:

(L*ARC*, *C*EN*C*¼*R*-He*R*D *C*ENY*A*S:) was (*C*eN¼*R**A*LE L*o**C*EK*A*L).

When spelled with a "d" or "du," this same (J) sound gets the British treatment and evolves into (DY). So the "residual effect of the individual graduation procedure" changes into the:

(*R*ESEDY*uA*L) effect of the (END*A*VWEDY*uA*L G*R*eDY*u*eS*A*N P*R*IZEDY*iR*).

Certain American consonant sounds do not exist in the languages of India and must be approximated by the speaker. Thus, (*T*) as in "there" is reshaped into (D) as in "dare." So if "they'd rather let those wither than bother bathing them," an Indian might find that:

(DeD *RAD¼R*) let (DoS VWED¼*R* DeN BoD¼*R* BeDEN¼ DeM).

Similarly, the (*t*) in "three" is modified into the (T) in "tree"—and "faithful through both thick and thin" emerges as:

(FeTFuL T*Ru* BoT TEK) and (TEN).

Another approximated sound is (Q), which this dialect transforms into (KV). Thus, if practitioners of Yoga "frequently acquire a quality of exquisitely quiet tranquility," being born in India, you would have to say that they:

(F*R*EKVANTLE AKVI*R*) a (KVALATE) of (EXKVESETLE KVIAT T*R*eNKVELETE).

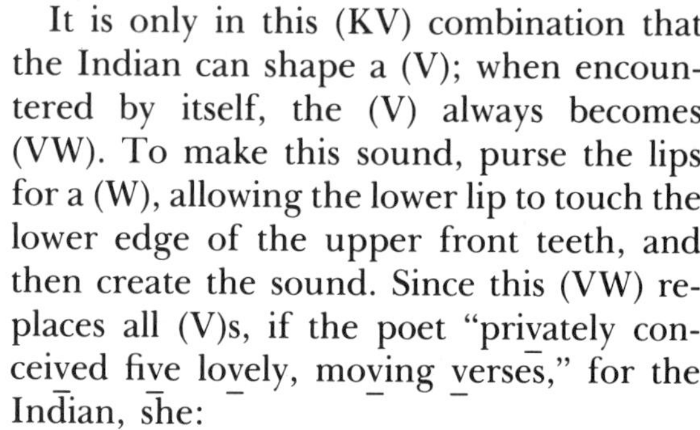

It is only in this (KV) combination that the Indian can shape a (V); when encountered by itself, the (V) always becomes (VW). To make this sound, purse the lips for a (W), allowing the lower lip to touch the lower edge of the upper front teeth, and then create the sound. Since this (VW) replaces all (V)s, if the poet "privately conceived five lovely, moving verses," for the Indian, she:

(P*R*IVWETLE KANZEVWD FIVW LAVWLE, M*u*VWEN¼ VWe*R*Z*e*S).

The same (VW) substitutes for all (W)s. So if a "whistling, wayward wind was twisting toward the highway," in the Indian dialect we would observe that a:

(VWESLEN¼, VWeVWA*R*D VWEND VWAS TVWESTEN¼ TAVWA*R*DS) the (HIVWe).

Peter Sellers, one of the most fluent of dialecticians, is pictured here in the role of an Indian physician in The Millionairess *(20th Century Fox, 1960). A thorough craftsman, Sellers kept his General Indian dialect pure and consistent: one of the best examples of "internalizing a dialect" on film.*

Music, Rhythm, and Pace

The Indian dialect is spoken two to three tones higher than American English and is clipped, ultra-clear, and slightly nasal. The pitch rises one-half tone on each stressed syllable (a full tone in an important word) and falls one-half tone immediately afterwards (a full tone at the end of a phrase). This results in a modified singsong quality reminiscent of Norwegian, in that the variation is regular and constant. These rises and falls are restricted generally to the same four notes, so the dialect seldom has a range exceeding two full tones.

All stressed syllables are drawn out in exact ratio to their tonal rise: a syllable which is raised a full tone is held twice as long as one raised only a half tone. Only one syllable in any word is accented. Indian is spoken at a slightly slower pace than American English and, while clipped, nevertheless retains a light and airy quality.

Observation and Notes

As for listening to the Indian dialect, there are no Indian actors I can point to. The Indian film industry is so different from both the British and the American that it is almost impossible for an actor to make the transition. What's more, there is hardly any motivation for such a move: with India's annual production averaging six hundred feature films, plenty of jobs are available for the talented. We can only turn to Indian ethnic centers and restaurants for authentic dialect models.

Ben Kingsley's dialect, however, in *Gandhi* is close enough to the authentic Indian dialect to be highly useful. And, if you get a chance to see a rerun of *The Millionairess*, don't miss the opportunity to record Peter Sellers's Indian doctor.

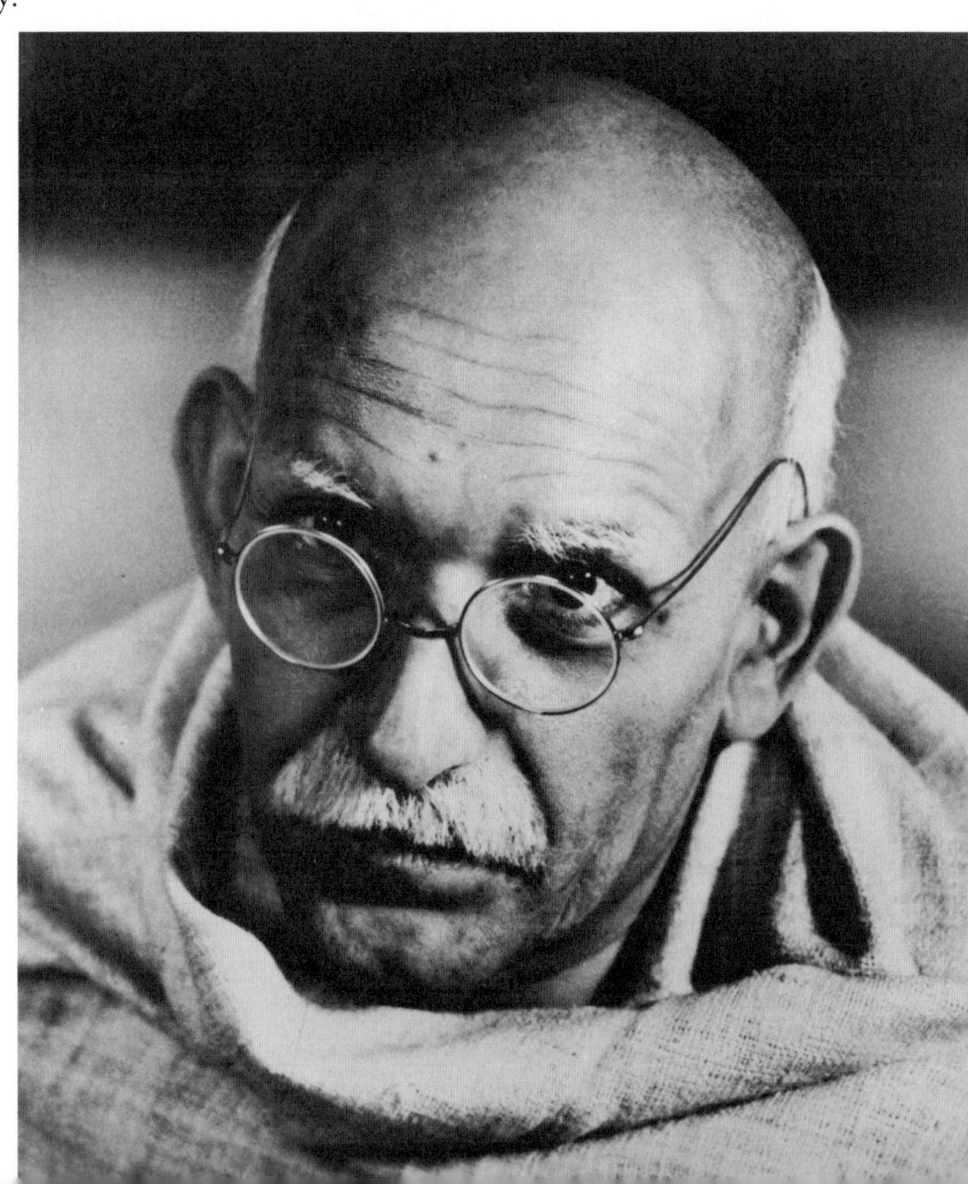

If you are watching Ben Kingsley's portrayal of Gandhi *(Columbia, 1982) for the first time, his dialect in the opening scenes may disappoint you. Kingsley quite accurately gave us a young Gandhi in South Africa who had set out to be a proper English lawyer, in speech as well as manner. As his Gandhi spent more and more time with his own people in India, Kingsley allowed his dialect to become more "General Indian." By the time Gandhi had reached the age shown here, the dialect is very close to General Indian. By that time, of course, you've been listening to* authentic *Indian dialects and subdialects from Indian actors for over two hours and should be able to capture their characteristic "music."*

GENERAL INDIA - BOMBAY, LESS EDUCATED - JAIPUR, UNEDUCATED

NEW DELHI, EDUCATED

GUIDE PAGES

	SOUND	General India	Bombay Less Educated India	Jaipur Uneducated India	New Delhi Educated India
Change in all positions: (came) KeM, (maintain) MeNTeN, (say) Se, (ate) eT	A	e	&	&	
OR change: Keim, MeiNTeiN, Sei, eiT	A				ei
Change in all positions: (easy) iSi, (here) HiR, (receive) RiZiVW, (me) Mi	E		i	&	
OR no change: ESE, HER, REZEVW, ME	E	E			&
No change: (ice) IS:, (buy) BI, (lie) LI	I	I	&	&	&
Change in all positions: (solo) SoLo, (old) oLD, (know) No, (toe) To, (sew) So	O	o	&	&	
OR change: SouLou, ouLD, Nou, Tou, Sou	O				ou
Change in all positions: (few) FYu, (cute) KYuT, (unit) YuNeT, (pure) PYuR	U	Yu	&	&	&
CHANGE: (fact) FeKT, (had) HeD, (man) MeN	a	e	&	&	&!
OR change in polysyllable: (elastic) ELAZTi:K, (bandana) BANDANA	a				A"?:
Change in prefix: (enact) ENeKT, (expect) EXPeKT, (endure) ENDYuR	e	E{	&	&	&
Change in all positions: (busy) BESE, (imprint) EMPRENT, (within) VWEDEN	i	E		&	
OR longer: Bi:Si:, i:MPRi:NT, VWi:Di:N	i		i:		&
Change in all positions: (copy) KoPE, (on) oN, (topnotch) ToPNoC, (shock) SoK	o	o			
OR change: KOPi, ON, TOPNOC, SOK	o		O	&	
OR change: KAPE, AN, TAPNAC, SAK	o				A
Change in all positions: (under) AND¼R, (blood) BLAD, (does) DAS, (what) VWAT	u	A	&	&	&
No change: (calm) KALM, (heart) HART	A	A	&	&	&
Change if spelled IR: (first) FARZT	E	A$ir	&	&	&
Change if " UR: (burn) BiRN, (urge) iRC	E	i$ur	&	&	&
Change if " OR: (work) VWuRK	E	u$or	&	&	&
Change if " ER: (her) HeR, (refer) REFeR	E	e$er	&	&	&
Change if " EAR: (learn) LARN (earn) ARN	E	A$ear	&	&	&
BUT drop when weak: (butter) BAT¼R	E	¼"½	&	&	&
No change: (predict) PRIDEKT	I	I	&	&	&
Change in all positions: (how) HOu, (down) DOuN, (out) OuT, (count) KOuNT	O	Ou	&		&
OR change: Ho, DoN, oT, KoNT	O			o	

		All 4
CHANGE: (soon) SuN, (move) MuVW, (true) TRu, (fruit) FRuT	U	u
CHANGE: (after) AFT¼R, (dance) DANS:, (laugh) LAF	a	A
IF spelled AL: (metal) MeTAL, (social) SoSAL	e	AL$al
IF " EL,LE: (apple) ePuL, (level) LeVWuL, (little) LETuL	e	uL$le
BUT DROP if spelled ER: (paper) PeP¼R, (over) oVW¼R	e	¼$er

Change in all positions: (above) ABAVW, (system) SEZTAM, (family) FeMALE	i	A	&!	&!	&
OR change as 2nd syllable: Si:ZTAM, FeMALi, (separate) SePAReT	i		2nd syl A	&	

Key:

C church	S show,sure	$ spelled	{ in prefix	" when
R trilled R	! excepting	& as shown	?: polysyllable	¼ drop
				½ weak

GENERAL INDIA - BOMBAY, LESS EDUCATED - JAIPUR, UNEDUCATED NEW DELHI, EDUCATED

GUIDE PAGES

	SOUND	General India	Bombay Less Educated India	Jaipur Uneducated India	New Delhi Educated India
Change in all positions: (call) KAL, (saw) SA, (door) DAR, (off) AF	o	A	&	&	
OR if spelled A,, AU or AW: KAuL, SAu	o				Au$a
OR spelled O,OA,OO, no change: DoR, oF	o				o$o
No change: (cook) KuK, (pull) PuL	u	u	&	&	&
Change in all positions: (oil) AEL, (voice) VWAES:, (boy) BAE, (join) JAEN	oE	AE	&	&	&
No change: (batch) BeC, (feed) FED	BCDF	BCDF	&	&	&
					All 4
Drop from ING suffix: (going) GoEN¼, (living) LEVWEN¼	G				¼ing)
No change	H				H
If spelled G change: (judge) JAC, (age) eC, (giant) CIANT	J				C$g
If " D: (individual) ENDAVWEDYAL, (procedure) PRIZEDYiR	J				DY$d
No change: (kill) KEL, (man) MeN	KLMN	KLMN	&	&	&
Change finally: (prop) PRoB, (up) AB, (pipe) PIB, (slip) SLEB, (step) STeB	P	.B		&	
OR change final: PROBP, ABP, PIBP	P		.BP		
OR change " : PRABP:, ABP:, PIBP:	P				.BP:
					All 4
CHANGE: (quite) KVIT, (equal) EKVAL, (square) SKVeR	Q				KV
TRILL: (rear) RER, (spring) SPRENG, (very) VWeRE	R				R
BUT drop final before consonant: (or not) A¼NoT (for some) FA¼SAM	R				.¼(¢
Change medially: (decide) DEZID, (basic) BeZEK, (ask) AZK	S				/Z
AND stronger finally: (cease) SES:, (yes) YeS:, (nice) NIS:	S				.S:
No change: (shut) SAT, (tissue) TESu	ST				S T
Change in all positions: (through) TRu, (healthy) HeLTE, (both) BoT	t	T	&		
OR change: SSRu, HeLSSi, BoSS	t			SS	
Or no change: tRu, HeLtE, Bout	t				t
Change in all positions: (other) AD¼R, (this) DES:, (with) VWED, (then) DeN	T	D	&		
OR change: ASS¼R, SSES:, VWESS, SSeN	T			SS	
Or no change: AT¼R, Ti:S:, VWi:T, TeN	T				T
Change in all positions: (have) HAVW, (visit) VWESeT, (never) NeVW¼R, (of) AVW	V	VW	&	&	
OR change: HAV:W, V:Wi:SeT, NeV:W¼R	V				V:W
Change in all positions: (where) VWeR, (always) ALVWeS, (was) VWAS, (we) VWE	W	VW	&	&	
OR change: VW:eiR, AuLVW:eiS, VW:AS	W				VW:
					All 4
No change	X				X
Change between vowels: (music) MYuSEK (lazy) LeSE (busy) BESE	Z				Sƒ
Change final if spelled S: (ears) ERS, (his) HES	Z				.S$s
Change in all positions: (azure) ASiR, (vision) VWESAN, (pleasure) PLeSiR	z	S	&	&	
OR change: eZYiR, V:Wi:ZYAN, PLeZYiR	z				ZY

Key:

(preceding	& as shown	¼ drop	R trilled R	ƒ between vowels
) in suffix	: stronger	/ medial	$ spelled	¢ consonant
		. final		

BRITISH WEST INDIAN

As I pointed out in the last chapter, though there are many similarities between General British West Indian and General Indian, you will be able to keep them apart as long as you remember that General Indian is a *dialect* while General British West Indian is a *variety*. This means that while Indians are *trying* to approximate the sound of a (to them) foreign language, the people of the British West Indies are speaking a language they have been taught in school and use every day.

The British West Indies are a chain of islands extending from Florida to Venezuela. The main islands in the group are Jamaica, Trinidad, the Windward Islands (including Grenada), Barbados, the Leeward Islands, and the Bahamas. Racially, the BWI is an extension of Africa: seventy-five percent of the people are descended from slaves brought to the Caribbean by the French, British, and Spanish. The second largest racial group comes from India. Indians are particularly well represented in the Windward Islands, and they make up about one-third of the population in Trinidad. This accounts for the fundamental resemblance between the West Indian variety and the Indian dialect. Other influences upon the BWI variety come from African languages, from Spanish, from British English, and from French.

Of the subvarieties covered, *Jamaica, Educated* is closest to both British and American speech, while *Grenada, Rural* is not only furthest from both those forms of English but also from the General British West Indian itself.

There are relatively few consonant changes in General BWI, and almost all can be found in Indian as well. Of course, the music of the BWI is quite distinct from Indian, but that is something we shall explore later. At this point, we'll look at the BWI handling of vowels, which includes the changing of eight of them and the shortening of eight others.

Vowel Changes

There are only two cases in which the vowel is lengthened. In the first, the (*u*) of "pull" is drawn out into a somewhat short (½) version of the (*U*) of "pool." Thus the observation that with the right makeup, "that woman could sure look good" becomes:

that (VW:*U*½MAN K*U*½D *SU*½*R* L*U*½K G*U*½D).

In Grenada, instead of extending the vowel, they interpolate an (i) as in "pill" before it—and the phrase comes out:

that (Vi*u*MAN Ki*u*D *Siu*¼ Li*u*K Gi*u*D).

In the second case the (i) in "pill" is elongated into a short (½) rendering of the "ee" (E) in "peel," so that the announcement that "the critic is visiting this district" ends up as:

the (K*R*E½TE½K E½S VWE½ZE½TE½N¼ DE½S DE½STR*E*½K¼).

In the Grenada version, the (i) is simply converted into the (*i*) sound of "normal"—and they would say that:

the (K*R*:*i*T*i*K *i*S W*i*Z*i*T*i*N¼ D*i*S D*i*ST*R*:*i*K¼).

In all other cases the characteristic tendency of BWI is to chop down or chop off the vowels. Two such abbreviations may be considered compensation reversals. Just as we saw (i) as in "pill" stretched into (E) as in "peel," the (E) is abridged into a long (:) version of (i) as in "pill." So if the girl thinks "these bikinis seem really neat," if she were from the BWI, she would say that:

(Di:S Bi:Ki:Ni:S Si:M *R*i:Li: Ni:T).

Similarly, the "oo" (*U*) of "pool" is modified into a stretched out (:) form of the (*u*) of "pull." Thus "his roomy, blue shoes soon grew too loose" turns into:

his (*Ru*:Mi:, BL*u*: *Su*:S S*u*:N G*Ru*: T*u*: L*u*:S).

Not all the BWI vowel abridgments are reversals. For example, while the (o) in "hot" remains unchanged, it also substitutes for the (*A*) in "heart." So if we want to report that "the harbor watchman guarded the large, dark barge's cargo," in the BWI variety we'd say that:

the (Ho¼B*eR* VW:o*C*M*A*N Go¼D*e*D) the (Lo¼J, Do¼K Bo¼J*e*S Ko¼GO½).

As you can see from "cargo," the diphthong (O) is reduced (½) in the BWI variety. This applies also to the diphthong (U) as in "huge." Grenadians, however, compress the double vowel even further, into (Y*u*), so "to use cute music" for them emerges as:

to (Y*u*S KY*u*T MY*u*ZiK).

As for the (O = *oU*) of "boat," they cut off the (*U*) element entirely, leaving just the "aw" (*o*) of "bought." So if they wish to complain that the "cocoa grows so slowly," they would gripe that the:

(K*o*K*o* G*R*:*o*S S*o* SL*o*Li:).

Another diphthong the BWI contracts is the (*O* = *AU*) in "now." The (*U*) is diminished to (*u*). Thus a "loud powwow about how to scrounge a couch" becomes a:

(L*Au*D P*Au*VW:*Au* *A*B*Au*T H*Au*) to (SK*RAu*NJ) a (K*Au*C).

However, the Grenadians alter the first part of the diphthong instead of the second one, resulting in an (a*U*) sound, and the phrase becomes:

a (La*U*D Pa*U*Va*U* *A*Ba*U*T Ha*U*) to (SK*R*:a*U*NJ) a (Ka*UC*).

The same difference in approach shows up with the "aw-ee" (*o*E) sound of "toy": in General BWI the *second* element is contracted; in Grenadian, the first. So if the "noisy, spoiled boy enjoyed annoying us," in General BWI we would describe how:

the (N*o*iZi:, SP*o*iLD B*o*i eiNJ*o*iD *A*N*o*iE½¼) us.

However, in Grenadian, it's how:

the (N*i*EZi:, SP*i*ELD B*i*E aNJ*i*ED *A*N*i*E*i*N¼) us.

The "ah-ee" (I) in "my" also reveals the difference between General BWI and Grenadian. In BWI, the "ee" ingredient is cut down to (i) as in "sit." So if you want to know "why my wife likes wild rides," you might ask:

(VW:*A*i M*A*i VW:*A*iF L*A*iKS VW:*A*iL¼ *RA*iDS).

In Grenada, on the other hand, they change *both* elements, and you would inquire:

(V*ii* M*ii* V*ii*F L*ii* KS V*ii* L¼ *R*:*ii*DS).

One last diphthong: the "ay" (A = eE) as in "mate" loses the (E) part entirely and prolongs (:) the (e). Thus, if "they may say payday's fairly late," being British West Indian you would suppose that:

(De: Me: Se: Pe:De:S F*A*¼Li: Le:T).

As "fairly" illustrates, when the (A) comes before an "r" it's transformed into "ah" (*A*) as in "mart"—and "their fair share of care" becomes:

(D*AR* F*AR* S*AR*) of (K*AR*).

This "ah" is a characteristic sound of the BWI. Take the (a) of "mat": if we're "glad that that man has his black cat back," in this variety we'd comment that we're:

(GLAD DAT DAT MAN HAS) his (BLAK KAT BAK).

"Ah" also replaces the (u) sound of "mutt." Thus, if "such trust must come from what was justly done," the British West Indian will suggest that:

(S*AC* T*RA*S¼ MAS¼ KAM F*RA*M VW:*A*T VW:*A*S JASTLi: DAN).

Finally, (*i*) as in "ago" also succumbs—and "normal families approve of mature companions" shifts into:

(No*R*MAL FAMALi:S *AP*R*u*:VW) of (M*A*C*u*:R KAMPANYANS).

A couple of vowels change to sounds that are *close* to "ah." There's the (*a*) of "aunt," which is broadened into a short (*A*½). So if he regrets that these "masterfully crafted glass flasks can't last," our man from the BWI must deplore that:

(M*A*½ST*i*¼F¼Li: K*RA*½FTeD GL*A*½S FL*A*½SKS K*A*½N¼ L*A*½S¼).

A second case in point is the "aw" (*o*) in "caught," which is reshaped into the (o) in "cot." Thus, if "the lords all ordered more strong war-horses," for those from BWI:

the (Lo¼DS oL o¼D*i*¼D Mo*R* ST*R*oN¼ VW:o¼-Ho¼SeS).

There are two last characteristic vowel changes. First, the (e) sound of "pet" is made into a diphthong by adding the (i) sound of "pit." So if "their best friends sent them an expensive bedspread," being from the BWI you would remark that:

their (BeiS¼ F*R*eiNDS SeiN¼ DeiM) an (eiXPeiNSE½VW BeiDSP*R*eiD).

If your character is Grenadian, you'd alter the (e) to the (a) sound of "pat" and say that:

their (BaS¼ F*R*:aNDS SaN¼ DaM) an (aXPaNS*i*W BaDSP*R*:aD).

Second, (*E*) as in "earn" is converted into (*i*) as in "ago." So if "her words were firm and terse," if British West Indian we'd say that:

(H*iR* VW:*i*¼DS VW:*iR* F*i*¼M) and (T*i*¼S).

Consonant Changes

The trilled "r" you saw in "her" and "were" is made by pressing the tip of your tongue against your upper gum ridge and voicing the letter until your tongue vibrates in a child's imitation of a motorcycle. Note that the "r" was *dropped* (¼) from "words," "firm," and "terse" in the last sentence. It was dropped because it was in the middle of a word preceding another consonant.

In contrast, the "g" sound is omitted *only* when it follows an "n" in the same word. Thus "a strong ringing song belongs" comes out as:

a (ST*R*oN¼ *R*E½N¼E½¼ SoN¼ Bi:LoN¼S).

You may have noted from "best," "sent," "can't," and "last" that final "t"s are eliminated when they follow other consonants. The same applies to "d"s. So if "he found this land cold and unkind," the BWI-born would point out that he:

(F*Au*N¼) this (LAN¼ KO½L¼ *A*N¼ *A*NKA*i*N¼).

Being at the end of a word also affects the "z" sound: if it is spelled "s," it is pronounced "s." So "does his pose please both those girls?" becomes:

(DAS HE½S PO½S PLi:S BO½T DO½S G*i*¼LS?).

You saw what happened to the "soft th" (*t*) in "both"; the same transformation changes "the three youthful athletes were thoughtful and faithful" into:

the (T*R*i: U½TF*U*½L *A*TLi:TS) were (ToTF*U*½L) and (Fe:TF*U*½L).

Similarly, the "hard TH" (*T*) in "those" is altered to (D). Thus "they clothed themselves with smooth leather" is converted into:

(De: KLO½D DeiMSeiLVWS VW:E½D SM*u*:D LeiD*eR*).

In "themselves" and "with" we run into two forms of (VW)—a sound produced by pursing the lips for "w," touching the bottom lip with the upper front teeth, and voicing the result. This sound replaces the "v" of "themselves," so that if "the love of private living survives in Vietnam," being born in the BWI, we'd say that:

the (LAVW *A*VW P*RA*iVWE½T LE½VWE½N¼ S*i*¼VW*A*iS) in (VWi:eiTN*A*M).

A stronger (VW:) is substituted for the "w" of "with"—and if she needs to find out "which way we will want to walk to work," the British West Indian would ask:

(VW:E½*C* VW:e: VW:i: VW:E½L VW:*A*N¼) to (VW:oK) to (VW:*i*¼K).

Understandably, (Q = KW) turns out as (KVW:). So if the press secretary "squashed a quantity of frequently asked questions quite quickly," someone from the BWI would report that he:

(SKVW:o*S*D) a (KVW:oNTE½Ti:) of (F*R*i:KVW:*A*NTLi: *A*½SK¼ KVW:ei*SCA*NS KVW:*A*iT KVW:E½KLi:).

Music, Rhythm, and Pace

We mentioned how the music of the BWI variety helps distinguish it from Indian dialect. As a matter of fact, this music is so distinctive that, like Italian and Swedish music, it is identifiable even without the help of vowel or consonant changes.

BWI is spoken one-and-one-half to two tones higher than American English. It has

Harry Belafonte, a New York-born actor, spent some of his early years in the West Indies. Though he could play most of his acting roles (such as in The World, the Flesh and the Devil, *MGM, 1959, shown here) "straight," for his portrayal in* Island in the Sun, *he had to reach back into his childhood for memories of the West Indian variety and its music. An accomplished singer-musician himself, he had no trouble producing a convincing West Indian character.*

Roscoe Lee Browne often interrupted his college teaching career for participation in A.A.U. events. Two American and one World Championships in track were followed by a career as a sales executive. Finally, he turned his considerable energies to acting. Unbelievably painstaking and thorough in his research and discipline (even in such roles as the one in Superfly T.N.T., *Paramount, 1973, shown here), the West Indian variety he adopted for* The Comedians *was so perfect as to be a model without compare.*

a wider range but much less up-and-down variety. Also, though echoing the "clipped" quality of British, it has a tendency to accent at least half of the syllables in any given polysyllable, with a much heavier stress than is used in either British or American speech. The rhythm this produces is the most important element in the BWI music.

Just as the syncopated beat of the calypso sets it off from other folk music, so the syncopated "dah/di/DAH/dah" is the hallmark of this variety. In this, as in the following examples, underlined syllables are stressed: underlined syllables in capital letters receive the primary stress, and non-underlined syllables are totally unstressed. Both prefixes and suffixes tend to get extra emphasis, the final syllable drops in tone, and the pace is steady and slow.

Without thinking of vowel or consonant changes, and keeping your syllables crisp and unslurred, pronounce the following words aloud:

Su/per/VI/sion, syn/co/PA/tion, ex/tra/DI/tion, in/ter/pre/TA/tion, re/pro/DUC/tion, cir/cum/STAN/tial, sub/li/MA/tion, im/po/SI/tion, e/VA/sion, trans/MI/ssion, con/FU/sion, fore/CLO/sure, dis/TRAC/tion, per/SUA/sion.

The slower, more relaxed pace of this variety reflects the general tenor of life in the British West Indies.

Observation and Notes

If you have a chance to see a production of *A Dream on Monkey Mountain*, you will get a deep, revealing, and eye-opening view into this life-style. When I saw this play, it starred Roscoe Lee Browne, an actor who earned my highest respect long before we shared discussions in the Directors' Section of Actors Studio West. Because of his versatile talent—both in acting and dialects—Browne has been cast in the best West Indian roles both in films and on television. And whenever you see one of his performances you will be listening to a true model of the British West Indian variety.

The only other dialect models I can think of are Harry Belafonte in his movie roles as a West Indian and the Reggae stars in their television interviews. So it's a good idea to keep reviewing the accompanying tapes. Good listening!

GENERAL WEST INDIES - TRINIDAD, LESS EDUCATED - GRENADA, RURAL JAMAICA, EDUCATED

GUIDE PAGES	SOUND	General West Indies	Trinidad Less Educated	Grenada Rural West Indies	Jamaica Educated W.I.
CHANGE: (age) e:J, (late) Le:T, (say) Se:	A	e:	&	&	
OR change: eiJ, LeiT, Sei	A				ei
OR before R: (care) KAR, (there) DAR	A	A(r	&	&	
CHANGE: (easy) i:Zi:, (he) Hi:, (see) Si:	E	i:	&	&	
OR shorten: E½ZE½, HE½, SE½	E				E½
CHANGE: (ice) AiS (night) NAiT (fly) FLAi	I	Ai			&
OR change: iiS, NiiT, FLii	I		ii	&	
SHORTEN: (old) O½L¼ (road) RO½D, (no) NO½	O	O½			
OR change: ouL¼, RouD, Nou	O		ou		
OR change: oL¼, R:oD, No	O			o	
OR change: eUL¼, R½eUD, NeU	O				eU
SHORTEN: (use) U½S (cute) KU½T (few) FU½	U	U½			&
OR change: YuS, KYuT, FYu	U		Yu	&	
CHANGE: (man) MAN, (at) AT, (sad) SAD	a	A		&	
OR change: MoN, oT, SoD	a		o		
OR change: MA½N, A½T, SA½D	a				A½
Change in all positions: (next) NeiX¼,	e	ei	&		
(end) eiN¼, (bread) BReiD, (said) SeiD					
OR change: NaX¼, aN¼, BR:aD, SaD	e			a	
OR longer: Ne:X¼, e:N¼, BR½e:D, Se:D	e				e:
Change in all positions: (busy) BE½Zi:,	i	E½			
(women) VW:E½ME½N, (it) E½T, (is) E½S					
OR longer: Bi:Zi:, VW:i:Mi:N, i:T, i:S	i		i:		&
OR change: BiZi:, ViMiN, iT, iS	i			i	
CHANGE: (on) o½N (pot) Po½T (stop) STo½P	o		o½		&
OR no change: oN, PoT, StoP	o	o		&	
Change in all positions: (uncut) ANKAT,	u	A	&	&	&
(does) DAS, (touch) TAC, (what) VW:AT					
CHANGE: (are) oR, (calm) KoLM, (spa) SPo	A	o	&	&	
OR no change: AR½, KALM, SPA	A				A
Change in all positions: (girl) Gi¼L,	E	i	&	&	
(earn) i¼N, (world) VW:i¼L¼, (her) HiR					
OR no change: GE¼L, E¼N, WE¼L¼, HER½	E				E
No change: (predict) PRIDE½K¼	I	I	&	&	&
CHANGE: (out) AuT (down) DAuN (how) HAu	O	Au			
OR change: AT, DAN, HA	O		A		
OR change: aUT, DaUN, HaU	O			aU	
OR change: AU½T, DAU½N, HAU½	O				AU½
Change in all positions: (tour) Tu:R,	U	u:		&	
(soon) Su:N, (do) Du:, (blue) BLu:					
OR shorten: TU½¼, SU½N, DU½, BLU½	U		U½		&
CHANGE: (laugh) LA½F, (dance) DA½NS	a	A½			
OR change: LoF, DoNS	a		o		
OR change: LAeF, DAeNS	a			Ae	
OR change: LAF, DANS	a				A
No change: (apple) oPeL, (dozen) DAZeN	e	e	&	&	&
Change in all positions: (above) ABAVW,	i	A	&	&	
(family) FAMALi:, (system) SE½STAM					
OR change: oBAV, FA½MoLE½, Si:SToM	i				o

Key: ½ weaken
C church (preceding R trilled R & as shown : stronger

GENERAL WEST INDIES - TRINIDAD, LESS EDUCATED - GRENADA, RURAL JAMAICA, EDUCATED

GUIDE PAGES

	SOUND	General West Indies	Trinidad Less Educated	Grenada Rural West Indies	Jamaica Educated W.I.
Change in all positions: (cause) KoS, (door) DoR, (off) oF, (saw) So, (all) oL	o	o	&	&	&
Change in all positions: (should) SU½D, (cook) KU½K, (pull) PU½L, (bush) BU½S	u	U½	&		
OR change: SiuD, KiuK, PiuL, BiuS	u			iu	
OR longer: Su:D, Ku:K, Pu:L, Bu:S	u				u:
CHANGE: (oil) oiL, (boy) Boi, (join) JoiN	oE	oi			&
OR change: iEL, BiE, JiEN	oE		iE	&	

		All 4
No change: (bunch) BANC	BC	BC
Drop final after consonant: (and) A½N¼, (hold) HO½L¼	D	.¼)¢
No change: (fifteen) FE½FTi:N, (fluffy) FLAFi:	F	F
DROP after N: (singing) SE½N¼E½N¼ (long) LoN¼ (hang) HAN¼	G	¼)n
No change: (hedge) HeiJ, (cool) Ku:L	HJKL	HJKL
No change: (mean) Mi:N, (mop) MoP, (nip) NE½P	MNP	MNP

	SOUND	General West Indies	Trinidad Less Educated	Grenada Rural West Indies	Jamaica Educated W.I.
CHANGE: (quit) KVW:E½T (equal) i:KVW:AL	Q	KVW:	&		
OR change: KViT, i:KVAL	Q			KV	
OR no change: KWi:T, E½KWoL	Q				KW
TRILL: (read) Ri:D, (very) VWeiRi:	R	R	&		
OR STRONG TRILL: R:i:D, WaR:i:	R			R:	
OR TAP: R½E½D, Ve:R½E½	R				R½
BUT drop medially before consonant: (dark) Do¼K, (turn) Ti¼N, (girl) Gi¼L	R	/¼(¢	&	&	&
OR drop finally: (here) Hi:¼, (fire) Fii¼, (are) o¼, (for) Fo¼, (our) A¼	R		.¼	&	
No change: (sash) SAS, (session) SeiSAN	SS	SS	&	&	&
Drop finally after consonant: (sent) SeiN¼, (best) BeiS¼, (fact) FAK¼	T	.¼)¢	&	&	&
Change in all positions: (think) TE½NK, (healthy) HeiLTi:, (both) BO½T	t	T	&	&	
OR no change: ti:NK, He:LtE½, BeUt	t				t
Change in all positions: (then) DeiN, (other) ADeR, (with) VW:E½D (that) DAT	T	D	&	&	
OR no change: Te:N, ATeR½, Wi:T, TA½T	T				T
CHANGE: (have) HA½VW (vow) VWAu (of) AVW	V	VW			
OR change: HoV:W, V:WA, AV:W	V		V:W		
OR change: HAeW, WaU, AW	V			W	
OR no change: HAV, VAU½, AV	V				V
CHANGE: (why) VW:Ai, (always) oLVW:e:S	W	VW:	&		
OR change: Vii, oLVe:S	W			V	
OR no change: WAi, oLWeiS	W				W
No change	X	X	&	&	&
Change finally if spelled S: (his) HE½S (ears) i:¼S (nose) NO½S (please) PLi:S	Z	.S$s	&	&	&
No change: (pleasure) PLeizeR	z	z	&	&	&

Key:
¼ drop / medial $ spelled (preceding & as shown
½ weaken . finally R trilled R) following : stronger
¢ consonant

PORTUGUESE

A glance at the following *GUIDE PAGES* will tell you that we approach Portuguese much as we did Spanish: as *two* dialects, each with its own subdivisions. Like Spanish, the Iberian version of the language has altered over the centuries, while the Latin American delivery is much closer to that of the original colonists. However, though Brazil declared its independence from Portugal about the same time the rest of South America won its freedom from Spain, it was a refugee Portuguese king who ruled the new "Empire of Brazil." The Portuguese royal line maintained Brazil's direct ties with "the mother country" for seventy more years. This has produced a similarity between the two dialects that justifies grouping them in one chapter.

The Portuguese never cared much about "race." Consequently, Brazil developed as the New World's only true "melting pot," with most of its present population so mixed that the only accurate description of them is "non-European." Aside from the Portuguese, the only major European influence on the dialect came from the huge influx of Italian immigrants that started during the last century.

Portugal was the first nation of explorers and colonists in the modern world and, until the second half of this century, it had colonies in Indonesia, China, Africa, and India. I was living in Lisbon at the time that rumblings of independence started to be heard from Goa, Portuguese India. My hotel was half full of wealthy and important Goans whom the government had brought over to convince that they were truly accepted as Portuguese—an experiment that backfired.

Though the Goans were the only ones who paid any attention to racial and color differences, the culture gap was much too great to be bridged. The Portuguese saw the visiting Goans as disturbingly different—and eventually as inferior—and began treating them as such. By the time they were ready to return home, none of the Goan visitors I talked to thought of themselves any longer as Portuguese; all were going back determined that Goa should have its independence.

Other aspects of Portuguese society disturbed these Goans. The "European" standard of living was no more evident in Portugal than it had been in India. Forty percent of the Portuguese were illiterate; most of the people lived in abject poverty. The select few who made up the ruling oligarchy fully supported the most corrupt and despotic government then in existence in Western Europe. We all became accustomed to the sight of heavy machine guns set up at street corners to intimidate possible "dissidents."

However, the Portuguese *did* go out of their way to be hospitable to me. And the soft accents of their dialect in English were beguiling—full of "sh" (*S*) and "zh" (*z*) sounds, with "S"s replacing "soft th's" (*t*) and "Z"s replacing "hard" (*T*) ones.

Later, coming in contact with Brazilians, I missed these "flowing" touches. I found that the Brazilians exchanged (*h*) for (H) rather than the Portuguese (H:), and that many more of their consonants were followed by a small "uh" (*e*½)—perhaps the influence of all those Italian immigrants. Also, though the characteristic Portuguese nasalization was still there, along with the Latinate (*A*), in general, the Brazilians used shorter vowel sounds.

Still, Brazil, as both a neighbor and an important commercial interest, plays a greater role in our national life than Portugal. We hear much more of its dialect than we do of the Portuguese. Therefore, most of the examples in this chapter are of the Brazilian dialect. The Iberian and Galician (from the northeast corner of Portugal) dialects will be described only as exceptions.

Vowel Changes

To the Portuguese-speaking, several pairs of vowels are hard to separate. For example, the "ee" (E) sound of "lead" changes to the (i) sound of "lid." Thus, if "we need easy, pleasing dreams," as Brazilians:

(*e*½Wi NiD = *e*½ iZi, PL ± iZęṆG*e*½ D ± *R*iMZ).

As you saw in "pleasing," when an (i) precedes a nasalized (Ṇ) or (Ṃ), it changes into a nasal (ę)—and "simple instincts" becomes:

(SęṂPeL ± *e*½ ęṆS*e*½T ± ęṆK*e*½T ± *e*½S*e*½).

However, in other cases, when the (i) receives *no* nasality (see Nasalization section, page 236), the Galicians reverse the first transformation we looked at, turning (i) into a short (E½)—so that "mystic women" comes out:

(ME½ST ± E½K*e*½ WE½MęṆ).

Nasalization also affects the "eh" (e) of "bent," making it into a nasal accented "ay" (Ạ) before a twanged (Ṃ) or (Ṇ). Thus, if she wanted to know about the "extent of the expenses we sent them," being from Brazil, she would ask about the:

(iXT ± ẠṆT ± *e*½) of the (iXPẠṆS*e*Z) we (SẠṆT ± *e*½ D ± ẠṂ).

You can see from "extent" and "expenses" that (e) becomes an (i) when it's in a prefix. In almost every other case, (e) as in "beg" evolves into (a) as in "bag." So if the "next card she read said 'Get well, my best, Peg'," if Brazilian-born, we would say the:

(NaXT*e*½) card she (*R*:aD = *e*½ SaD = *e*½ GaT ± *e*½ WeL ± *e*½) my (BaS*e*½T ± *e*½, PaG*e*½).

As "well" shows, (e) does *not* alter before (L).

In a fine example of "compensation reversal" (see page 28), the (a) in "bag" shifts into the (e) in "beg." So "Baghdad has had magic lamps" emerges as:

(BeGD ± eD = *e*½ *h*eZ *h*eD = *e*½ Me*z*iK*e*½ L ± eṂP*e*½S*e*½).

In Iberian Portuguese, however, the (a) in "bag" becomes in the "ah" (*A*) of "bargain" and the phrase becomes:

(B*A*GD ± *A*D = *e*½ H:*A*S½ H:*A*D = *e*½ M*Az*½i:K*e*½ L ± *A*ṂP*S*½).

Another pair of reversible vowels is "aw" (*o*) as in "caught" and (o) as in "cot." In Brazil and Galicia, (*o*) ends up as (o) when it is spelled "a," "au," or "aw." So if we were "taught to call all warlike causes false," as Brazilians, we were:

(T ± oT ± *e*½) to (KoL ± *e*½ oL ± *e*½ Wo*R*:L ± *A*iK*e*½ Ko*Z*e*Z* FoL ± *e*½S*e*½).

Iberians and Bahians (as well as other rural Brazilians) reshape (*o*) into (o) when it is spelled "o," "oa," "oo," or "ou." So if "his boss ordered more strong horses brought," *they* will say:

his (BoS o*R*D ± *eR*D = *e*½ Mo*R* ST ± *R*oṆG*e*½ H:o*R*:SeZ B*R*oT ± *e*½).

In the reversal, the same group exchanges the (o) for an (*o*). So if we admire the price "Tom got on that solid block of topnotch bonds and common stocks," if we were from Portugal, we would speak of how much:

(T ± *o*Ṃ Go*T* ± *e*½ *o*Ṇ) that (So*L* ± i:D = *e*½ BL ± *o*K*e*½) of (T ± *o*PNo*C* BoND ± Z) and (K*o*MęṆ ST ± *o*K*S*½).

Most *Brazilians*, however, change the (o) to a nasal (ǫ) before a nasalized (Ṃ) or (Ṇ), and might describe what:

(T ± ǫṂ GAT ± *e*½ ǫṆ) that (SAL ± iD ± *e*½ BL ± *A*K*e*½) of (T ± *A*P*e*½NA*C* BAND = *e*½Z) and (K*A*MęṆ ST ± *A*K*e*½S*e*½).

As you can see from "got," when they *don't* nasalize (o), the broaden it to an (*A*).

This "ah" (*A*), in one form or another, is a

trademark of the Portuguese dialect. In its nasal form (*Ą*), it substitutes for "ay" (A) as in "rain" whenever that sound precedes a nasalized (Ṃ) or (Ṇ). Thus, if his "namesake maintains the same painful aims," our Brazilian would remark that his:

(NĄṂSeKe½ MĄṆT±ĄṆZ) the (SĄṂ PĄṆFuL±e½ ĄṂZ).

As you saw from "namesake," when it doesn't take on a nasal color, the "ay (= eh-ee)" diphthong is shortened to a mere "eh" (e). So "they may take away eight pale gray chairs" turns out as:

(D±e Me T±eKe½ AWe eT±e½ PeL±e½ GRe CeRZ).

Another double vowel that they nasalize into (*Ą*) before (Ṃ) or (Ṇ) is the "ow" sound of "town." So, if the "brown clown bounced down the mountain," being Brazilian-born we would report that the:

(BRĄṆ KL±ĄṆ BĄṆSe½T±e½ D±ĄṆ) the (MĄṆT±¼N).

When it *doesn't* get a nasal accent, an initial or medial (*O*) receives an added little burst of air (*e*½). So if you want to ask "how our crowd now can allow doubts about housing," in this dialect you would inquire:

(hA Oe½R KROe½D=e½ NA) can (AL±A D±Oe½T±Se½ ABVOe½T±e½ hOe½ZęṆGe½).

Note that in "how," "now," and "allow" a final "ah-oo" gets cut down to just "ah" (*A*).

This non-nasal (*A*) also takes the place of the (u) in "cut," and if they can't "trust such dumb numbskulls to unplug their stuck plumbing," those from Brazil would complain that they can't:

(T±RASe½T±e½ SAC D±AṂ NAṂSe½KAL±e½Z) to (AṆPe½L±Ge½) their (ST±AKe½ PL±AMęṆGe½).

In Bahia and Portugal, however, (u) is transformed to the "aw" (*o*) of "caught," and the above phrase becomes:

(T±RoST±e½ SoC' D±oṂ NoṂSKoL±S½) to (oṆPL±oGe½) their (ST±oKe½ PL±oṂęṆGe½).

Another vowel sound replaced by "ah" (*A*) is (*i*) as in "ago." Thus, if he "approved combining vanilla with bananas in a natural balance," the Brazilian-born would explain that he:

(APe½Ru;VD=e½ KAMB:AiNęṆGe½ VANiL±A) with (BANeNAZ) in a (NeCER½AL±e½ BEL±ęṆSe½).

As you can see from "balance," the (*i*) sound changes to a nasal "eh" (ę) when it comes before a nasalized (Ṃ) or (Ṇ). So a "system of companion sciences" ends up as a:

(SiSe½T±ęṂ) of (KęṂPeNYęṆ SAięṆSeZ).

Finally, the (*a*) sound of "aunt" is also shaped into "ah," but this time in a shorter version: (*A*½). Thus, if the "half-masked lass's frantic dancing charmed and enchanted us," we might say that the:

(hA½Fe½-MA½Se½Ke½T±e½ L±A½ZeZ FRA½ṆT±iKe½ D±A½ṆSęṆGe½ CA½RMD=e½) and (ĄṆCA½ṆT±eD=e½) us.

The shortening of the normal "ah" (*A*) as in "charmed" holds wherever you find that sound.

The Portuguese-speaking also reduce the diphthong "ah-ee" (I = *A*E) to (*A*i). So if "in my mind I finalized my five wisest designs," if I were from Brazil, I'd advise that:

in (MAi MAiND=e½ Ai FAiN¼L±AiZD=e½ MAi FAiV e½WAiZiSe½T±e½ D±iZAiṆZ).

This tendency to trim diphthong changes "y-oo" (U) to (Y*u*), and if after being betrayed "you view few humans as useful, valuable, beautiful, or pure," being Portuguese-speaking:

(Yu VYu FYu YuMęṆZ) as (YuSe½FuL±e½ VEL±YuBVeL±e½, BYuT±iFuL±e½) or (PYuR).

In Portugal and in Bahia, the double vowel "oy" (*o*E) as in "toy" is also compressed, coming out (*o*i). So if I showed him how to "avoid destroying his boyish, unspoiled, joyful voice," as a Portuguese, he would have seen how to:

(*A*VoiD=*e*½ D±i:ST±*R*oiçṆG½) his (Boii:*S*, oṆSPoiL±D=*e*½, *z*½oiF*u*L±*e*½ Voi*S*½).

In the rest of Brazil, however, "oy" undergoes a complete transformation into the triphthong (Oi), and the above phrase becomes to:

(*A*VOiD=*e*½ D±iS*e*½T±*e*½*R*OiçṆG*e*½) his (BOii*S*, *A*ṆS*e*½POiL±*e*½D=*e*½, *z*OiF*u*L±*e*½ VOiS*e*½).

Two vowel changes remain. In the first, the "oo" (*U*) in "pool" changes into a version of the (*u*) in "pull," which is formed much farther forward (;) in the mouth. Thus, if the "shooting crew soon moved to cooler rooms," a Brazilian-born person would comment that the:

(*Su*;T±çṆG*e*½ K*e*½*Ru*; *Su*;Ṇ M*u*;VD=*e*½ T±*u*; K*u*;L±*eR* *Ru*;ṂZ).

Second, the "oh" (O) of "coat" evolves into a short rendition (½) of the "aw" (*o*) of "caught." So if we'd rather "postpone towing both those old rowboats solo," being from Brazil, we'd rather:

(P*o*½S*e*½T±*e*½P*o*½Ṇ T±*o*½çṆG*e*½ B*o*½T= D±*o*½Z *o*½L±*e*½D=*e*½ *R*:*o*½BV*o*½T±*e*½S*e*½ S*o*½L±*o*½).

Consonant Changes

Whereas we form our "d"s, "l"s, and "t"s with our tongues touching the gum ridge behind our upper front teeth, the Portuguese-speaking shift the tongue down to the teeth themselves. For example, if a "d" is in the middle of a word and between vowels, or if it precedes an "r," this dialect calls for an interdental (D=) in which the tip of the tongue is *between* the teeth. So if the "lady drew faddish dresses with wider, hidden padding," in our dialect we would observe that the:

(L±eD=i D=*Ru*; FeD=i*S* D=*R*aZeZ) with (*e*½WAiD=*eR*, *h*iD=çṆ PeD=çṆG*e*½).

At the end of a word, or medially before any consonant but "r," this interdental (D=) receives the addition of a little puff of sound (*e*½). Thus, if she "would gladly trade a good bed for a gold band," if Brazilian, you would point out that she:

(*e*½W*u*L±*e*½D=*e*½ GL±eD=*e*½L±i T±*R*eD=*e*½) a (G*u*D=*e*½ BaD=*e*½) for a (G*o*½L±*e*½D=*e*½BeND=*e*½).

In rural Portugal and Galicia, however, one drops (¼) every final "d" that follows a consonant other than "r," so the sentence ends "for a (G*o*L±*e*½¼ B*A*N¼)." At the beginning of a word, or medially after a consonant, the "d" is *upper dental* (D±), with the tongue touching the back of your upper front teeth. So that "handouts do induce dependency" ends up as:

(*h*eND±*O*e½T±*e*½S*e*½ D±*u*; iND±Y*u*S*e*½ D±iPaND±çṆSi).

This *upper dental* handling of "l" results in a "thicker" sound. At the beginning of a word, or medially before a vowel, "l" is pronounced with the tongue pressed against the back of your upper front teeth. So if the judge is "unwilling to let lawless killers loose," to a Brazilian, he's:

(*A*N*e*½WiL±çṆG*e*½) to (L±aT±*e*½ L±oL±iS*e*½ KiL±*ER*:Z L±*u*;S*e*½).

This form, generally followed by a puff of sound (L±*e*½), occurs even where we would *not* normally pronounce "l" at all. Thus, if he "could talk calmly half the night," the Brazilian would say that he:

(K*u*L±*e*½D=*e*½ T±oL±*e*½K*e*½ K*A*½L±*e*½ML±i *hA*½L±*e*½F*e*½) the night.

These "l"s occur not only in the middle of a word, preceding another consonant, but also at the end of a word. So a "well-built school in a level field" turns out to be a:

(*e*½WeL±*e*½ BiL±*e*½T±*e*½ SK*u*;L±*e*½) in a (L±aVeL±*e*½ FiL±*e*½D=*e*½).

One last letter that becomes upperdentalized is "t," so "it's important to get started

right" is made into:
(iT±e½Se½çMPo½RT±eNT±e½ T±u; GaT±e½ ST±A½RT±eD=e½ R:AiT±e½).

We can see from "it's," "important," "get," and "right" that the (T±) takes an (e½) both before another consonant and at the end of a word. This is not the case, however, in Galicia, where a final (T±:) is just pronounced more strongly.

Another consonant that comes out stronger is the Iberian reading of our "h." Thus "he had overheard her unhappy, hopeless history," for a Portuguese is:
(H:i: H:AD=e½ oVERH:ERD=e½ H:ER oNH:APi:, H:oPL±i:S H:i:S½T±AR½i:).

While rural and Galician Portuguese drop the "h" sound entirely, Brazilians turn it into (*h*), articulating the above sentence as:
(*h*i *h*eD=e½ o½VER*h*ERD=e½ *h*ER AN*h*ePi, *h*o½Pe½L±iSe½ *h*iSe½T±AR½i).

This (*h*) sound is made by arching the back of your tongue until it almost touches your soft palate (as for a "k") and allowing the air to hiss through the narrowed opening.

The last consonant to receive heavy stress is "b." This occurs in the middle of a word whenever it precedes a vowel and follows any consonant except "s." So that "emboldened, the unbeaten barbarians embarked on unbending combat" shifts into:
(iMB:o½L±e½D±aND±e½), the (ANB:iT±¼N BA½RB:eR½içNZ iMB:A½RKe½T±e½) on (ANB:aND±çNGe½ KAMB:eT±e½).

As with many other consonants, when they are either final or medial before another consonant, "b" takes an (e½). However, either between vowels or following an "s" and preceding a vowel, "b" opens into (BV)—a sound made by starting to say a "b" but not quite bringing the lips together. So, if the Old Testament shows us "rebellious disbelievers stubbornly disobeying their rabbis' taboos," being born in Brazil, we read of:
R:iBVeL±YASe½ D±iSe½BViL±iVeRZ ST±ABVER:NL±i D±iZo½BVeçNGe½) their (R:eBVAiZ T±eBVu;Z).

The Portuguese, on the other hand, add a little (e½) whenever a medial "b" precedes "d," "l," "r," "s," or "t." Thus "probably absent" is made into:
(PRoBVABVe½L±i: ABVe½SANT±e½).

The Galicians even make initial "b"s into (BV)s—and a "baseball bat" emerges as a:
(BVez½BVoL±e½ BVAT±:).

The (BV) also replaces "v" sounds among the rural Portuguese; their variation of a "love of living" is a:
(L±ABV ABV L±i:BVçN¼).

In contrast, Galicians substitute (B) for "v," resulting in a:
(L±oB oB L±E½BçNGe½).

It's not that the Portuguese-speaking can't handle a "v"; indeed, the rural Portuguese and *all* Brazilians turn "f" sounds into (V)s at the end of a word when the following word begins with a vowel. Thus, if they "laugh at stiff odds," these people:
(L±A½V) at (ST±iV AD=e½Z).

Before a consonant, however, "f" adds on the characteristic (e½), modifying "half-life" to:
(*h*A½L±e½Fe½-L±AiFe½).

In the "kw" sound of (Q), most Brazilians also exchange (V) for the "w" part. So if I "quieted their frequent quarrels quite quickly," in Brazilian dialect I'd announce that I:
(Ke½VAiAT±iD±e½) their (FRiKe½VçNT±e½ Ke½VA½R½eL±e½Z Ke½VAiT±e½ Ke½ViKe½L±i).

You probably noticed that the "k" part of (Q = kw) added an (e½). This holds true both in Portugal and Rio de Janeiro, though those from Rio leave the "w" part alone, so the announcement above becomes:

I (Ke½WIAT ± i:D = e½) their (FRi:Ke½WęṆT ± e½ Ke½WAR½eL ± S½ Ke½WIT ± e½ Ke½Wi:KL ± i:).

As you might suspect by now, a "w" by itself is always *preceded* by (e½), except when it follows a vowel. So "meanwhile, each one was wishing for windier weather," for the Brazilian is:

(MiNe½WAiL ± e½, iC e½WAN e½WAZ e½WiSęṆGe½ Fo½R e½WiND ± ieR e½WaD ± eR).

Before we leave the ubiquitous (e½), we should note that it also follows *all* final (G), (K), (P), or (S) sounds, as well as medial (K), (P), and (S) sounds when they precede other consonants.

There are certain characteristic exceptions in the Iberian handling of (S) sounds. For instance, medially or finally, when preceding "b," "d," "g," "l," "m," "n," "r," or "v" sounds, (S) is altered into a short version (z ½) of the "s" in "measure." If we want these "disgraceful yes-men to cease misleading the boss-man," if we were born in Portugal, we might demand that these:

(D ± i:z½GRA½SFuL ± e½ Yaz½MẠṆ Si:z½ MI:z½L ± i:D = ęṆGe½) the (Boz½MAN).

At the end of a word, before "f," "k," "p," "s," or "t" sounds or at the end of a phrase, the Portuguese replace the (S) sound with a soft "sh" (S½). So if "his Swiss friend found his peace plan useless," to a Portuguese:

his (Se½Wi:S½ FRaND = e½) found his (Pi:S½ PL ± AṆ Yuz½L ± i:S½).

To a Galician, however:

the (PE½SS PL ± AṆ) was (Yuz½L ± E½SS),

since they pronounce *this* "s" with the teeth far enough apart to give it an "sh" flavor. Finally, between vowels the "s" sound ends up as a (Z). So if a Brazilian student has no worries "aside from passing basic classes," she would confess to being anxiety-free:

(AZAiD = e½) from (PeZęṆGe½ BeZiKe½ KL ± A½ZeZ).

The "s" sound also enters into one of the pronunciations of "x," and while Brazilians seem to have no trouble with *any* rendering of this letter, the Portuguese shape (X = ks) into "sh" (S) next to any consonant. Thus, "Experienced Marxists expect expert excuses," evolves into:

(i:SPi:R½i:ęṆST ± e½ MARSi:ST ± S i:SPaKT ± e½ i:SPERT ± e½ i:SKYuZeS½).

The Portuguese also delete the "g" sound from (X = gz), so if the corporation wants to give its "existing execs exacting exams," in this dialect you would say it will give its:

(i:Zi:ST ± ęṆGe½ i:ZaKYuT ± i:VZ i:ZAKT ± ęṆGe½ i:ZAṂS½).

Look back at "excuses" and "exams." Do you see how the final "z" sound is changed to a soft "sh" (S½)? This is what the Portuguese do with any "z" sound at the end of a phrase, or at the end of a word *if* the next word starts with an "f," "k," "p," "s," or "t" sound. Thus, "These flowers surprise Tom's friends," becomes:

(Zi:S½ FL ± Oe½ERS½SERPRIS½ T ± oṂS½ FRaND ± S½).

The Galician reading of this substitution is a sort of "s-sh" (SS).

The "z" sound undergoes a completely different change when it is medial or final preceding a "b," "d," "g," "l," "m," "n," "r," or "v." In these positions, the Portuguese approach it as a light version (z½) of the "s" in "measure." So if the "cosmetic business wasn't puzzling over his dazzling wisdom," if we were from Lisbon, we would remark that the:

(Koz½MaT ± i:Ke½ Bi:z½Ni:S e½Woz½NT ± e½ Poz½L ± ęṆGe½) over (H:i:z½ D ± Az½L ± ęṆGe½ Wi:z½D ± ęṂ).

People from Lisbon and Rio de Janeiro use this same (*z*½) to take the place of (J) sounds as in "judge." However, all other Portuguese and Brazilians employ the *full* (*z*). So "He just gradually changed the subject to strange religions" transforms into:

He (*zA*ST±*e*½ G*Rezu*;L±i *C*ẠṆ*z*D=*e*½ D±*A* SABe½*z*aK*e*½T±*e*½) to (ST±*R*ẠṆ*z* *R*:iL±i*z*ȩṆZ).

Did you notice what happened to the "hard TH" in "the"? This replacement by an *upperdental* "d" (D±) occurs throughout the dialect. So if you'd "rather bother with those than these," being Brazilian, you'd explain that you'd:

(*R*:*A*½D±*eR* BAD±*eR* *e*½WiD± D±*o*½Z D±eṆ D±iZ).

On the other hand, if you were Portuguese you'd use (Z) for (*T*) and:

(*R*:*A*Z*eR* BoZ*eR* *e*½Wi:Z Z*oz*½ Z*A*Ṇ Zi:*S*½).

You'd also convert "soft th" (*t*) into (S), transforming "The athlete thought it worthwhile to think things through" into:

(Z*A* *A*SL±i:T±*e*½ SoT±*e*½) it (*e*½W*ER*:S*e*½WIL±*e*½) to (SȩṆK*e*½ SȩṆG*S*½ S*Ru*;).

Brazilians, however, employ the interdental (T=) for (*t*), resulting in:

(D±*A* eT=L±iT±*e*½ T=*o*½T±*e*½) it (*e*½W*ER*T=*e*½W*A*iL±*e*½) to (T=ȩṆK*e*½ T=ȩṆGZ T=*Ru*;).

The "trilled r" (*R*) as in "through" is made by pressing your tongue against the gum ridge behind your upper front teeth and then voicing the sound until the tongue vibrates, producing a facsimile of a machine gun or motorcycle. The sound may be abbreviated (*R*½) to a single "tap" or it may be extended (*R*:); indeed, this dialect uses all three forms. Initially, or medially before "l," "n," "s," or another "r," the prolonged (*R*:) is employed. Thus "irresolute persons rarely return to rural residence," for a Brazilian would be:

(i*R*:aZ*A*L±*u*;T±*e*½ P*ER*:SȩṆZ *R*:e*R*:L±i *R*:iT±*ER*:N) to (*R*:*u*;*R*½*A*L±*e*½ *R*:aZiD=ẠṆS*e*½).

As you saw from "rural," a medial "r" between vowels is only lightly tapped (*R*½). So if it's "very arid around Arabia," the Brazilian-born would speak of it being:

(V*ER*½i e*R*½iD=*e*½*AR*½O*e*½ND=*e*½ *AR*½eBVi*A*).

Please note: Galicians draw out (*R*:), when it comes between vowels, rather than diminish it. Except as noted above, a medial "r" or a final one gets normal trilling (*R*) and "ev'ry Spring brought more dry weather," turns out as:

(aV*R*i SP*e*½*R*ȩṆG*e*½ B*Ro*½T±*e*½ M*o*½*R* D±*R*Ai *e*½WaD±*eR*).

Nasalization

The last characteristic process to be considered is Portuguese nasalization. The only consonants affected are "m" and "n." Both become nasalized before any other consonant except "b" or "d" (the Galicians also exclude "g," "k," "p," and "t") and are sounded through the nose rather than the mouth. Thus, if he was "unconvinced that the infringement on his invention was inconsequential," a Brazilian would comment that he was:

(*A*ṆKȩṆVȩṆS*e*½T±*e*½) that the (ȩṆ F*e*½*R*ȩ Ṇ*z*MẠṆT±*e*½ ǫṆ) his (ȩṆVẠṆSȩṆ) was (ȩṆKǫṆSiK*e*½VẠṆS*A*L±*e*½).

As "on" and "invention" show, *final* "m"s and "n"s are also nasalized. So "Some comfortable homes seem completely timeless," comes out:

(S*A*Ṃ K*A*ṂF*ER*T±*A*B:L±*e*½ *ho*½ṂZ SiṂ KȩṂP*e*½L±iT±*e*½L±i T±*A*iṂL±eS*e*½).

Music, Rhythm, and Pace

The music of these dialects is light and flowing. Both Brazilians and the Portuguese speak one-and-a-half tones higher than we do, but while the Portuguese range the scale only a little more than we, the Brazilians use a much wider range. This musical freedom is reflected in the Brazilian samba. If you have the chance, listen to a number of samba recordings; then compare them with the more somber, restricted measure of the Portuguese fado.

Though both Brazilians and Portuguese stress the next-to-the-last syllable in any multisyllable word, the Brazilians speak only slightly more briskly than we, while the Portuguese are quite rapid in their delivery.

Observation and Notes

When it comes to models for Brazilian dialects, all I can recommend are telecasts of old Carmen Miranda films. For the Portuguese, their local consulate may be able to recommend restaurants or other businesses open to the public where you can listen in. Of course, the same applies to the Brazilian consulates. In addition, listen to the accompanying tapes carefully and practice the new sounds until you absorb them.

For a pure Brazilian dialect, all of the films that Carmen Miranda made in the 1940's (which keep popping up on late-night TV) give us great exposure to the real thing. Also search your local record store for LP albums of comedy shows of that period, such as The Jack Benny Show, *on which she made many appearances.*

GENERAL BRAZILIAN PORTUGUESE - RIO DE JANEIRO, EDUCATED BRAZILIAN BAHIA, RURAL BRAZILIAN

GUIDE PAGES

	SOUND	General Brazilian Port.	Rio de Janeiro Educated	Bahia Rural Brazilian Port.
Change in all positions: (vacate) VeKeT±e½, (age) ez, (say) Se, (fail) FeL±e½, (day) D±e	A	e		&
OR shorter: VA½KA½T±e½, A½z½, SA½, FA½L±e½	A		A½	
BUT before nasalized M or N: (mainly) MA̦N̦L±i, (nameless) NA̦M̦L±aSe½, (came) KA̦M̦, (sane) SA̦N̦	A	A̦(M̦,N̦	&	&
Change in all positions: (see) Si, (be) Bi, (easy) iZi, (need) NiD=e½, (these) D±iZ	E	i	&	&
Change in all positions: (my) MAi, (buy) BAi, (I'll) AiL±e½, (night) NAiT±e½, (try) T±RAi	I	Ai	&	&
Change in all positions: (slow) SL±o½, (old) o½L±e½D=e½, (solo) So½L±o½, (no) No½	O	o½		
OR change: SL±o, oL±e½¼, SoL±o, No	O			o
OR no change: SL±O, OL±e½D=e½, SOL±O, NO	O		O	
Change: (use) YuZ, (few) FYu, (unit) YuNiT±e½	U	Yu	&	&!
OR change medially: (pure) PuR, (cute) KuT±e½, (music) MuZi:Ke½, (feud) FuD=e½	U			/u
Change in all positions: (as) eZ, (knapsack) NePe½SeKe½, (bad) BeD=e½, (glad) GL±eDe½	a	e	&	&
CHANGE: (bed) BaD=e½, (read) R:aD=e½, (leg) L±aGe½, (neck) NaKe½, (said) SaD=e½	e	a!(1		&
OR longer: Be:D=e½, R:e:D=e½, L±e:Ge½, Ne:Ke½	e		e:!(1	
BUT change in prefix: (exit) iXiT±e½, (enact) iNeKe½T±e½, (expense) iXPA̦N̦Se½	e	i{	&	&
AND before nasalized M or N: (men) MA̦N̦, (them) D±A̦M̦ (encourage) A̦N̦KER½iz (mental) MA̦N̦T±eL±e½	e	A̦(M̦,N̦	&	&
BUT no change before L: (wealthy) e½WeL±e½T=i (tell) T±eL±e½, (fell) FeL±e½, (sell) SeL±e½	e	e(1	&	&
LONGER: (busy) Bi:Zi, (critic) KRi:T±i:Ke½, (mystic) Mi:Se½T±i:Ke½, (if) i:Fe½	i			i:
OR no change: BiZi, KRiT±iKe½, MiSe½T±iKe½	i	i	&	
& spelled I before nasalized M or N: (in) e̦N̦, (imprint) e̦M̦PR½e̦N̦T±e½, (insist) e̦N̦SiSe½T±e½	i	e̦(M̦,N̦	&	&
CHANGE: (got) GAT±e½, (odd) AD=e½, (fog) FAGe½, (topnotch) T±APe½NAC, (not) NAT±e½	o	A	&	
OR change: GoT±e½, oD=e½, FoGe½, T±oPe½NoC	o			o
AND before nasalized M or N: (on) o̦N̦, (compact) Ko̦M̦PeKe½T±e½, (gong) Go̦NGe½	o	o̦(M̦,N̦	&	&
Change in all positions: (touch) T±AC, (up) APe½, (love) L±AV, (what) e½WAT±e½	u	A	&	
OR change: T±oC, oPe½, L±oV, VoT±e½	u			o

		All 3
SHORTER: (heart) hA½RT±e½, (calm) KA½L±M̦, (swan) Se½WA½N̦	A	A½
No change: (learn) L±ER:N̦, (girl) GER:L±e½, (her) hER	E	E
No change: (predict) PRID=iKe½T±e½, (propose) PRIPo½Z	I	I
CHANGE initially & medially: (our) Oe½R, (loud) L±Oe½D=e½	O	-/Oe½
AND change finally: (now) NA, (how) hA, (vow) VA	O	.A
AND before nasalized M or N: (downtown) D±A̦N̦T±A̦N̦	O	A̦(M̦,N̦

Key:

& as shown	- initial	! excepting	h loch,ich	z measure
: stronger	/ medial	(preceding	= interdental	R trilled R
½ weakened	. finally	{ in prefix	± upperdental	, nasalized

GENERAL BRAZILIAN PORTUGUESE - RIO DE JANEIRO, EDUCATED BRAZILIAN BAHIA, RURAL BRAZILIAN

GUIDE PAGES	SOUND	General Brazilian Port.	Rio de Janeiro Educated	Bahia Rural Brazilian Port.
Change in all positions: (two) T±u;, (soon) Su;N̦, (group) GRu;Pe½, (blue) BL±u;	u	u;		&
OR no change: T±U, SUN̦, GRUPe½, BL±U	u		u	

		All 3
CHANGE: (staff) ST±A½Fe½, (bath) BA½T=, (ask) A½Se½Ke½	a	A½
No change: (apple) ePeL±e½ (dozen) D±AZeN̦ (level) L±aVeL±e½	e	e
CHANGE: (above) ABVAV, (family) FeMAL±i, (extra) iXT±e½RA	i	A
BUT before a nasalized M or N: (opinion) APiNYe̦N̦	i	e̦(M̦,N̦)

	SOUND	General Brazilian Port.	Rio de Janeiro Educated	Bahia Rural Brazilian Port.
If spelled A,AU,AW: (saw) So, (cause) KoZ, (war) e½WoR, (all) oL±e½, (draw) D±Ro	o	o$a au aw	&	&
If spelled O,OA,OO,OU: (or) o½R, (broad) BRo½D=e½, (door) D±o½R, (court) Ko½RT±e½	o	o½$OA ooOou	&	
OR no change: oR, BRoD=e½, DoR, KoR¼	o			o
FORWARD in mouth: (book) Bu;Ke½, (could) Ku;L±e½D=e½, (pull) Pu;L±e½, (woman) Vu;Me̦N̦	u			u;
OR no change: BuKe½, KuL±e½D=e½, PuL±e½	u	u	&	
Change in all positions: (joy) zOi, (voice) VOiSe½, (noise) NOiZ, (boy) BOi, (toy) T±Oi	oE	Oi		&
OR change: z½oi, VoiSe½, NoiZ, Boi, Toi	oE		oi	

		All 3
No change initially: (back) BeKe½, (but) BAT±e½, (by) BAi	B	-B
BUT STRONGER medially: (number) NAMB:eR (rainbow) R:eNB:o½	B	/B:!
EXCEPT between vowels: (maybe) MeBVi, (sober) So½BVeR	B	≠BV
AND after S, before a vowel: (baseball) BeSe½BVoL±e½	B	BV)s(*
AND medially before consonant: (absent) eBe½SA̦N̦T±e½	B	/Be½(¢
& finally: (suburb) SABVERBe½ (robe) R:o½Be½ (bob) BABe½	B	.Be½
No change: (church) CERC , (future) FYuCeR	C	C

UPPERDENTALIZE initially & medially: (under) AND±eR, (day) D±e, (dry) D±RAi, (dumb) D±AM̦	D	-/D±!	&	&
BUT INTERDENTALIZE between vowels: (deduct) D±iD=AKe½T±e½, (credit) KRaD=iT±e½	D	≠D=	&	&
AND before R: (address) eD=RaSe½	D	D=(r*	&	&
BUT medially before a consonant: (advise) eD=e½VAiZ, (bedside) BaD=e½SAiD=e½	D	/D=e½ (¢	&	&
AND finally: (did) D±iD=e½, (mind) MAiND=e½	D	.D=e½	&	&!
OR drop after a consonant: MAiN̦¼, (and) A½N̦¼	D			.¼)¢

		All 3
Change medially before a consonant: (after) A½Fe½T±eR	F	/Fe½(¢
AND finally: (if) iFe½, (rough) R:AFe½, (life) L±AiFe½	F	.Fe½!
BUT " before vowel: (off of) o½VAV, (laugh at) L±A½VeT±e½	F	.V(*

Change finally: (big) BiGe½, (leg) L±aGe½	G	.Ge½	&	&!
OR drop finally after N: (along) AL±oN̦¼, (sang) SeN̦¼, (among) AMoN̦¼, (ring) R:e̦N̦¼	G			.¼)n
CHANGE: (he) hi, (have) hA½V, (how) hA	H	h		&
OR change: h½i, h½A½V, h½A	H		h½	

Key:

z measure	h ich,loch	R trilled R	! excepting	= interdental
¼ dropped	: stronger	¢ consonant	(preceding	± upperdental
; forward	½ weakened	* vowels	) following	, nasalized
$ spelled	- initial	≠ between "	/ medially	. finally

GENERAL BRAZILIAN PORTUGUESE - RIO DE JANEIRO, EDUCATED BRAZILIAN BAHIA, RURAL BRAZILIAN

GUIDE PAGES

	SOUND	General Brazilian Port.	Rio de Janeiro Educated	Bahia Rural Brazilian Port.
CHANGE: (judge) zAz, (gradual) GRezu;eL±e½	J	z		&
OR change: z½Az½, GRez½UeL±e½, (age) A½z½	J		z½	
				All 3
Change medially before a consonant: (action) eKe½Se̦N̦	K			/Ke½(¢
AND finally: (kick) KiKe½, (clock) KL±AKe½, (ache) eKe½	K			.Ke½
UPPERDENTALIZE: (love) L±AV, (willing) e½WiL±e̦N̦Ge½	L			L±
BUT before consonant: (old) o½L±e½D=e½, (self) SeL±e½Fe½	L			L±e½(¢
AND finally: (all) oL±e½, (feel) FiL±e½, (well) e½WeL±e½	L			.L±e½
AND add where silent: (half) hA½L±e½Fe½, (talk) T±oL±e½Ke½, (could) KuL±e½D=e½ (balmy) BA½L±e½Mi (walk) e½WoL±e½Ke½	L			+L±e½ "¼
NASALIZE before consonant except B or D: (empty) A̦M̦Pe½T±i, (aimless) A̦M̦L±aSe½, (flimsy) FL±e̦M̦Zi, (simple) Se̦M̦PeL±e½	M			/M̦(¢ ! b d
AND finally: (him) he̦M̦, (bomb) Bo̦M̦, (same) SA̦M̦, (gem) zA̦M̦	M			.M̦
NASALIZE before consonant except B or D: (mainly) MA̦N̦L±i, (inside) e̦N̦SAiD=e½, (lunch) L±AN̦C, (sink) Se̦N̦Ke½	N			/N̦(¢ ! b d
AND finally: (town) T±A̦N̦, (then) D±A̦N̦, (motion) Mo½Se̦N̦	N			.N̦
Change medially before a consonant: (improve) e̦M̦Pe½Ru;V	P			/Pe½(¢
AND finally: (pipe) PAiPe½, (up) APe½, (stop) ST±APe½	P			.Pe½
CHANGE: (quick) Ke½ViKe½, (equal) iKe½VAL±e½	Q	Ke½V		&
OR change: Ke½WiKe½, iKe½WAL±e½	Q		Ke½W	
				All 3
STRONG TRILL initially: (write) R:AiT±e½, (read) R:iD=e½	R			-R:
TRILL medial & final: (are) A½R, (dry) D±RAi, (for) Fo½R	R			/.R!
BUT STRONGER before L,N,R,S: (poorly) Pu;R:L±i, (carry) KeR:i, (mournful) Mo½R:N̦FuL±e½, (worsen) e½WER:SeN̦	R			/R:(l n r s
AND TAP between vowels: (very) VaR½i, (story) ST±o½R½i	R			*R½
Change between vowels: (basic) BeZiKe½, (icy) AiZi	S			*Z
BUT change medially before a consonant: (ask) A½Se½Ke½, (crisp) KRiSe½Pe½, (last) L±A½Se½T±e½, (best) BaSe½T±e½	S			/Se½ (¢
AND finally: (mouse) MOe½Se½, (nice) NAiSe½, (use) YuSe½	S			.Se½
No change: (show) So½, (sure) Su;R, (motion) Mo½Se̦N̦	S			S
UPPERDENTALIZE: (take) T±eKe½, (into) e̦N̦T±u;	T	T±	&	&
BUT medially before consonant: (restless) R:aSe½T±e½L±ASe½, (softly) So½FeT±e½L±i	T	/T±e½ (¢	&	&
AND finally: (it) iT±e½, (tight) T±AiT±e½	T	.T±e½	&	&!
OR DROP finally after consonant: (sent) SA̦N̦¼, (fact) FeKe½¼, (left) L±aFe½¼, (part) PA½R¼	T			.¼)¢
CHANGE: (three) T=Ri (both) Bo½T= (thin) T=e̦N̦	t	T=		&
OR change: T=tRi, BOT=t, T=te̦N̦	t		T=t	
CHANGE: (they) D±e (other) AD±eR (with) e½WiD±	T	D±		&
OR change: D±TA½, AD±TeR, ½WiD±T	T		D±T	
No change: (visit) ViZiT±e½ (involve) e̦NVAL±e½V	V	V	&	&
CHANGE: (we) e½Wi, (why) e½WAi, (which) e½WiC	W	e½W	&	
OR change: Vi, VAi, Vi:C	W			V
No change: (measure) MazeR	XZz	XZz	&	&

Key:

C church	- initial	: stronger	, nasalized	= interdental
+ add to	/ medial	½ weakened	! excepting	± upperdental
" when	. finally	& as shown	(preceding	¢ consonants
¼ drop	; forward	R trilled R	) following	* vowels
				*̸ between "

LISBON, IBERIAN PORTUGUESE - SINTRA, RURAL IBERIAN PORTUGUESE

BANDO, GALICIAN PORTUGUESE

GUIDE PAGES

	SOUND	Lisbon Iberian Portuguese	Sintra Rural Iberian Port.	Bando Galician Portuguese
SHORTEN: (age) A½z½, (say) SA½, (fail) FA½L±*e*½	A	A½		
OR change: ez, Se, FeL±*e*½	A		e	&
BUT before nasalized M or N: (mainly) MA̧ŅL±i:, (nameless) NA̧M̧L±aS, (sane) SA̧Ņ, (came) KA̧M̧	A	A̧(M̧,Ņ	&	&
CHANGE: (see) Si: (easy) i:Zi: (need) Ni:D=*e*½	E	i:	&	
OR shorten: SE½, E½ZE½, NE½D=*e*½	E			E½

		All 3
No change: (I'll) ILe½, (night) NIT±*e*½, (buy) BI, (my) MI	I	I
CHANGE: (old) *o*L±D=*e*½, (solo) S*o*L±*o*, (know) N*o*, (toe) T±*o*	O	*o*
CHANGE: (unit) Y*u*Ni:T±*e*½, (few) FY*u*, (music) MY*u*Zi:K*e*½	U	Y*u*
CHANGE: (as.) *A*S½., (bad) B*A*D=*e*½, (at) *A*T±*e*½, (man) M*A̧Ņ*	a	*A*
CHANGE: (neck) NaK*e*½, (said) SaD=*e*½, (read) *R*:aD=*e*½	e	a!
BUT when in prefix: (exit) iZi:T±*e*½, (enact) iNAKT±*e*½	e	i{
& before nasalized M or N: (them) ZA̧M̧, (mental) MA̧ŅT±*e*L±*e*½	e	A̧(M̧,Ņ
BUT no change before L: (fellow) FeL±*o*, (tell) T±eL±*e*½	e	e(l

	SOUND	Lisbon Iberian Portuguese	Sintra Rural Iberian Port.	Bando Galician Portuguese
LONGER: (critic) K*R*i:T±i:K*e*½, (busy) Bi:Zi:	i	i:	&	
OR change: K*R*E½T±E½K*e*½, BVE½ZE½	i			E½
BUT before nasalized M or N: (in) e̜Ņ, (him) H:e̜M̧, (insist) e̜ŅSi:ST±*e*½, (swim) S*e*½We̜M̧	i	e̜(M̧,Ņ	&	&
CHANGE: (stop) ST±*o*P*e*½, (got) G*o*T±*e*½, (on) *o*Ņ	o	*o*	&	&
Change in all positions: (up) *o*P*e*½, (touch) T±*o*C, (love) L±*o*V, (what) *e*½W*o*T±*e*½, (us) *o*S	u	*o*		&
OR change: *A*P*e*½, T±*A*C, L±*A*B, *e*½W*A*T±*e*½, *A*S	u		*A*	
No change: (heart) H:*A*RT±*e*½, (calm) K*A*L±M̧	*A*	*A*	&	&
No change: (learn) L±*E*R:Ņ, (girl) G*E*R:L±*e*½	*E*	*E*	&	&
No change: (predict) PRID=i:KT±*e*½	*I*	*I*	&	&
Change initially: (our) *O*e½R, (out) *O*e½T±*e*½	*O*	-*O*e½		
OR " " : *A*R, *A*T±*e*½, (owl) *A*L±*e*½	*O*		-*A*	
& " medially: (loud) L±*O*e½D=*e*½ (house) H:*O*e½S	*O*	/*O*e½	&	
& " finally: (now) N*A*, (how) H:*A*, (vow) V*A*	*O*	.*A*	&	
OR no change: *O*R, *O*T±:, L±*O*D=*e*½, ¼*O*S, N*O*, ¼*O*	*O*			-/.*O*!
BUT before a nasalized M or N: (bounce) BA̧ŅS, (downtown) D±A̧ŅT±A̧Ņ, (count) KA̧ŅT±*e*½	*O*	A̧(M̧,Ņ	&	&

		All 3
CHANGE: (do) D±*u*;, (soon) S*u*;Ņ, (group) G*R**u*;P*e*½	*U*	*u*;
CHANGE: (staff) ST±*A*F*e*½, (class) KL±*A*S, (ask) *A*S½K*e*½	*a*	*A*
No change: (apple) *A*P*e*L±*e*½, (dozen) D±*o*Z*e*Ņ	*e*	*e*
CHANGE: (above) *A*BV*o*V, (family) F*A*M*A*L±i:, (extra) iST±*RA*	*i*	*A*
BUT before nasalized M or N: (opinion) *A*Pi:NYe̜Ņ, (motion) M*o*Se̜Ņ, (system) Si:ST±e̜M̧, (science) SIe̜ŅS, (ocean) *o*Se̜Ņ	*i*	e̜(M̧,Ņ

	SOUND	Lisbon Iberian Portuguese	Sintra Rural Iberian Port.	Bando Galician Portuguese
If spelled A,AU,AW: (saw) So, (cause.) KoS., (all) oL±*e*½, (draw) D±Ro, (talk) T±oK*e*½	*o*			o$a au aw
OR no change: S*o*, K*o*S½., *o*L±*e*½, D±R*o*, T±*o*K*e*½	*o*	*o*$a	&	
If spelled O,OA,OO,OU: (or) o*R*, (broad) B*R*oD=*e*½, (court) Ko*R*T±*e*½, (door) D±o*R*	*o*	o$oOA ou oo	&	
OR no change: *oR*, BV*o*RD=*e*½, K*o*RT±*e*½, D±*oR*	*o*			*o*$o

Key:

¼ dropped	S show, sure	C church	z measure
- initial	, nasalized	; forward	& as shown
/ medial	! excepting	$ spelled	*R* trilled R
. finally	(preceding	: stronger	= interdental
	{ in prefix	½ weakened	± upperdental

LISBON, IBERIAN PORTUGUESE - SINTRA, RURAL IBERIAN PORTUGUESE BANDO, GALICIAN PORTUGUESE

GUIDE PAGES		Lisbon Port.	Sintra Rural	Bando Galic.
FORWARD: (book) Bu;Ke½, (could) Ku;L±D=e½	u		u;	
OR longer: BVu:Ke½, Ku:L±D=e½, (pull) Pu:L±e½	u			u:
OR no change: BuKe½, KuL±D=e½, PuL±e½	u	u		
CHANGE: (joy) z½oi (voice) VoiS (noise) NoiZ	oE	oi	&	
OR shorten: zoE½, BoE½S, NoE½Z	oE			oE½
Change initially: (back) BVAKe½, (but) BVoT±:	B			-BV
OR no change initially: BAKe½, BoT±e½	B	-B	&	
STRONGER medially: (number) NoMB:eR	B	/B:	&	&!
OR no change medially after M or N: NoMBeR	B			/B)mn
AND change between vowels: (maybe) MA½BVi:	B	≠BV	&	&
AND after medial S: (baseball) BA½z½BVoL±e½	B	/BV)s	&	&
AND before D,L,R,S,T: (obtain) ABVe½T±A̦N̦, (absent) ABVe½SA̦N̦T±e½, (subdue) SoBVe½D±Yu	B	/BVe½ (dLrSt	&	&
& finally: (suburb) SoBVERBe½, (robe) R:oBe½	B	.Be½	&	&
No change: (church) CERC, (future) FYuCeR	C	C	&	&
UPPERDENTALIZE initially & medially: (under) oND±eR, (day) D±A½, (dry) D±RI, (dumb) D±oM̦	D	-/D±!	&	&
BUT INTERDENTALIZE between vowels: (deduct) D±i:D=oKT±e½, (credit) KRaD=i:T±e½	D	≠D=	&	&
AND before R: (address) AD=RaS	D	D=(r*	&	&
& change final: (did) D±i:D=e½ (need) Ni:D=e½	D	.D=e½	&!	&!
OR drop after a consonant: (board) BoR¼, (mind) MIN̦¼, (cold) KoL±e½¼, (card) KAR¼	D		.¼)¢	
OR except after R: BVoRD=e½, KARD=e½	D			.¼)¢!r
Change finally: (if) i:Fe½, (rough) R:oFe½	F	.Fe½	&!	&
OR finally before vowel: (off of) oVABV	F		.V(*	
Change finally: (big) Bi:Ge½, (leg) L±aGe½	G	.Ge½	&!	&
OR drop from ING: (coming) KAMe̦N̦¼ (going) Goe̦N̦¼	G		¼ing)	
STRONGER: (he) H:i:, (have) H:AV, (how) H:A	H	H:		
OR drop: ¼i:, ¼ABV, ¼A (household) ¼Oe½S¼oL±¼	H		¼	&
CHANGE: (judge) z½oz½, (giant) z½Ie̦N̦T±e½, (gradual) GRAz½u;eL±e½, (wage) e½WA½z½	J	z½		
OR change: zAz, zIe̦N̦¼, GRAzu;eL±e½, e½Wez	J		z	&
				All 3
Change finally: (kick) Ki:Ke½ (clock) KL±oKe½ (ache) A½Ke½	K			.Ke½
UPPERDENTALIZE: (love) L±oV, (willing) e½Wi:L±e̦N̦Ge½	L			L±
AND add where silent: (half) H:AL±Fe½, (talk) T±oL±Ke½	L			+L±"¼
BUT finally: (all) oL±e½, (feel) Fi:L±e½, (well) e½WeL±e½	L			.L±e½
NASALIZE before consonant except B or D: (empty) A̦M̦PT±i:, (aimless) A̦M̦L±aS, (flimsy) FL±e̦M̦Zi:	M	/M̦(¢ ! b d	&	&
AND finally: (him) H:e̦M̦ (bomb) BoM̦ (same) SA̦M̦	M	.M̦	&	&!
OR except before B,D,G,K,P,T: (same place) SeM PL±eS (come to) KoMT±u; (prime cut) PRIMKoT±:	M			.M̦!(b dGkPt
NASALIZE before consonant except B or D: (lunch) L±oN̦C, (mainly) MA̦N̦L±i:, (inside) e̦N̦SID=e½	N	/N̦(¢ ! b d	&	&
AND finally: (town) TA̦N̦ (then) ZA̦N̦ (motion) MoSe̦N̦	N	.N̦	&	&!
OR except before B,D,G,K,P,T: (gain time) GeN T±IM̦, (run by) R:oNBVI, (bone dry) BVoND±RI	N			.N̦!(b dGkPt

Key:

	& as shown	" when	(preceding	
+ add to	: stronger	z measure	) following	! excepting
½ weaken	S show,sure	- initial	) in suffix	¢ consonant
¼ dropped	R trilled R	/ medial	= interdental	* vowels
; forward	, nasalized	. finally	± upperdental	≠ between "

LISBON, IBERIAN PORTUGUESE - SINTRA, RURAL IBERIAN PORTUGUESE

BANDO, GALICIAN PORTUGUESE GUIDE PAGES		Lisbon Port.	Sintra Rural	Bando Galic.
				All 3
Change finally: (pipe) PIPe½, (up) oPe½, (stop) ST±oPe½	P			.Pe½
CHANGE: (quick) Ke½Wi:Ke½, (equal) i:Ke½WeL±e½	Q			Ke½W
STRONG TRILL initially: (raw) R:o, (rain) R:ĄŅ	R	-R:	&	&
TRILL medially & finally: (are) AR, (dry) D±RI, (for) FoR, (prove) PRu;V, (or) oR	R	/.R!	&	&
BUT before L,N,R,S: (worse) e½WER:S, (turn) T±ER:Ņ, (poorly) Pu;R:L±i:, (carry) KAR:i:	R	/R:(1 n r s	&	&
AND LIGHT TAP between vowels: (very) VaR½i:	R	ǂR½	&	
OR STRONG TRILL: BaR:E½, (story) ST±oR:E½	R			ǂR:
Change between vowels: (basic) BA½Zi:Ke½	S	ǂZ	&	&
AND " medial & final before B,D,G,L,M,N,R,V: (dismiss) D±i:z½Mi:S, (useless) Yuz½L±aS, (nice guy) NIz½GI, (face value) FA½z½VAL±Yu	S	/.z½ (bDgL mNrV	&	&
& finally before F,K,P,S,T: (yes sir) YaS½SER, (close friend) KL±oS½FRĄŅD=e½, (peace plan) Pi:S½PL±ĄŅ, (ice cream) IS½KRi:M̦	S	.S½(f kPsT	&	
OR change: YaSSER, KL±oSSFRĄŅ¼, PE½SSPL±ĄŅ	S			.SS(f
& at end of phrase: (nice.) NIS½., (use.) YuS½.	S	..S½	&	
OR change: NISS., YuSS., (mouse.) MOSS.	S			..SS
CHANGE: (show) Co (sure) Cu;R (motion) MoCȩŅ	S		C	
OR no change: So, Su;R, MoSȩŅ	S	S		&
UPPERDENTALIZE: (take) T±A½Ke½, (into) ȩŅT±u;	T	T±	&	&
BUT change finally: (it) i:T±e½ (tight) T±IT±e½	T	.T±e½	&!	
OR stronger finally: E½T±:, T±IT±:	T			.T±:
OR drop after consonant: (sent) SĄŅ¼ (part) PAR¼	T		.¼)¢	
				All 3
CHANGE: (three) SRi:, (both) BoS, (thin) SȩŅ, (math) MAS	t			S
CHANGE: (they) ZA½, (other) oZeR, (with) e½Wi:Z	T			Z
CHANGE: (visit) BVi:Zi:T±e½ (involve) ȩŅBVoL±BV	V		BV	
OR change: BE½ZE½T±:, ȩŅBoL±B, (of) oB	V			B
OR no change: Vi:Zi:T±e½, ȩŅVoL±V, oV	V	V		
CHANGE: (we) e½Wi: (why) e½WI (which) e½Wi:C	W	e½W	&	&
"Z" for "GZ" sound: (exact) iZAKT±e½, (anxiety) ĄŅZIeT±i:, (exist) iZi:ST±e½	X	Z 4 gz	&	
AND change next to consonant: (next) NaST±e½, (mixture) Mi:SCeR, (expect) iSPaKT±e½	X	SI¢	&	
OR no change: iGZAKT±:, NaKST±:, ME½KSCeR	X			X
Change medial & final before B,D,G,L,M,N,R,V: (newsman) NYuz½MAŅ, (plays down) PL±A½z½D±ĄŅ, (wisely) e½WIz½L±i:, (his best) H:i:z½BaST±e½	Z	/.z½ (bDgL mNrV	&	
OR change: NYuzMAŅ, PL±ezD±ĄŅ, e½WIzL±E½	Z			/.z(b
& finally before F,K,P,S,T: (does for) D±oS½ FoR, (was past) e½WoS½PAST±e½, (is caught) i:S½KoT±e½, (his best) H:i:S½BaST±e½	Z	.S½(f kPsT	&	
OR change: D±oSFoR, e½WoSPAST±:, E½SKoT±:	Z			.S(fK
& at end of phrase: (size.) SIS½. (rose.) R:oS½.	Z	..S½	&	
OR change: SIS., R:oS., (please.) PL±E½S.	Z			..S
No change: (measure) MazeR, (vision) Vi:zȩŅ	z	z	&	&

Key:	4 for	¢ consonants	- initial	! excepting
& as shown	C church	* vowels	/ medial	(preceding
: stronger	½ weaken	ǂ between "	. finally	I before or after
R trilled R	; forward	= interdental	.. " in phrase	
, nasalized	¼ dropped	± upperdental		) following

NOW THAT YOU'RE A DIALECTICIAN . . .

As I stressed in the opening chapter, this book is not aimed at academicians nor designed to settle esoteric questions of phonetics. It is aimed exclusively at *you*, the actor or actress, and designed specifically to make your performances more convincing and your quest for work easier and more fruitful.

Of course, your professional reputation also helps to determine how hard you have to fight to get that part you want so badly. Study and practice make it possible to keep improving that reputation—and, used correctly, this book can make that practice pay off. In this chapter, you'll see how practice, reputation, and work are all intertwined, interactive, and interdependent.

"Work" is what it's all about for us in the entertainment industry: without it we can't communicate our talent, fulfill our ambitions, or satisfy our creative longings—without it we don't eat.

Primarily, this work will come from "franchised" talent agents; second, from advertising agencies, local advertisers, and from film editors. I understand the confusion you're probably feeling at this point, the anxious questions going through your mind: "Where do I find these people? How do I get to them? What do I do? What do I say to them when I *do* reach them? How do I open the right doors?

But bear in mind that you are a dialectician: You now have skills that you can demonstrate easily and quickly, skills which give you a clear advantage over actors who can only show off their voice quality or emotional range.

You have only to open your mouth and, within one minute, you can amuse, intrigue, and fascinate your interviewers. Seldom will they be satisfied with only sixty seconds of your performance. As you change from dialect to dialect, you are creating the "magic" that seduced them into this business in the first place: the ability of one person to turn him- or herself into many, many people—a Swedish count one moment and an Indian houseboy the next—a London bobby, a Colombian plantation owner, a Russian diplomat, an Italian street vendor—all these and more, right in front of their eyes.

The last time I returned to the United States (after an eight-year absence), I didn't have many contacts left in the industry, but I did manage to latch onto a dialects dubbing job. The editor in charge of the dub was sufficiently satisfied with my work to recommend me to a top voice-talent agent. It took quite a few phone calls, but I finally got the interview.

After listening to the voice-field's foremost agent give me his (obviously) standard three-minute lecture on why they couldn't take on any more people for representation, and how stiff the competition was and how hard it was to get work, I thanked him and handed him my Dialects Proficiency resume. On a single sheet, it listed over one hundred dialects and varieties (where fifty, or even fifteen, would have been plenty). He raised a skeptical eyebrow and said, "You're kidding."

"Not in the least, amigo," I replied in my best Mexican dialect, and then launched into a patter that covered four more dialects and varieties. Then I said, "Now *you* pick one." Still skeptical, he chose Indian. I did that, carried on with a few more, and ended by illustrating the differences between Austrian, Berlin, and Rhineland German. By now, it had become a game, with him as an enthusiastic participant. After five minutes of this, I asked him, "*Now* what do you think of my chances?" I left that office with an agency contract.

Why did I hold myself down to five minutes? Because I knew his time was limited and because after five minutes of rapid dialect switching the differences between accents become blurred to the listener.

I'm aware that you may not have a contact to direct you to a good voice-talent agent, but don't despair. Your local branch of AFTRA (American Federation of Television and Radio Artists) will furnish you with a list of "Franchised Talent Agents" as will your local Screen Actors Guild. A telephone book will help you locate these guilds, as will the *Academy Directory*, which can be found in any big city library. The library should also be able to furnish information on how to contact local recording studios and advertising agencies. They in turn can tell you which of the talent agencies in your area specialize in "voice people."

At the time of this writing, in Los Angeles the leading voice-talent agencies are Abrams-Rubaloff; Carey-Phelps-Colvin; William Morris; William Cunningham & Associates; Charles H. Stern, and probably the best known, Wormser, Heldfond & Joseph. One further note: of all the casting agents in Hollywood, Bob Lloyd is known as the "Voice Caster."

The sales managers at local recording studios *might* be cooperative enough to let you know which advertising agencies are booking the most nonmusical recording time—especially those who are heaviest into radio ads. The recording studios that have dubbing facilities can also put you on to film or TV editors who might use your talents.

Watch local TV advertising and listen to the radio ads of your local merchants. Ask yourself if you can come up with any ideas using your dialect skills that would bring more spark to someone's advertising. Bear in mind that humor and novelty are attention grabbers. Try your hand at some and, if they're not downright embarrassing, find a way to get them to that local merchant. And don't agonize over whether someone will steal your brilliant idea. Remember, you're selling yourself as a voice actor, not an ad writer.

If you live in or near New York or Los Angeles, see if you can get someone at your Motion Picture Editors Guild local to help you. Find out which studio editors specialize in dubbing. Usually these editors will combine sound-effects skills with dialogue-editing ability. The same goes for free-lance editors; they are the ones most often used to dub English-speaking dialogue into foreign feature films. Since those films were shot abroad, they are an excellent source of many potential dialect roles.

In this situation, if you have a variety of different voices in your repertoire, it can be both helpful and lucrative. In one World War II saga that was dubbed, I did seven British voices, seven German, and four French. After three weeks I walked away exhausted but "flush."

Once you've used your phone book, your library, and your local professional guilds and associations to locate your "targets," it's time to prepare your campaign. It's best to aim only at those located no more than half-a-day's travel away; missed interviews can cool a contact's interest very fast.

Prepare a presentable resume; once again, the library can guide you on how this is done. If you lack professional acting experience, emphasize how many dialects you can speak. Don't send out a "blind" resume; always address it to someone in the organization who is in a position to hire you or offer you representation. After four to five working days, follow up the resume with a personal phone call. Your object is to get an interview, remember, so whet their appetites and curiosity (a dialect or two here wouldn't hurt).

If a major voice-talent agency is your goal, it's a good idea to send a "demo" tape to start things off. Just as with musical groups and vocalists, a good demo can get you quick interest and attention. But do it right. Prepare a script that will show variety, include humor, and be fast-paced enough to hold the interest (but not too fast to be intelligible). Your script should run *no more* than five minutes. Then put out the money for decent recording facilities and an engineer (don't worry: it won't cost you as much as it would cost a vocalist). Take the time to do it, and redo it until your demo is perfect.

Once you get the interview, prepare for it. Remember, you're not auditioning for a modeling assignment and you're not trying to impress anyone with how far-out you can look. Nothing should distract your audience from what you want them to concentrate on—your *dialect* skills. Know what you want to say, but don't forget how to listen. If you pay attention, they'll let you know what bores them and what impresses them. They'll even let you in on their personal interests; if their words don't reveal them, their office decor will. If you really do have an interest in common, it won't hurt to say so. But don't dwell on it; you're there as a professional, not a "buddy." Above all, don't bluff about having knowledge or interests you don't really have!

Even if you've done everything right up to this point, your search for work is far from over. In fact, in our field it's *never* over. You have to expand your contacts continually through more personal interviews. And you have to follow up every personal interview with a monthly phone call. (If they want you to check in more frequently, they'll let you know.) Being in "the right place, at the right time" consists of no more than being in enough different places at enough different times.

Since waiting is part of the "game," what else can you do in the meantime? Unfortunately, the first thing that occurs to many actors is socializing. Resist the impulse to be "on"; socialize with your contacts only if you have interests in common. Remember, until you get the first job with any particular contact, you're employable only as long as you're personally interesting. After the first success with them in a working situation, you're employable no matter how little you have in common with them.

There is, however, one type of socializing that can't go wrong, and that's after an evening in which you've entertained your contact. If you are going to make a professional appearance (especially in a "prestige" workshop), make sure you invite *one* contact (no more) for each evening you perform. In your invitation, suggest that the person join you for a quick drink (or coffee) afterwards, if he or she has the time. If your performance has intrigued, amused or moved your contact, your guest may stretch out that "quick drink" into real communication—if only to be close to the "magic" you created for a little longer.

I mentioned prestige workshops. This is where you want to be *seen*. As to where you want to do your practice work, that's up to you. Consider local theatrical groups. Is there one in which you think you can expand your talents? Take on greater challenges? Especially keep an eye out for any group staging a play with a role in dialect. They'll find that role hard to cast, and *you'll* find yet another chance to PRACTICE.

To learn which plays have dialect parts, it's back to your friendly librarian. You might be steered to *My Fair Lady, A View from the Bridge, Anastasia, Fiddler on the Roof*, or *I Remember Mama*. Another source is Samuel French, a play-publishing house with an enormous selection and a bookshop in Los Angeles at 7623 West Sunset. Their listing often breaks plays down into categories and supplies enough information so that you can determine its potential as practice material.

If you're auditioning for an extensive part in dialect, it's good to have one of these scenes "in your back pocket," so to speak. That way you don't have to "go away and come back when you've got it." Many screenplays are also now published, any number of which have good dialect parts.

Lastly, there is the dialect joke. This doesn't have to be offensive; it can be warm, loving and insightful, if only you stay "inside the character." If you are going to create a stand-up comic routine, let it be from the point of view of the character speaking the dialect, as Richard Pryor does and as Freddie Prinze did. If you are going to do more than one dialect, create a character for each one and give that character enough stage time so that he can "establish" himself with the audience.

With humor as your wedge, you can enter into areas where reputation can be built without being a nightclub star. Try out your routines on your nontheatrical friends. Volunteer to entertain organizational luncheons (if you're good enough, they'll promote you to dinners). Do your routines for charity drives. Do them anywhere and everywhere that you can find a respectable "establishment" audience—and especially where you know there will be a lot of businessmen in attendance, preferably with their wives.

Much if not all of the last paragraphs has been devoted to *creating a reputation* as much as to *practice*. But a professional reputation can be destroyed more easily than it can be built. The cardinal rule that will protect your reputation against all onslaughts is: *Never promise what you can't deliver*!

If the time *does* come when someone offers you a "paid turn" at the local cocktail bar or even a bit on local cable TV, keep that cardinal rule in mind. Remember, also that you're not a stand-up comic yet, just a dialect actor working on building a professional reputation.

Creating a reputation doesn't stop when you turn professional, or even when you're an established dialectician. Every pleased employer is another opportunity to add to your reputation. If you've done an exceptional job and your employer knows it, don't press for further employment (if it's there, they'll tell you). Instead, turn your happy boss into an enthusiastic booster. Everybody likes to spread the good word, especially when it reflects well on their own "good judgment."

Strike while the glow lingers; ask if you can refer another (or others) to them for their recommendation. *If* there seems to be a decent opening, find out if someone they know in the field might be able to use you in the future. But don't push it; let *them* get the idea of making that casual phone call. Lead them gently, and they'll do your P.R. for you—and be glad of the chance.

PRACTICE WORD LIST—1

A	able	satiate	pain	o	honest	polyglot	got
	ache	tailgate	rate		odd	topnotch	lock
	age	vacate	shame		omelette	bonded	not knot
	aid	waylay	snake		on	clock	pocket
	aim	baby	table		operation	collar	polish
	air	blade	away		opposite	combine	pot
	eight	break	day		oxen	common	shock
	heyday	cake	say		oxide	compact	shop
	maintain	late	Saturday		concoct	copy	solid
	namesake	maybe	they		hobnob	drop	stop
	placate	nail	yesterday		hopscotch	fog	top
I	eye	linotype	right	E	easy	receive	these
	ice	twilight	side		each	release	be bee
	I'd	crime	while		ear	reveal	early
	idolize	desire	by buy		east	theory	free
	I'll	kind	cry		eat	heat	he
	I'm	like	die		either	here	me
	iodine	line	fly		emit	indeed	sea see
	island	mind	lie		erase	seem	secretary
	dynamite	nice	my		believe	steam	she
	finalize	night	tie		degree	steel	tree
	likewise	pipe	try		greasy	teach	we
U	unit	cute	news	O	oar	solo	total
	use	dual	pure		oath	boat	whole hole
	useless	fuel	shrewd		oboe	bone	blow
	you	feud	stewardess		old	coal	fellow
	you'll	huge	tune		only	gold	grow
	you're	humor	chew		overthrow	note	know no
	youth	immune	cue		oh owe	polo	show
	allude	jewel	few		own	road	slow
	amusement	lewd	lieu		cocoa	roll	snow
	beautiful	mule	new		postpone	slope	so sew
	chewed	music	value		potato	smoke	toe
e	enact	express	men	a	act	knapsack	happy
	end	extend	neck		add	madcap	lad
	endure	extent	next		afghan	ransack	mad
	every	bedstead	read red		am	bad	magic
	exam	bed	said		amnesia	cat	man
	excel	bell	send		angry	fact	map
	excess	dead	sense		as	flag	nap
	exempt	fled	smell		at	flat	pan
	expect	leg	them		Bagdad	glad	pat
	expend	let	well		bandana	had	snack
	expense	memory	wet		cataract	hammer	stamp

PRACTICE WORD LIST—2

i			
	if	distill	kick
	imprint	distinct	lid
	in	English	lift
	infringe	mystic	milk
	inquisitive	privilege	ring
	insist	within	stick
	instill	bill	still
	instinctive	bit	sympathy
	is	brick	this
	it	busy	visit
	critic	dig	women

U			
	oodles	move	wound
	oolong	poor	blue
	ooze	room	do
	boot	root	drew
	cruel	rule	flew
	fool	school	glue
	fruit	soon	knew
	groove	soup	screw
	group	spoon	shoe
	lose	tool	to two
	moon	tour	true

u			
	ugly	numskull	gun
	umpire	among	love
	uncut	blood	onion
	under	bug	rub
	undone	but	scrub
	unjust	button	sudden
	unplug	color	thus
	unsung	cut	touch
	up	does	was
	us	front	what
	hubbub	govern	young

e			
	added	frighten	often
	aided	glamor	onion
	ambulance	gorgeous	paper
	apple	heighten	person
	bullet	labor	reason
	caper	level	rhythm
	certain	major	simple
	dozen	metal	social
	facial	muscle	title
	fertile	nation	trouble
	fragrance	neighbor	vigilance

A			
	alms	car	mark
	arc	card	market
	are	carve	palm
	argument	charge	regard
	army	far	star
	art	garden	start
	gala	harbor	swamp
	afar	heart	swan
	alarm	large	wand
	bizarre	largo	watch
	calm	march	spa

o			
	all awl	broad	horse
	always	call	long
	autumn	cause	lord
	awful	cough	loss
	off	court	sort
	order	dog	talk
	ought	door	tall
	foreswore	false	walk
	forethought	floor	war
	Warsaw	form	law
	board	halt	saw

I			
	precaution	proclaim	precede
	precipitate	produce	predict
	precocious	profanity	prepare
	preposterous	profound	pretend
	pretentious	progress	prevail
	profession	prohibit	prevent
	proficiency	project	propel
	propensity	propose	protect
	proportion	propriety	protest
	prospective	protract	provide
	provisional	prolong	provoke

E			
	earn	current	separate
	err	dirty	servant
	irk	first	skirt
	urge	girl	stir
	merger	heard	turn
	perverse	her	were
	purser	learn	word
	burn	nerve	work
	butter	purpose	world
	comfort	refer	worm
	concern	return	worse

PRACTICE WORD LIST—3

O	ounce	count	round
	our hour	crowd	sound
	out	doubt	town
	outbound	down	trousers
	outing	foul	allow
	outlet	found	cow
	owl	frown	endow
	about	loud	how
	amount	mountain	now
	brown	powder	plow
	cloud	power	vow

oE	oil	joint	toilet
	oily	joyful	voice
	oyster	loiter	voyage
	avoid	loyal	alloy
	boiling	moist	annoy
	choice	noise	boy
	coil	point	destroy
	coin	poison	employ
	coyly	royal	enjoy
	exploit	soil	joy
	join	spoil	toy

a	after	brass	laugh
	anchovy	can't	mask
	and	craft	past
	answer	dance	path
	ant	fast	plant
	ask	flask	rather
	aspen	gather	staff
	astral	grasp	stand
	athletic	half	task
	bath	land	telegraph
	branch	last	transplant

C	church	digestion	each
	chain	future	lunch
	change	hatchet	match
	charm	itching	much
	cheap	ketchup	ranch
	chest	lecture	search
	chief	orchard	speech
	child	pinching	such
	chin	picture	teach
	choice	preacher	touch
	bachelor	watchman	which

i	above	balance	political
	addition	combine	science
	afraid	companion	system
	ago	company	camera
	alarm	connection	comma
	approve	family	drama
	attack	immature	extra
	avoid	machine	idea
	awake	natural	mama
	banana	normal	sofa
	pajama	opinion	umbrella

F	fife	friend	if
	fifteen	from	laugh
	fluffy	coffee	life
	fall	left	off
	farm	nephew	roof
	fat	office	rough
	fear	offside	safe
	feeling	orphan	scarf
	few	phase	self
	fine	zephyr	stiff
	fold	enough	wife

u	beautiful	hook	push
	book	instrument	pussycat
	brook	insurance	put
	bush	likelihood	should
	childhood	look	stood
	cook	manhood	took
	could	outlook	umlaut
	cushion	overlook	wolf
	foot	pitiful	woman
	full	pull	wood
	good	puller	wool

H	hothouse	here	forehead
	household	high	inherit
	hair	his	inhibit
	hand	hope	likelihood
	hard	house	manhood
	has	how	overhear
	hate	who	perhaps
	have	ahead	redhot
	he	anyhow	rehearse
	head	behave	somehow
	help	behind	unhappy

PRACTICE WORD LIST—4

K		
cake	keep	sky
character	kill	sticky
clerk	accent	ache
clock	accept	ask
coke	active	desk
cork	bobcat	ink
corncob	bucket	make
cucumber	circle	neck
kick	direction	risk
kink	fact	stomach
come	mankind	think

J		
judge	danger	damage
judgement	enjoy	dodge
genius	gradual	edge
general	individual	language
George	logic	manage
giant	major	age
giraffe	procedure	range
jelly	religion	sponge
jewel	residual	stage
joy	suggestion	strange
jump	bridge	urge

B		
baby	because	obtain
barb	bite	rainbow
bib	break	submit
blab	but	club
blurb	by buy	grab
bob	absent	robe
boob	emblem	rub
bubble	habit	scrub
bulb	husband	sob
suburb	maybe	tube
bath	number	verb

L		
lilt	blue	told
lull	brilliant	willing
skillful	bulb	all
land	calm	call
law	clean	control
laugh	elder	ill
lead	field	rail
leaf	halt	school
list	help	tell
low	million	till
alms	silver	well

D		
added	dual	middle
dead	address	and
deduct	bedtime	bad
deed	body	bird
dependent	credit	cold
did	endure	food
died	field	had
drained	good	made
dread	handler	mind
day	hurdler	need
dress	induce	said

M		
humdrum	my	arm
maim	amber	comb
ma'am	chimney	flame
mom	embarrass	frame
mum	empty	game
man	impress	him
married	limit	same
meal	summer	seem
meet	swamp	some sum
milk	tempted	time
move	alarm	warm

G		
goggle	grass	along
going	green	bag
groggy	again	big
gurgle	angle	coming
singing	bigtime	gag
get	disgust	leg
give	forget	living
glad	forgive	meeting
glass	maggot	morning
go	regret	pig
grain	together	song

n		
anchor	include	drink
ankle	income	flunk
anxious	increase	ink
blanket	monkey	junk
conquer	shrunken	rank
donkey	sunken	sink
encore	thinker	spank
encounter	trinket	stink
encourage	uncle	thank
frankly	wrinkle	think
function	bank	zinc

PRACTICE WORD LIST—5

Q		
quack	quiet	frequent
quail	quit	inquire
quake	quite	liquid
quality	acquaint	misquote
qualm	banquet	request
quantity	bequeath	require
quart	conquest	sequel
quarter	earthquake	square
quell	equal	squash
question	equator	squeak
quick	equity	tranquil

R		
disregard	alright	tomorrow
rare	art	turnip
rear	coarsen	unrest
regular	dry	very
roar	grey	are
rural	hearing	cure
read	organ	fire
ready	park	for
rich	poorly	hire
write	spring	or
wrong	story	wire

S		
cease	sit	decide
closeness	sleep	disguise
dismiss	smile	disrupt
sauce	snake	insect
slice	speak	instead
space	stop	misbehave
spice	swing	across
stress	ask	base
useless	basin	face
civil	beefsteak	nice
say	best	yes

S		
shush	action	tissue
champagne	attention	brush
charade	conscious	cash
chef	discussion	dish
chute	issue	fish
ship	motion	foolish
shirt	official	harsh
show	position	moustache
shut	punishment	rush
sugar	sensual	smash
sure	special	wish

N		
condition	name	ornate
known	near	until
nine	need	again
none	nip	can
noon	amnesia	even
noun	and	in
saneness	any	pen
knife	inmate	run
knock	money	sign
knot not	only	son sun
nail	onto	then

ś		
artsy	outside	westside
bitesize	outskirts	cents
eastside	outsmart	contents
fatso	outspoken	oats
heartsick	outspread	pants
hotseat	outstrip	quartz
jetset's	patsy	quits
jetstream	Scotsman	sports
jetsum	sportsman	sits
lightsout	statesman	tights
outset	waits	waltz

P		
paper	place	impress
peep	play	napping
people	poor	open
pep	price	respect
pipe	program	space
pop	put	cup
pup	compare	slip
page	complete	soap
past	copper	step
paste	expel	stop
pin	gap	up

ŧ		
thief	athlete	bath
thin	breathless	birth
thing	deathly	breath
think	faithful	death
thought	healthy	earth
thread	lethal	growth
three	nothing	month
throat	ruthless	mouth
through	sympathy	north
thunder	toothache	south
anthem	wealthy	worth

PRACTICE WORD LIST—6

V	involve	voyage	conceive	*T*	that	breathing	bequeath
	revive	advertise	curve		the	either	breathe
	revolve	canvas	drive		them	farthest	clothe
	valve	cover	five		then	father	loathe
	verse	ever	gave		there	feather	mouthed
	vest	living	give		they	leather	seethe
	view	nerveless	love		this	mother	sheathe
	visit	never	of		those	other	smooth
	voice	oven	solve		though	rather	soothe
	vote	over	wave		thus	whether	writhe
	vow	private	you've		bathing	bathe	with
X	anxiety	experience	ax	W	walk	which	farewell
	buxom	expert	box		was	whistle	forward
	complexion	exude	complex		water	why	meanwhile
	exact	luxuriant	fix		way weigh	will	nowhere
	examine	luxurious	flax		we	window	reward
	example	luxury	fox		weak week	always	subway
	exchange	Marxist	mix		weight wait	anywhere	swim
	excuse	next	sex		west	away	thruway
	execute	oxen	six		what	between	toward
	executive	oxide	tax		when	beware	twist
	exist	taxi	wax		where	everywhere	unwilling
T	important	tell	into	Z	zeal	bazaar	does
	interrupt	thoughtful	little		zebra	business	flowers
	straight	tie	strictly		zephyr	busy	gaze
	taste	trade	winter		zero	lazy	his
	taught	battle	fact		zest	music	nose
	test	better	get		zinc	poison	please
	ticket	bolted	left		zip	present	rise
	tight	bottle	part		zone	prison	size
	tilt	committee	rest		zoo	puzzle	use
	treat	detail	salt		zoom	result	was
	take	empty	sit		absorb	advise	wise

z	Asia	conversion	exclusion	inversion	pleasure	television
	azure	decision	excursion	leisure	Polynesian	transfusion
	aversion	delusion	fusion	measure	precision	treasure
	collision	diversion	illusion	Persian	profusion	version
	conclusion	division	inclusion	perversion	provision	vision
	confusion		intrusion		revision	

INDEX

ABOUT THE AUTHOR

Actor, writer, director, producer, teacher, Don Molin has, in his career, spanned the entire spectrum of theatre arts. From the age of 17 when he joined the army and was recruited for the Counter Intelligence Corps (becoming for six months the army's youngest counterspy), he has been writing, directing and/or producing plays for radio, television and stage. His unique and extensive knowledge of dialects grew out of teaching English as a second language, when it was essential that he identify each vowel and consonant sound that his students were substituting for the correct sounds in English. This invaluable experience was supplemented by long periods of travel in Europe as well as in the United States and years of residence in such countries as Germany (ages 17 and 18 when he worked for Armed Forces Radio); Sweden (first on a scholarship to the University of Stockholm and later as actor, writer, director for Swedish National Broadcasting and the Royal Dramatic Theatre); and for shorter periods in Turkey, Monaco, Spain, Portugal and Finland (as a theatre consultant). For close to 10 years he spent most of his time as a dialectician: dubbing, doing voice-overs, dialect acting, tutoring. He eventually joined one of the largest independent sound-editing firms of Hollywood and helped to organize the industry leader in independent post-production, Intent International. He became Managing Director of this company, which worked on such projects as the Oscar-winning *The Last Picture Show* and *Cabaret*, as well as the Cannes Jury prize winner, *Johnny Got His Gun*. Molin went on to head the Literary Department of the JMA Agency and to create the Literary Department of the Wormser agency. One of the founders of the Directors' Section of Actors Studio West, Molin has continued to direct and produce his own projects, package them, and keep involved in creative assignments throughout his busy career. This book, the culmination of many years of note-taking and observation, has been 15 years in the making.

VOWEL SYMBOL GUIDE

Symbol	How to Pronounce the Symbol if You Are from the U.S.	the U.K. Canada	Australia N.Z.
O	as in “old,” “only” and “show”	o + *U*; both the “aw” (*o*) and “oo” (*u*) elements receive equal stress and value.*	
O	as in “out” and “clown”	*A* + *U*; both the “ah” (*A*) and the “oo” (*U*) elements receive equal stress and value.*	
o	as in “stop” and “trot”	Similar to the “a” in “father” but only half as long.	the o of “off”
o	as in “horse” or “warm”	Similar to the “aw” sound of “off” or “loss” only longer.	Shorter version of the “aw” sound in “order” or “for.”
*o*E	as in “boy” or “oil”	Both elements receive equal stress and value; the second element is a full “ee” (E) sound.*	
U	as in “you” or “music”	Y + *U*; the “y” as in “yet” is short and, together with the “oo” (U) element, is formed *entirely* in the front of the mouth.*	
U	as in “fool” and “brew”	This is a pure “oo” sound as in “fool” with *no* other vowel elements involved. The vowel is not sounded until the lips have been rounded. Having only one part, no part of it originates in the back of the mouth cavity.	Longer version of the “oo” in “fool” produced entirely in the front of the mouth.
u	as in “up” and “color”	As a London executive pronounces the u of “up” and “cut”; as one from Suffolk pronounces the u of “pull.”	As in “up” or “cut”
u	as in “cook” and “could”	Similar to the u in “full” and “push,” but farther back in the mouth.	

*The elements of an American diphthong are so closely tied that the two parts always blend into a single sound.

KEY TO SYMBOLS

&	as indicated previously
$	when spelled
4	for the sound; in place of
"	when
#	open sound; mouth open
·;	pronounced forward in the mouth
%	liquid sound
!	excepting; except
-	initially; at the beginning of a word
--	at the beginning of a sentence
/	medially; in the middle of a word
.	finally; at the end of a word
..	at the end of a phrase
@	glottal stop; air stopped in the throat
(	preceding
{	in a prefix
)(	before or after
)	following
}	in a suffix
+	add to
,	nasalized
:	stronger; more drawn out
½	weakened; shortened
¼	dropped; omit the sound
?	when used in a monosyllable
?:	in polysyllable
¢	consonant(s)
¢:	voiced "
¢½	unvoiced "
₡	between "
*	vowel(s)
⁎̸	between "
C	as in church
n	as in bank, ink
S	as in shop, sure
s	as in outset, sits
t	as in think, bath
T	as in this, that
z	as in measure
=	interdentalized; pronounced with the tongue between the teeth
±	upperdentalized; pronounced with the tongue touching and behind the upper teeth
∓	lowerdentalized pronounced with the tongue touching and behind the lower teeth
h	as in the Scottish loch, or the German ich; the position of G or K with air hissing through a narrow opening
R	trilled "r"; tongue rapidly tapping the upper palate behind the teeth, as when imitating a steam drill's sound
r	uvular "r"; as when one makes a gargling sound

VOWEL SYMBOL GUIDE

<table>
<tr><th rowspan="2">Symbol</th><th colspan="3">How to Pronounce the Symbol if You Are from</th></tr>
<tr><th>the U.S.</th><th>the U.K. Canada</th><th>Australia N.Z.</th></tr>
<tr><td>A</td><td>as in “day” or “baby”</td><td>e + E; both the “eh” (e) and “ee” (E) elements receive equal stress and value.*</td><td>(like the a in “comrade” as pronounced in Brisbane or in N.Z.)</td></tr>
<tr><td>A</td><td>as in “father” or “garden”</td><td colspan="2">Similar to the a in “are” or “swan” but shorter, like the a in “was”</td></tr>
<tr><td>a</td><td>as in “happy” or “had”</td><td>As pronounced at Oxford in the words “act,” “happy” and “had”</td><td>As in “after” or “ask”</td></tr>
<tr><td>a</td><td>as in “after,” “ask,” “plant” or “France”</td><td>Doubled (or longer) Oxford “a” (see above); like the a in “after” or “can’t” in the Norfolk dialect.</td><td>Similar to the “a” of “ask” or “after,” but doubled or longer.</td></tr>
<tr><td>E</td><td colspan="3">as in “free,” “please,” “eat” or “steam”</td></tr>
<tr><td>E</td><td>as in “learn” or “herb”</td><td colspan="2">Like the e in “her” and the “o” in “word”</td></tr>
<tr><td>e</td><td colspan="2">as in “bed” and “next”</td><td>Similar to the e in “end” or “well” but longer.</td></tr>
<tr><td>e</td><td colspan="3">as in “level” or “gorgeous”</td></tr>
<tr><td>I</td><td>as in “island” or “light”</td><td colspan="2">A + E; the second element is the long sound “ee” (E); both the “ah” (A) and “ee” (E) elements receive equal stress and value.*</td></tr>
<tr><td>I</td><td colspan="3">like the e in “predict” and the o in “propose”</td></tr>
<tr><td>i</td><td colspan="2">as in “lift”</td><td>As in “in,” “with,” or the second syllable of “insist.”</td></tr>
<tr><td>i</td><td colspan="3">as in “ago”</td></tr>
</table>

*The elements of an American diphthong are so closely tied that the two parts always blend into a single sound.